Narrating Media History

Based on the work of media historian, James Curran, *Narrating Media History* explores British media history as a series of competing narratives.

This unique and timely collection brings together leading international media history scholars, not only to identify and contrast the various inter-relationships between media histories, but also to encourage dialogue between different historical, political and theoretical perspectives including liberalism, feminism, populism, nationalism, libertarianism, radicalism and technological determinism.

Essays by distinguished academics cover television, radio, newspaper press and advertising (among others) and illustrate the particularities, affinities, strengths and weaknesses within media history. Each section includes a brief introduction by the editor, with discussion topics and suggestions for further reading, making this an invaluable guide for students of media history.

Michael Bailey teaches media history and cultural theory at Leeds Metropolitan University.

Communication and society
Edited by James Curran

Narrating Media History

Edited by
Michael Bailey

 Routledge
Taylor & Francis Group

LONDON AND NEW YORK

First published 2009
by Routledge
2 Park Square, Milton Park, Abingdon, Oxon OX14 4RN

Simultaneously published in the USA and Canada
by Routledge
270 Madison Ave, New York, NY 10016

Routledge is an imprint of the Taylor & Francis Group, an informa business

Editorial selection and material © 2009 Michael Bailey
Chapters © 2009 the contributors

Typeset in Bembo by
Taylor & Francis Books
Printed and bound in Great Britain by
TJ International Ltd, Padstow, Cornwall

British Library Cataloguing in Publication Data
A catalogue record for this book is available from the British Library

Library of Congress Cataloging in Publication Data
Narrating media history / edited by Michael Bailey.
  p. cm. – (Communication and society)
Includes bibliographical references and index.
 1. Mass media–History. I. Bailey, Michael.
  P90.N258 2008
  302.2309–dc22
                      2008004518

ISBN10: 0-415-41915-8 (hbk)
ISBN10: 0-415-41916-6 (pbk)
ISBN10: 0-203-89295-X (ebk)

ISBN13: 978-0-415-41915-4 (hbk)
ISBN13: 978-0-415-41916-1 (pbk)
ISBN13: 978-0-203-89295-4 (ebk)

Contents

Illustrations

Tables

Figures

Acknowledgements

Parts of Hugh Chignell's chapter are reprinted from an earlier article 'The Birth of Radio 4's *Analysis*', *The Journal of Radio Studies* 13 (1), 2006, pp. 89–102, by permission of the Taylor & Francis Group.

The editor would also like to thank all of the contributors, whom it has been a pleasure to work with. My thanks go also to Natalie Foster and Charlotte Wood at Routledge for their patience and invaluable support.

Contributors

Michael Bailey teaches media history and cultural theory at Leeds Metropolitan University. He has published widely on the history of the early BBC, and is currently working on the 1984/85 miners' strike and a co-authored study of Richard Hoggart. He is an honorary member of the Goldsmiths Media Research Programme, the international advisory board for the Louis le Prince Interdisciplinary Centre for Cinema, Photography and Television, University of Leeds, and Visiting Research Fellow at the ESRC Centre for Research on Socio-Cultural Change (CRESC) at The Open University.

Adrian Bingham is a lecturer in modern history at the University of Sheffield. He is the author of *Gender, Modernity, and the Popular Press in Inter-War Britain* (Oxford University Press, 2004) and *Family Newspapers? Sex, Private Life, and the British Popular Press 1918–1978* (forthcoming). He is currently working on a project with Martin Conboy exploring the journalism of the *Daily Mirror* in the period 1935–69.

Menahem Blondheim teaches communication and American history at the Hebrew University of Jerusalem, and serves as director of the university's Smart Family Institute of Communication. After gaining a BA from the Hebrew University and MA and PhD degrees in history from Harvard University, he consulted and was an entrepreneur in the communication sector of the high-tech industry.

Hugh Chignell is reader in radio at The Media School, Bournemouth University, where he is also a member of the Centre for Broadcasting History Research. His doctoral research was on BBC Radio 4's *Analysis* programme, and he is currently working on a history of British current affairs radio. He is co-chair of the Southern Broadcasting History Group. Publications include various journal articles on radio history and *Key Concepts in Radio Studies* (Sage, 2008).

James Curran has been professor of communications at Goldsmiths, University of London, since 1989, and has held endowed visiting chairs at

Penn, Stanford, Stockholm and Oslo Universities. He is the author or editor of eighteen books about the mass media, some in conjunction with others. These include *Media and Power* (2002), *Power without Responsibility*, 6th edition (2003), *Mass Media and Society*, 4th edition (2005) and *Culture Wars* (2005). He is the director of the Goldsmiths Media Research Programme, supported by a £1.25 million grant from the Leverhulme Trust.

Daniel Day is a PhD student at the Communication and Media Research Institute of the University of Westminster in London and a researcher on volume six of the official history of the BBC, currently being written by Professor Jean Seaton. Funded by the Arts and Humanities Research Council, his dissertation examines the evolution of BBC 'regional' broadcasting from the late 1960s to the late 1980s. His research/teaching interests include broadcasting history, the media and identity and political communication. He is also on the editorial board of the journal *Westminster Papers in Communication and Culture*.

David Deacon is reader in media and politics at the Department of Social Sciences, Loughborough University. He has published widely in the fields of media sociology and political communication. His publications include *Researching Communications: a Practical Guide to Media and Cultural Analysis*, 2nd edition (with Michael Pickering, Peter Golding and Graham Murdock) and *Taxation and Representation: The Media, Political Communication and the Poll Tax* (with Peter Golding). His forthcoming book on *British News Reporting of the Spanish Civil War* will be published in 2009 by Edinburgh University Press.

Mark Hampton is associate professor of history at Lingnan University (Hong Kong) and a fellow of the Royal Historical Society. He is the author of *Visions of the Press in Britain, 1850–1950* (2004) and co-editor with Joel Wiener of *Anglo-American Media Interactions, 1850–2000* (2007). He is a co-editor of the journal *Media History* and modern reviews editor for *H-Albion*. He is currently preparing a book manuscript on 'Hong Kong and Britishness, 1945–97'.

Su Holmes is reader in television at the University of East Anglia. She is the author of *British TV and Film Culture in the 1950s* (Intellect, 2005), *Entertaining TV: The BBC and Popular Programme Culture* in the 1950s (Manchester University Press, 2008) and co-editor of *Understanding Reality TV* (Routledge, 2004), *Framing Celebrity* (Routledge, 2006) and *A Reader in Stardom and Celebrity* (Sage, 2007). Her key research and teaching interests are in British television history, contemporary popular television genres and the subject of celebrity.

Elihu Katz is trustee professor at the Annenberg School for Communication at the University of Pennsylvania and professor emeritus of sociology and communication at the Hebrew University of Jerusalem.

Jamie Medhurst is director of learning and teaching and lecturer in film and television history at the Department of Theatre, Film and Television Studies, University of Wales Aberystwyth. He teaches, researches and publishes on broadcasting history and issues of television and national identity.

Jeffrey Milland read PPE at Wadham College, Oxford. After graduating in 1962, he spent nearly forty years working in television, initially as a journalist, then as a producer and director. In 2005, he successfully completed a PhD on the origins and consequences of the 1962 Pilkington Report on broadcasting in the Historical Studies Department of Bristol University, where he went on to teach contemporary British history. He is now working towards an MA in aesthetics in the Philosophy Department of the University of Southampton.

Graham Murdock is reader in the sociology of culture at Loughborough University. He has been a visiting professor at the University of California at San Diego, The Free University of Brussels, Bergen University and Stockholm University, and is a former head of the Political Economy Section of the International Association of Media and Communication Research. His work has been translated into nineteen languages. He has a longstanding interest in the relations between innovations in media and social and cultural transformations and is currently researching the social impact of digital communication technologies. His latest book (co-edited with Janet Wasko) is *Media in the Age of Marketisation* (2007).

Julian Petley is professor of film and television at Brunel University. He has published widely on film and media studies. His most recent publication is a co-authored book with James Curran and Ivor Gaber, entitled *Culture Wars: the Media and the British Left* (University of Edinburgh Press, 2005). He is also principal editor for *Journal of British Cinema and Television* and a member of the editorial board for *British Journalism Review*.

Michael Pickering is professor of media and cultural analysis in the Department of Social Sciences at Loughborough University. He has published in the areas of cultural history and the sociology of culture as well as media analysis and theory. His recent books include *History, Experience and Cultural Studies* (1997), *Researching Communications* (1999/2007), co-written with David Deacon, Peter Golding and Graham Murdock, *Stereotyping: The Politics of Representation* (2001), *Creativity, Communication and Cultural Value* (2004), co-written with Keith Negus, *Beyond a Joke: The Limits of Humour* (2005), co-edited with Sharon Lockyer, *Blackface Minstrelsy in Britain* (2008) and *Research Methods for Cultural Studies* (2008).

Paddy Scannell is professor of communication at the University of Michigan, where he moved in 2006 after many years at the University of

Westminster. He is a founding editor of *Media Culture & Society* which began publication in 1979. He is the author, with the late David Cardiff, of *A Social History of British Broadcasting* (Blackwell, 1991) and of *Broadcast Talk* (Sage, 1991) and *Radio, Television and Modern Life* (Blackwell, 1996). He is currently working on a trilogy, the first volume of which, *Media and Communication*, was published by Sage (UK) in June 2007. Its companion volume, *Television and the Meaning of 'Live'*, is nearing completion, while the final volume, *Love and Communication*, is still in its early stages.

Stefan Schwarzkopf is a PhD candidate at Birkbeck College (School of History) and lecturer in marketing and communications at Queen Mary College, London. His thesis is on the history of the British advertising industry between 1900 and 1939. His research interests are in the relevance of political and social concepts for the study of marketing, the history of marketing in general, and the development of European advertising in particular. He has published on Cold War advertising communication, on the transatlantic relationships between British and American advertising, on the history of market research and on the reception of Ernest Dichter's 'Motivation Research' in postwar Britain.

Foreword

Elihu Katz

It is a rare honour for a student of media effects to be invited to introduce a book on media history. The best explanation for this seeming anomaly is that the book, and this foreword, are dedicated to James Curran who, almost alone among his peers, has encompassed the entire field of media studies and understands the relationships among its parts.

In tribute to James, I will try to rise to the occasion. I will attempt to show that media histories, including those recorded in these pages, have direct bearing on the study of media effects, and vice versa. Indeed, I believe that all of media studies aims to unveil effects, whether it be audience research, content analysis, technological theories, or institutional histories. These branches of media study – whatever their other uses – seek, respectively, to comprehend the reach, the rhetoric, the technical, and the organizational production of influence. I am not so much referring to persuasive influence – not the kind that concentrates on immediate change of opinions, attitudes, and actions – but on the kind of long-run effects that describe Curran's interest in media history, that is "how the media contribute to the making of modern Britain." And one should add, in deference to the radical narrative, how these institutions may interact to avert change!

Blissfully ignorant as I am of most media history, allow me to share several reactions to the enlightening set of combative papers collected here.

Let me begin by pointing out some of the parallels between these narrative histories and the several "schools" of research on media effects (Katz 2001; Katz *et al.* 2003). The radical narrative, obviously, echoes the neo-Marxism of the Frankfurt School, as well as some of Birmingham and Glasgow. The technological narrative corresponds almost exactly to the Toronto School of Innis (1951) and McLuhan (1964), as well as their disciples and critics. The anthropological narrative encompasses a variety of nation-builders from the Chicago School (e.g., Wirth 1948), their predecessors (e.g., Tarde 1898) and descendants (e.g., Cardiff and Scannell 1987; Anderson 1991). Effects of the liberal narrative may be found among students of the "cognitive turn" (see Beniger and Gusek 1995), who are occupied with diffusion (Rogers 2003), agenda-setting (McCombs and Shaw 1972), the knowledge gap (Tichenor *et al.* 1970) and, more generally, with providing the kinds of information that underlie deliberative democracy. The populist and feminist narratives find their parallel in the functional analysis − begging your pardon − of cultural studies, including so-called gratifications research (Blumler and Katz 1974), reception theory, research on resistance, women's studies, and the like. The divisions among these schools, as indeed among the narratives, are often blurred, but the parallel between them is reasonably clear. If the narrative approach tends toward the historical, the schools of effect have a sociological bent, even if there are crossovers on both sides.

The interesting byproduct of this comparison is the revelation − obvious to some, but not to me − that the historical approach supplies the ingredient that is most lacking in the study of effects, namely *time*. From the earliest days of empirical research on mass communication, emphasis has been placed on the short run − that is, on persuasive effects, on "campaigns" − not only because these were of interest to politicians and advertisers, but because they were *measurable*. It is easy to answer the question whether this or that advertisement affected the behavior of some subsample of the population, while it is very difficult indeed to measure the impact of the introduction of commercial broadcasting on consumer culture. How shall we answer the question whether public television has enfranchised the viewer? How shall we discover whether the introduction of television broadcasting in Israel or in Ireland strengthened or weakened the renaissance of national culture and language in those nations?

Historians of the media, willy-nilly, help to answer such questions − even if this may not be their intent. The narrative histories in this book come even closer to providing answers, because they are themselves interested in high-lighting effects. At the very least, these histories provide over-time observations and informal "measures" that allow for falsifying or confirming expectations, whether popular or scholarly. The ironic finding that abolishing the stamp tax and other government fetters "freed" the British press to move *closer* to the conservative establishment is one such example.

Methodological purists in the effects tradition have shied away from such "data" because of their imprecision, their unrepeatability, and their frequent contradictions. Although the Columbia School from which I hail is thought to be narrowly focused in this way, it is worth noting that the founder him-self, Paul Lazarsfeld, belies this image (Katz 2004). He taught us "how to read a book," by which he meant that the prose of philosophers and historians may be recast as "hypotheses." One of his favourite examples − and now one of mine − was the social psychologist Gabriel Tarde (1898; also see Katz *et al.* 1998) whose observations on late nineteenth-century France offer a wealth of directives for research on effects. Tarde proposed that the rise of newspapers: (1) consolidated the nation, drawing attention to its center; (2) overthrew the king, by challenging his ability to separate the parts of the kingdom from each other; (3) constrained parliament to supplant regionalism by majority rule, in response to the new we-feeling of nationhood; (4) supplied a daily or weekly agenda for public discussion in cafes and salons; and (5) percolated public opinion by intermixing reading and talk. In fact, Lazarsfeld *et al.*'s (1944) discovery of the "two-step flow of communication," echoes Tarde's proposition that newspapers are without influence unless they are the subject of conversation.

Indeed, Tarde's "public sphere" (press–conversation–opinion–action) reappears in Habermas fifty years later, although Habermas is not much aware of his predecessor. As for the contribution of the press to nation-building, Anderson (2006) reiterates Tarde, while Carey (1989) makes the same claim for the telegraph as Cardiff and Scannell (1987) do for radio. Here is comparativism in action – in defiance of the assumption that history consists only of unique cases. Often enough, one stumbles on evidence of similar long-term effects, much as Curran calls for in this volume. Thus, the press not only allows for the over-time observation of single cases, but provides a basis for comparisons across media and across societies. I agree that we should not get bogged down in determinisms, but "data" are certainly available from multiple sites for the study of the interaction between media technologies and other social institutions.

Further examples of the workings of ostensibly similar processes may be found in all of the nations that have adopted the British or French systems of public broadcasting. Placing these side by side to compare their similarities and differences may begin to interest even the methodological purists.

To consider the long-run effects of television now that its prime is almost past, Paddy Scannell and I have assembled a group of media effects scholars to think together. We are reviewing some of the hypotheses that accompanied the new medium when it was launched, in its heyday, and now that it is changing form and function. We have found some beautiful hypotheses. Meyrowitz (1985) proposes, for example, that television, given its accessibility to all, has "abolished secrets," that is, that children know as much about their parents as their parents know about them, and that the same thing is true for the mutual awareness of the sexes, of politicians and their publics, etc. Or consider the proposition that broadcasting (radio as well), having moved politics "inside," has displaced ideology by personality, and emasculated the political parties.

But while we have found interesting long-run hypotheses, we cannot find the long-run studies that set out to track their validity over time, nor do we find many scholarly narrative histories that have tried to cope. Methodologically, there have been several such attempts, and they are worth noting here, although not all of them have been applied to television: (1) The most famous, perhaps, is Eisenstein's (1979) attempt to identify those social institutions that underwent major change shortly after the appearance of the new technology of print. Whereupon she asked – with respect to religion (Protestantism), science (astronomy), and scholarship (of the Renaissance) – whether the printing press might be at least partly responsible for these changes. This is a method that resonates with James Curran's proposal in this book, although it has not, so far, been applied to broadcasting; (2) A somewhat similar attempt was made in Israel, where a team of researchers conducted an elaborate survey of attitudes, values, and leisure behaviors on the eve of the establishment of television, and repeated the same study twenty years later at the point at which commercial television was being introduced (Katz and Gurevitch 1976). We examined each of the changes in order to consider which of them might be attributable to the two decades of (public) broadcasting. While we arrived at certain conclusions (Katz et al. 1997), we were stymied in our attempt to sort out television-related changes from equally powerful innovations such as the change in the percentage of women working, the introduction of a shortened working week, an overall rise in living standard, and several wars! The finding that Israelis had become more materialistic and more present oriented seemed to coincide with prior expectations – but it is clear that this method is hardly satisfying in itself; (3) Gerbner, Gross and their associates (Gerbner et al. 2002) developed still another method that they call "cultivation research," by means of which they compare the views of "reality" held by "heavy" and "light" viewers in order to test the hypothesis that reality as portrayed on television (that the "world is a dangerous place," for example, or the number of policemen in the city) would coincide more closely with the reality of the heavy viewers. Brilliantly, they infer a long-range effect from this short-run methodology. But there is plenty to worry about here, too.

In short, we need each other.

Editor's introduction

Michael Bailey

The inspiration for this collection of essays has its origins in the work of James Curran. Widely respected as a communications scholar of international repute, Curran has been at the forefront of media research for some thirty-odd years now, providing a source of intellectual inspiration for students and colleagues alike.[1]

Noted for his extraordinarily wide-ranging and polymathic approach to mass communications – he is the (co)author or (co)editor of eighteen books that draw upon a variety of different methodologies, intellectual traditions and academic disciplines – Curran is probably best known for his contribution to media history. Unlike some media scholars who, judging by their research, live in a perpetual state of historical amnesia, for Curran, history and media studies are fundamentally connected insofar as one can only really begin to understand the contemporary media landscape if one knows something about how communication technologies – and their social uses – have changed over time. Such knowledge is not only useful in terms of better understanding the world in which we live. It is also useful in terms of acquiring a concrete understanding of the social relations of media production and consumption apropos the historical development of modern liberal democracies and their political economies. In short, past media systems and practices continue to inform media systems and practices in the present day. And if we want to change those systems and practices, we have to comprehend their past history, for the past and the present are inextricably intertwined.

Curran's (e.g. 1977 and 1978a) own accounts of British press history are exemplary for the way in which they continue to inform our awareness of the British newspaper industry in the present day. Prior to him reappraising standard interpretations of the historical emergence of a 'free' press from the nineteenth century onwards, it was very hard for contemporary media scholars to think outside – much less challenge – the prevailing orthodoxy that would have us believe that the emergence of a commercially funded popular press was an essentially democratizing development, not only for press journalism, but for society at large. Thanks to Curran, we now know this explanation to be overly simplistic in that it fails to take into account the way in which market forces have helped to contain democracy by effectively silencing radical opinion and political criticism. Furthermore, without this critical understanding, it would make the case for contemporary press reform even more difficult than it already is.

However, when Curran wrote his seminal essays on the history of the British press in the 1970s, he was one of only a handful of media historians. In fact, the phrase 'media history' was still relatively uncommon, even among those with an interest in such academic foci. It was with this in mind that Curran (1991: 27) famously noted, over fifteen years ago now, that historical research has tended to be the 'neglected grandparent of media studies', in the sense that it is uncared for, marginalized and visited only occasionally. Even then, visits are often fleeting and performed reluctantly.[2]

This neglect is undoubtedly due to the complexities of historical research, particularly for those who do not have an academic background in history. For the inexperienced, historical enquiry can appear difficult and cumbersome, not unlike some grandparents! One can understand why media students might opt to write an essay about the contemporary media, rather than trying to familiarize themselves with their antecedents. Media history can also appear unfashionable and uninteresting. Why spend time with your frumpy grandparents when you can be hanging out with your infinitely more chic contemporaries. There is also the question of relevance: most media students choose to study the media in the hope that they will secure a job in the media industries. Hence the often asked question: what use is media history for somebody who wants to work as a media practitioner in the rapidly changing digital age?

Yet another reason for the relative underdevelopment of media history is to do with the disciplinary formation of media studies (see O'Malley 2002). Historically, the birth and early development of British media studies was an unlikely symbiosis of functionalist sociology, western Marxism and literary criticism, with history as the poor relation.[3] This unevenness was further exacerbated following the establishment of the Centre for Contemporary Cultural Studies at the University of Birmingham in 1964. Although some extremely important and interesting media research was carried out by many of its early members, not least by Stuart Hall, much of the work produced was largely concerned with theory, textual analysis and audience studies, in short the ideological effects of mediated representations (see Hall *et al.* 1992 [1980]). Consequently, a great deal of media research has tended to be ahistorical, according little if any attention to the historical materiality of one's object of analysis.

While some of the above points remain pertinent to the way in which media history is perceived, recent developments bode well. One might even go as far as to say that media history has undergone something of a renaissance, to the point where one can now, arguably, talk about the subject as a mainstream field of study (cf. Hampton 2005). As well as a notable increase in media history-related conferences, there has been a significant growth in the number of contributions to the field, not just from communication scholars but also from historians (recent publications include Bingham (2004), Briggs and Burke (2002/2005), Cannadine (2004), Chapman (2005a), Conboy (2004), Hallin and Mancini (2004), Hampton (2004) and Holmes (2005), among others). The rise of cultural history has no doubt assisted in this symbiotic interaction between 'media' and 'history', as has the recent growth of history programmes made for television (see Champion 2003), or what has been dubbed 'telehistory'.

All things considered, the future of media history looks a great deal brighter than it did just a decade ago. Curran (2004: 33) himself was markedly more optimistic about the subject's growing popularity in a recently published article on the 'Rise of the Westminster School', noting that 'it was relatively easy to document alternative ways of viewing the role of the media in the development of modern British society…something that had been almost impossible a quarter of a century earlier'. Of course, Curran has played a significant part in stimulating this surge in academic interest. Indeed, the document that he is referring to is an essay he himself wrote, entitled 'Rival Narratives of Media History' (see Curran 2002).[4] As well as reiterating the need for communication scholars to take media history more seriously, even more significant is Curran's mapping of different media historiographies – liberal, feminist, populist, anthropological, libertarian, radical and technological determinist – in an effort 'to present media history as a series of competing narratives'. In synthesizing what were previously narrowly focused accounts of individual mediums into opposing theoretical models of interpretation, he has provided us with a highly original and commanding overview of British media development over the last 300 years.[5]

However, it is important to point out that Curran is not advocating Nietzschian-type perspectivism or an inane postmodern celebration of historical relativism. He is not suggesting that we collapse media history into a beguiling myriad of intertexuality and free-floating signifiers, to the point whereupon the past, or any semblance of the past, is simply determined by a historian's ideological point of view. Instead, what he proposes is that we critically evaluate each narrative by attending more closely to the dichotomy of fact and interpretation, or to paraphrase E. H. Carr (2001 [1961]: 23), to steer carefully between the Scylla of 'history as an objective compilation of facts' and the Charybdis of 'history as the subjective product of the mind of the historian'.

Starting from this premise, *Narrating Media History* represents an attempt to critically engage with Curran's foregoing taxonomy, not only to identify and contrast the various articulations between media histories, but also to encourage dialogue between different historical, political and theoretical perspectives. The book is divided into seven sections, with each section comprising a brief introduction and two essays – published here for the first time – that illustrate the particularities, strengths and weaknesses of one of the aforementioned narratives. In some cases, contributors make a compelling case for their respective narrative, while others tread more carefully by offering a more holistic account, thus reflecting some of the ambiguities and continuing uncertainties of the field as it is developing currently. In addition to these essays, the book is framed with a reworked version of Curran's original essay, updated in the light of recent developments in the field. Finally, while the book falls short of realizing Curran's original clarion call for 'a new synthesis', it is my hope that it will nevertheless contribute to a wider process whereby new narratives of media history are realized, thus developing the field of study yet further.

Notes

1 Before becoming professor of communications in the internationally renowned media department at Goldsmiths College, University of London, Curran started his academic career as one of the pioneers of the first media studies degrees in the UK, at what was then the Polytechnic of Central London (later renamed the University of Westminster in 1992) in the mid-1970s. Along with other key members of what has since been characterized as the Westminster tradition of media studies – e.g. Nicholas Garnham, Vincent Porter, Jean Seaton, Paddy Scannell, Colin Sparks, John Keane, Brain Winston and Steven Barnett, among others – Curran was instrumental in broadening the development of media scholarship during its formative years, not least as a founding editor of *Media, Culture & Society* and co-author (with Jean Seaton) of *Power Without Responsibility*, both of which quickly and justifiably became, and remain, essential reading for media researchers.

2 Alternatively, media history is a subject that, to quote Anthony McNicholas (2003: 15), 'dare not speak its name'. Consequently, those who teach media history have had to approach the subject with caution, avoiding any direct reference to the h-word! When the subject does speak its name in lectures and seminars, one is still occasionally greeted with looks of uncertainty, anxious mumblings or, worse still, complete silence!

3 For a fuller discussion of the complexities of the various conflicts and points of academic synergy between the above disciplines, see Abrams (1982), Burke (1980), Lepenies (1992) and Williams (1962 [1958b]).

4 An abridged version of the essay was published as 'Media and the Making of British Society, c. 1700–2000' (Curran 2002b).

5 Similarly, Mark Hampton (2005: 240) recently noted that 'Curran's taxonomy and call for synthesis…could be a major field-defining moment'.

Chapter 1

Narratives of media history revisited

James Curran

It was a happy chance that took me to see *Copenhagen*, a play that re-enacts, from different perspectives, fateful interchanges between a Danish and a German physicist during the 1930s and 1940s. It gave me the idea of presenting British media history as a series of competing narratives, in the opening chapter of my book, *Media and Power* (Curran 2002). The book was translated into five languages and led directly to this volume, which explores media history in terms of my proposed 'rival' narratives.

In adopting an unconventional formula for a literature review, I was responding to what seemed to me to be three underlying problems. British media history is highly fragmented, being subdivided by period, medium and interpretive tradition. It is often narrowly centred on media institutions and content, leaving the wider setting of society as a shadowy background. And media history has not become as central in media studies as one might expect, given that it pioneered the study of the media. So I was looking for a way of integrating *medium* history into a general account of media development, connecting these to the 'mainframe' of general history and conveying how media history illuminates the role of the media in society – in the present, as well as in the past.

In returning to the subject of my essay some six years after it was first written, I shall attempt to do two things. I will briefly restate the essay's central themes, although in a new way by concentrating primarily on recent research. I will also suggest, with great diffidence, possible new directions in which media history might develop in the future, including the reclaiming of 'lost narratives'.

Dominant tradition

Any review of British media history must begin with its leading and longest established interpretation – the liberal narrative. This was first scripted, in its initial form, in the nineteenth century, and comes out of the hallowed tradition of 'constitutional' history which examines the development of Britain's political system from Anglo-Saxon times to the present.

Key landmarks in Britain's constitutional evolution are said to be the defeat of absolutist monarchy, the establishment of the rule of law, the strengthening of parliament and the introduction of mass democracy in five, cautious instalments. It is also claimed that the media acquired a 'constitutional' role by becoming the voice of the people and a popular a check on government.

This constitutional elevation is usually recounted in terms of two inter-twined narrative threads. The first of these records that the press became free of government control by the mid-nineteenth century, and its emancipation was followed by the liberation of film and broadcasting in the mid-twentieth century. The second thread is concerned with how independent media empowered the people. Recent historical work has focused on the latter theme, so this is what we shall concentrate upon.

There is broad agreement among liberal media historians that the rise of a more independent press changed the tenor and dynamics of English politics. Newspapers increased their political content during the eighteenth century and successfully defied the ban on the reporting of parliament during the 1760s. This enabled newspapers to shine a low wattage light on the previously private world of aristocratic politics. People outside the political system could observe, through the press, factional battles among their rulers. How spectators reacted to these battles began to matter, as increasing references in the later eighteenth century to the wider public testify. In a more general sense, the rise of the press was part of a profound shift, in which it came to be accepted that the general public had the right to debate and evaluate the actions of their rulers. Some publications also directly attacked corruption and oligarchy, functioning as pioneer watchdogs monitoring the abuse of official power. In short, the growth of public disclosure through the press rendered the govern-mental system more open and accountable.[1]

The expansion of the press after the end of licensing in 1695 also con-tributed, it is argued, to the building of a representative institution. During the eighteenth century, newspapers mushroomed in different parts of the country and expanded their readership. An increased number of newspapers published views as well as news reports, seeking to speak for their readers. By the 1850s, following a period of rapid expansion and enhanced independence, the press allegedly came of age as an empowering agency. Its thunder echoed down the corridors of power.

However, the central unanswered question at the heart of this eloquent liberal narrative is precisely *who* was being represented by this 'empowering' press. A much favoured answer, over a quarter of a century ago, was the dynamic forces of the 'new society', that is to say primarily the middle and working classes in the expanding urban centres of the 'first industrial nation'.[2] This interpretation stressed the progressive nature of the evolving press, the way in which it broke free from the political agenda of the landed elite and supported campaigns to reform the institutions of British society. Indeed, in some versions of this argument, the growing power of the press helped to usher in a new political order that reflected the changed balance of social forces in British society.

This beguiling interpretation has been undermined from two different directions. Revisionist histories of nineteenth-century Britain increasingly emphasize continuity rather than radical change. They point to the embedded nature of the *ancien regime* before the extension of the franchise; the powerful pull of Anglicanism, localism and tradition; the incremental, uneven nature of the industrial revolution; and, above all, the landed elite's continued dominance of political life until late into the nineteenth century.[3] Meanwhile, historical research has drawn attention to the continuing importance of the conservative press (which greatly strengthened in the last quarter of the eighteenth century), the diversity of the nineteenth-century newspapers and the tenuous evidence that the press strongly influenced political elites and public policy, save in special circumstances (Black 2001). The thesis that an independent press, representative of a transformed society, helped to forge a new political order now looks distinctly unconvincing.

So whom did the press represent? The undermining of the claim that the later Hanoverian press championed a progressive social alliance has encouraged a return to a traditionalist Whig view of the press as the voice of an indeterminate 'public'. Typical of this shift is Hannah Barker's (2000) now standard textbook which argues that newspapers gained a larger, more socially diverse readership and came to be shaped primarily by their customers. 'The importance of sales to newspaper profits', she writes, 'forced papers to echo the views of their readers in order to thrive' (ibid.: 4). By 1855, she concludes, 'the newspaper press in England was largely free of government interference and was able – with some justification – to proclaim itself as the fourth estate of the British constitution' as it informed and represented public opinion (ibid.: 222).

However, some liberal historians remain rightly uneasy about viewing the press as the voice of an undefined public. Jeremy Black, for example, argues that 'the press was at best a limited guide to the opinions of the public' and should be viewed as connecting to 'public opinions rather than public opinion' (Black 2001: 107). This more nuanced view enables him to conclude that 'public culture' (in which the press was central) became less representative of political difference after the 1850s (ibid.: 192). Other liberal historians point to the growing interpenetration of journalism and politics in the second half of the nineteenth century and early twentieth century when much of the national press became an extension of the party system (Seymour-Ure 1977; Boyce 1978). The liberal historian Stephen Koss (1981/1984) even argues that the British press did not become representative of the public until the late 1940s and 1950s when national newspapers allegedly shed their close party attachments.

But if the Whig conception of the press as a fourth estate looks vulnerable, there is another interpretation waiting in the wings. In 1982, Brian Harrison wrote an erudite essay assessing the role of the pressure group periodical in the nineteenth and twentieth centuries. He showed that these modest, and widely overlooked, publications helped to sustain public interest groups 'through three major functions: inspirational, informative and integrating' (Harrison 1982: 282). They inspired some converts to the cause; they armed activists with factual ammunition and sustained commitment; and they sometimes helped to unify reforming movements. By contributing to the functioning and effectiveness of pressure groups, the minority political press contributed to the development of a pluralist democracy.

This is an important line of argument that can now be extended, with the help of more recent research, to the earlier period. The eighteenth-century press provided the oxygen of publicity for political campaigning centred on petitions, addresses, instructions (to MPs), public meetings and concerted demonstrations (Brewer 1976; Black 2002; Rogers 2006). These fostered a 'modern' style of politics based on public discussion and participation, rather than on personal relationships, clientelist networks and social deference. Sections of the press aided this new politics by conferring prominence on leading campaigners, by communicating their arguments and demands and by mobilizing public support. They contributed in other words to the building of an infrastructure of representation based on collective organizations.

In the nineteenth century, radical newspapers contributed to the growth of trade unions; reformist publications sustained a growing multiplicity of interest groups; and a new, party-aligned press helped to transform aristocratic factions in parliament into mass political parties. This last development – often attracting disapproval from liberal press historians – represented a crucial contribution to the building of a key institution of democracy. Political parties became key co-ordinating organizations within the British political system: they aggregated social interests, formulated political programmes that distributed costs and redistributed resources across society, and defined political choices for the electorate.[4]

A view of the press as an agency contributing to the building of civil society is subtly different from, and more persuasive than, a traditional conception of the press as the ventriloquist of the public. Yet, arguments and evidence supporting this alternative interpretation are to be found in numerous radical as well as liberal accounts (for example, Hollis 1970 and Black 2002). These portray the press as contributing to the development of civil society organizations *through which different publics were represented*. Implicitly, they also depict civil society rather than the press as the main locus of representation.

Mark Hampton (2004) has adopted a questioning view of traditional liberal press history in another way. In a notable book, he documents the mid-Victorian elite vision of an educative press that would recruit large numbers of people to 'politics by discussion'. This gave way, he shows, to growing disenchantment when newspapers became more commercial and sensational, and large numbers of people turned away from 'liberal' enlightenment. After 1880, the educational ideal was increasingly replaced by a view of the press as a representative institution – something that Hampton, drawing on radical press history, largely rejects.

His chapter in this volume can be read as an account-settling epilogue to his book. In effect, he concludes that the twentieth-century press may not have measured up to the unreal expectations of Victorian visionaries, nor fulfilled the heroic destiny assigned to it in Whig history, yet neither should the press's democratic role be written off as an illusion. There were times during the twentieth century – most notably during the South African War, the onset of the Cold War in the 1940s and the 1970s debate about economic management – when the British press offered multiple perspectives. This enriched public debate and manifestly contributed to the functioning of democracy.

Some liberal historians also argue that the educational mission of the press may have faltered, but it was absorbed by radio and television. The rise of public service broadcasting, it is claimed, diminished the knowledge gap between elites and the general public, aided reciprocal communication between social groups and fostered the development of a public interest-oriented, policy-based discourse of democratic debate.[5]

The countercharge to this is that public service broadcasting was locked into a paternalistic style of journalism, a view that is in effect endorsed in Hugh Chignell's essay in this book. However, his contention is that BBC radio introduced more popular styles of journalism, particularly during the 1960s, in response to social change, competition and the possibilities created by new technology. This popularization produced a furious reaction from elite critics, who were placated in the 1970s by the development of a more analytical, research-based form of journalism on BBC Radio 4. The implication of this study is that the BBC learnt to develop different registers of journalism, which responded to the divergent orientations of different audiences.

Liberal media historians usually shrug off criticism by ignoring it. Both Hampton and Chignell are unusual in that they incorporate critical arguments from different intellectual traditions. In doing so, they provide more guarded and persuasive liberal histories.

Feminist challenge

The dominance of the liberal narrative is now challenged by the rise of feminist media history. This argues that the media did not become fully 'independent' when they became free of government, because they remained under male control. And far from empowering the people, the media contributed to the oppression of half the population. This feminist interpretation is thus not merely different from the liberal one but directly contradicts it.

It comes out of a historical tradition that documents the subordination of women in the early modern period when wives, without ready access to divorce, could be lawfully beaten and confined by their husbands, and when women did not have the same social standing or legal rights as men. It describes the struggle for women's emancipation and advance as a qualified success story in which women gained new legal protections, greater independence and improved opportunities, but in a context where there is not yet full gender equality. Its account of the development of media history is told as an accompaniment to this narrative.

Feminist media history is now the fastest growing version of media history. So, this return visit will focus primarily on recent feminist media research that is revising the pioneer version of feminist media history.

This pioneer version argued that popular media indoctrinated women into accepting a subordinate position in society. It did this primarily by portraying men and women as having different social roles, with men as breadwinners and women as mothers and housewives. As the *Ladies Cabinet*, a leading women's journal, apostrophized in 1847: woman 'is given to man as his better angel...to make home delightful and life joyous' and serve as a 'mother to make citizens for earth' (cited in White 1970: 42). This understanding of the proper role of women was justified in terms of the 'natural' differences between the sexes, established by divine providence. During the course of the nineteenth century, this gender discourse was given a turbo-boost by being articulated to discourses of class and progress. Images of femininity were linked to those of elegant affluence, while understandings of domestic duty were associated with the moral improvement of society. Traditional gender norms were upheld by family custom, peer group pressure and education, and rendered still more coercive by being reproduced in mass entertainment – including media produced especially for women.

This pioneer version also stresses the underlying continuity of media representations of gender from the nineteenth century through to the late twentieth century. The main concerns of women were defined, according to this account, as courtship, marriage, motherhood, home-making and looking good. There were minor shifts of emphasis over the years (for example, a stress on being a professional housewife and mother in the 1930s, 'make do and mend' in the 1940s and 'shop and spend' in the 1950s). But the central message remained, it is argued, essentially the same. Women's concerns were projected as being primarily romantic and domestic; men and women were depicted as being innately different; and women who transgressed gender norms were generally portrayed in an unfavourable light. The functionalist cast of this argument is typified by Janet Thumim's analysis of postwar film. 'Our exploration of popular films', she concludes, 'shows that screen representations in the period 1945–65 performed a consistently repressive function in respect of women. There are, simply, no depictions of autonomous, independent women either inside or outside the structure of the family, who survive unscathed at the narrative's close' (Thumim 1992: 210). Popular media, in short, consistently sustained patriarchy.

This stress on the continuity of social control is now being challenged within the feminist tradition. First, revisionist research is drawing attention to women's active resistance to patriarchal domination through the creation of their own media.[6] In particular, Michelle Tusan shows that a women's press grew out of a dense matrix of women's associations and single-issue campaigns in Victorian Britain. Originating in the 1850s, the women's press confounded Lord Northcliffe's observation that 'women can't write and don't want to read' (cited in Tusan 2005: 99) by gaining a significant readership before the First World War. Its leading publications reported news that was not covered in the mainstream press, developed women-centred political agendas and advanced alternative understandings of society. Even when the women's press was in decline during the 1920s, it still boasted the early *Time and Tide*, a weekly that published a satirical 'Man's Page' and thoughtful commentary by leading feminists from Virginia Woolf to Rebecca West. Eclipsed in the 1930s, the women's press was reborn in the 1970s.

Second, revisionist research argues that representations of gender changed in meaningful ways in response to wider changes in society. Thus, Adrian Bingham (2004) attacks the standard view that the popular press sought to contain the advance of women during the interwar period. A narrow focus on women's pages, he argues, ignores the diversity of viewpoints that were expressed in the main body of popular daily papers. Although reactionary sentiments were sometimes voiced, the prevailing view expressed in the interwar press was that there should be no going back to the prewar era. Women's increased freedom from restrictive social codes and dress was generally welcomed; successful women in public and professional life were depicted both prominently and positively; the greater independence, assertiveness and athleticism of 'modern women' was widely presented as being part of a generational change and an inevitable step towards greater gender convergence; there was an increased stress on the need for a companionate marriage and for an appropriate adjustment of traditional male behaviour; and women were invested, in a variety of ways, with greater prestige (not least as newly enfranchised citizens).

However, this scholarly study acknowledges that change was not unidirectional or across the board. Fashion, housewifery and motherhood still dominated the women's pages. The women's movement was under-reported; feminism itself was frequently said to be outdated and 'superfluous'; and the Rothermere press opposed votes for women under thirty. Women were more often presented in sexualized ways, which had no counterpart for men. But, although Bingham's assessment stresses complexity and diversity, his conclusion is that the interwar popular press adopted, overall, a more enlightened view of gender.

Third, revisionist research has drawn attention to the ambiguity or 'textual tension' of some media representations. This argument is not new and can be found in earlier studies of eighteenth-century ballads (Dugaw 1989), nineteenth-century women's magazines (Beetham 1996) and twentieth-century women's films (Landy 1991), which sometimes provided, it is argued, a space in which women could imagine a different gender order or express a veiled form of protest. But while this argument is not original, it has become both more prominent and more explicitly linked to social change. For example, Deborah Philips and Ian Haywood (1998) draw attention to popular 1950s women's novels that featured women doctors. These heroines were held up for admiration and were even portrayed as builders of a brave new world inaugurated by the post-1945 welfare state. But they were also presented as being traditionally feminine, and their careers were implicitly viewed as being an extension of women's traditional caring role. These books, according to Philips and Haywood, were pleasurable partly because they offered a mythological resolution to conflicting impulses, one embracing change and the other harking back to the past.

Deborah Philips (2006) extends this argument in a subsequent study. In her account, 1980s 'sex and shopping' novels celebrated women's advance, without questioning the structures of power that held women back. 1990s 'Aga saga' novels reverted to domesticated romance, while expressing unmistakeable dissatisfaction with contemporary men. And some early 2000s 'chick lit' novels depicted successful women in search of still more successful men. Philips argues that these novels responded, in different ways, to contradictions in feminine sensibility: between hoping for a future where things would be better for women and clinging to aspects of the past.

Fourth, revisionist research points to a different denouement of the feminist narrative. Instead of arguing that media representations of gender remained fundamentally the same, the case is now being made more often that a sea-change took place from the early 1980s onwards. A growing number of TV series – made or shown in Britain – featured independent women with successful careers as sympathetic objects of identification and portrayed them as being strong, capable and appealing (Cooke 2003; Lotz 2006). Teen magazines emerged that expressed female sexuality in new, more open ways (McRobbie 1996). But traditionalist representations of gender also persisted (Macdonald 1995). Depictions could also mislead by implying that gender equality had been achieved: indeed, as one analyst wryly notes, women in the fictional world of television have advanced further than women in real life (Boyle 2005). Some seemingly 'progressive' lifestyle journalism also had conservative undertones, urging women to take control of their lives in individualistic ways rather than seeking to change society through collective action (Blackman 2006). The complexity of the media shift that took place, and of responses to it, is perhaps best conveyed by the popular TV series *Sex and the City* (1998–2004). It is interpreted very differently: as a beacon of 'third wave' feminism (Henry 2004) and as a return to a reactionary past (McRobbie 2005). But, whichever view is taken, the series staged a running debate about what women should expect out of life between four friends, each of whom initially espoused a different position: home-centred traditionalism, romantic idealism, sex without commitment and qualified feminism. This was part of its appeal. It is also what made it emblematic of a more questioning orientation towards gender relations in the media at the turn of the century, compared with even twenty years before.

This feminist narrative, in its revised form, does not dispute the past role of the media in socializing women into the norms of patriarchy. But the contours of this narrative, and its ending, are changing in response to new research. David Deacon's contribution to this book can be read as contributing to this revisionist drift. He documents how female journalists, mostly from privileged backgrounds and with influential male patrons, made a breakthrough in the 1930s by breaching a traditional male preserve: the reporting of war. Even so, female journalists were still encouraged to concentrate on the everyday lives of ordinary people and to report war as an extended human interest story.

Michael Bailey's essay in this book sits more uneasily within the revisionist feminist canon. He argues that the BBC sought to educate women into being efficient housewives and informed mothers during the interwar period. However, the BBC's briefing was more than just helpful advice because it was also a way of making women internalize a sense of domestic duty and of feeling guilty if they fell short of the standards expected of 'modern women'. The BBC's domestic education is thus viewed by him as psychologically coercive and strongly conservative in reaffirming women's place in the home. This is a subtly different interpretation from Adrian Bingham's 'take' on similar press content during the same period, which he characterizes as an extension of newspapers' discourse of modernity that rejected a return to the reactionary past, and as advice that rendered domestic labour 'more acceptable to the "modern woman"' (Bingham 2004: 105).

It is an indication of feminist history's growing influence that both contributors to this section of the book are men, as this tradition was once largely the preserve of women. Research is also developing into the evolution of masculinity in a way that shadows, and supports, the feminist narrative.[7] In short, a new way of viewing the media's evolution has come into being that takes account of one of the most important social developments of the last 150 years – the advance of women. It requires media history to be rewritten.

Radical challenge

The liberal tradition is also assailed from another direction. Writers of radical media history attack the same vulnerable point of the liberal narrative as feminist critics: the assumption that the media switched allegiances from government to the people when the media became 'free' from official control. Radical media history argues that, on the contrary, mainstream media remained integrated into the underlying power structure and continued to support the social order.[8]

This version of media history comes primarily out of a historical account that records the rise of an organized working class movement in the first half of the nineteenth century. This movement became more radical, won increasing support and developed its own popular press, which conferred publicity on working class institutions and radical causes, and encouraged its readers to view society in more critical ways. However, these early working class militants, and their subsequent heirs, were defeated. Consequently, when Chartist demands for equal citizenship were broadly met, this did not lead to the building of an equal society (Hall 1986).

Radical media historians seek to understand the part played by the media in this 'containment'. In particular, they seek to explain why the media supported the social order when they were no longer under direct government control. In essence, their answer boils down to three arguments. The market developed as a system of control (not as an engine of freedom, as in the liberal narrative). The rise of *mass* market newspaper entry costs in the period 1850–1918 contributed to the consolidation of unrepresentative, business control of the press (and also of the music hall and, later, film and television industries). The media's growing dependence on advertising also disadvantaged the left, while the development of media concentration curtailed choice.

Elites exerted influence on the media through state institutions, principally by informal processes rather than legal coercion. A professionalized apparatus of news management developed, beginning with the introduction of the lobby system in 1885 and culminating in the enormous expansion of state public relations in the period after 1980. Coalitions between political factions in government and press controllers were constructed, as during the Chamberlain and Thatcher eras. Above all, elites set the parameters of political debate in broadcasting through their ascendancy over state institutions, especially parliament and the civil service.

Dominant groups also influenced the culture of society and, in this way, shaped the content of the media. The prevailing ideas of the time, from the intensification of nationalism in the eighteenth century, the rise of imperialism in the nineteenth century, the diffusion of anti-communism during the Cold War to the triumphalist neo-liberalism that followed, have tended to support, it is argued, the existing disposition of power and privilege. Media staffs were controlled, in this view, through the air they breathed.

This narrative is recounted, in part, in Julian Petley's essay in this volume. It continues to be enriched by new studies – to take just three such studies almost at random: further research into the radical press during its heroic Chartist phase (Allen and Rushton 2005); an illuminating study of the role of the media in the transformation of Queen Victoria into the 'Mother of her People' and symbol of imperial and industrial greatness (Plunkett 2003); and a radical, Foucauldian analysis of how the BBC sought to 'train and reform the unemployed as docile but efficient citizens' during the 1930s (Bailey 2007a: 464).

This historical tradition has unstitched the more vulnerable seams of traditional liberal history. It also makes an insightful contribution to a historical understanding of why socialism was defeated in Britain. But it suffers from one central defect: its failure to acknowledge that the reformist heirs of the early working class movement succeeded in the twentieth century in significantly modifying the social system. Moreover, a progressive alliance did so partly as a consequence of securing an extensive hearing – even support – from a section of the media system. Simplistic arguments about the 'refeudalization of society' after 1850, linked to a very simplistic sketch of a subordinated media system, as in Jurgen Habermas' (1989 [1962]) classic radical account no longer seem satisfactory – even to the author himself (Habermas 1992). In short, the traditional radical narrative needs to pay more attention to political success rather than to failure, and to the media's involvement in progressive change. To this, we shall return.

Populist challenge

The populist tradition of media history has an ambiguous relationship to the liberal orthodoxy. It describes the development of the media as a prolonged escape story – not from government but from a cultural elite that sought to impose its taste and judgements on the people. The denouement of this populist history is that the people obtained more of what they wanted from the media: entertainment rather than high culture and uplift.

This interpretation connects to two themes in the general history of Britain. One documents the erosion of deference to authority (whether based on birth, wealth, occupation or age). The other charts the development of a market society in which life became better, and class dominance was subverted by consumer power. These two themes are entwined to provide the filament of the populist media narrative. This describes a popular revolt against a cultural hierarchy, and claims that it succeeded as a consequence of the 'egalitarian' power of the consumer in a world made better by mass consumption.

The core of this narrative is based on specialist studies that record the triumphs of the entertainment-seeking public over high-minded Victorian elites and their heirs: registered for example in the advent of the 'new journalism' in the 1880s, the stocking of light fiction in public libraries, the expansion of popular music on radio and the cumulative popularization of television. This narrative has as an important subsidiary theme a celebration of the pleasure people derived from the media.

New studies continue to fill out this narrative. Thus, a recent study of the rise of a consumer society in nineteenth-century Britain portrays the growth of popular journalism as part of an efflorescence of 'bright colour, light and entertainment' (Flanders 2006: xvii) in which life became more fun, fuller and richer – enhanced by the retail revolution and the rise of football, mass tourism, bestselling books and the music hall.

Similarly, another populist study argues that the expansion of popular music through the gramophone, radio and dance hall immeasurably improved the quality of life in interwar Britain, just as cheap food, electricity and better housing also did. The enormous pleasure derived from popular music was allegedly a direct consequence of its commercialization. 'In an important sense', writes James Nott (2002: 227), 'the application of the profit motive to cultural production was democratic'. It meant that music was directed towards what people wanted, rather than what disapproving – and sometimes snobbish and racist – cultural gatekeepers thought was worthy. Nott also argues that commercial popular music during this period had vitality, affirmed the ordinary, connected to popular romanticism and produced sounds and songs that have lasted.

Jeffrey Millard's essay in this volume comes from the same intellectual home. He documents the sometimes patrician, paternalistic and platitudinous thoughts of those who shaped, in the 1950s and 1960s, a public service broadcasting regime that embraced both commercial and public television. The advent of digital television is now undermining, he argues, this paternalist framework of regulation, and is offering people more of what they want.

The populist tradition of media history also continues to spawn celebrations of popular media content, as being connected to the real lived experiences of ordinary people and as validating popular taste (for example, Hills 2005; Wilson 2005). The assumption is that it was in the public interest for the media to have provided whatever the public enjoyed: the customer was always right. But this tradition's narrow focus on consumer satisfaction disregards the media's role in enabling democratic self-government (prompting clashes with liberal historians),[9] classifies our concerns about the media's support of inequality (causing conflicts with radical historians) and sometimes fails to engage adequately with issues of cultural quality (leading to disputes with post-Leavisites). Yet, despite its flaws, populist media history illuminates the life-enhancing pleasures generated by the rise of the media.

Nation building

The liberal, feminist, radical and even populist traditions belong recognizably to the same intellectual family. They recount media history in relation to the evolution of different forms of power – political, social, economic and cultural – and intersect or confront one another, either implicitly or explicitly. However, there are three other narratives that have only a tangential relationship to this core of media history. Yet, these offer versions of media history that are illuminating.

The anthropological narrative, inspired by the insight that the nation is partly a cultural construct, explores the role of the media in fostering national identity. The United Kingdom is a relatively 'new' nation: created formally (although there had been a prior build-up) through the political union of

England and Wales with Scotland in 1707 and the constitutional union of Britain and Ireland in 1801 (followed by a messy divorce with most of Ireland in 1920–21). The emergent media system, it is argued, played a significant part in bonding this collective of nations and forging a sense of being 'British'.

Thus, print media helped to foster a British national identity in the eighteenth century principally through Protestant bigotry and antagonism towards Catholic France (with whom Britain was at war for much of the century) (Colley 1992). This identity became overlaid subsequently by a strong sense of imperial superiority, expressed in a hubristic and racist understanding of national character, as well as by widely diffused images of Britain as a rural arcadia that persisted even when Britain became highly urbanized (Mackenzie 1984; Richards 1997). However, the decline of Protestantism and the dismantlement of the Empire after 1945 undermined the traditional conception of Britishness, while conventional visualizations of Britain as an unchanging Constable painting did not accord with a new stress on modernity. With difficulty, and still in a contested form, a weaker national identity emerged after the 1960s, a time when the United Kingdom joined the European Union and was exposed to increased globalizing influences. This took the form of a multicultural, multiethnic, plural understanding of Britishness. Thus, the optimistic claim of this media narrative is that British national identity, forged originally through religious hatred and racist imperialism, evolved to include people of all religions and none, and to embrace people of different ethnic backgrounds.

Recent research has extended this argument, giving it greater depth and detail. For example, James Chapman's (2005b) examination of British historical films between the 1930s and 1990s argues persuasively that these films say as much about the time they were made as about the past. Among other things, his study draws attention to a deepening sense of national decline during the 1950s. Richard Weight's (2003) study of patriotism between 1940 and 2000 describes the attempt made in the 1980s, with strong press support, to reverse this sense of national decline through the projection of Britain as a recuperated nation, the victor of a short, exciting war (Falklands), and regenerated through a return to traditional values (with an implied single ethnicity). This failed to capture permanently the national imagination, Weight argues, and gave way by the 1990s to a looser, more inclusive and multiple understanding of Britishness. However, a sense of being British has always been mediated through other identities, including class, gender, region and membership of the nations of Scotland, Wales and Ulster. As Paul Ward (2004) argues, there is an underlying continuity in the fractured and mediated nature of British national identity between 1870 and the present.

Indeed, more critical attention is now being given to media and identity in the 'national regions'. This has produced groundbreaking research into Englishness. Richard Colls (2002) argues that a sense of Englishness was buried inside the mythologizing of the 'Anglo–British imperial state' and came to be viewed as synonymous with Britishness. But this equation of England and Britain was undermined first by the death of imperialism (in which all countries of the United Kingdom had a shared investment) and then by political devolution. However, the English found difficulty in expressing their subnational identity partly because readily available images of England were so outdated. As Richard Colls eloquently puts it, 'island races, garden hearts, industrial landscapes, ecclesiological villages, fixed properties, ordered relationships, native peoples, cultural survivals, northern grit, southern charm, rural redemption, rule Britannia – all these discourses persist, but with less conviction' (Colls 2002: 380). This portrait of 'Englishness' as a buried, inarticulate consciousness accords with Krishan Kumar's (2003) subsequent study, which argues that an English identity was deliberately repressed for the sake of imperial and national unity (with clear parallels to Austria and Russia).

Historical exploration of Englishness has been accompanied by renewed interest in Welsh and Scots national identity (and a boom in good, revisionist books about Irish nationalism that lies outside this review). Especially notable is a study of the media in Wales (Barlow et al. 2005). The Welsh region of the BBC (radio) was established in 1937; a Welsh ITV company in 1958; a unified Welsh BBC television service in 1964; and the Welsh television channel, Sianel Pedwar Cymru (S4C), in 1982. All these initiatives came about partly as a consequence of Welsh nationalist pressure and helped to sustain a distinctive Welsh identity. S4C played an especially important role in supporting the declining Welsh language (which is now spoken only by 20 per cent of Welsh people).

But these developments should not obscure the extent of national (and predominantly English) domination of Britain's media system. In 2002, 85 per cent of daily morning papers bought in Wales came from across the border (Barlow et al. 2005: 47). In 2003, less than 10 per cent of the output of BBC1 and 2 and ITV1 (HTV) was produced specifically for Welsh consumption, and much of this was accounted for by news (Barlow et al. 2005: 144, table 6.2). While emphasizing the complex factors in play in sustaining rival national identities, this study highlights just how important the national integration of the United Kingdom's media system has been in supporting an overarching British national identity.

The increased attention given to 'regional nationalism' is thus an important feature of the way in which the anthropological narrative is developing. This is probably a response to the revival of separatism and the establishment of the Scottish Parliament and Welsh National Assembly in 1999. Day's and Medhurst's essays in this book reflect this shift of focus.

Culture wars

The libertarian media narrative arises from different developments in British society. There was a sustained decline in religious belief and observance from the later nineteenth century onwards. The increasing de-Christianization of Britain, combined with greater individualism fostered by market development, contributed to the advance of social liberalism in the 1960s. This was fiercely resisted by traditionalists who sought to turn the clock back. A titanic battle between social conservatives and social liberals ensued that provides the central theme of the libertarian narrative for the second half of the twentieth century.

The best documented part of this narrative is provided by research into the social reaction that took place against 1960s social liberalism. This highlights the role of the media in generating moral panics about a succession of deviant groups from the 1960s through to the 1980s. The media presented these groups in stereotypical and exaggerated ways; represented them to be part of a deeper social malaise; mobilized support for authoritarian retribution; and recharged in promethean ways social conservatism (Hall et al. 1978; Cohen 1980; Golding and Middleton 1982; Hall 1988).

Recent work, within the libertarian narrative, updates this narrative and offers a different provisional ending. Thus, one study examines the emergence of a new kind of left in municipal politics – owing more to 1960s counter-culture than to Marxism or Methodism – which was symbolically annihilated in the media during the 1980s. Yet, its political agenda and some of its once controversial policies became almost mainstream in the early 2000s when the 1960s generation gained control of leading public institutions. This outcome 'was because in Britain – unlike America – progressives were winning major battles in an unacknowledged culture war' (Curran et al. 2005: 286).

If this study suggests that the tide of social reaction receded after the 1980s (although this did not extend to issues arising from immigration and terrorism during the early 2000s), another survey reappraises the concept of moral panic, the *deus ex machina* of the radical libertarian narrative. Chas Critcher (2003) argues that some moral panics were prevented through opposition and expert intervention (as in the 1980s, over AIDS); some were deflected from authoritarian repression towards harm minimization (as in the 1990s, over raves and ecstasy); and some led to ritualistic illusions of effective action (as when the complexities of child abuse were reduced, in the late 1990s and early 2000s, to a hue and cry against 'stranger paedophiles'). The concept of moral panic, concludes Chas Critcher, is an 'ideal type' which, in reality, takes different forms and has different outcomes. This is a significantly different position from the depiction of the moral panic as a mechanism for the reassertion of the 'control culture' that featured in his earlier co-authored work (Hall et al. 1978).

The libertarian narrative exists only in embryonic form and is in need of more work and clearer definition. However, one can obtain a glimpse of how it can be projected back in time through research into media representations of our groups. These helped to establish boundaries in terms of what society was willing to accept or tolerate.

In the case of sexual minorities, there has been a clear change over time. During the 1880s, there was a press-supported outcry against gay men (accompanied by the strengthening of penal legislation), followed by a comparable crusade against lesbians in the 1920s. Representations of sexual minorities continued to be strongly hostile until there was a softening of media homophobia in the 1960s (accompanied by the partial de-criminalization of gay sex). Even so, gay people were often presented on British television in the 1970s as being either silly or threatening. The 1980s witnessed a dichotomization in TV drama: positive portrayals of gay men tended to be confined to those who appeared reassuringly asexual, while the sexualized were more often projected in strongly negative ways. It was only at the turn of the century that gay people were more often featured as 'ordinary' (Gleeber 2004; cf. Cooke 2003). The symbolic turning point was the British television series, *Queer as Folk* (1999–2000), a soap opera set in Manchester's gay village. It portrayed, in bright primary colours, a young generation of gay men as intelligent, attractive, heterogeneous and 'normal': free of shame or concealment and relatively untouched by the stigmata of traditional celluloid representation. The perspective of the series' narrative, the gaze of its camera, even its sex scenes normalized rather than pathologized being gay. It marked a milestone of social change, followed by legislation in the early 2000s that ended some forms of continuing discrimination against gays and lesbians.

Another way in which the libertarian narrative can be extended over time is through studies of moral regulation of the media. There was draconian censorship in the first half of the twentieth century (especially in relation to sex, morality and bad language), but this tended to diminish overall during the second half. Here, the two relevant studies in this volume, by Bingham and Holmes, complexify the libertarian argument in an interesting way. They extend an understanding of moral regulation to include issues such as protection of privacy; reveal that the impulse to censor came from the left as well as the right; and show that the media deflected these assaults on their freedom partly through self-censorship.

Technological determinism

The last of the alternative interpretations of media history, technological determinism, transcends national frontiers and represents a proposed 'master narrative'. Instead of seeing the media as being linked to change, it portrays the media – or rather its communications technology – as being the origin and fount of change.

There are a number of classic studies advancing this position. Innis (1951) argues that each new medium of communication changed the organization of society by altering dimensions of time and space. Eisenstein (1979) maintains that the printing press contributed to cultural advance in early modern Europe by preserving and making more widely available the intellectual achievements of the past. McLuhan (1964) claims that the rise of electronic media fostered a 'retribalized', syncretic culture by simultaneously re-engaging the human senses. Meyrowitz (1985) argues that the universality of television changed social relations by demystifying the 'other'.

This tradition is now being renewed through accounts which argue that the internet is fundamentally changing the world. The internet, we are told, is 'blowing to bits' traditional business strategy (Evans and Wurster 2000); rejuvenating democracy (Tsagarousianou *et al.* 1998); empowering the people (Poster 1995); inaugurating a new era of global enlightenment (Stratton 1997); transforming human sensibility (Turkle 1997); rebuilding community (Rheingold 2000); generating a self-expressive culture (Anderson 2006); and undermining, with interactive television, established media empires (Negroponte 1996).

I have discussed technological determinism in relation to the internet elsewhere (Curran and Seaton 2003; Curran 2008), and there is not sufficient space here to do more than register briefly two points. First, the evidence strongly suggests that the offline world influences the online world – in particular its content and use – more than the other way round. Second, this should not lead us to accept a social determinist position, the mirror opposite of technological determinism, which is now gaining ground. This last sees the internet – and by implication all new communications technology – as merely an extension of society reproducing, in a closed loop, its culture and social relations. This misses the point that the specific attributes of internet technology (its international reach, cheapness, interactivity and hypertextuality) make a difference. It also tends to present society as a simplifying abstraction, instead of investigating the ways in which the architecture, content, use and influence of the internet have been shaped by interacting and contending forces within society that have evolved and changed over time.[10]

Wider issues in relation to new media are explored in three essays in this book. Scannell makes an eloquent case that communications technology – viewed in conjunction with technology in general – has built a better world, not least by extending communicative sensibility. Murdock and Pickering address one aspect of this claim, arguing that the telegraph and photography have not automatically promoted communication and understanding through killing distance: in fact, photography has sometimes impeded understanding through objectification, while the telegraph has been used to extend control. Blondheim concludes that the starting point of many influential accounts – their view of communications technology as autonomous – is misleading, weakening their claims.

Lost narratives

Where does this leave us? The obvious next step is to construct alternative syntheses of the seven narratives in a battle of meta-narratives. However, rather than recapitulate my own outline version (Curran 2002), it is perhaps more useful to reflect upon what has been left out of this review.

I set about writing my original essay, after some initial difficulty, by listing on a sheet of paper key trends in British history and then reflecting upon what the available media historical literature said in relation to each of these. Some trends I had to omit because there was not enough evidence and argument to sustain a linked media historical account. The six trends that survived this winnowing process were: (1) national unification; (2) mass democracy; (3) defeat of socialism; (4) advance of women; (5) rise of consumer society; and (6) decline of moral traditionalism/religion.

But this leaves out important developments in the history of Britain in which the media played a part. It is worth drawing attention to four 'lost narratives', in particular, which failed to make the shortlist. They merit further investigation.

The most glaring omission is the building of the welfare state, linked to a 'reformist' narrative of media development. Adapting rather freely a celebrated essay by the social democratic theorist, T. H. Marshall (1950), it is possible to see British history as an evolving, collective struggle for securing human rights: civil rights (notably the right to assembly and equal justice), political rights (the right to vote), social rights (including access to free health care and social security) and cultural rights (including access to 'cultural privilege', public affairs information and symbolic representation). The first of these two struggles had been largely (but not wholly) won by 1918. The period from 1918 to the present marked the intensification of the collective battle for social and cultural entitlements. Late nineteenth- and early twentieth-century advances in social welfare were greatly extended in the 1940s to include state protection 'from the cradle to the grave'. In the cultural sphere, nineteenth-century advances – free elementary schools, public libraries, parks, museums and galleries – were extended in the twentieth century through the expansion of free education, public service broadcasting, cultural subsidies and the creation of the free world wide web.

This historical perspective bears some resemblance to that proposed by Graham Murdock (1992, 1999). McKibbin's fine study (1998) is a key source for this narrative, showing the way in which a solidaristic working class culture, supported by popular entertainment, reached its zenith of confidence and influence in the 1940s. Elements of this narrative are to be found in Curran and Seaton (2003), which dwells, in three chapters, on the early 1940s, a time when much of the media system (including a radicalised section of the war-time press) contributed to building a consensus in favour of a consolidated welfare state. This study also differentiates between the positive role of public service broadcasting (including *regulated* commercial TV) and the web and the negative role of a debased press, a theme partly shared with other histories (Eldridge *et al.* 1997; Williams 1998). This critical celebration of public service broadcasting is supported by other studies documenting the development of innovative public service TV journalism (Tracey 1983; Holland 2006), the BBC's struggle to defend public service virtues under siege (Barnett and Curry 1994), public service television's extension of symbolic representation in the second half of the twentieth century (Williams 2004) and, of course, Briggs' (1961–95 [2000 reprint]) history of the BBC. More generally, there is a strong historical tradition of policy analysis (O'Malley 1994; Goodwin 1998; O'Malley and Soley 2000; Freedman 2003; Tunney 2007) that examines successful and failed attempts to reform the media and to resist neo-liberal transformation (although some of these authors would object vehemently to being characterized as 'reformist' historians). There are rich secondary materials available for the development of a reformist media history, especially in the twentieth century. But these are currently too fragmented and, more importantly, their perspectives are too internally divided for this proto-history to make it into the 'canon' of established media historical narratives. But there is a gap here that needs to be filled.

The second missing dimension is a narrative that describes the distributional battles between social classes in terms of power, status and material rewards, and describes the evolving role of the media in relation to these. Surveying the last two centuries, there have been two major losers: the aristocracy, which used to rule Britain (but does so no longer), and the working class, which was once a powerful political, economic and cultural force but has now contracted, subdivided and in important respects lost ground. The great victors have been key sectors of the middle class best adapted to the globalizing economy. A class media narrative can be constructed for the nineteenth century, but – because of the present state of research and shifting fashion – it loses coherence by the later twentieth century. In essence, this would be a more ambitious version of the radical narrative we have already.

The third lost dimension is the rise of the British economy (and associated gains in living standards and job creation) paired with an economic history of the British media. Britain became the 'first industrial' nation, was overtaken by the United States and then evolved into a prosperous service-based economy. This has parallels with the development of British media which it would be interesting to explore. Imperial Britain played a key role in the development of telegraph technology and of news agencies; the United States, not Britain, pioneered industrialized, mass journalism; Hollywood locked horns with, and defeated, the British film industry by 1910; Britain failed to capitalize on the construction of a pioneer digital computer in 1944 and its prominent role in the development of packet-switching network technology during the 1960s; yet, Britain became (and remains) the second biggest exporter of television programmes in the world and played a significant role in the development of the web. Whether similar processes were at work in the successes and failures of the British media, and of the British economy, remain a largely unexplored avenue of research. Stefan Schwarzkopf's essay in this book, examining the context of the American takeover of the British advertising industry, is a pioneer contribution to this narrative.

A fourth theme was half in and half out of my review. This featured a technological determinist view of new communications technology in a supranational context. It was not possible to present an alternative version of this perspective in a UK context, given the existing nature of research. Good historical work has been done in this general area, but primarily limited to researching influences shaping communications technology, and their use, mostly in other countries.[11] But it would be interesting to develop a nuanced account of how new communications technology changed British politics, culture and social relations.

Retrospect

In short, what I came up with was necessarily highly selective. It offered an account determined by what was available rather than what was needed. But, hopefully, its portrayal of how the media contributed to the making of modern Britain – as a series of competing narratives – will provoke further discussion and serve as an antidote to the mind-numbing narrowness of too much media history.

Of course, specialist studies provide the essential building blocks of all areas of enquiry. But it is also important to advance a tradition of media history that seeks ambitiously to situate historical investigation of the media in a wider societal context. In due course, this approach should widen the context still further through comparative research. There are a growing number of media historical studies, especially in America, that make explicit comparisons across national frontiers (for example, Starr 2004 and Nerone 2006). Pioneer comparative media histories (Briggs and Burke 2002/2005; Chapman 2005a) have now surfaced. However, the most ambitious of these (Briggs and Burke 2002/2005) falters when it enters the nineteenth century. Perhaps the next phase of comparative media history should begin by identifying key trends that leading western nations had in common, and recount the role of the media in relation to these. Indeed, the sequel to this admirable book might be called *Narrating Western Media History*, to be followed by a third volume entitled *De-Westernizing Media History*.

Notes

1 See in particular Harris (1996) and Barker (1998).
2 For example, Read (1961), Perkin (1969) and a more recent airing of this argument, Brett (1997).
3 Among others, Clark (1985), Price (1999) and Cannadine (2000).
4 Political theorists differ in where they locate political parties within their conceptual maps. Parties are perhaps best viewed as being half in and half out of civil society: indeed, ideally, conduits between civil society and the state.
5 The classic exposition of this interpretation is provided by Scannell (1992).
6 This is the key point made in DiCenzo's (2004) critique of my original essay.

7 See, for example, the pioneering study by John Tosh (1999).
8 While space does not permit a full exposition of this and subsequent narratives, they are presented more fully (and more extensively sourced) in my original essay running to over fifty pages (Curran 2002).
9 See for example the elaborately polite debate between Wiener and Hampton in Hampton *et al.* (2006).
10 For a fine historical exemplification of this argument, see Turner (2006).
11 See, for example, Abbate (2000), Flichy (2002), Turner (2006) and Winston (1998). Only the last of these relates to the British context.

The liberal narrative

Introduction

A defining characteristic of many historical accounts of media development is their tendency to present an essentially liberal interpretation of the complex interaction between media institutions and wider socio-political relations and processes. One aspect of this narrative is that the media has become increasingly free from state interference and politically independent. Starting with the press in the mid-nineteenth century, liberal media historians argue that the abolition of the so-called 'taxes on knowledge' and other financial restrictions was a defining moment in the establishment of a 'fourth estate', a phrase that is still used to this day – particularly by newspaper journalists and proprietors – lest we forget the historical struggle to secure press freedom and the continuing threat of state censorship.

Although the term itself is usually attributed to T. B. Macaulay, a well-known Victorian parliamentarian and historian, the idea of the press as the fourth estate of the realm was born out of the development of Western liberalism between the seventeenth and nineteenth centuries. Normally associated with the writings of John Milton, John Locke, Adam Smith, Jeremy Bentham, James Mill and John Stuart Mill – at least within a British context – liberalism is best understood as a political ideology that places special emphasis on individual and civil liberties (e.g. free enterprise and the freedom of speech and political assembly) in the quest for prosperity, happiness and enlightenment.

One of the necessary conditions for ensuring the aforementioned, according to classic liberal theory, is that the polity be made up of a plurality of representative institutions that facilitate critical debate and democratic decision-making. Of these institutions, liberal thinkers consider the press to be fundamental to the formation of public opinion and a trustworthy bulwark against political corruption and social injustices. In other words, the press has a constitutional role to play, which is to facilitate and strengthen the wider process of democratization – still in its infancy – by making government and other power elites more accountable to the public. However, it can only fulfil this role if it has unlimited freedom of expression, which has since been interpreted as an argument for absolute market freedom, including the freedom to self-regulate.

While the foregoing arguments still form the basis for the classic liberal defence of press freedom, some liberal media historians are critical of the way in which the press has become increasingly commercial and populist, arguing that the golden age of journalistic professionalism peaked in the late Victorian period, culminating in W. T. Stead's advocacy for 'government by journalism'. Although *laissez-faire* economics secured press freedom and facilitated the expansion of the British press, on the other hand, Adam Smith's 'invisible hand' was failing to promote the public interest. The main reason for this is that, as the press became increasingly industrialized, it fundamentally altered the nature of its ownership, resulting in more and more of the local and national press being owned by a handful of enterprising individuals, otherwise known as press barons (e.g. Rothermere, Northcliffe, Beaverbrook, Harmsworth), whose prime concern was to sell as many newspapers as possible, thereby increasing their advertising revenue and profit margins.

It is at this point in the liberal narrative that we see the emergence and development of a more socially responsible media, viz. public service broadcasting in the 1920s, under the aegis of the BBC. Like the press, broadcasting was soon heralded as yet another estate of the realm, the 'fifth estate'. Commonly perceived as an exemplary public institution whose principal role is essentially a democratizing one, liberals have argued that broadcasting has been invaluable in contributing to the ongoing cumulative empowerment of the people. The BBC's public service ethos, especially its commitment to educating and informing its listening public, is particularly important in this respect, not least because it filled the void created by an increasingly commercialized press. That this coincided with early twentieth-century extensions of the franchise is of further importance for liberal historians; if representative democracy and parliamentary sovereignty were to function in a meaningful way, it was imperative that the newly enlarged electorate be politically informed and taught how to be responsible citizens. Liberal media historians have also argued that broadcasting has helped to facilitate communication between different social groups who might not otherwise have anything in common, thus mitigating any extreme antagonistic social relations.

Unlike the press, broadcasting has always been subject to an unusual degree of public control and officialdom in comparison with other media, the press in particular. For a start, licence to broadcast has always been regulated by state-appointed regulatory bodies. Broadcasters also have a statutory obligation to ensure that programmes observe certain standards of taste and decency, among others. Having said this, although broadcasters have come under a good deal of pressure from governments in the past, and continue to do so, liberal historians argue that they have nearly always resisted such pressures, thus asserting their editorial autonomy and commitment to impartiality and representing a diversity of competing social interests. Curran (2002a: 5) probably best sum-marizes the way in which liberal histories of broadcasting have been woven together to illustrate the above: the lifting of the ban on broadcasting con-troversial issues in 1928; the consolidation of the BBC's status during the Second World War; the coming of commercial television in 1955; the aboli-tion of the 'fourteen day rule' forbidding broadcast coverage of any issue that was due to be debated in parliament within the next fortnight; the BBC's refusal (unlike during the 1926 General Strike) to capitulate to government official policy during the Suez crisis and the Falklands conflict; through to the recent spat surrounding the war on Iraq and the controversial Hutton Report.

Both the chapters in this section contribute openly or by implication to this debate, while also questioning some of the broad-brush accounts one often associates with liberal histories of media development. Mark Hampton's opening essay offers an authoritative and thought-provoking reappraisal of the liberal narrative in the context of the twentieth-century British press. Contrary to the widely held belief that the press ceased its democratizing role from the late nineteenth century onwards, Hampton suggests that radical criticisms of the popular press have possibly overstated its influence and political bias. He argues that the press is still a key facilitator of public debate, especially during moments of crisis. However, while he thinks that liberal accounts of press history are valuable in aiding our understanding of how the press and other related media have developed – and ought continue to develop – he argues for what he calls a 'post-radical' liberal narrative of media history that is con-text specific and takes account of the possible articulations between liberal–pluralist and radical approaches to the study of the media. In doing so, he draws upon the rich empiricism of existing historical case studies of the newspaper press, on the one hand, and contemporary media theory, on the other.

Hugh Chignell provides an interesting analysis of the ebb and flow of change and reaction in BBC current affairs radio. Starting with the 1930s, he argues that there was a progressive shift from the elitist programmes that characterized much early radio to a more inclusive and democratic approach to current affairs broadcasting. Such changes were particularly noticeable in the 1950s and 1960s, a period that saw all kinds of challenges to traditional BBC cultural values, including innovations to current affairs and news–related talks. Chignell also notes the ways in which the BBC became less deferential to political authority, evident in the organization's coverage of foreign affairs, and its institutional support for the satire boom of the 1960s. Like Hampton, he too argues for a more nuanced liberal narrative, one that is more accepting of populist changes, rather than judging such developments to be undemo-cratic, just because they are not explicitly educational. His main focus, how-ever, is a case study of the 1970s *Analysis* programme, which signified a return to non-populist current affairs broadcasting. On the one hand, such develop-ments were clearly elitist and no longer aimed at the listening public in general. Yet, *Analysis* was also an attempt to uplift and challenge the listening public into thinking more deeply about contemporary affairs. How one interprets this contradiction is precisely what this book is about.

Further reading

For those interested in the history of liberalism as political theory, and its renaissance in the late twentieth century, see Callinicos (2007) and Heywood (2007) for wide-ranging introductions to the key ideas and most current debates. For a discussion of the early development of liberalism and, more crucially, liberal theories of press freedom, Siebert *et al.* (1963) is widely regarded as essential reading. Equally important is Habermas' (1989) account of the public sphere in the work of John Stuart Mill and Alexis de Tocqueville. As well as summarizing the key writings of traditional liberal theorists, J. B. Thompson (1995) reformulates the liberal emphasis on the freedom of expression into what he calls *the principle of regulated pluralism*; see also Boyce (1978), Briggs and Burke (2002), Bromley and O'Malley (1997), Keane (1991) and Williams (2003).

Although subtly different in terms of narrative and emphasis, liberal histories of the press are plentiful, of which the following are key: Aspinall (1973), Barker (1998, 2000), Boston (1988), Cranfield (1978), Harris (1996), Koss (1981/1984) and Somerville (1996). Just as the press became increasingly free from state interference, a similar narrative exists for British cinema: see, for example, Mathews (1994), Pronay (1981, 1982), Pronay and Croft (1983) and Richards (1997b), among others. This said, not all liberal media historians are critical of state intervention. Although disparaging of government censorship, a good many of the aforementioned are in fact broadly supportive of state support in the form of public funding and subsidies, particularly for media or cultural institutions that have an educational rationale. This is particularly so in relation to the BBC: see, for example, Briggs (1961–95), Crisell (1997), Scannell (1992) and Wyndham Goldie (1977). Probably the most rounded example of this particular narrative, with regard to a variety of media, and the arts in particular, is Janet Minihan's (1977) *The Nationalisation of Culture*.

Chapter 2

Renewing the liberal tradition

The press and public discussion in twentieth-century Britain[1]

Mark Hampton

James Curran's essay, "Rival Narratives of Media History," attempts to place a widely disparate scholarship on the British mass media since 1700 into six ideal types. Given that British media history can hardly be said to constitute a "field" in the strongest sense of the term – it does not center around a common set of debates or key texts, and many scholars engaging in media history do not necessarily think of themselves as "media historians" – the most important function of Curran's monumental essay is a taxonomical one: he names the categories as they already exist, sometimes implicitly, in the scholarly literature. With these categories framed explicitly, we are able not only to try to adjudicate between them, but to question the categories themselves. This chapter examines the liberal narrative in the context of the twentieth-century British press, arguing that it carries significant explanatory power. It does so by taking on board much of the radical critique, indeed welcoming it as a corrective to some of the more naïve and unrealistic claims of the liberal position, and arguing for what I will call a "post-radical" liberal narrative of media history.

The liberal narrative of media history, like all six of Curran's narratives, is often implied and assumed by its proponents, rather than argued directly. This means, of course, that *historical* scholarship written within the framework of the liberal narrative will not necessarily bear a close resemblance to liberal scholarship concerning the *contemporary* media – for not only is the former often undertheorized, but the latter is often unhistorical (Curran 1991: 27; 2002a: 3). On the other hand, given Curran's role as a prominent critic of the liberal theory of the media, we can expect that his own statement of a liberal narrative of media history will not merely have been assembled from previous scholarship, but will have been informed by contemporary theory. At the same time, both contemporary media scholarship and twentieth-century media history have been shaped by categories drawn from nineteenth- and twentieth-century commentators on the press (Negrine 1994: 20). For both of these reasons, our attempts to evaluate the liberal narrative of media history need to be informed by both contemporary theory and empirical evidence concerning specific media in specific historical contexts.

The liberal theory has come under much deserved criticism among British and American scholars (McChesney 1999; Curran 2002: 79–103). Despite this, Curran has argued that radical scholars of the contemporary media, by arguing too much among themselves even while moving toward traditionally liberal positions (for example by questioning media "influence" and by demonstrating that power was more dispersed through society than previously assumed), have effectively allowed the liberal position to attain predominance by default, at least in some circles (2002: 107–26, 146–47).[2] The implication is that the liberal premises, that media reflect rather than shape society and that markets (eventually) ensure that audiences' wishes are honored, could not stand up to rigorous scrutiny. According to Curran (2002: 147), following revisionist radicalism's deconstruction of earlier radical scholarship, the latter's insights are being "smothered;" "What is needed is a reformulation, which both salvages these insights and also takes account of criticism."

Curran makes this point in the context of discussing the past generation of *contemporary* media studies, rather than in his "rival narratives of media history" essay, and he is advocating a radical synthesis that accommodates radical, more than liberal, criticism. But a broadly similar point can be made about the liberal narrative of media history: there is a need for a liberal narrative that accommodates the insights of radical scholarship. Curran argues that the rival narratives rarely address each other, and he calls for a synthesis of the five optimistic narratives (including the liberal) and the more pessimistic radical narrative. This chapter more modestly asks, in the context of the twentieth-century British press, whether the "liberal narrative" depends on myopically ignoring radical scholarship's pointed critiques of ownership concentration and the democratizing power of the market, or if a place exists for a liberal analysis of media history that takes radical critiques seriously. It argues that a nuanced, context-specific version of the liberal narrative is supported by the development of the twentieth-century newspaper press in Britain.

According to Curran (2002: 4–5), the liberal narrative entails that the development of the mass media "enormously strengthened" the process of democratization, both through the media's struggle to become independent of government and through free media's empowering of ordinary people. With regard to the press, the liberal narrative has a lengthy pedigree, and present-day scholars and pundits who argue from this perspective often reproduce the narrative of political activists from the Levellers to the 1850s campaigners against "Taxes on Knowledge."[3] At the center of this narrative is a conception of the press as an educational institution that facilitates the rational public discussion of serious ideas (Siebert *et al.* 1963: 39–71; Keane 1991; Hampton 2004: 48–74; Winston 2005). It rests on the assumption that market competition will ensure that alternative voices will have a chance to be heard, and that the better ideas will, in the long run, prevail. Historically, its proponents have believed that any excesses attributable to the marketplace paled in significance to the dangers of tyranny resulting from state regulation. With the emergence of the New Journalism and the press barons at the end of the nineteenth century, according to Curran (2002: 6), the liberal narrative of the press as an aid to the democratic process "trails off" in studies of the press and relocates in liberal studies of public service broadcasting. For this reason, locating a liberal function in the twentieth-century British press is particularly significant.

Given its emphasis on rational discourse of public affairs, proponents of the liberal narrative would seem to find less to value in the twentieth-century British press than would proponents of the radical or populist narratives, for whom (respectively) the growth of entertainment values in popular newspapers signify either a distraction from the exercise of power (Chalaby 1998: 183–93) or an indication that the press was becoming more democratic in focusing on topics in which working class readers were actually interested (McNair 2000; Conboy 2002). Whereas for the populist scholar, the increasing competitiveness of the newspaper industry ensured that papers catered to readers' desires, for the radical scholar, the increasing concentration of ownership, reliance on advertising revenues, and the requirement for either mass circulation or affluent readers have meant that key political perspectives have been effectively silenced.

The development of the twentieth-century press thus seems well suited to a debate between advocates of the radical and populist narratives. From the perspective of the liberal narrative, in contrast, twentieth-century newspapers present three key problems, each of which has been illuminated by the radical critique. First, regardless of whether the human interest, sex and scandal emphasis of twentieth-century popular newspapers constituted the distraction claimed by the radicals or the populist validation claimed by the democratic populists, it certainly did not look like the discursive aid to parliamentary self-government envisioned by liberal reformers in the 1850s and 1860s.

Second, even on those pages devoted to serious political news, newspapers' performance has not always justified the triumphalism of the liberal narrative. In particular, newspapers' weakness as a liberal, educational agent can be seen in their inability to discuss such a fundamental topic as war and peace comprehensively and rationally, as several focused studies have argued. For example, in the years before the First World War, at the same time that Lord Northcliffe's papers vilified Germany, a wide range of newspapers, in covering the wars of the early twentieth century, provided "distance" and "denial" for their readers, failing to offer a substantial picture of the dead and wounded but instead presenting war as sport and pacifism as unnatural (Wilkinson 2003). Whereas Edwardian newspapers are blamed for failing to prepare the First World War generation for the realities of war, the papers of the 1930s are blamed for failing to provide an open debate between the advocates of appeasement and the supporters of confronting Hitler; rather, the press largely supported appeasement, both in accordance with government wishes and as a result of journalists' aversion to another war (Gannon 1971; Cockett 1989). Although the actual policies advocated in these two cases contradict each other (and although Wilkinson's study of the Edwardian period focuses on cultural images of war rather than editorial foreign policy advocacy), what unites the two cases is their insufficiently vigorous presentation of important political views on a crucial issue. In each case, moreover, within a few years, a consensus had emerged that the poorly represented view was the correct one. More recently, John Richardson (2004) shows that even the broadsheet press has resorted to negative stereotyping in its coverage of topics related to Islam, rather than providing comprehensive and balanced information and editorial views, a result that he ties to the views of elite journalists and affluent audience members.

Third, whereas nineteenth-century liberals assumed the market would provide the diversity of editorial viewpoints required by the liberal narrative, radical scholars of newspaper political economy have emphasized the ever-increasing concentration of media ownership during the course of the twentieth century, resulting by the end of the century in newspapers owned by multinational corporations whose primary interests might not lie in Britain, or even in media (Tunstall 1996). The nineteenth-century liberal ideal of the press implied that anyone with a view to peddle could start his or her own paper, and the marketplace of ideas would determine success; as radical scholars have argued, rising entry costs and the expanding reliance on advertising revenues gave Big Business increasing influence over editorial content (Political and Economic Planning 1938: 188–99; Curran and Seaton 2003: 346–62). In this atmosphere, even high-circulation newspapers could be squeezed out of the market if their editorial views ran foul of corporate concerns. Much as the early twentieth-century Liberal Party was squeezed between the parties of Capital and Labour, the liberal narrative would seem to be outflanked by the populist and radical narratives in relation to twentieth-century press history.

Yet despite these obvious limitations in relation to the twentieth-century press, I would suggest that the liberal narrative retains significant explanatory power, within carefully delimited constraints. First, in deference to the radical critique, proponents of the liberal narrative have to acknowledge the incomplete level of democratic participation. Both the liberal and the populist narratives may be similarly optimistic, but they should not be confused; it need not be part of the burden of the liberal narrative to argue that markets are infallible, or that consumer choice equals democracy. Second, and following closely from this point, the liberal narrative must own up to the fact that it is not a totalizing narrative: much editorial content in the press has little if anything to do with the project of democratic self-government. These are limitations of the liberal narrative, not devastating problems for it; the fact that not all newspaper content serves a project of liberal self-government should not distract us from those cases in which it does.

Third, a revised liberal narrative needs to employ a more flexible definition of "rational discourse," one more receptive to the overlap between human interest and public affairs. In pointing out that "less than 20 per cent of the content of the national popular press is allocated to political, economic and social issues," Curran has further argued:

> Admittedly, gossip about TV stars in the tabloid press may be said, in a circuitous way, to contribute to a normative debate about changing social relations. But this is not what is meant by liberal theorists when they repeat age-old phrases about the press being a vital source of public information and life-blood of democracy.
>
> Curran and Seaton (1981 [2003]: 347)

This is true enough, but I would argue that this is a question to be settled on a case-by-case basis through historical content analysis supplemented, where possible, by examinations of reader response; we must not rely on similarly "age-old phrases" about "false consciousness" or "dumbing down." To take one example of the ways in which our understanding of "rational discourse" might be expanded, Michelle Tusan has shown that the Edwardian suffrage paper, *Votes for Women*, drew on the "human interest story" made popular by the New Journalism to emphasize social injustice that could be addressed only by giving women the vote (Tusan 2005: 159). More recently, Martin Conboy's (2006) examination of the early twenty-first-century British tabloid has shown that celebrity cases can be used to address important social issues, such as domestic violence, although he argues that, in practice, the celebrity event tends to overwhelm the broader issue.

Finally, the liberal narrative needs to reconsider the significance of what Chalaby calls the "polarization" between popular and quality journalism (1998: 167; see also Sparks 1988, 1991; Seymour-Ure 1996: 26–27), followed by their reconvergence in the "tabloidization" of the quality press in the 1990s (Bromley 1998a). How one makes sense of elite- and mass-market segmentation depends as much on a scholar's theoretical bent and temperament as it does on any sort of empirical evidence: the choice of a less politically oriented paper can be viewed as media-driven fatalism or political passivity, on the one hand, or a reader's own reasonable acceptance of the basic political framework combined with a rational lack of interest in politics, on the other. A realistic liberal narrative has to avoid the extremes of regarding readers of the popular press either as powerless victims or as participants in a democratic undertaking simply by virtue of exercising consumer choice.

All of these limitations entail moving away from a perfectibilist standard of politics by public discussion. From the perspective of the (revised) liberal narrative, the press can have an important role in promoting a democratic politics by public discussion without doing so in every newspaper title, or in every edition; and it can do so even if not every reader wishes to participate. Indeed, given historical liberalism's dynamic nature, it is only fitting that the liberal narrative of media history, and the liberal media ideal that undergirds it, should be more flexibly defined.[4]

With these revisions in mind, the evidence suggests that the press in twentieth-century Britain has often, but not always, operated in ways suggested by Curran's "liberal narrative." This is a large topic, and because of space it cannot be addressed comprehensively here. I will devote most of the remaining space, therefore, to a single major point of tension between the radical and liberal narratives, the quantity and quality of political information available in popular newspapers, including the question of political balance. During the early twentieth century, for example, a leftist critical tradition emerged that argued that the commercial press, as the mouthpiece of big business, was to blame for Labour's inability to get elected, and Norman Angell argued in 1922 that, even if Labour were elected, a hostile press would render their victory meaningless (Angell 1922; Hopkin 1978). Following Labour's landslide election victory in 1945, party leaders' belief that press opposition made it impossible for them to carry out their mandate was one of the factors prompting them to order the first Royal Commission on the Press (O'Malley 1998: 87; Moore 2007). More recently, *The Sun* was blamed for turning the 1992 election away from Labour leader Neil Kinnock, who had enjoyed a substantial lead in the polls, and ensuring the Conservative re-election. Following a steady barrage of anti-Labour editorials and stories, including one entitled "Why I'm Backing Kinnock, by Stalin," the largest mass circulation paper devoted a full page on election morning to the headline "If Kinnock wins today, will the last person to leave Britain please turn out the lights" (Thomas 2005: 87, 103). Not surprisingly, Kinnock and his supporters blamed a right-wing popular press for their loss.

This portrayal of the press's relationship to the Labour Party supports the radical narrative of the media's facilitation of social control. In this model, the media engenders consent through consumerism and selective portrayal of politics, and steadily attacks the Labour Party because of its potential threat to the capitalist social order. But as James Thomas' recent work suggests, the relationship of the popular press to the Labour Party has been far more complicated than this portrayal allows. For one thing, the press's overwhelming hostility to Labour between 1979 and 1992 represented a qualitatively new phenomenon that was the contingent result of political developments in the Thatcher era, rather than any sort of inevitable outcome of commercial press ownership. Between 1945 and 1949, even as Labour supporters complained that it could not receive a fair hearing from the capitalist press, Thomas (2005) shows that it actually held its own. When the press was at its most partisan, between 1945 and 1951, Labour was well represented, and during the era of relative "consensus," even nominally pro-Tory papers often employed frames that favored Labour candidates over Conservative ones. The historically contingent support Labour often enjoyed depended upon muting radicalism, certainly, and it is not necessarily evidence for a journalistic polis of the Victorian ideal. But it is important evidence of a popular press that has been relatively reflective of the two postwar mass parties.

It might be objected that, although it has been shown that longstanding claims regarding the inherent and overwhelming hostility of the popular press to the Labour Party have been overstated, there is a difference between supporting the Labour Party in particular contexts and supporting the labour movement. Certainly, from the perspective of the radical narrative, New Labour's adoption of more market-friendly policies and its championing of "Third Way" views over Keynesianism seem to serve as evidence that a capitalist press is structurally biased against the interests of labour and, thus, on basic bread-and-butter questions of economic power, presents a one-sided range of opinion, rather than the diversity of viewpoints required by the liberal narrative. Rather than two (or more) dissimilar parties shaping newspaper debate, concern for favorable newspaper coverage helped to stimulate a convergence of the two parties' policies (Tunney 2007). This point illustrates Kingsley Martin's (1947: 45–46) argument that capitalist ownership of the press would naturally tend to promote pro-capitalist perspectives; as he asked in 1947, "Why should anyone try to bribe a millionaire in order to make him a capitalist?"

At one level, it would be difficult to dispute that (as radical scholarship argues) the commercial press supports dominant interests, nor is this point surprising. But even here the radical critique has tended to understate the opportunities for alternative voices to be heard, both in the mainstream and in the alternative press, and to shape the dominant political debates. Again, this is historically contingent, a matter to be settled by specific empirical scholarship as much as by theory. Even in periods in which pressures to conformity were at their highest, such as during particular wars, the commercial press was often able to offer critical perspectives. During the South African War, for example, despite a concerted attempt by the government to portray its critics as unpatriotic, and despite widespread manifestations of jingoism, *The Manchester Guardian* was able not only to maintain a consistent anti-war line, but also to redefine "patriotism" in such a way as to demand a critical politics by public discussion, and to help shape the debates on imperialism following the war. Moreover, despite its unpopular position on the war, and the temporary decline in circulation that the paper sustained, it was able to support this critical message by carving out a commercial niche: its superior shipping news (Hampton 2001). This is not to minimize the overwhelming support that the elite and popular press gave to the war (Beaumont 2000; Helly and Callaway 2000; Potter 2003: 36–55), or to suggest that the government was immediately constrained by a debate between its journalistic supporters and its opponents. But multiple perspectives were maintained in an important critical debate, thus contributing to evolving publicly held perspectives on Empire. More broadly, while several scholars have emphasized the everyday barrage of imperial propaganda during the age of New Imperialism (Mackenzie 1984;

Richards 1990: 119–67), recent scholarship has shown that not only alternate perspectives but ample specific information about empire was available in the elite and popular press (Startt 1991; Kaul 2003).

Similarly, during the Cold War, despite the Labour government's early support for the American side and anti-Soviet propaganda (Jenks 2006), Tony Shaw dismisses both the "commonly held view that a consensus on the threat posed by Soviet communism swiftly emerged among Britain's opinion-formers in the wake of VE Day," and the "traditional impression of the popular press as simplistic in its coverage of politics and international affairs" (Shaw 1998: 83). Rather, he sees the popular press in the early Cold War as divided among strident anti-Russian papers (e.g. the *Daily Mail*), foreign policy "realist" papers that countenanced a postwar Russian sphere in Eastern Europe (e.g., the three major Beaverbrook papers), and an "internationalist" school (ibid.: 73). For both the popular press and the broadsheets, fluidity and multisided debate eroded only with the Czechoslovak coup in 1948 (see also Foster 1990).

The twentieth-century press facilitated critical debate not only on questions of foreign policy, but on economic policy as well. Even in the second half of the twentieth century, when ownership concentration and newspapers' integration into multinational companies with interests in broadcasting and non-media industries had reached an advanced state (Tunstall 1996), it proved possible for non-dominant opinion to break into the mainstream press and to challenge and even reshape dominant points of view. During the 1970s, despite the power of printing unions, monetarist think tanks were able to challenge the dominance of the Keynesian consensus. Richard Cockett has described the process by which monetarist ideas developed by the Institute of Economic Affairs were disseminated through the *Daily Telegraph*, the *Financial Times*, and *The Times*, particularly through the conversions of journalists Samuel Brittan, Peter Jay and William Rees-Mogg (Cockett 1995: 184–88). Although it might appear counterintuitive to portray the intellectual vanguard of Thatcherism as evidence supporting Curran's liberal narrative, particularly given that the triumph of its ideas in recent media policy is taken as a key manifestation of exactly the sort of loss of worker/citizen control that the radical critique decries, for present purposes what is important is that the press was an agency in which dominant economic policies were challenged. Moreover, the influence of monetarist think tanks in getting their viewpoints into the press is paralleled in the 1980s and 1990s by trade unions and public interest groups employing public relations to get their message into a post-Wapping commercial press – an ability ironically facilitated by corporate cost-cutting measures that leave understaffed newspapers looking for "information subsidies." While corporations have much deeper pockets than unions or public interest groups, the latter have similarly been able to take advantage of this opening (Davis 2002).

The 1979 election, and the five years or so leading up to it, is an interesting example of the limits of the liberal narrative, and of the ways in which the liberal and radical narratives overlap and risk talking past one another. At the risk of simplification, there is an extent to which press coverage of partisan politics in the 1970s exemplifies the bifurcation between elite and popular that radical critics and liberal theorists have constructed since the end of the nineteenth century (Hampton 2004: 98–99). While *The Times* was giving Sir Keith Joseph and the Centre for Policy Studies a platform for turning the Conservative Party against its recent Keynesian heritage (Cockett 1995), the *Daily Express* was presenting a Labour Britain "UNDER SEIGE," with "MILES OF MISERY" and "CHAOS ON ALL SIDES" (Thomas 2005: 78). This returns us to two points made earlier: first, the liberal narrative, to be a helpful model for understanding the development of the British press, need not be equally applicable to all contexts; second, the liberal narrative has to account for, rather than being juxtaposed with, sensationalism.[5]

What these examples suggest is that the twentieth-century British press has, in particular contexts, provided alternative viewpoints and information of the sort necessary to shape political debate. This further suggests that the liberal narrative has to be removed from any Whiggish triumphalism: rather than a steady advance in democratic participation and political rights, the press has better filled a liberal role in some cases than in others, and always imperfectly. Yet even this point marks only a starting point for considering the press's role in promoting a liberal politics by public discussion. Beyond the bare documenting of cases in which the commercial press was able to provide the information necessary to a politics by public discussion, further empirical work is needed in at least four areas that have only been addressed sketchily here. First, how has vigorous journalistic debate, when it has occurred, shaped government policy? Second, where this is possible to discover, how have readers participated in the debate, whether through letter-writing, choice of which papers to read, or otherwise (Bromley 1998b)? Third, how have alternative papers, including single-issue papers, shaped discourse in the mainstream press? Fourth, how has the growth of public relations and modern Government "spin" (Barnett and Gaber 2001; Davis 2002; Moore 2006) affected the range of opinion available in the press – as presumably the government, different corporations, public interest groups, and trade unions, all of which engage in information management, will not pay to put the *same* opinions into the press? Each of these questions requires specifically focused historical case studies.

While acknowledging that more empirical work needs to be done in order to test Curran's liberal narrative explicitly, based on the examples cited here, we can tentatively draw at least two conclusions concerning the twentieth-century British press. First, such examples as the South African War, the early Cold War, and the contest over economic thought in the 1970s suggest that journalistic debate tends to be most vigorous during certain pivotal moments in which elite opinion is most sharply divided, such as when a consensus is breaking down and another has not yet taken shape.[6] This observation has a tautological quality, but not entirely so – particularly once the possibilities for alternative media to influence elite opinion are taken into account. Theoretically, this point also raises a "chicken or egg" question, for it will not always be easy to disentangle the extent to which journalistic discourse is undermining consensus or an unraveling consensus is reshaping journalistic discourse. But it is certainly consistent with the liberal narrative that the press would tend toward promoting conflict at certain times (or regarding certain issues), while on other occasions "manufacturing consent," in the liberal Walter Lippmann's famous phrase.

Second, we need to distinguish between the liberal narrative as a *meta-historical* "grand narrative" that Curran has identified as one of the six narratives through which media historians tell their story, on the one hand, and as a *historical* topic, on the other hand. By this I mean that, along with such factors as the political economy of the press, the professional organization of journalism, and the political–legal environment, we need to see the liberal narrative of media history as an autonomous cultural factor that has shaped the history of the British press in the twentieth century, and not merely as a contemporary framework for studying the past. The liberal narrative, moreover, is a common heritage over which no political faction holds a monopoly. While those calling for press reform, and lamenting the conservative effects of tabloid celebrity culture, have found their foil, at least implicitly, in nineteenth-century models of the public sphere and denunciation of tyranny (Hampton 2004), opponents of press reform (or opponents of the BBC) have drawn on the longstanding equation of freedom of the press with non-intervention by the state (O'Malley 1997). This discourse, in turn, continued to find support – sometimes, in particular contexts – in the "really existing" liberal political function of the twentieth-century British press.

Notes

1 My thanks to David Karr for his valuable suggestions on an earlier draft.

2 It is not clear in what sense Curran thinks the liberal perspective has been allowed to predominate in discussions of the contemporary media. Although liberal media ideals remain powerfully normative, there seems to be widespread agreement that political communication is in a crisis of a sort that would undermine these ideals (see McNair 2000: ix–x, 1–13).

3 A recent example of a fairly uncritical rendering of the liberal narrative is Copeland (2006).

4 As Freeden (2005: 15) argues, "One can never understand liberalism if one assumes that it is a monolith in its postulates, assumptions, and values." See also Kloppenberg (1998: 3–20) for similar points in the context of American liberalism.

5 See Bingham (2004) for an impressive, historically contextualized counterexample to the assumption that sensationalism in the popular press is inherently socially conservative.

6 This mirrors the point made by Hallin (1989: 10), in the context of American media during the Vietnam War, that journalists become more "detached or even adversarial" in situations of political conflict, whereas in "situations in which political consensus seems to prevail," journalists tend to uphold the "dominant political perspective."

Chapter 3

Change and reaction in BBC Current Affairs Radio, 1928–1970

Hugh Chignell

Current affairs captures something unique about British broadcasting. Like public service broadcasting, it serves to differentiate British from American media and, also like public service broadcasting, it is influenced more by broadcasting values than by audience ratings. A search for the origins of current affairs radio begins with the 'topical' talks of the 1930s that addressed political issues of the day, usually with the utmost caution. As Scannell and Cardiff (1991) describe, there were some attempts under the first Head of Talks, Hilda Matheson, and her successor, Charles Siepmann, to address social problems (most notably unemployment and homelessness), but the decade was marked by increasing caution and, in the words of Asa Briggs (1965: 148), a 'swing to the right'. By the beginning of the Second World War, topical talks were in a fairly moribund state and completely unprepared for what was to come. One of the factors that jerked the BBC out if its complacency was the popularity of the Nazi propagandist, William Joyce ('Lord Haw-Haw'), who attracted audiences of over a quarter of the adult population. The BBC's response was to employ the novelist J. B. Priestley to deliver a series of topical talks after the *Nine O'Clock News* entitled *Postscript to the News*. Sian Nicholas (1996: 61) accounts for Priestley's success (a 'national sensation') in these terms:

> The popularity of the *Postscripts*, and Priestley's transformation into the radio personality of 1940, indicates as much the dissatisfaction of the British people with what they were being offered as they do the undoubted craft of the author. In 1940 the Ministry of Information and the BBC were clearly failing to provide the information and the support that a people at war demanded. Not surprisingly, the listening audience wanted to know what was going on; they wanted to be talked with, not talked to. Above all, they welcomed diversity of opinion: in a war that was going to affect almost every aspect of their lives. The British people could not be expected to carry on as usual and trust to their leaders for the rest.

From the high-mindedness of 1930s talks to the plain speaking, 'talking with' of Priestley's *Postscripts*, there is clearly a shift from improving and, at times, frankly elitist output to a form of current affairs commentary that was more democratic and far more responsive to audience needs. The purpose of this chapter is to explore other similar – and less well known – developments in BBC radio talk and current affairs up to and including the 1970s, while also raising questions about the extent to which a more democratic and inclusive approach was established, as is widely assumed.

Change in the 1950s

The 1960s are commonly seen as the decade of the most pronounced social and cultural change in Britain. There are numerous accounts, however, which show that the 1950s was also a decade of change and innovation and one in which earlier orthodoxies were undermined (see for example Marwick 1998; Tracey 1998). A range of factors contributed to this progressive shift in the BBC, not easily summarized here, although some of the most important catalysts can be identified. For a start, changes in social relations and processes from the end of the war to the 1960s challenged the arrogance and elitism of the BBC and 'brought into question the authority of the whole hierarchy of values on which the Reithian system of control, consensus and ethos itself depended' (Burns 1977: 43). The breaking of the BBC's monopoly with the arrival of ITV in 1955 further contributed to this change. By offering an alternative to BBC television, ITV forced a re-examination of BBC practices and values; indeed, as Janet Thumim (2004: 53) points out, the depiction of the BBC as 'stuffy' and 'highbrow' was part of Independent Television's sales pitch, 'in order to lure viewers to their own, supposedly more accessible, offerings'. In his account of the decline of public service broadcasting, Michael Tracey (1998: 76) sees the replacement of the ultra-Reithian William Hayley as Director-General of the BBC by Sir Ian Jacob as of critical importance. Hayley's most notable achievement had been the creation of the Third Programme, which in its uncompromisingly high cultural output 'allowed not the slightest tinge of populism' (ibid.: 69). Jacob had very different ideas about broadcasting and was wholeheartedly committed to the television service, unlike his predecessors. The dramatic rise in the popularity of television in the 1950s was itself a populist development that challenged Reithian values.

Radio was also experiencing some serious self-examination partly because of the success of television and the commercial challenge from Radio Luxembourg. Broadcasting 'family' output on long wave, Luxembourg pioneered the highly popular quiz shows *Take Your Pick, Double Your Money* and *Opportunity Knocks* before they transferred to ITV (Street 2002: 199). Faced by hugely increased competition, the BBC's Director of Sound Broadcasting, Lindsay Wellington, set up the Sound Working Party in 1956 to suggest a way forward. The resulting report was, according to Briggs (1995: 39–40), essentially anti-Hayley, anti-Reith and anti the old BBC. The report included the stridently anti-Reithian declaration that, in future, BBC Radio should 'seek to cater for the needs and tastes of its audiences without seeking, as it perhaps had done too much in the past to alter and improve them' ('The Future of Sound Broadcasting in the Domestic Service' quoted in Briggs 1995: 40). Similarly, the American commentator Burton Paulu (1956: 121) provides us with an understanding of why change was necessary. Writing in the 1950s, he felt that what the Talks Department needed were 'audience aware producers', 'showmen' rather than 'high-minded scholars'. He thought that it was among these 'purveyors of culture and education' that the least realistic understanding of the audience was to be found and hoped (with some prescience) that the growing competition from television would encourage democratic change.

Technology also came to the aid of those who wanted to change current affairs output. Although the BBC was comparatively slow to convert from disc to magnetic tape, by 1955 tape had largely replaced the disc (Briggs 1979: 582). The impact of tape recording had the potential to solve many problems identified in the 'current affairs crisis' and the perceived failure of talks to be genuinely topical. For example, tape recording made it possible to provide material from around the world and greatly improve the variety and topicality of programme content. Indeed, by facilitating a move to more actuality, recording took production increasingly away from the studio and thereby undermined the traditional studio-based talk.

Faced with the problem of producing topical, news-related talks and armed with the new weapon of the Midget tape recorder, BBC Talks launched its new talks magazine *At Home and Abroad* in 1954. An extract from the *BBC Handbook* of the time describes the programme:

> The new magazine programme, *At Home and Abroad*, can accommodate up to ten talks in two half hour periods, providing authoritative comment on, and explanation of, subjects which may only have made news on the day of broadcast.
>
> *BBC Handbook* (1955: 54)

In other words, *At Home and Abroad* was a new and more accessible form of current affairs radio, an alternative to the didactic radio talk and the predecessor to the most important of all radio current affairs programmes, *Today*. It owed its success partly to its magazine structure, its division into a sequence of relatively short segments that allowed the listener to drop in and out of the programme. The magazine format can be traced back to the radio magazines of the war such as *The Kitchen Front*, which provided a mainly female audience with domestic advice. Unlike the more sustained single-subject talk, the magazine acknowledges the fact that its audience is often engaged in other activities and that radio is a 'secondary' medium.

One final feature of the liberal and more democratic culture of the 1950s (and moving into 1960s) was the decline in deference towards those in positions of power. The Suez crisis of 1956 contributed to that sense that those in authority could be questioned and denied; this was a mood that was fully expressed in the satire boom of the early 1960s. *At Home and Abroad* had its moments of controversy which greatly upset those in power. In October 1954, the programme's editor, Stephen Bonarjee, arranged an interview with the Cypriot leader, Archbishop Makarios, who led the Enosis movement for union with Greece and was seen as a communist agitator by the Churchill government. Makarios had been interviewed on BBC television, and Bonarjee had characteristically seized the opportunity to get his own interview. The result was a furious response from Churchill to the Chairman of the BBC:

> I do not consider that the BBC should be used for the publicizing of people hostile to this country and the gratuitous advertisement of their case…I cannot believe that men with so distinguished a record of service as yourself and Sir Ian Jacob could have been content to stand by and see the BBC used to exploit anti-colonial prejudice for the satisfaction of those whose greatest wish is to destroy the British Commonwealth and Empire.[1]

Churchill was appalled that the adventurousness of BBC current affairs, and its greater international reach, had led to the airing of Makarios' anti-British views. Bonarjee's ambition for *At Home and Abroad*, to be topical and to get the most important voices, had led him to seek out and record an enemy of the British government. The daring and innovation of the programme would become a characteristic of the current affairs magazines that followed in the 1960s.

News and current affairs in the 1960s

Under the progressive leadership of Hugh Carleton Greene (Director-General, 1960–69), who had been head of News and Current Affairs, the 1960s were undoubtedly a progressive decade for BBC news and current affairs radio. Greene's liberalism can be traced back to his exposure to prewar German decadence, and he had a much more *laissez-faire* attitude to his producers than his Reithian predecessors. When he took over as Director-General 'he declared that the BBC under him should be fully alive to the temper of the times' (Hendy 2007: 19). At a time when the influence of Reith was still strong in the BBC, Greene was prepared to take risks and to be ahead of public opinion; hence his support for innovative and even controversial pro-grammes such as *That Was the Week That Was* and *Steptoe and Son*. In radio news and current affairs, Greene made a decisive and important intervention soon after his appointment. He closed down *At Home and Abroad* and the solidly factual *Nine O'clock News* (which had been in existence since the 1920s) and created a daily news and current affairs programme, *Ten O'clock*. Briggs

(1995: 327) records the complaints made about this fusion of fact and comment including a letter to *The Times* from the Archbishop of Canterbury. Despite the protests over *Ten O'clock*, Greene further consolidated news and current affairs under the Editor of News and Current Affairs in June 1960, a role which he then absorbed into his own as Director-General. The anxieties expressed about these changes are important if only because, to the modern listener, so used to news and comment in one programme, they are difficult to comprehend. The author and critic, Joanna Richardson, was particularly critical of the abolition of the *Nine O'clock News*:

> The BBC should keep news and comment absolutely distinct. It should not concede too much to popularity; and it should cater for listeners… who like to have the news straight, and form their own opinions.
>
> Quoted in Briggs (1995: 328)

This concern that news and comment should be kept separate was the orthodox view in the BBC but one that Greene and certain senior managers of BBC radio were clearly prepared to challenge. One of the managers who supported the fusion of news and comment and the general thrust towards a more accessible current affairs output during this period was Frank Gillard (Director of Sound Broadcasting 1963–70). Gillard was something of a radio visionary. His varied background included a celebrated career as a BBC war correspondent, his time spent away from the constraints of the BBC in London at West Region (where among other innovations he created *Any Questions*) and his inspiring encounter with American local radio, which made him into an enthusiastic supporter of that cause (Briggs 1995: 620). As Director of Sound Broadcasting, Gillard quickly established his credentials as a man of action by abolishing both *Children's Hour* (1927–64) and the Features Department. As Features had been the home of some of the most innovative and challenging radio, servicing almost exclusively the Third Programme and staffed by some of radio's most famous names (including Laurence Gilliam, Louis McNeice and D. G. Bridson), its abolition was a brave if perhaps unsurprising move as Bridson (1971: 295) himself confessed:

> …the end of the Features Department came as no great surprise to me: I merely deplored it as yet another wrong decision at the top, this one more likely than any other to put an end to the kind of radio I valued.

Indeed, the closure of the Features Department was an iconic moment in the reinvention of BBC radio. Radio features were at their best a creative form of radio art originally devised in the prewar years. They represented the most challenging and uncompromising form of radio, which often combined poetry, classical music and drama. The demise of the radio feature reflects the fact that this heady mix was far removed from the more audience-aware radio favoured by Gillard. His later introduction of BBC local radio further widened and deepened the engagement of those outside the traditionally elite and metropolitan BBC.

Gillard's partner in the reform of BBC radio was Gerard Mansell (Chief of the Home Service 1965–67 and the first Controller of Radio 4). Like Gillard, Mansell had not come from BBC radio's natural London centre at Broadcasting House but had spent the previous fourteen years at Bush House, the home of External Services. Greene's creation of the 'news plus current affairs' *Ten O'clock* challenged the orthodox BBC division of news from comment, and Mansell shared Greene's views that news and comment should be fused together:

> We should seek to break down these barriers, which are largely artificial, and move towards an integrated 'news show' formula in which all these ingredients are fused, as I am sure they can be without losing either the well established authority and reputation of BBC news or the all important separation of news and comment.
>
> Mansell quoted in Hendy (2007: 44–45)

Influenced by listening to French radio which he took as his model (Mansell was born and educated in Paris), he favoured not only the further integration of news and comment but also a more informal and conversational style of presentation employing unscripted speech. This aspiration translated into the creation of the controversial news and current affairs programme, *The World at One*, in 1965. The programme epitomised Mansell's desire for a more informal, urgent and 'newsy' style produced by a carefully chosen team of producers not recruited from the Talks and Current Affairs Group and who were 'less hide-bound by questions of balance, correctness and deference, and much more inclined to be controversial' (Hendy 2007: 48). But the most controversial component of *The World at One* was the presenter, graphically described here by Hendy (2007: 48–49):

> William Hardcastle, who had been a Washington Correspondent for Reuters after the War and an Editor of the *Daily Mail*…was a large, beetle-browed, untidy person, cigarette-smoking, hard-drinking and shirt-sleeved, and he brought to *The World at One* some of the urgency and heat of Fleet Street. His breathless delivery mangled the conventions of measured speech that still held sway across most of the Home Service, and prompted a regular flow of complaint by disappointed listeners.

Perhaps the main reform for which both Mansell and Gillard were responsible was the move towards 'format' or 'generic' radio. In Reith's BBC, an eclectic mix of output was a defining feature of public service broadcasting. The listeners would find themselves listening to quite unexpected programmes, sometimes challenging or educational, and this contributed to the Reithian mission to educate, inform and entertain. Format radio, on the other hand, was far more attentive to audience demand, and that audience even included youth. 'Pirate Radio' had started with Radio Caroline in 1964 beaming pop music to huge audiences of young people in Britain mainly from ships moored in the North Sea. In June 1967, legislation dealt with the pirates by making it illegal to service their ships (Street 2002: 109). A few months later, BBC Radio 1 was launched. At the same time, Gillard renamed his other networks and so Radios 1, 2, 3 and 4 were born. Meanwhile, Mansell was in the business of not only transforming and popularizing radio news and current affairs but also, in line with the policy of format radio, bringing as much as possible of it to Radio 4, which was emerging as the main place for news and current affairs. He had started down that road with the introduction of *The World at One* and then *The World This Weekend* two years later. He had ambitions to transfer more news and current affairs output to Radio 4 in order to make it the main provider of BBC news and current affairs on either radio or television.

This change towards more 'generic' networks appears to fit a move towards a type of radio that was responsive to a diversity of audience demand, a process that culminated in *Broadcasting in the Seventies*, a distinctly non-Reithian document published in 1969. The document had a particular impact on Radio 3, which became almost exclusively a music network relying increasingly on records. Almost all speech content on Radio 3 was transferred to Radio 4. What was left of mixed programming would survive only on Radio 4, and the whole policy of format radio, targeting specific audiences with discrete programme content, was made explicit. Within weeks, the Campaign for Better Broadcasting was launched to fight the changes. In a letter to *The Times* signed by Sir Adrian Boult, Professor Max Beloff, Jonathan Miller, Henry Moore and others, the gravity of the attack was well expressed:

> [The BBC's policy] seriously threatens the unique role the BBC has played in the cultural and intellectual life of the country [and would] prove disastrous to the standards and quality of public service broadcasting…the issues involved transcend any individual or group interest and we feel that only by organizing all dissent into a unanimous voice will there be any hope of affecting a fundamental change of heart at the BBC which is proceeding with its plans despite the evidence of public dismay.
>
> Briggs (1995: 785)

The fight against the proposals contained in *Broadcasting in the Seventies*, organized by the cultural elite of the time, was partly driven by the concern that the reorganization of radio into generic networks would dilute the quality of output, in particular on Radio 3. There was also concern that mixed programming was being abandoned. Eventually, the outburst against the proposals died down. It probably helped that, at the end of the year, Frank Gillard retired and was replaced by Ian Trethowan, an altogether less radical manager of BBC radio than his predecessor. The promotion of Mansell to Director of Programmes and the arrival of a new Controller of Radio 4, Tony Whitby, shortly followed this. Like Trethowan, Whitby was also considered a safe pair of hands, as evidenced in his championing of a return to non-populist current affairs programmes. It is to such programmes that I now turn.

Compromise and reaction in the 1970s

By the beginning of January 1970, the mood in BBC radio was one of compromise, not least because BBC management was, in the words of Briggs (1995: 800), 'anxious...to reduce contention'. In January, the new Controller of Radio 4, Tony Whitby, had arrived in post having been proposed by Trethowan. He appeared to have the right qualities to 'reduce contention': intelligent and charismatic, he was also an Oxbridge graduate with a particular interest in the work of Matthew Arnold, a literary tradition which Reith himself had subscribed to some fifty years previously. With the BBC still bruised after the uproar over *Broadcasting in the Seventies*, this was a good time to introduce on Radio 4 a demanding, single-subject current affairs programme, reminiscent of an in-depth Radio 3 documentary. Whitby's answer was to commission the talk-based current affairs programme *Analysis*. Ian McIntyre, the first and main presenter of the programme in its early years, takes this view:

> What had been going on in the background, in the BBC at the time was the changeover from the old format of the Home Service and so on, to the networks, to a sort of streaming which they said was to be generic broadcasting...and in all the uproar about this, one cause of concern was what was going to happen to serious current affairs broadcasting, so in a way, the idea for *Analysis* was that it should be a sort of demonstration of good faith to the listener that there were going to be serious things done.[2]

So *Analysis*, in McIntyre's words, would be 'serious', a demanding listen that would stretch the listener and also feature important people as contributors discussing the main current affairs issues of the day. *Analysis* was also the result of a decision to move Radio 3-style talks programmes from the newly 'formatted' Radio 3 to the more mixed Radio 4. So the 'serious' *Analysis* with its Radio 3 heritage would signal clearly to the members of the Campaign for Better Broadcasting and their supporters that they were wrong to think that the quality of public service broadcasting had been damaged. The new current affairs programme would enshrine the traditional ideas of quality as formulated by Reith.

The four men directly responsible for creating *Analysis* were Tony Whitby (Controller, Radio 4), Ian McIntyre, an occasional presenter of talks programmes on Radio 3, Lord Archie Gordon (Editor, Talks and Documentaries Radio) and the producer, George Fischer. McIntyre had joined the BBC in the early 1950s and worked on *At Home and Abroad*. He had been appointed by the Controller of Talks Division and BBC traditionalist, John Green, with whom he shared a conservatism about current affairs broadcasting. Green and McIntyre and their close colleagues represented traditional, anti-populist BBC values, including concern about the combination of news and comment in magazine formats. From the 1950s, McIntyre presented occasional talks and documentaries for the Third Programme. It was this freelance work in the rarified atmosphere of Talks that helped build the informal alliances which then spawned *Analysis*.

Another factor in the creation of *Analysis* was the reaction to the huge growth in journalistic or news-based current affairs exemplified by William Hardcastle's *The World at One*. Ian McIntyre supported the traditional BBC distinction between news and current affairs to the extent that he defined himself as *not* a journalist.

> Journalists were people who worked for newspapers, and there were some people who had come from newspapers and worked in the BBC's News Division, and they called themselves journalists, some of them, but we did not regard ourselves as journalists, we regarded ourselves as current affairs broadcasters, and it was a very different sort of animal really. The business of journalists was to get the news and present it. Our business was to get behind the news, and dig and illuminate and go a bit further, and they were very, very distinct disciplines, we thought. News didn't agree, and were resentful that we made the distinction, but it was a distinction we made.[3]

McIntyre's argument here is based on a sense of his own identity grounded in the old talks/news bifurcation of the prewar BBC. There was more to *Analysis*, however, than the confirmation of McIntyre's identity and, indeed, his criticisms of BBC journalism were shared by others. The proliferation of news-based current affairs, encouraged by Mansell in the pursuit of a more accessible BBC radio, may have at times produced superficial, secondhand accounts of events. Michael Green, an early *Analysis* producer who went on to create *File on Four* and become Controller of Radio 4, expresses the commonly held view that a great deal of journalism was and is superficial and derivative:

> There was a group of people in Broadcasting House who took a very sceptical view of the journalism made in Broadcasting House which they thought was superficial...this drove them to another pole which said 'how are we going to put into the network something which people will find more challenging, less superficial, more demanding, more

authoritative, more first hand?' I would certainly take the view that much of journalism now, as then is derivative and second hand...broadcast journalism is essentially a rewrite agency...and at that time the tide of daily journalism was engulfing people and the end result was a bit unsatisfying for some listeners and they wanted something a bit more challenging.[4]

The thoroughness with which *Analysis* presenters researched their programmes was seen (especially by Fischer and McIntyre) as in marked contrast to the hasty and ill-researched work of radio journalists. It was a deliberate reaction to the hastiness of fusion programmes such as *The World at One* in its self-consciously meticulous use of primary evidence and in-depth research. *Analysis* was a very demanding and *ambitious* programme made by people who, like their inspiration, John Reith, had little or no time for the corrupting triviality of television. McIntyre and Fischer in particular were driven by their commitment to getting the most distinguished contributors and basing their programmes on the most rigorous research. This 'driven' quality to their work perhaps signalled not only an attempt to outdo the much disliked journalistic competition but also to show superiority over television.

In addition, *Analysis* was purely a speech programme; there was rarely any 'actuality'. *Analysis* was similar to its forerunners in Radio 3 and the Third Programme including those made by McIntyre and Fischer in the 1960s. The pace of *Analysis* also contrasted with the briskness of far more popular magazine programmes such as *The World at One* and *Today* (1970–). For example, the 1974 *BBC Handbook* talks of the 'more leisurely, considered and reflective' style of *Analysis*: the one-to-one interviews were tellingly referred to as 'conversations'. Elsewhere, Whitby wrote a series of articles about the new schedule on Radio 4 in the *Radio Times*. His mission for *Analysis* is particularly revealing:

We've got to accustom the audience to the fact there will be tougher programmes in the new Radio 4 than there were in the old one. Between 9 and 10 in the evening, the fare will tend to be more thoughtful, tougher in intellectual terms, and will include material previously thought of as Third Programme. Let's take an example. *Analysis* is the new current affairs documentary which I shall put on Friday nights at 9.15. Now my brief for the programme is – to be true to your subject. Say what you want to say, say it clearly, lucidly, in a form that a reasonably intelligent, reasonably well informed person can understand. Aim at excellence, and at nothing else. There's no word about the size of the audience in that brief. If it gets a low audience figure, I shall not be surprised. So the programme is protected to that extent. If it gets a larger audience I shall be delighted. There is no reason why it shouldn't – anybody can tune in to the radio at 9.15 on a Friday night.

The Radio Times (12 March 1970)

Whitby makes explicit here the Radio 4 inheritance from Radio 3. *Analysis* is described as an example of this 'tougher' and 'more thoughtful' programme. The suggestion that 'excellence' is more important than any consideration of the audience is typically Reithian. The rather throwaway remark that 'anybody' could listen is perhaps a little disingenuous. A rather more realistic view of the audience, explicitly underlining its elitist aspirations, is provided by Greville Havenhand who was both producer and the series editor in the mid-1970s:

> ...you were aiming at an elite audience...you were actually aiming at opinion formers, and because the average Joe Public wasn't going to turn on to a programme like that at eight o'clock on a Thursday evening for three quarters of an hour...you could have made it a popular programme but it wouldn't have been popular...you were aiming at a certain intellectual level that would appeal to these people.[5]

In other words, the creation of *Analysis* can be seen as running entirely counter to earlier more democratic and inclusive trends. It satisfied the needs and concerns of an elite audience and reaffirmed traditional, Reithian values, values that enshrined not only conventional approaches to a news/current affairs separation but also a belief in the supremacy of radio over television. Interestingly, it was not alone in this attempt to reassert traditional radio values. The epic 26-part *Long March of Everyman* was an extremely ambitious history of the common man bristling with ambition; it even attempted to breathe life back into the old radio features tradition and was repeated twice in its entirety. Other examples of an apparent attempt to reaffirm quality and standards in Radio 4 output at about the same time were the major drama series *A Century of Modern Theatre* (including Ibsen and Strindberg), a 13-part anthology, *The Modern British Poets* and a remake of *Under Milk Wood* with Richard Burton.

Conclusion

Curran argues that in the liberal narrative the advent of broadcasting in the twentieth century was a development that broadened and deepened democracy. He identifies three claims made by liberal historians: that broadcasting 'diminished the knowledge gap between the political elite and the general public' (2002a: 6), that changes in the style and tone made for greater inclusivity and, finally, that developments in broadcasting enabled different social groups to talk to each other. There is evidence in the history of BBC radio to support these claims (as Curran shows), and the liberal narrative provides us with an interesting and certainly plausible broad-brush account of the development of BBC current affairs radio. The success of Priestley's wartime talks, the introduction of the magazine format and the fusion of news and comment in the brasher and more conversational news and current affairs programmes of the 1960s do fit a populist–liberal history. Spurred on by the rise of television (including ITV) and competition from Radio Luxembourg and the pirates, BBC radio marched to a far less exclusive and more audience-aware tune. It is, however, a potentially misleading gloss on the shifting sands of broadcasting values as they evolved during the first fifty years of the BBC. What is perhaps missing in liberal histories is an account of *reaction* to trends that some vigorously opposed. In the case of radio, the reaction came in the form of an opportunist coup to reverse the tide of history and put Reithian values back on the agenda. Furthermore, although the magazinization of speech radio and the breaking of the old news/comment taboo were the result of a far greater sensitivity to public tastes, the priorities of men such as Mansell and Gillard were survival and even success in difficult times for radio. Although they may have presided over the streamlining of the networks, they also made space for more serious programmes, the uncompromisingly cerebral and exclusive current affairs programme, *Analysis*, among others.

Notes

1 BBC Written Archive Centre, File R5/107.
2 Ian McIntyre, personal communication, 26 February 1999.
3 Ian McIntyre, personal communication, 26 February 1999.
4 Michael Green, personal communication, 27 October 2000.
5 Greville Havenhand, personal communication, 30 October 1998.

The feminist narrative

Introduction

Although it is common nowadays to talk about feminisms (e.g. first-wave, second-wave, third-wave, radical, socialist, liberal, psychoanalytic, to name but a few), each of them is essentially concerned with explaining and challenging women's oppression and sexual inequality. Hence, most feminist studies see patriarchy – the rule of the father – as the main historical form of social division and site of political contestation. Furthermore, within this patriarchal culture, many feminists regard the family as the chief institution for mediating between the individual and the social status quo, as it is within familial relations that identities based on sex and age take on their sharpest definitions. Such analyses typically portray family life as a prison in which women – *qua* housewives, mothers and daughters – are confined to a life of domesticity and reproduction.

The historical representation and idealization of women as the servile domestic is largely attributable to the Victorian poet, Coventry Patmore, and his domestic epic *The Angel in the House* (1854–62). Of course, the angel ideal not only affected women in the domestic sphere. This quasi-canonization of women as homely saints greatly restricted women's participation in the workplace and public life generally. That women were second-class citizens for much of the nineteenth century and the early twentieth century is unquestionable. And while working class males were still far from equals with their middle class counterparts, they had at least secured significant advances in their social and political rights. Women, on the other hand, regardless of their social class, were still not citizens for much of this period insofar as they did not have the same educational rights, voting rights, property rights or, even, union rights. Hence what is sometimes referred to as 'two spheres' ideology.

Not surprisingly, the media has played a significant part in reinforcing these traditional ideas about domesticity and familial relations, a view that is endorsed in Michael Bailey's contribution to this section. The main thrust of Bailey's chapter is to argue that women's political duty in the early twentieth century continued to be defined in terms of their activity in the private sphere, as it was in the nineteenth century. Even though women were now permitted 'to put a cross on a ballot paper', their principal civic responsibility was still conceived to be one that necessarily involved self-sacrifice in support of husband, family and nation. The crucial difference between the two periods was that, in the early twentieth century, the home was constructed as a source of alternative power, a space for women to make decisions that could affect the life of the nation. They were thus exhorted to identify the domestic realm of the home with the political and social well-being of the nation. The reality, however, was that women were still excluded from positions of any real power; and what political agency they did have in the form of enfranchisement was not sufficient to alter the hegemonic gendered social roles that continued to define women as housewives and mothers.

More specifically, Bailey illustrates how broadcasting during the interwar period was complicit in maintaining or redefining feminine subjectivities for the good of the nation's moral and physical well-being. Like other media technologies, broadcasting sought to capture and to regulate the rhythm of women's daily life, by simultaneously domesticating and gendering certain cultural practices, reinforcing demarcations between the spheres of public and private and thereby establishing the home as a site for cultural governance. In other words, the recovery of traditional family moral values was dependent, to a large extent, on the part that women would have to play in transmitting the cultural values of broadcasting into the *sanctum sanctorum* of the home. Hence the importance accorded to household talks for women listeners, particularly ones that addressed public health issues such as nutrition, domestic economy, mothercraft, childcare, etc. All such programmes were aimed at increasing public awareness of body politics and, more specifically, providing the necessary instruction for a new generation of mothers and housewives, reinvigorating and reinforcing hegemonic familial ideals and practices.

The chapter by David Deacon is a more subtle interpretation of this particular narrative and is in keeping with more recent feminist scholarship. The main focus of his chapter is an examination of the important and distinctive contribution made by female journalists in the reporting of the Spanish Civil War in the UK and USA news media. As well as providing biographical details about the key female correspondents who directly reported on the war in Spain (e.g. Virginia Cowles, Gerda Taro, Martha Gellhorn, Hilde Marquand and Nancy Cunard), Deacon's analysis shows that many of the female correspondents shared remarkably similar views of their reporting roles and responsibilities. In the main, these were to provide empathetic insights into the everyday lives of the civilians caught up in the conflict. The remainder of the chapter considers the immediate and deeper reasons for this shared emphasis upon the everyday, emotional experiences of civilians. For this focus in the female correspondents' work, although to some extent self-determined, also reflected a pragmatic appreciation of the edicts of the international news market and the uncertainties of their employment status.

Further reading

Those interested in feminist media history would do well to familiarize themselves with women's social history to acquire a better understanding of the key issues and debates within this broader field of study and its relationship with the emergence and subsequent development of feminist theory and criticism. Useful overviews of feminist women's history in Britain include: Bennett (2007), Caine (1997), Dyhouse (1981, 1989), Giles (1995), Lewis (1984, 1986), Purvis (1991, 2000) and Rowbotham (1973). Of these, Sheila Rowbotham's *Hidden From History* is widely regarded as the catalyst for women's history. There are also a handful of dedicated journals, e.g. *Women's History Review, Journal of Women's History* and *Gender and History*.

In terms of media history, there are a growing number of feminist interpretations, some of which are largely concerned with the oppressive ideology of media representations and their effects on women, while others focus more on the ways in which women actively resist patriarchal media practices or, indeed, ways in which the media have become progressively supportive of the 'modern woman'. For analyses of the newspaper press and women's popular literature, see Bingham (2004), Braithwaite (1995), Chambers *et al.* (2004), Gorham (1982), Holland (1998), Leman (1980), Tinkler (1995), White (1970) and Winship (1987). Examples of feminist film histories include Doane (1987), Geraghty (2000), Gledhill (1987), Gledhill and Swanson (1996), Kaplan (1980) and Lloyd and Johnson (2003). Surprisingly, in spite of the growing popularity of television studies, feminist television histories are relatively few. Furthermore, what work there is tends to concentrate on the arrival of television in the domestic home space in the 1950s, for example Holmes (2005), Leman (1987) and Thumim (1998, 2002); cf. Baehr (1980) and Wheatley (2005). Similarly, radio – ever the Cinderella medium – remains underdeveloped as a specific field of study. This said, there is a scattering of specialized publications, autobiographies and passing references: see, for example, Leman (1996), Giles (2004), Hilmes (2007), Matheson (1933), Murray (1996) and Shapley (1996); Mitchell (2000) is especially informative and includes an assortment of feminist radio histories.

Maria Dicenzo (2004) provides an interesting and lucid critique of Curran's original attempt to summarize the feminist narrative by problematizing the way in which he overlooked 'feminist media', that is to say alternative media that are produced to overtly challenge the patriarchy of the mainstream media (something Curran addresses, incidentally, in his introductory chapter for this book). Publications of this sort include: Baehr and Ryan (1984), Beetham (1996), Cadman *et al.* (1981), Chambers *et al.* (2004), Dicenzo (2000, 2003), Doughan and Sanchez (1987), Harrison (1982), Kaplan (1983), Mercer (2004), Mitchell (2000), Oram (2001), Tusan (2005) and Winship (1987).

Finally, there is an ever-expanding body of contemporary feminist-informed media theory and criticism. The following references are just a very small random sample of some quite recent publications that usefully summarize and/or advance this canon of work: Brunsdon (2000), Brunsdon *et al.* (1997), Gill (2006), Hollows and Moseley (2006), Johnson (2007), Kaplan (2000), McRobbie (2006), Shattuc (1997) and Thornham (2000). The very latest scholarly research and book reviews can be found in *Feminist Media Studies*.

Chapter 4

The angel in the ether

Early radio and the constitution of the household

Michael Bailey

Marr'd less than man by mortal fall,
Her disposition is devout,
Her countenance angelical;
The best things that the best believe
Are in her face so kindly writ
The faithless, seeing her, conceive
Not only heaven, but hope of it.

Coventry Patmore, *The Angel in the House*, 1854

The state of unrest in family life, so prevalent today, due largely to the greater variety of outside interest, which tend to bring about the disappearance of the links which formerly bound the members of the group together, has long been a matter of profound concern. Something was evidently needed to make home attractive and to revive the waning interest in common action by the family. Radio performs this function admirably, and there is no doubt that it can, and will, effectively neutralise, to a considerable extent, some of the more serious tendencies of the changing home.

C. W. Kimmins (*Radio Times*, 16 July 1923)

Introduction

The one social institution more or less universal throughout modern Western societies is the family. Nearly every human being is born into a family, has ancestors, parents, brothers and sisters, kindred, and will quite probably, in later life, form new familial relationships – to wife or husband, to children, even grandchildren. Furthermore, assembled around the constituent relationships inherent in any family are several primary functions fundamental to social processes, namely the sexual, the economic, the reproductive apropos socialization and the educational (see Morgan 1975). And while there are other social institutions that have some bearing upon one or more of these social processes, no institution but the family fulfils and reinforces one and all; it is the main locus of people in relation to most other things.

The significance of this in terms of women's history is that the family increasingly becomes a focal point for a plethora of discursive practices aimed at regulating the everyday practices of domesticity and the private sphere of the home (see Lewis 1986; Dyhouse 1989; Purvis 2000, among others). More specifically, women become the home's moral cornerstone, widely perceived as integral to ensuring the physical and moral well-being of the family and the nation generally, making possible a regularization of everyday life.

This idealization of women as domestic angels has proceeded apace since the nineteenth century. Having said this, for all the pressures towards the continuing domestication of women in the early twentieth century – working class women especially – women's education would have to take account of their enhanced role as democratic citizens with the long-awaited arrival of universal adult suffrage in 1918 and the further enlargement of enfranchisement in 1928. At this historical juncture, two contradictory political rationalities come together for the first time. On the one hand, women were still needed to fulfil their traditional private domestic role as home-makers. On the other hand, it was important that women were better equipped to understand matters of public importance and fulfil their newly acquired democratic responsibilities.

How to reconcile these two hitherto diametrically opposed spheres was now a matter of increasing importance, which brings me to what is the main hypothesis of this chapter: early radio, under the aegis of the BBC, permitted a fusion of the two spheres. It educated women in their newly ascribed civic function, while simultaneously addressing them as mothers and housewives located in the private sphere, thus amplifying Victorian idealizations of women.

Home sweet home: radio and hearth

In terms of broadcasting histories, Shaun Moores (1988) probably best describes broadcasting's early relationship with the family and home, not least the somewhat startling revelation, given the ubiquity of broadcasting technologies in the present day, that the acceptance of wireless into the interior home space was a gradual, not immediate, process. The main reason for radio's initial unpopularity as a domestic form of cultural activity was to do with the way in which the technology was gendered. Initially, the innovation of wireless was a masculine hobby located in the male-dominated sphere of technology and science: early broadcasting literature was highly technical and virtually incomprehensible to anybody who did not have an interest in electrical engineering; listening in was restricted to a single listener using headphones, which, more often than not, were monopolized by the male head of the house. Consequently, women were excluded from the early years of broadcasting, which probably explains why so many experienced wireless as, to quote Lesley Johnson (1981: 161), 'an unruly guest', 'upsetting daily routines and interfering in family relationships'.

All this changes with the advent of the loudspeaker, making it possible for the whole family to listen together. The advent of domestic electricity meant manufacturers had more scope and incentive to improve wireless' technical componentary and mechanical appearance: do-it-yourself wireless kits were gradually replaced by ready-made wireless sets, mounted in a variety of furniture cabinets (cf. Butsch 1998). Non-technical wireless magazines (e.g. *The Broadcaster*, *Radio Times* and *The Listener*) began to appear and presented the reader with weekly articles, advertisements and cartoons that portrayed broadcasting as a quintessential family activity (see Briggs 1981). This and greater emphasis on broadcasting content, symbolized by entertainment programmes aimed at different family members, did much to elevate wireless' social status as a household consumer durable. Hence, by the 1930s, broadcasting was the primary form of domestic entertainment and assumed a central place of cultural importance in most homes, as evidenced by the significant increase in the number of licence holders (see Briggs 1979: 279). In short, and to quote Peter Black (1972), radio becomes 'the biggest aspidistra in the world'.

The acceptance of wireless as an everyday household object, as opposed to it being a 'miraculous toy' for male adults and their sons, made broadcasting the ideal medium for organizing domestic life and bringing the family together around the 'radio hearth'. Broadcasting became both cause and occasion for visits between friends, relatives and neighbours (see Briggs 1981: 26–53; Frith 1983: 110–12). For example, the report of a BBC-sponsored survey into the effects of broadcasting on the quality of individual, family and social life noted that wireless had 'taken its place as a normal feature of home life' among all social classes (Jennings and Gill 1939: 39). Moreover, by increasing 'the attractiveness of the home', it was felt that broadcasting had tempered those uses of leisure thought to be licentious or disorderly: 'comparatively few people now spend a whole evening in a public house, as they want to get home to the wireless. The children also play less in the streets than formerly… because they like to listen to the wireless programmes' (ibid.: 21). Similarly, in an article entitled 'Wireless and Domestic Life', G. H. Grubb ventured to suggest 'that a wider use of wireless…will bring us back to that state of national life, the old love of home and family, which has always been such a bulwark against aggression of all kinds for the British people' (*Radio Times*, 2 May 1924). In other words, wireless was a safeguard against the perceived decline in social mores and the unity of family interests.

However, this recovery of family moral values was dependent, to a large extent, on the part women would have to play in transmitting the cultural values of the BBC into the *sanctum sanctorum* of the home. Radio, like the broader project of home-making, needed a feminine touch. Women listeners were thus interpellated by gendered broadcasting discourses as housewives and mothers with civic responsibilities: keeping the husband out of the pub by making the home an attractive alternative, ensuring the physical well-being of the family, the rearing and moral education of children, among others. This articulation of public and private roles was an ideal function for a medium publicly produced but consumed in private (cf. Lacey 1994). Women could go about their everyday domestic chores while simultaneously being educated in issues of political and social importance. Broadcasting reinforced and rationalized the housewife's timetable of work, with occasional 'natural pauses' so that more effective listening could be undertaken. And located in such pauses was programming for women, otherwise known as household talks.

Programming the housewife: Home Service[1]

Initially, household talks were broadcast in the afternoon. Eventually, after much experimentation with timing, in the summer of 1930 household talks moved to a regular slot between 10.45 am and 11.00 am.[2] Women were expected to turn on their wirelesses for the weather forecast and morning service and continue listening during their daily household routine. Although including news from parliament and other countries, more frequent topics were housecraft, child welfare and cookery. This was in spite of women listeners expressing a clear preference for talks on general topics, not cookery or house-keeping hints, when once invited to send in their opinions as to what broadcasting matter they thought most suitable for household talks.[3] Having said this, there is also evidence to suggest that a large number of listeners came to enjoy listening to household talks, in particular ones that gave details of recipes or where listeners were invited to contribute recipes and hints of their own (BBC WAC R51/239).

Household talks were supplemented with the introduction of women's 'home pages' as a regular feature in the *Radio Times* from March 1934. Although articles varied and included a diversity of subjects, perhaps the most interesting regular feature, in terms of the way in which it sought to discipline women listeners, was a column by the home economist, Elizabeth Craig. In her first article (*Radio Times*, 30 March 1934), she instructed housewives how to plan their working day by breaking it down into an ordered succession of prescribed domestic responsibilities as follows:

7 am	Draw curtains. Open windows. Clean dining room and living room.
8.15 am	Prepare breakfast…
8.30 am	Serve breakfast
9 am	Turn down beds. Clear away breakfast things. Wash up, and return everything to its proper place, polished and ready for the next meal. Leave breakfast table tidy and chairs in position. Tidy kitchen premises.
10 am	When you do your own shopping shop at once…
11 am	Make beds. Clean bedroom or bedrooms, staircase if you have one, and hall and passages and bathroom, etc.

12 noon	Prepare midday meal and lay table.
1 pm	Serve midday meal.
2 pm	Clear away, wash up, return everything to its place, polished and ready for next meal.
3 pm	(a) Clean kitchen premises. Set and cover tea-tray. Wash out tea-cloths and finish any odd jobs. (b) Prepare everything as far as possible for evening meal.
NOTE:	Spend 30 minutes attending to your toilet, your hair and hands, changing your clothes and seeing to immediate necessities.
4.30–5.30 pm or 6 pm	Free to entertain or rest, etc., unless there are children to see to.
6 to 7 pm	Prepare evening meal and prepare bedrooms for the night.
7 or 7.30 pm	Serve meal.
8.30 pm	Clear away, wash up, return everything to its proper place, etc.
9 or 9.30 pm	Free again.

Another example of the interpellation of women as housewives was a broadcast entitled 'The Art of Easing Housework' (*The Listener*, 9 October 1929). It reminded housewives that the home was not 'just a place for cooking, washing and cleaning', but also 'a place where children are brought up, and where adults can come back happily to their rest and recreation'. As well as to themselves, housewives 'owe it to others to try and ease your housework', so they would not neglect other family members. Essential to 'the art of easing housework' was to 'make a definite plan, a timetable, for the work you have to do, get it down in black and white'. Doing so would improve one's 'methods of work' and reduce 'the time taken'. As an incentive, women were encouraged to 'compete with yourself' and to 'make a game of finding short cuts', for 'two minutes a day mean twelve hours in a year'(!).

In both of the above instances, one is immediately stuck by the extraordinary attention to temporal regulation and the regimental-like discipline with which the BBC exalted women to go about their housework. In fact, this organization of time was a recurring theme in many of the women's talks and wireless literature generally. Just as the industrial labourer was subjected to the virtues of punctuality and the discipline of the factory whistle, broadcasting was instrumental in institutionalizing 'the domestication of standard national time' to order and demarcate the day's social activities (Moores 1988: 38).[4] For women especially, there was now a more clearly defined time to work and a time to play. If they were to be diligent housewives, it was imperative that they learn to conduct their lives by hours, minutes and seconds. Idleness or frivolous pleasure was not permitted. And the best disciplinary method with which to manage the activity of female listeners was to prescribe particular temporal regularities in the form of a timetable whose *raison d'être* was to, as pointed out by Foucault (1991: 149), 'establish rhythms, impose particular occupations [and] regulate the cycles of repetition'. In other words, household talks and the accompanying literature constituted a mode of 'disciplinary time', a means with which to train women in the art of efficient time-keeping and hence good house-keeping.

A doctor in the house: managing health through the family

Another aspect to women's talks was the concern with public health. It was early recognized that broadcasting could play a significant part in maintaining a healthy populace. Hilda Matheson, then Director of Talks, thought that 'broadcasting can do a great deal to make effective the modern campaign for preventative medicine' (Karpf 1988: 32). This was especially important in the 1920s and 1930s when it was widely feared that the nation's physical well-being was underdeveloped and a liability to the country's security in the event of another major military conflict. Building a healthy nation was crucial to ensuring a strong nation-state and empire. Hence, the establishment of the Ministry for Health in 1919 and other attendant postwar welfare reforms.[5]

Military and imperial rationalities were not the only reason for raising the public's consciousness about public health. Equally important, and in some ways related, was the state's efforts to increase national efficiency, particularly economic productivity. A regular broadcaster on health issues was George Newman, Chief Medical Officer of the Ministry of Health.[6] In one particular broadcast, Newman argued that personal health was one of the main 'contributions to national prosperity and the wisest kind of economy', citing ill-health as a cost to the worker, the employer and the state (*The Listener*, 4 November 1931). Indeed, Newman calculated that if one were to add up the number of days workers were absent from work in 1930, a total of 26½ million weeks were lost owing to sickness, which, as he went on to point out, was 'more than all the time lost to industry in all the trade stoppages, strikes and lock-outs put together'. Hence Newman's belief that, just as Chadwick had taught the necessity of the 'sanitary idea', the chief aim for early twentieth-century social reform was to instil in the public what he called the 'health idea', that is to say, 'the discovery by every individual of a systematic way of health for himself or for herself'. In short, it was imperative that the public learn that 'to attain health is a discipline and not a spree'.[7]

This discipline–health couplet was further expounded in a series of twelve talks broadcast in the winter of 1932, entitled 'The Doctor and the Public'. One of the talks was given by Thomas Horder, one of the foremost members of the medical profession. Among other things, Horder considered a healthy body synonymous with a healthy mind. In other words, he proposed that health was impossible without morals. Hence it was 'easier for the disciplined man [sic] to keep his health than for the undisciplined' (*The Listener*, 5 October 1932). Women were especially instructed how to best discipline their children in body and mind, as adult health depended upon 'the habits that have been formed during childhood and youth'. For Horder, health was thus 'very much bound up with education', education here understood to mean not only 'the giving of instruction', but also 'the formation of the mind, the regulation of the passions and the establishment of principles'. In short, health was 'inseparably bound up with the conduct of life'. Indeed, the listener was reminded that just as 'order is heaven's first law, it is the first law of health also'. Just as godliness was equated with cleanliness in the nineteenth century, so too was it equated with healthiness in the twentieth century.

What the above illustrates is the extent to which governmental prescriptions for new norms of health were entered into the private space of the family as everyday practices of household management so as to incite individuals to be responsible for the hygienic management of bodily functions, habits, personal environment and the welfare of all those whose health depended upon the hygienic conduct of others. Nikolas Rose (1985: 146–51) has described this governmental rationality as a 'neo-hygienist' strategy, a fusion of nineteenth-century *laissez-faire* liberalism and early twentieth-century Liberal collectivism. Moreover, the habits and conducts of the body promoted by neo-hygienism were intrinsically moralistic. Being healthy implied responsible and con-scientious habits about cleanliness, regular meals and temperance. In other words, early twentieth-century welfarism deployed the family as a technology of 'responsibilization', a means for disseminating sober habits and good conduct.

More than this, the housewife in particular was entered into medical dis-course as family doctor. Hence, women listeners were constantly instructed in practical health care. The family would not only be subject to a professional medical gaze but also the discreet and ubiquitous gaze of the mother, fur-nishing them with a social status previously unavailable (cf. Donzelot 1980). In some ways, this was related to the way in which broadcasting represented a paradoxical challenge to the patriarchal authority of the head of the house. What father said now had to be reconciled with what 'Auntie' said. And for the most part, wireless was saying that, in household matters at least, mum knows best. In this sense, household talks were potentially empowering for women, inasmuch as they were invested with a 'natural' authority. If they wanted extra household income, it was because they were acting on instruc-tion, and not out of personal impertinence or whim. Such contradictions opened up a 'transitional space' between public and private that women could, potentially, occupy and exploit to subvert traditional gendered relations of power. However, this ought not to be understood as a direct affront to the patriarchal authority of the father, much less that of the state. Rather, women were still essentially confined to the private sphere, but accorded a new role as medical auxiliary and emissaries of life-affirming cultural values and practices.

Feeding the nation: managing family budgets

Despite the emergent emphasis on public welfare, many twentieth-century public health reformers continued to equate ill-health with bad household management and malnutrition, rather than poverty (Karpf 1988: 35–37). Having said that, how to provide a population with enough nutrients in times of economic hardship was the main political issue for much of the interwar period, not least because putting food on the table represented the main struggle for most working class families during this period. Which ever way one looks at it, it was widely realized that fit bodies, and a healthy nation, could not be built up on empty stomachs.[8] Needed was an angel in the house capable of performing minor miracles in the art of domestic economy with very frugal resources.

Hence, women listeners were also educated in the importance of nutrition, especially for themselves and their children, receiving frequent advice on family budgeting. Talks were more often than not presented under the rubric of 'national health' and 'progress' (e.g. Newman 1939: 322–59). The importance of this was stated by Edward Le Gros Clark, an eminent anatomist, in one of many internal BBC memos relating to talks on nutrition:

> ...we are on the eve of a great movement of reform in this country; and the motto we shall take will be...if everyone could be properly fed, the progress in health and happiness would be even more remarkable than the progress we made last century when we made our vast sanitary reforms, laid down our drainage systems and guaranteed our water supplies free from contamination.
>
> BBC (WAC R51/359)

As well as addressing scientific and policy-related issues, nutrition talks were supplemented by information about diets for different levels of income in relation to food prices. A deluge of BBC publications accompanied morning talks, many selling in their thousands: *Home, Health & Garden* (1928); *Choosing the Right Food* (1933); *Economical Cookery* (1933); *The Wise Penny – Hints on Economical Marketing & Recipes* (1934); and *Shopping & Cooking* (1935). The BBC even appealed on air for listeners to submit details of their family budgets, based on actual expenditure. Fifty were received and analysed, and the results were discussed in a special issue of *The Listener* (15 July 1931). Although the conclusions that could be drawn from such limited evidence were tentative, by calculating per capita expenditure on food, a dietician could none the less surmise the standard family's probable nutritional state *vis-à-vis* the family's cost of living. The main recommendation was that the minimal cost per person expenditure on food ought to be one shilling (five pence) per day. Anything less than this merited some kind of intervention, if only to give advice. The BBC felt that it had to maintain standards even when dealing with food matters. There was also the additional point of interest that the figures had been gathered together through the agency of broadcasting and that they might form the basis for future investigations.

However, this kind of project attracted criticism for its class bias and patronising tone, both evident in the advice given in a series of talks by Margaret McKillop in April 1924 on 'The Family Budget on A Weekly Wage':

> The Father should be in regular employment; both parents need to be sober, steady and unselfish; then the money has to be laid out, and all the items put down afterwards, with regularity, careful planning, and a good deal of orderliness and perseverance, so that to hand in a budget at all is evidence of good housekeeping.
>
> *The Listener* (24 April 1929)

Not surprisingly, working class women objected to being lectured on how best to spend what frugal resources they had while middle class housewives were more or less free to spend what they liked. Catherine Byworth, a listener from St Leonards-on-Sea, stated as much in a letter addressed to the editor of *The Listener.*

> ...how irritating it is to hear people talking about the best way of spending a minimum wage of 30s per week on a family of four...It is only the poor mother of only two who knows what a struggle for existence it is year in and year out and never able to have a week's holiday...It is not human to preach to people who have so little sunshine in their lives.
>
> *The Listener* (19 June 1929)

Similarly, trade union official and founding member of the British Communist Party, Walter Hannington (1936: 60–61), criticized the way in which the reports of Medical Officers of Health discussed working class diets using bourgeois pseudo-scientific terms, thus excluding working class women from what was essentially a public issue about poverty and economic hardship.

> We frequently come up against insidious propaganda, which I believe has been encouraged by the Ministry of Health, to the effect that it is not the amount of income to the household that is too low, but...the ignorance of the average working-class housewife in regard to food values and the art of cooking, resulting in the loss of the nutritive qualities of the food, which is responsible for the present ill-health that pervades so many working-class homes. It is indeed interesting to read of the well-to-do women assuming the right to instruct the working-class mother on the way she shall spend the 4s or less on twenty-one meals a week.

Such sentiments were more widespread; working class mothers especially objected to being made to feel inadequate (see Wilson 1977: 125). To many working class women, the series of early twentieth-century welfare strategies, of which broadcasting was one, were as offensive and insulting as the patronising charity interventions of the nineteenth century.

Government by numbers: surveying the family

Despite its critics, the BBC continued to research the state of the nation. Of the many subjects upon which social investigators, the BBC included, wanted to have more detailed returns from the public, *The Listener* (27 January 1932) argued that none was 'of more immediate interest than the changes which we believe to be taking place today in family life':

> how is it being affected by present-day economic conditions, by the emancipation of women and their entry into industry, by changed ideas on the subject of sex, by changed conditions of health, and even by such radical alterations in the amenities of home life as are brought by modern inventions like the wireless?

One outcome was a series of talks on 'Changes in Family Life', initiated and organized by William Beveridge and broadcast over a six-week period between February and April 1932. As well as providing a general historical overview of the family, the talks considered the importance of certain familial relationships: marriage and its relation to occupation and size of family; the relationship between the family and the population; the economic functions of family; family income and its use; the employment of married women; changes in the legal position of married women; state provision for children and elderly people; a family's use of leisure, and so on.

One of the talks was a discussion between William Beveridge and Mrs J. L. Adamson about the emancipation of married women. During the discussion, Beveridge happened to mention that one of the people who filled in the family form objected to the way wives no longer behaved as many husbands' mothers had done. Adamson countered the objection by stating that women were now citizens and entitled to public life, even if that meant disagreeing with their husbands in politics. The debate then developed into an argument about the private and public roles of women.

> W.B.: They can disagree about things like politics without upsetting anybody. Where one puts a cross on a ballot paper does not matter much. But where one puts the sideboard or the gramophone matters a great deal.
> J.L.A.: No, no, Sir William, to my mind it is more important where one puts a cross on a ballot paper than the position of the sideboard or gramophone.
> W.B.: I am sure you are an exceptional woman, Mrs Adamson. But what about more serious family problems – about the place of living, the use of leisure, and the place for holidays, the education of the children...
>
> *The Listener* (6 April 1932)

At one level of analysis, Beveridge's remarks are straightforward sexism. The family, especially the mother, is located firmly in the private sphere with only a tangential relation to the public sphere. At another level of analysis, Beveridge's obsession with how a family functions through the placement of children and household objects can be understood as a transparent expression and rearticulation of the angelic ideal. That is to say, women's role was defined in relation to the maintenance of population and hence the nation. The main problem for Beveridge and others was how to reconcile women's demands for greater emancipation with the fundamental regeneration of society.

Accompanying the series was a questionnaire issued to the listening public. More comprehensive than the census, it was a collaboration between the BBC and the London School of Economics (BBC WAC A/254). Among other things, respondents were asked to note changes in past and present generations. Revealing questions were also asked about the occupations and earnings of husband and wife. Whereas the husband was simply asked to provide information about his employment, the wife was asked to provide the same information before and after marriage. The inference was that paid employment was a problem, as she had to explain why she worked and for how long, what arrangements she made for childcare and domestic help, etc.

Anxiety about the potential disintegration of the family was evident in a *Listener* (6 April 1932) editorial on the survey. Among other things, it pondered whether economic change has wrought 'a corresponding alteration of emphasis on moral values', with 'loosening of the bonds of family discipline and respect, and some extension of individual liberty or licence in conduct'. The overall concern with such changes was 'whether the family as a social institution can adapt itself to them and survive unharmed'? More than this, it was suggested the state may have to intervene so that perhaps

> …we shall see the State recognise that it cannot allow the disintegration of the family, either from the moral, economic or biological point of view. If there is a movement to deurbanise and decentralise human civilisation – a movement which will be powerfully aided by the new cultural forces such as broadcasting – we may confidently expect that family life will be revivified, and parenthood will again become a normal and attractive ambition and duty for most citizens. Thus the changes which we are witnessing may, if properly guided, be forces to enrich rather than to destroy the oldest of human associations – the home.

The significance of the above from a feminist point of view is twofold. First, affirmed here and elsewhere is the primacy of the family–home couplet as a sphere of socio-political urgency. The politics of the private sphere were very much a public issue. Second, while women secured some significant political and social gains during the interwar period, the household and family remained the main sites for ensuring the continuation of female domesticity and women's subordination.

Conclusions

At the turn of the twentieth century, family life was to be intensified. To regulate a population and its conduct, the private sphere, with the family at its heart, increasingly becomes an object of early welfarist strategies. It was made to be more careful and self-conscious about its own internal dynamics and relations, all according to hygienist and pedagogical norms. The family's contingencies, deviancies and regularities were measured, quantified and interpreted into techniques of government that sought to simultaneously regulate the corporal activities of individual bodies and the social activities of populations. Consequently, the family was no longer an autonomous social institution composed of independent individuals. Rather, a whole series of values and privileges emerged that transformed the family into an agent for maximizing social economy and social order. Women in particular were perceived as absolutely integral to enabling a regularization of everyday conduct and thus targeted as instruments for conveying the norms of the state (healthy, regular and disciplined conduct) into the private sphere. Such developments served to regulate inter- and intrafamilial relations: families would police themselves and each other. This policing of families, government through the family, was instrumental to maintaining a particular socio–political order.

Even at its most liberal and reformist, the BBC was implicated in the con-tradictions of such welfare reforms, especially in its conception of family life. It sought to regulate the organization of family life by reinvigorating hegemonic familial ideals and practices, simultaneously domesticating and gendering cer-tain cultural practices, reinforcing demarcations between the spheres of public and private, and thereby establishing the home as a site for cultural govern-ance. Hence, much broadcasting during the interwar years addressed its women audience as mothers and housewives. Among the earliest regular programme slots were 'household talks'. Deliberately broadcast at times that reflected the daily timetable and 'natural' breaks of the average housewife, these talks defined women's political duty in terms of their domestic activity in the private sphere, according them little role in the public sphere of politics. Indeed, women were exalted to identify the domestic realm of the home with the political and social well-being of the nation. The relationship between wireless and women listeners during the interwar period is all the more interesting when one bears in mind that it is during this period that women finally acquired the right to vote on equal terms with men, thus signalling the long-awaited arrival of universal adult suffrage. Just when women were slowly entering the public world of politics through the extension of the franchise, public service broadcasting ascribed women listeners a social role confined to the domestic sphere of family and home. Understood thus, early broadcasting was one of many domestic technologies during this period whose intended use was, in part, to regulate and direct women's behaviour and conduct for patriarchal reasons of state.

Notes

1 The initial organization of women's (and children's) talks was the responsibility of Ella Fitzgerald, who joined the BBC in April 1923 as Central Organizer. One of her first tasks was to form a Women's National Advisory Committee of representative women who could make useful suggestions with regard to speakers, subjects, timing of programmes, etc. The Committee first met in January 1924. Its jurisdiction over women's talks, however, was short-lived. At the end of 1924, general supervision and matters of policy were absorbed by Talks, which came under the control of J. C. Stobart, then Education Director (BBC WAC R6/219 and R51/646).

2 The subject of what was the most suitable time for household talks was widely discussed in various internal memoranda. Even when it was agreed that the 10.45 am slot appeared to be most popular, there were further experiments with the timing of women's talks. For example, for a few months in January 1932, some of the morning talks were given at 1.45 pm, as it was felt that was more convenient than the earlier morning talks. It was even suggested that domestic talks be given in the evening, not least because it would enable the BBC to reach women in full-time work who could not listen in the morning. Interestingly, in an internal memorandum dated 18 September 1935, it was hinted that a further reason for having household talks in the evening would be to cater for middle class interests in the home, something that was not provided for in the morning talk broadcasts as it was felt to be inappropriate given that the majority of listeners were working class housewives (see BBC WAC R51/239 and R51/646).

3 The invitation was made following a suggestion made at the first Women's Committee meeting that a debate be staged by two of the committee members with a view to ascertaining female listeners' opinions on the timing and subject matter for women's talks. As a result, it was found hat 75 per cent of listeners wanted talks on general topics, while the remaining 25 per cent wanted talks concerning the home, but not cookery or household hints (BBC WAC R51/646).

4 For a fuller analysis of the institutionalization of time–work discipline, see Thompson (1967).

5 To an even greater extent than the Boer war, the First World War strengthened the case for state intervention in the field of public health, prompting some social historians to argue that many early twentieth-century welfare reforms can only be properly understood in the historical context of the then prevalent imperial consciousness (see Wilson 1977: 100; Fraser 1982: 164–67).

6 It should be noted that relations between the BBC and the Ministry of Health were not always amicable. This was partly to do with the latter's attempts to dominate public health broadcasts to which the BBC occasionally objected (see Karpf 1988: 38–43).

7 This change in 'the rules of health' was similarly noted in the editorial of the same issue of *The Listener* in which Newman's broadcast was transcribed. Emphasizing the virtues of cleanliness, exercise and diet, the editor argued that being vigilant about one's health was more to do with 'the adoption of a few common-sense habits and precautions' than it was 'the multiplication of restrictions, exercises, ablutions and other health ceremonies'. In other words, the discourse of health and its disciplinary apparatus was presented as a natural state of affairs, it was 'what-goes-without-saying'. And it was from this premise that the editorial – and broadcasting generally throughout the interwar period – affirmed Newman's recommendation that, 'Good health should be regarded as a duty of individual citizenship, and not merely as a lucky accident'.

8 How to develop a wise nutrition policy was widely discussed in both houses of parliament. The following extract from a speech by Kingsley Wood in the House of Commons, dated 8 July 1936, was typical of the concern expressed by all political parties: '…there is a great scope for activity and advance. Malnutrition in the true sense

of the term exists and must be fought, and it is manifest that we must continue to pay increasing attention to the nutrition of the nation as a potent weapon against disease and a great instrument for the promotion of mental and physical efficiency and well-being'. Lord Horder, speaking in the House of Lords, 10 November 1936, was even more candid: 'Let the Government have faith that if the people of Britain are given the modest requirements of security at home and the security of sustenance, their sturdy common-sense will do the rest…and I would remind your Lordships that democracy, especially a democracy asked to be physically fit, also advances on its stomach' (BBC WAC R51/359).

Chapter 5

'Going to Spain with the boys'

Women correspondents and the Spanish Civil War

David Deacon

> Me, I am going to Spain with the boys. I don't know who the boys are, but I am going with them.
>
> Martha Gellhorn (1937)

Introduction

This chapter examines the role of women correspondents in the reporting of the Spanish Civil War.[1] Such an analysis has, I believe, intrinsic historical value. Although labelled a civil war, it was a conflict that implicated all the major international powers of the day. But the Spanish Civil War was about more than power politics. From the outset, it was recognized as a battle of ideas, ideals and ideologies, which meant that issues of mediation and representation assumed crucial importance. As will be shown, any adequate analysis of the role of the international news media needs to consider the distinctive and significant contribution made by women correspondents. More broadly, I hope this case study makes a small contribution towards elaborating what James Curran (2002) identifies as 'feminist narratives' of media history, particularly as they apply to understanding the roots and evolution of foreign correspondence in general, and war reporting specifically. These domains have been dominated historically by men and, particularly with regard to the reporting of armed conflict, it is often claimed that they are infused by masculinist values. As Dafna Lemish (2005: 275) recently put it: 'It is mostly men who perpetrate the violence, organise a violent response, and present media stories about it'.

Although it is difficult to dispute the general legitimacy of this observation, we need to be wary of overgeneralization. One can readily think of many striking contemporary exceptions to the proposition that war stories are male stories. For example, in the UK, there is the influential and prestigious presence of female journalists such as Orla Guerin, Maggie O'Kane and Kate Adie. Furthermore, there is a historical lineage to female foreign correspondence that can be traced back to the 1840s (see Sebba 1994). An important aspect of the recognition that 'the media politics of gender deserve more attention than they have received to date' (Carter *et al.* 1998: 3) is the development of an historically informed perspective that retains, and where necessary recovers, understanding of the past contributions, achievements and trials of women working in these male-dominated environments. Central to this project is the need to examine the extent to which these pioneering women introduced different values and perspectives from their male counterparts, and the reasons for these differences.

Women journalists in Spain

The Spanish Civil War began in July 1936 with the rebellion of Nationalist forces commanded by General Francisco Franco and ended with the defeat of the Republican government in April 1939. Women correspondents represented a small minority of the international press corps that gathered in Spain to witness the events during this period.[2] Table 5.1 lists those women I have firmly identified as having visited Spain and provided editorial copy for international news organizations during the war. This list should not be seen definitive for two reasons. It is biased towards British and North American news organizations, which reflects the focus of my wider research into the journalistic representations of the conflict in these contexts (Deacon 2009, forthcoming).

Table 5.1 Female correspondents, their affiliations and areas of operation in the Spanish Civil War.

Republican sector only	• Kitty Bowler (*The Manchester Guardian* and *The Toronto Star*)
	• Hilde Marchant (*Daily Express*)
	• Helen Wilkinson (*Daily Worker*)
	• Dorothy Parker (*New Masses*)
	• Eleanor Packard (United Press)
	• Lorna Wood (*The Manchester Guardian*)
	• Nancy Cunard (*The Manchester Guardian*)
	• Josephine Herbst (*New York Times*)
	• Helen Seldes (*New York Times*)
	• Martha Gellhorn (Colliers)
	• Barbro 'Bang' Alving (*Dagens Nyheter*)
	• Martha Huysmans (*Peuple*)
	• Gerde Taro (*CeSoir, Vu, Life*)
	• Charlotte Haldane (*Daily Worker*)
Republican then Nationalist sector	• Virginia Cowles (*Sunday Times* and *New York Times*)
Nationalist then Republican sector	• Eleanor Packard (United Press Bureau)
Nationalist sector only	• Frances Davis (*Daily Mail* and *Chicago Daily News*)
	• Sheila Grant Duff (*Chicago Daily News*)

Furthermore, the list probably excludes the names of other women who worked for Anglo-American news organizations during the war.[3] But if the list is not comprehensive, it can be said to include those women whose reporting had most public impact during the conflict and whose contributions have endured over time.

Most of these female correspondents reported from Republican-held territories. To some extent, this differential distribution mirrored a general numerical imbalance in the international news net, which in turn reflected the different attitudes the combatants had towards foreign journalists and their work. Nationalist news management was often autocratic and inflexible, and journalists were treated with suspicion and antipathy ('A Journalist', 1937). They were expected to relay Franquist propaganda uncritically, and those who incurred the displeasure of the Nationalist news managers could expect rough treatment. The intimidation and expulsion of correspondents was also evident in Republican-held territories, but these threats were less concerted and not strategically conceived. Journalists had more freedom of movement and, in general terms, Republican news management was framed by a political rather than a military culture, which reflected a clear perception of the need to communicate with international audiences. Within this context, a further gender-specific factor worked to marginalize the presence of female correspondents in Nationalist territories. Most of the women worked for left-wing or left-of-centre newspapers, many of which were banned or restricted by the Nationalists.

However, these structural factors only provide a partial explanation as to why more female reporters covered the war from the Republican side. In particular, they do not address the political agency of these women and how this affected their professional practices. To generate such insight, there is a need to look more closely at the personal and professional lives of these correspondents.

Personal histories, professional choices

Most of these female correspondents came from privileged backgrounds and were highly educated. Nancy Cunard was the only child of an English baronet and was educated in private schools across Europe. Martha Gellhorn and Kitty Bowler came from wealthy professional families, and both attended the women's university *Bryn Mawr* based in Philadelphia. Gerda Taro was born into 'a bookish family' in Germany and studied in a commercial school in the Weimar Republic prior to its downfall (Kershaw 2002: 24). Virginia Cowles was able to pursue a journalistic career in Europe as a result of a large personal inheritance (Sebba 1994: 94), and Sheila Grant Duff was the daughter of a lieutenant-colonel and a baronet's daughter and studied at Oxford University. Such advantages in wealth, class and cultural capital no doubt helped to compensate for the barriers of gender discrimination to some extent, as at that time journalism was deemed an occupation of fairly low social status (even the elite realms of foreign correspondence) (see Cox 1999).[4]

What these women shared was an antipathy to class and gender conventions and a strong affinity with progressive and left-wing politics. Some had sought to channel their political energies through journalistic activities prior to the outbreak of war in Spain, whereas others became involved in reporting the conflict through more circuitous and serendipitous routes. Virginia Cowles started her career on a small journal called *Entre Nous* in 1931. Two years later, she started working as a freelancer for the Hearst Press, and then began travelling around Europe filing reports for the Hearst papers on a pay-for-publication basis. Prior to Spain, she visited Italy and Libya and interviewed Mussolini (Sebba 1994: 94–95). Martha Gellhorn abandoned her university studies early to pursue a career as a writer and journalist. In the early 1930s, she travelled Europe as an aspiring foreign correspondent, filing reports for a variety of magazines and newspapers in the US. Sheila Grant Duff graduated from Oxford University in 1934 and became an apprentice of the renowned foreign correspondent Edgar Mowrer of *The Chicago Daily News*, who was at that stage based in Paris.

Other women correspondents had more tenuous connections with journalism prior to the war. During the 1920s, Nancy Cunard had been involved in a wide range of cultural and artistic activities in Europe. In the late 1920s, she founded the Hours Press and became immersed in a range of progressive political causes, in particular the American civil rights movement (Chisholm 1979: 200–44). She visited Spain on several occasions during the war and was a key figure behind the publication of 'Authors Take Sides on Spain', which invited leading literary figures to state their political allegiances in the conflict. Her journalistic involvement only came at the end of the war, when, covering her own personal expenses, she reported on the internment and mistreatment of Republican refugees on the Franco-Spanish border in January and February 1939 for *The Manchester Guardian*. Her correspondence with the paper's editor clearly reveals her professional uncertainty and inexperience: 'Now, I really would feel relieved to know if the articles I have sent are suitable. Give me some criticism, some suggestion – are they too long or too much about refugees?'[5]

Regardless of their journalistic experience, the female correspondents had little professional status within their news organizations. Apart from Hilde Marchant, who was a staff correspondent at the *Daily Express*, all the women were employed on a freelance basis, and most secured their commissions after they had arrived in Spain. For example, Frances Davis was an aspiring freelance journalist based in Paris, who rushed to Spain at the start of the war having given little prior thought as to who the combatants were or what issues were at stake. Her recruitment as a special correspondent for *The Daily Mail* came about accidentally. In the earliest days of the war, she teamed up with a group of male correspondents that included *The Daily Mail*'s correspondent, Harold Cardozo. The journalists made daily forays over the Franco-Spanish border into the war zone by car and, when it was not possible for the group to return to their French base, Davis took responsibility for couriering the copy over the border. After a lengthy solo trip returning Cardozo's copy, she had to remonstrate strongly with *The Mail*'s London desk to get them to take the story. Her tenaciousness created an impression, and she was offered a job by the paper's editor:

> I will carry credentials. I am not excess baggage in a car. I'm not a free-lance doing mail columns. I'm Davis of the *Daily Mail*.
>
> Davis (1940: 101)

Unlike Davis, Martha Gellhorn was initially drawn to Spain for the struggle rather than the story, but she too gained her commission with *Collier's* magazine after her arrival and almost by accident. As she later recollected:

> I went to Spain with no intention of writing anything about it…And then somebody said, why don't you write about life in Madrid? So I just wrote a piece about daily life in Madrid where shells used to hit our hotel everyday, things like that. And sent it off to a friend of mine who worked on *Colliers* and the next thing I saw I was on the masthead as a war correspondent.[6]

It is a measure of their junior status that none of the women was recruited to provide daily news. This was often the source of some frustration, as deadlines would have lent discipline and opportunities in their news-gathering activities (e.g. Davis 1940: 84; Cowles 1941: 21; Herbst 1991: 139–40). Instead, the role of the women correspondents was to provide 'colour stories' (Davis 1940: 103): reportage that provided human interest and personal context to the hard news stories about political manoeuvrings and military conflicts in the Iberian peninsula.

'Reportage' is a term that is often conflated with 'reporting' but is actually a distinctive form of journalistic discourse. Whereas reporting requires the eradication of the journalist's position, in reportage, the author occupies centre stage. As Noel Monks (1955: 95–96), writing two decades after he reported on the conflict for *The Daily Express*, observed:

> These were the days in foreign reporting when personal experiences were copy, for there hadn't been a war for eighteen years…We used to call them 'I' stories, and when the Spanish war ended in 1939 we were as heartily sick of writing them as the public must have been of reading them.

If reportage was a cornerstone of Anglo-US news coverage, reportage from women seemed to have a distinctive quality. Rather than describing the drama and horrors of open combat, their reports focused more frequently upon the impact of the war on ordinary people and their everyday lives. Virginia Cowles (1941: 55) said she was 'much more interested in the human side – the forces that urged people to such a test of endurance'. Martha Gellhorn wrote about 'the ordinary people caught up in the war'.[7] Both Josephine and Hilde Marchant were separately encouraged by their editors to provide a 'women's angle' on the effect the war was having on daily life (Sebba 1994: 91 and 148). According to Angela Jackson (2002: 132), these concerns represented more than just a difference of emphasis:

> Women's writing on Spain frequently allowed space for the personal, and empathy, in many cases overrode detachment. This should not be dismissed as a mere trick for propaganda purposes, aiming to obscure objectivity by an appeal to the emotions. It was, in many cases, a reflection of a different agenda.

It is striking how consistently this empathic approach translated into active sympathy, even advocacy, for the Republic. Many of the women arrived in Spain with their allegiances clearly established. Sheila Grant Duff (1982: 151) felt a 'passionate commitment to the cause of Spanish freedom' and in 1937 was sent in to Nationalist territory to discover the fate of the journalist Arthur Koestler, who was then under sentence of death. On this occasion, Duff's lack of status and experience were seen by her senior colleagues as advantageous, as she would be unknown to Nationalist authorities who were antagonistic towards *The Chicago Daily News*. So successful was she in slipping under the radar and into the confidences of the military, she was invited to witness the summary execution of Republican prisoners. She immediately appreciated the conflict this created:

> For a journalist it would be a sensational *coup*; for a spy it would really be seeing what Franco's men were at; for a human being it would be to stand and watch people whom I regarded as friends and allies being put to death in cold blood. I knew I would not be able to live with it. I did not go.
>
> Grant Duff (1976: 81–82)

Martha Gellhorn's affinity for the Republic endured throughout her life and was unaffected by the vicissitudes of historical revisionism. She claimed never to have read a book on the war because, whatever their factual accuracy, they could not capture 'the emotion, the commitment, the feeling that we were all in it together, the certainty that we were right' (quoted in Knightley 1975: 103).

Other female correspondents developed pro-Republican sympathies as a result of their experiences. For example, Virginia Cowles (1941: 55) said that when she first arrived in Spain she 'had no "line" to take on Spain as it had not yet become a political story for me'. However, it was not long before some strong opinions about the protagonists began to take shape. In Republican Madrid, she took a 'great liking to the Spanish people' (ibid.: 35), but later experienced feelings of 'revulsion' when witnessing the end of Franco's Basque offensive, on a press trip organized by the Nationalists to the front at Gijon (ibid.: 85). Although Frances Davis only reported the civil war from the Nationalist sector – and therefore had no equivalent opportunity for making direct comparisons – she, too, came to dislike the Francoists and their supporters. She later wrote of her relationship with Captain Gonzalo de Aguilera, who was a senior Nationalist press officer: 'I know him for my enemy, and I am his. Everything that has made me is death to him; everything that has made him is death to me' (Davis 1981: 159).

The difference between those women who arrived in Spain with strong allegiances and those who developed them through their experiences seems to have had some impact upon how they defined their professional roles and responsibilities. Gellhorn memorably dismissed journalistic conventions of balance and neutrality as 'all that objectivity shit' (Moorehead 2003: 150) and was unapologetically partisan in her coverage. Similarly, Nancy Cunard saw no reason to mask her outrage at the treatment of the Republican refugees on the French border or her disgust at meeting victorious Falangist troops (Chisholm 1979). In contrast, Victoria Cowles sought to remain dispassionate in her coverage, maintaining an obligation 'to give both sides a fair hearing' (Sebba 1994: 103) despite her personal dislike of the Nationalists.

Which republic?

Despite these differences, an overwhelming majority of these women supported the Republican cause. This begs the question as to which parts of the Republic they supported, for the Popular Front was a complex amalgam of communists (Stalinist and anti-Stalinist), socialists, liberals, regional Nationalists and anarcho-syndicalists, and these participants held very different political visions of the purpose and conduct of the war. For the more radical elements, the war was about realizing a genuine social revolution in Spain, based on the wholesale redistribution of land and the formation of collectives. For the more liberal and conservative elements, the war was about preserving liberal democracy against Fascist aggression, a line supported by the Stalinist Communists largely because of the geopolitical interests of the Soviet Union at that time.

In the accounts of the male correspondents who reported on the war directly and were broadly sympathetic to the Republican cause, one typically finds conditional appraisals of the competing factions. Put simply, both radical and liberal correspondents supported the more conservative political forces and shared a deep distrust of the more radical components of the Republican movement (e.g. Steer 1938: 178; Matthews 1938: 286; Buckley 1940: 275; Fischer 1941: 404; Monks 1955: 90–93; North 1958: 140). Such variable and conditional endorsements of the political factions within the Popular Front are signally absent from the accounts the women correspondents provided of their time in Spain. Rather, these women seemed to connect with a broader and undifferentiated conception of the Republic and its values.[8] As Josephine Herbst (1991: 135) put it: 'I have never had much heart for party polemics, and it was not for factionalism I had come to Spain'. But why did these women tend to identify so strongly and unconditionally with the Republic?

One of the indisputably revolutionary elements of the Popular Front was its commitment to gender equality and female emancipation (Nash 1995; Ackelsberg 2005). These ideals contrasted starkly with the chauvinistic codes of traditional Spain, which sequestered the lives of women and which the Nationalists were determined to defend (see Knickerbocker 1936: 44; De la Mora 1939: 53–123). This is not to suggest that these women were disengaged from the wider political issues at stake in the Spanish war – these women were as acutely aware of the anti-Fascist implications of the conflict as their male colleagues – but rather that the gender politics of the conflict added a further powerful connection and identification with the Republic.

A further question is: why did women's reportage focus so much upon the inner lives and lived experiences of the 'ordinary' citizens of the Republic? One way of explaining this is to invoke those strands of feminist theory that identify deep-seated psychological gender differences, such as Carol Gilligan's (1982) proposition that men are governed by rationalistic concerns about rules and justice whereas women are naturally orientated to an ethics of caring, which privileges emotions, relationships and empathy. However, there is a strong essentialist logic in such explanations that has been criticized by many contemporary feminist theorists (e.g. Oakley 1998; Lister 2003). Moreover, it deflects attention from the material reasons that compelled these women to focus on the politics of the everyday in their writing. As noted, most female correspondents were freelancers with tenuous contractual arrangements with their news organizations. This lack of status restricted their news-gathering opportunities, and many voiced their frustrations at being denied the access, accreditation, transportation and communication facilities provided for their senior male colleagues. However, without the pressures of daily deadlines, these women had more opportunity to integrate with local people and absorb the local culture. There was some inevitability, therefore, that these everyday observations and interactions became a central subject of their work. In Josephine Herbst's (1991: 139–40) words:

> If I had been a regular correspondent, I would have been obliged to show something for each day. But I was on a special kind of assignment, which meant I would write about other subjects than those covered by the news accounts…I did a lot of walking around, looking hard at faces. There was almost nothing to buy except oranges and shoelaces, and all this seemed

wonderful to me. The place had been stripped of senseless commodities, and what had been left was the aliveness of speaking faces.

Male mentors

Many women correspondents formed close professional, and sometimes personal, relationships with male colleagues. Lorna Wood, Helen Seldes and Eleanor Packard were all married to senior male journalists and came to Spain because of their partner's deployment to the region.[9] Kitty Bowler entered into a relationship with Tom Wintringham, who initially came to Madrid as a military correspondent for the *Daily Worker*, was an influential figure in the British Communist party and had a key role in the establishment of the International Brigades. Gerde Taro had been the partner, colleague and agent of Robert Capa before the war and collaborated with him in photo-journalistic work in Spain until her death in July 1937.

The most famous journalistic alliance forged in the Spanish war was between Martha Gellhorn and Ernest Hemingway. They became lovers soon after Gellhorn's arrival in Madrid in March 1937, and this generated some resentment among the other international journalists gathered in the Hotel Florida in Madrid because it delivered Gellhorn greater opportunities in terms of transport and access to influential sources than she would otherwise have had had she remained unattached (Herbst 1991: 138; Moorehead 2003: 142). Gellhorn herself admitted to an element of pragmatism in her relationship with Hemingway. As she dryly commented: 'I was just about the only blonde in the country. It was much better to belong to someone'.[10] The cynicism of this remark needs to be placed in the context of the subsequent, acrimonious breakdown of her relationship with Hemingway, and it is not my intention to suggest that it typifies a calculating motivation on the part of these women correspondents to cultivate male contacts purely out of professional self-interest. Rather, these relationships demonstrate that for all the pioneering, feminist spirit of these women, and despite the spirit of gender equality at the heart of the Republic, their professional environment was highly patriarchal, and their status and opportunities were restricted and facilitated by their male contacts, both in the field and 'up line' in the editorial departments of their news organizations.

Valuing women's perspectives

The significance of editors in the allocation of these women's roles and the use of their copy links to a final question regarding the role of women correspondents in the war. Why were news organizations so interested in obtaining female perspectives on the war? Despite the low professional status of these women, newspapers often used their contributions prominently, and frequently emphasized the gender of the author. For example, Frances Davis' articles for the *Daily Mail* in 1936 were frequently by-lined 'Only woman correspondent with patriot armies' and, on several occasions, her gender itself became a topic for coverage (e.g. 'A girl looks at a battle', *Daily Mail*, August 1936). Nancy Cunard's dispatches in 1939 on the plight of Republican refugees at the Spanish–French border and their internment by the French authorities dominated *The Manchester Guardian*'s international coverage for several days. As noted previously, Hilde Marchant and Josephine Herbst were instructed by their editors to provide a woman's perspective on the war.

A range of factors explains this 'low status–high profile' paradox. The first relates to the intense competitiveness and circulation wars of the newspaper industry in the late 1930s, particularly in the UK. Specifically, this was manifested in strenuous attempts by newspapers to dramatise and personalise their coverage of foreign affairs to attract and retain readers (Gannon 1971: 3). The inclusion of women's perspectives was often used strategically to vitalize foreign coverage. More generally, the 1930s saw an intensification in the 'feminization of news' that had began with the Northcliffe revolution at the start of the twentieth century (Tusan 2005: 243). This 'New Journalism' was based on a recognition of 'women consumers as an important audience on their own terms' (Carter *et al.* 1998: 1) and involved the inclusion of 'softer' news stories – items and features related to lifestyle, human interest and celebrity issues. Here again, the inclusion of feminine perspectives on the personal, emotional and domestic consequences of international events was seen to assist in connecting with these lucrative female markets.

Broader cultural trends also framed the editorial appetite for the kind of empathic reportage of everyday events that these women correspondents provided. The 1930s saw the emergence of the mass observation studies,[11] the documentary film movement[12] and new photo-journalist publications such as *Life* and *Picture Post* that in their separate ways shared an interest in delineating the details and dramas of ordinary lives.

A final reason why women's views of the Spanish Civil War were valued related to the nature of the war itself. Across Europe, and in the UK in particular, political and public opinion in the 1930s 'was overshadowed and, to a great extent, determined by an obsessional and, in retrospect, exaggerated fear of air attack' (Morris 1991: 48). This 'air fear' assumed that significant advances in aircraft and bombing technology meant that nations would be defeated by devastating and irresistible aerial assaults on civilian populations. In 1932, the British Prime Minister Stanley Baldwin delivered the apocalyptic warning to the House of Commons: 'The bomber will always get through. The only defence is in offence, which means that you have to kill more women and children more quickly than the enemy if you want to save yourselves'.[13] This conviction was a central pillar of Britain's subsequent policy of appeasement towards the German and Italian dictatorships. As the Spanish Civil War represented the first 'total war' on European soil, in which 'the shadow of the bomber' removed distinctions between front line and home front, and combatants and civilians, it was inevitable that there would be immense public and media interest in the impact these assaults had on citizens' lives and morale.

Conclusion

This chapter has examined the important and distinctive contribution that women correspondents made to the coverage of the Spanish Civil War in the international news media. This is not the first study to identify a distinct emphasis and quality to female war reporting and foreign correspondence through history (e.g. Sorel 1999). Indeed, such differences are still identified today. In 1999, Victoria Brittain, deputy foreign editor of *The Guardian*, asserted:

> Men's response to fear is usually bravado, and in war some male journalists do the same: they become obsessed with weapons and start identifying with the military, in the hope of feeling stronger themselves. Women's response is to identify with the people whose lives are shattered.
>
> Cited in McLaughlin (2002)

The legitimacy of such distinctions is not accepted by all. For example, McLaughlin (2002: 170) argues: 'it is certainly wrong to suggest that there is a strict gender difference in style between men and women reporters'. The basis of his objection is that there are plenty of examples in war coverage that do not conform to the pattern, i.e. cases where men provide compassionate reportage about the human and emotional costs of military conflict, and examples where women provide dramatic and significant hard news scoops. With reference to Spain, one can certainly find such exceptions.[14] Nevertheless, the tendency for male correspondents to focus on dramatic military events and high-altitude political manoeuvrings in their coverage of the Spanish Civil War and for female correspondents to concentrate on the war's impact on ordinary lives behind the lines is so obvious that it cannot be ignored. However, I share McLaughlin's concern about the suspicion of essentialism in many accounts that identify absolute gender differences in war reporting and, indeed, journalism in general. This is not just because it does a disservice to the 'good guys' on the international newsbeat, but because these distinctions can inadvertently demean and patronize women's contributions. As Ann Oakley (1998: 725) notes, the logic of such reasoning '…is likely to be the construction of "difference" feminism where women are described as owning distinctive ways of thinking, knowing and feeling, and the danger is that these new moral characterisations will play into the hands of those who use gender as a means of discriminating against women'.

It is not necessary to resort to essentialism to explain why these gender distinctions occurred in Spain. Although highly educated, these women lacked status within their occupational field and were often reliant on the grace-and-favour of male colleagues and editors. This restricted their news-gathering opportunities, in terms of both access to senior political figures and physical mobility. Thus, their interest in reporting the impact of the war on everyday lives was to some extent a case of making a virtue of necessity. Certainly, when some of these women were provided with opportunities to visit the front, they exhibited an equivalent appetite to their male colleagues for observing and reporting battles. They also matched them for bravery and, occasionally, recklessness. On one occasion, this ended in tragedy when the photo-journalist Gerda Taro was crushed to death by a tank during the military retreat of Republican forces from Brunete in July 1937.

Despite the subordinated status of women journalists, news organizations valued and encouraged the production of a female perspective of the war. In part, this represented intensification in the general 'feminization' of news during this period, but it also revealed specific public and political interest in the experiences of citizens in coping with the traumas of total war. In this respect, these micro-narratives about everyday experience – which can be seen as symptomatic of the exclusion of women correspondents from wider public affairs – had a subtle but profound impact upon international power politics and military planning. By the late 1930s, the 'air fear' that shaped the foreign policy of European democracies through the mid-1930s started to lose credibility. A key reason for this was the eyewitness testimony provided by journalists in Spain, many of them women,[15] which showed that civilian morale was stiffened rather than destroyed by air attack and that the devastating impact of incendiaries and bombs could be mitigated by effective air raid precautions. By late 1938, press and political discourses in the UK had shifted decisively towards the development of air raid precautions to help defend civilian populations (Morris 1992: 65). Thus, by identifying resilience and stoicism amid the trauma and suffering, female reportage helped to fortify the political and public will of democratic nations as they prepared to confront the terrible trials in prospect. It is a striking illustration of how the politics of the personal are not only of intrinsic importance, but can also have major, if unforeseen, 'macro' political consequences.

Notes

1 This chapter draws on research funded by the ESRC (grant reference RES 000-22-0533).
2 Women accounted for 10 per cent of the British and North American correspondents whom I have definitely identified as having been present in Spain at some stage of the conflict
3 For example, in his account of his traumatic incarceration by Nationalist forces in 1937, Arthur Koestler describes meeting a woman who acted in a dual capacity as both a nationalist press officer and correspondent for the Hearst Press in the USA (Koestler 1938: 284–88). Unfortunately, I have yet to identify her.

4 Hilde Marchant was a notable exception in this respect, coming from a working class background.
5 3 February 1939, letter from Cunard to W. P. Crozier, *The Manchester Guardian* archives.
6 Quoted in *Great Lives*, BBC Radio 4, 16 January 2007.
7 'Martha Gellhorn: On the Record', BBC4 broadcast, 24 May 2004.
8 Jackson notes that this distaste for factionalism was common among many other women activists who were involved in offering practical and political support to the Republic (2002: 85).
9 Their partners were, respectively, Joseph Swire of Reuters, George Seldes, a radical freelance journalist who submitted copy to the *New York Post*; and Reynolds Packard of the *New York Times*.
10 'Martha Gellhorn: On the Record', BBC4 broadcast, 24 May 2004.
11 The first mass observation study commissioned by the British government examined public attitudes to the abdication crisis, but soon expanded into a broad anthropological investigation of the interior lives of British citizens (Hubble 2005).
12 The British Documentary movement, founded by the Scottish film-maker John Grierson and sponsored by the British governmental agencies, was also at its most influential during the late 1930s. This movement was defined by its commitment to social realism in film and conveying the experiences of 'real places and real people' (http://www.britmovie.co.uk/history, accessed 20 March 2007).
13 Hansard, 5C/270, 10 November 1932: 632.
14 See, for example, the compassionate reportage by Louis Delaprée who highlighted the suffering of the citizens of Madrid (1937).
15 See, for example, an article by Charlotte Haldane published in the *Daily Mirror* (8 March 1938: 14) relating her observations on the effects of the bombing of civilians in Madrid and the most effective defence against its worst effects. She concludes: 'Mothers who want to protect their babies in the next war must be prepared to fight for such protection now'.

The populist narrative

Introduction

The populist history of the media is essentially a celebratory narrative that has its roots in the late nineteenth century, whence we see the beginnings of what is usually characterized as the 'rise of the consumer society'. Part of the drive towards mass consumerism was the marketization of the media – indeed culture generally – which populists see as a positive development. The reason for this is that, as media and culture became more responsive to popular demand, there occurred an attendant change in social mores and cultural practices, such as the decline of socio-cultural deference and the birth of consumer sovereignty, both of which are taken to be democratizing, especially for the 'popular masses'.

Prior to this, it has been argued that the production and regulation of cultural practices and values were monopolized by a cultural elite composed of middle class professionals and an avant-garde intelligentsia. Although a residue of this cultural elitism remained well into the twentieth century, the authority of these 'cultivated elites' was slowly eroded as culture became increasingly commercialized. Although not quite the proletariat dictatorship that Marx had envisaged, for some social commentators and cultural critics, the popularization of the media and everyday culture was nevertheless a 'revolt of the masses', bringing about greater cultural egalitarianism and de-subordination.

The other driving force behind this 'cultural revolution' was the growing influence of American popular culture. However, American civilization failed to inspire confidence among Britain's cultivated elites, particularly its crass democratic appeal and valorizing of egalitarian values. Others objected to the way in which American populism played upon the common, baser instincts. They particularly loathed America's commodifying of culture and the consequent undermining of their own cultural ascendancy. Fear that American influences would usurp traditional British cultural and social values was perhaps the defining characteristic of early twentieth-century cultural pessimism.

The commercial mass media was thought by many cultivated elites to be the main instrument of Americanization. Popular daily newspapers began copying American tabloid techniques; mass advertising became a ubiquitous art form; respectable British popular music was usurped by ragtime and jazz. In short, the mass media in Britain became increasingly subject to American investment and cultural influences, particularly during the interwar period. Moreover, American culture was especially popular with the British working classes, partly because it treated them 'as equals'. Even the BBC began to adopt a more inclusive mode of public address and to provide more regular light entertainment, specially during and after the Second World War. However, America's domination of Britain's film industry was probably the cause for most alarm. Fears of American domination of British film resulted in the British government inaugurating protectionist policies in an attempt to stem the flow of American films. Some American films were even censored, on the grounds that they were either immoral or politically controversial.

Not surprisingly, these debates continue to attract intense political and scholarly debate, thus reflecting contemporary anxieties about the influences of foreign competition on the British economy and its culture. In the first of the chapters in this section, Stefan Schwarzkopf looks at the introduction of commercial television in Britain in 1955. More crucially, he argues that it has been little noticed that the advertising boom which followed in the wake of commercial television was the beginning of the long decline of some of the largest British advertising agencies. In this process, many of the large British advertising agencies lost ground to the more experienced and better equipped American agencies such as J. Walter Thompson and McCann-Erickson. In other words, the ardent ideological support for the case of commercial television shown by some representatives of the British advertising industry eventually helped prepare the field for the growth of American agency networks in the UK, which by the early 1960s had bought up and merged with the majority of their once powerful British rivals. Hence Schwarzkopf's contention that radical media historians have failed to understand that, for the most part, the British advertising industry was in fact reluctant to embrace televisual advertising. That is to say, only a minority of advertisers showed any real interest in the new medium, which would suggest that the case for this seemingly 'popular' technology was as much political as it was commercial.

The other chapter in the section, by Jeffrey Milland, in some ways follows on from the above insofar as it focuses on the Pilkington Report and the subsequent fallout between commercial television and the British political establishment. Published in 1962, Pilkington can be understood as one of the most influential texts produced in Britain in the first decades of mass broadcasting, in the period after the BBC had lost its monopoly and before new technology allowed a profusion of cable and satellite channels. More crucially, Milland argues that Pilkington constituted the essence of an attitude towards broadcasting, dominant for thirty years among the country's social and intellectual elite, which can be described as both liberal and paternalist. 'Liberal' because it insisted that broadcasting institutions must be open to the widest possible range of ideas and opinions, while remaining, as far as possible, unaffected by the profit motive; 'paternalist' because it declared, first, that certain programmes were 'good' and others 'bad' and could be recognized as such by initiates, and, second, that broadcasting and morality were inextricably entwined, with a duty incumbent on broadcasters to concern themselves with 'the moral condition of society'. Milland asks how it was that the liberal/ paternalist narrative achieved such dominance. How, in particular, in a democratic society, did Conservative governments, eager to win elections but torn between paternalism and populism, come to acquiesce in a broadcasting system that tried to marginalize the profit motive and regularly neglected popular taste? And, at a time when deference was widely thought to be dead, or dying, how was it that deference to the tastes of the educated middle class was enforced on the great majority of television viewers much of the time on all available channels?

Further reading

Although their renderings of the 'cultivated elites' are somewhat different, LeMahieu (1988) and Carey (1992) form the backbone for this particular narrative (cf. Ortega y Gasset, for whom the 'revolt of the masses' was a cultural disaster). Other contributors to this narrative are surprisingly few. Among them, see Bromley (1991), Conboy (2002), Lee (1976) and Wiener (1996) on the Americanization of the Victorian British press, the attendant rise of 'new journalism' and the continuance of tabloidization in the twentieth century (cf. Hampton 2004 for an analysis of what the cultivated elites thought about the British press, c.1850–1950). See Camporesi (1990a, b) on the influence of American broadcasting on the BBC during the interwar period; Cardiff (1980), Cardiff and Scannell (1986), Scannell and Cardiff (1991) and Frith (1983) on the gradual popularization of radio up to and including the 1940s; Chapman (1992) on the introduction of mixed scheduling shortly after the Second World War, the popular demand for pirate radio among Britain's youth in the 1960s and the eventual arrival of the first licensed, popular music radio channel – Radio 1 – in 1967. For an overview of similar developments in relation to film and television, see Swan (1987) and Holmes (2008).

The above should be supplemented with what are essentially related historical accounts of 'de-subordination' and the rise of 'the consumer society'. For a cultural history of the decline of deference and the breakdown of the postwar consensus in Britain, see Hewison (1995) and McKibbin (1998). For a history of consumerism and affluence, see Bermingham and Brewer (1995), Brewer (1997), Brewer and Porter (1993), Hennessy (2006), McKendrick *et al.* (1983) and Offer (2006); Richards (1990) offers a highly theorized analysis of commodity spectacle in Victorian Britain; see also Lancaster (1995), Miller (1981) and Williams (1982) for a cultural history of mass consumption and the department store.

This body of literature should be read alongside what are essentially sociological accounts of the so-called 'consumer society', usually in relation to cultural consumption and identity: see, for example, Baudrillard (1998), Bauman (1988), Douglas and Isherwood (1996), Featherstone (1991), Giddens (1991), Lury (1996), Miller (2001), Nava *et al.* (1997) and Slater (1997). Similar discussions and debates are to be found within the populist cultural studies canon: see, for example, Fiske (1989a, b), Hebdige (1979), Radway (1987) and Willis (1990); cf. Golby and Purdue (1984), Hall (1981), Hall and Whannel (1964) and Williams (1961, 1976) for an altogether more subtle and thoughtful discussion about the 'popular' *vis-à-vis* the historical development of British popular culture.

Classic critiques of modern consumer society and the commoditization of culture include Adorno (2001), Galbraith (1958), Hoggart (1958), Leavis (1979[1930]) and Packard (1977); see also Fine and Leopold (1993). Of these, Leavis and Hoggart are occasionally characterized as representatives of the 'cultivated elites' insofar as their criticisms are largely based upon notions of quality and judgement. Following in this Leavisite tradition, although from a more radical perspective, Curran (2002a: 107–26), Garnham (1998) and McGuigan (1992) offer what are undoubtedly the most palpable, contemporary critiques of 'cultural populism'.

Chapter 6

'A moment of triumph in the history of the free mind'?

British and American advertising agencies' responses to the introduction of commercial television in the United Kingdom.

Stefan Schwarzkopf

My telly – right or left

The introduction of commercial television in Britain in September 1955 has attracted intense scholarly debate in media studies and media history circles (Buscombe 2000; Dickason 2000; Thumim 2001; Turnock 2007). These debates reflect contemporary anxieties about the influence of purely commercial interests on the public sphere. Drawing on James Curran's typology of media historical narratives, a dualism of interpretations has established itself around the advent of commercial television. On the one hand, populists have argued that commercial television has brought more variety and programme diversity, and that it is as responsible and professional as its historical counterpart, the BBC. On the other hand, commercial television is seen by some media scholars as a social ill that has created a ruthless caste of media owners, whose final interest lies not in providing resources for citizenship and civil society, but merely in ratings and profits (Groombridge 1972; Murdock 2005). This radical narrative identifies a powerful 'pressure group' behind the introduction of commercial television, consisting of representatives of consumer goods industries, Conservative MPs and the advertising industry at large (Mayhew 1959; Jenkins 1961: 17–33; Wilson 1961: 133–45; Sampson 1962: 580–619; Bakewell and Garnham 1970; Williams 1974: 68–70, 86–96; Curran and Seaton 1981: 226–49).

In this chapter, I argue that both narratives need to be revised. Taking contemporary arguments around commercial advertising, increased consumer choice and 'the people's will' as a starting point, I argue that media historians have failed to acknowledge that, on the whole, the British advertising industry was reluctant to embrace the potential of television as a new advertising medium. Technically unprepared, managerially incompetent and unwilling to make the necessary financial investments to deal with television advertising, a large number of British agencies failed to adapt to a new era in advertising. I also argue that the introduction of commercial television in the United Kingdom was not at all a moment in British history at which market and commercial demands won over politics and civil society, a description often used by critical media historians. On the contrary, only a minority of 'the advertising interest' actually showed keen interest in the new medium, while the majority found itself overpowered by the political imperative represented by a Tory government, which suggests that the realm of politics played a more significant role in shaping the relationship between popular culture and (media) consumption than hitherto acknowledged.

Setting the scene: the pressure group takes form

The first postwar Labour government committed itself to building a society based on universal social services, full employment in nationalized industries, technological innovation and a more efficient distribution of wealth. Arguably, advertising did not fit well into the new vision of a rational and efficient Britain. Instead of putting vital economic resources into fancy packaging, expensive posters or gimmicky radio jingles, Labour politicians and many consumers thought that these resources should be put into the improvement of production facilities in order to produce better products at lower prices that could be exported to earn badly needed dollars for the nation. When statisticians found in 1948 that advertisers had spent almost £125 million that year on advertising – at a time when housewives had to queue for oranges and butter – many people insisted that these millions would be better spent on rebuilding bombed schools or caring for injured servicemen (Silverman 1952). In the wake of these findings, Labour's Chancellor of the Exchequer, Stafford Cripps, proposed a tax on advertising, which the industry only narrowly avoided by submitting to a scheme of voluntary reductions in advertising. From the advertiser's point of view, the increased powers of the state and of Whitehall officials in deciding what types of products should be available at what price smacked of socialism and prevented consumers from deciding for themselves what they wanted (Harris and Seldon 1959). The debates between an embattled advertising industry that felt misunderstood and a pugnacious Labour movement peaked around the early 1950s, when consumers, politicians and advertising agencies were drawn into the maelstrom of the cultural Cold War (Schwarzkopf 2005). It is important to remember this background of ideologies to understand why contemporary writers and politicians lumped industries, advertising agencies and Conservative politicians together into a giant conspiracy when trying to explain why commercial television was introduced in Britain.

Not surprisingly, early debates about advertising on television were strongly influenced by popular anxieties about the undue influence of commercial interests on broadcasting and fears of growing American dominance over British culture (Curran and Seaton 1981: 239–49; Hebdige 1988: 45–76;

Black 2001, 2003: 94–104; Thumim 2004: 12–17, 40–42). When the Tory government White Paper on Broadcasting and the subsequent Memorandum on Television Policy were discussed in the Commons and the House of Lords, an imposing alliance covering members of all parties in both Houses formed itself and began to single out 'advertising interests' as the major evil force behind all these endeavours. Lord Reith compared advertising-sponsored television to smallpox, bubonic plague and the Black Death. Aneurin Bevan publicly denounced advertising as the 'evil consequence of a society which in itself is evil'.[1] Crucially, it was widely claimed that the lobbying work for the introduction of commercial television was mainly undertaken by Tories who were active in the business of advertising. Among them were Ian Harvey, Under-Secretary of State at the Foreign Office, MP for Harrow East and a Director of Crawford's; John Rodgers, MP for Sevenoaks, Chairman of the British Market Research Bureau and Director of the J. Walter Thompson agency (JWT); Patrick Hannon, MP for Moseley (Birmingham), Chairman of the Birmingham-based poster advertising company Sheffield's and President of the National Union of Manufacturers; Frank Patrick Bishop, MP for Harrow Central and Advertising Manager of *The Times*; R. Hornby, MP for Tonbridge and in the employment of JWT; Ian McArthur, MP for Perth and Associate Director of JWT; W. F. Martin Maddan, MP for Hitchin and Director of Television Audience Measurement Ltd (TAM); and R. G. Page, MP for Crosby and Director of Greenwood's Advertising (Jenkins 1961: 17f; Wilson 1961: 133–45). These and other Conservative MPs, who constituted the back-bench pressure group that was mainly responsible for pushing the Television Act through both Houses, were not even too careful in hiding their involvement in an industry that was supposedly to profit directly from the introduction of commercial television. The trade journal *Advertiser's Weekly* celebrated them regularly as 'our advertising MPs'.[2] Indeed, the Labour MP Chris Mayhew did statistical research in *Hansard* and found that some 80 per cent of all parliamentary speeches, questions and interruptions in relation to the Television Bill were made by MPs who held prestigious positions in the world of advertising, marketing and media (Jenkins 1961: 19).[3]

This said, the opponents of the Television Bill consisted not only of Labour MPs and peers – who, incidentally, might have been accused of being biased towards a media monopoly of the state – but also of Liberal and Conservative dignitaries. In fact, almost the entire leadership of the Conservative Party of the early 1950s – Winston Churchill and Lords Halifax, Waverley, Brand and Salisbury – were opposed to what they saw as an organized attempt at undermining the cultural hegemony of the 'cultivated classes' over those classes favouring what Churchill called a 'tuppenny-ha'penny Punch and Judy show'. Thus, both the traditional Conservative elites and the Labour movement and their intellectual vanguard among journalists and writers identified the advertising industry as an evil-minded, but nevertheless carefully planned, well-prepared group of individuals who would drive British society down the path of this new age. When Clive Jenkins tried to answer the question in 1961 as to who really wanted commercial television to happen in the first place, his answer was unambiguous: 'It was the advertising agencies' (Jenkins 1961: 17). Such criticisms culminated in the publication of H. H. Wilson's *Pressure Group* (1961), now a seminal account of the arrival of commercial television, which reiterated the claims that powerful right-wing advertising agents and their clients press-ganged Parliament and the nation into adopting the Television Act of 1954 (Wilson 1961: 133–45).

An industry dragging its feet

Evidence from agency archives and contemporary trade journals, however, sheds a different light on the ability of agencies to embrace the potentials of the new medium. Most advertising agencies had indeed a political tendency towards attacking the BBC monopoly. Yet at the same time they were reluctant, if not unwilling, to actually prepare themselves to offer their clients a television advertising service. In 1958 and 1959, the LSE Research Fellow Walter Taplin studied the reaction of around 270 manufacturing firms and retailers towards television as a new advertising medium. In his survey, Taplin found that 'there is no good reason to believe that much forethought had gone into the questions of the use of television for advertising purposes', on the part of both the advertisers and their agents (Taplin 1961: 22). Taplin's survey showed that only 20 per cent of his respondents had considered using television as an advertising medium before 1954, and the vast majority (60 per cent) only even began to consider television advertising after it was introduced in September 1955. Of the surveyed firms, a mere 36 per cent began to make factual investigations into television before September 1955, while 61 per cent began such investigations after ITV went on air. The survey also found that agencies often 'dragged their feet' when consulted by clients with regard to the new medium. Moreover, and rather surprisingly, the suggestion that the possibilities of television advertising should be investigated did not come from the advertising agencies. The more apprehensive advertisers tended to discuss TV advertising first within their own organizations and only brought in the agency at a later stage. At this moment, however, agencies had to deal with a *fait accompli* (Taplin 1961: 28–30).

This impression is corroborated by evidence from within the professional body of the advertising agencies, the Institute of Practitioners in Advertising (IPA). The Institute had discussed the issue of commercial advertising already in the late 1940s but began to deal with the question in earnest only after the publication of the White Paper on Broadcasting in July 1952 – suggesting that it was political forces that pushed advertising into a certain direction rather than the other way around. At a meeting in July 1952, Hubert Oughton, President of the IPA and Managing Director of Crawford's, warned the Institute's member agencies that the 'the general public would judge very critically the way in which sponsored television was handled'. He believed that 'relatively few agencies' would probably make use of sponsored television and that it would be 'a long time before the new medium could become valuable other than as a novelty in its early stages'. Oughton therefore advised his colleagues that, because of public scepticism, 'the advertising business should avoid any move which savoured of panic or controversy'.[4]

Of course, this was merely a polite form of advising the Institute's member agencies that the IPA should not be seen to press the matter of commercial television publicly and at the political level, as 'neither advertisers nor their agents intended to be jockeyed into the position of advocating competitive television'.[5] Secretly and outside the framework of the IPA, an advisory panel on commercial television was formed in 1952, consisting of representatives of those few agencies that intended to press ahead in the matter. This group only became formalized as the IPA Television Advisory Panel after the government published its Memorandum on Television Policy in November 1953.[6] In January 1955, with nine months to go before commercial television went on air, it became clear that neither most IPA member agencies nor the Institute itself had enough information about air-time buying standards, regulations for agency remuneration, audience measurement techniques, etc., so that a letter had to be written to Robert Fraser, the ITA's Director-General, indicating that the agencies were not ready yet for commercial advertising.[7]

Evidence from within advertising agencies supports this view of an industry that failed to anticipate the arrival of a new advertising medium and then reacted in panic. One such example is the large and well-established agency Samson Clark. Samson Clark had been founded in 1896 and, in 1952, served around 130 clients, among them Aspro, the British aircraft industry, Ilford films, the Milk Marketing Board, Waterman pens and Debenham's department stores. Samson Clark's largest client was the pharmaceutical company that produced Aspro. Throughout the period between the early 1920s and the 1960s, Aspro was by some distance the largest advertiser in the UK in the category of aspirins and other pharmaceutical products (*Advertiser's Annual* 1937: 46). When in December 1953 a board member of Samson Clark raised the question of providing TV advertising services for their clients, mainly Aspro, his proposal to establish a TV department was rejected as the 'likelihood of commercial television during the next few years was remote'.[8] More than half a year later, in July 1954, Samson Clark's client Aspro informed the agency that they wished to use television as an advertising medium as soon as it was made available by the authorities. At this moment only, in late July 1954, the decision was taken to 'advertise for a young man to develop this department'.[9]

Three weeks later, however, Samson Clark was informed by Aspro that the British–American agency Masius & Ferguson would now be in charge of all advertising: Samson Clark had lost their largest client. The agency was informed that Masius & Ferguson had been 'backwards and forwards to the

United States during the past two years in connection with TV advertising' and that Samson Clark were simply 'too slow'.[10] Samson Clark's internal structure was altogether geared to an old age of advertising in print, not on air. In the week in which the first TV commercials were screened into the homes of thousands of British viewers in September 1955, Samson Clark's governing board discussed at great length the details of a new rooftop for their printing plant in Stevenage. It took Samson Clark until 1961 before they produced their first television commercial.[11]

Some of the larger and more modern advertising agencies in the UK, such as Colman Prentis & Varley (CPV) – which was in charge of Tory party campaigns in the 1950s – were reluctant to engage in the new medium on the grounds of ethical and financial considerations. John Hobson, who had started in advertising in 1930 and later worked with CPV wrote (quoted in Henry 1986: 425–33):

> I remember that I myself was extremely worried about these new developments because, being concerned for the general image of advertising, I feared it would not be improved when beamed into the public's living room... Agency reaction was by no means unanimous. While some were enthusiastic about the future potential of the medium, others, including some major agencies, thought it would be a nine days' wonder...Some went into it with eagerness. The less enthusiastic carefully segregated their television staff from their main business activities, so as to be able to drop them with the minimum of disruption when the nine days' wonder flopped.

Other large and established British agencies such as Mather & Crowther (agent for British Home Stores, Sainsbury's, Singer sewing machines and HP Sauce) also had considerable problems in managing the transition into the TV age. When the young copy-writing trainee Winston Fletcher, who had joined Mather & Crowther in 1959, was given a tour of the newly formed TV department, he was surprised to find ex-BBC radio producers now in charge of TV production: 'Even in my innocent ignorance, I had dark suspicions that television was more concerned with pictures than with sound, but it seemed impertinent to point this out to the pedagogic luminaries who knew so much about wavelengths and decibels, so I listened intently if uncomprehendingly' (quoted in Henry 1986: 421–22). Many agencies in the late 1950s suffered from this severe lack of specialists with sufficient experience of this new medium. In sheer desperation, British agencies resorted to bringing in people from the BBC, from cinema, theatre and photography. At great cost, American advisers and TV consultants were flown in from Chicago and New York. Often, however, these American 'TV experts' were not worth their money: US television advertisers had a particular strength in devising sponsored programmes, yet the 1954 Television Act demanded that advertisers would supply 'spot' advertising of around thirty to sixty seconds only. As a result, many British agencies that were guided by American advisers created commercials that looked more like cinema movies, some of them with a length of up to two minutes (Tunstall 1964: 87–89; Berkman 1987; Nevett 1992; Samuel 2001: 67–72).

This evidence of course raises the question as to why the advertising industry as a whole was so markedly unenthusiastic about television advertising. In the following section, I argue that this reaction can be explained by using a rational choice and organizational learning approach.

The cosiness of the competitive lock-in

The advertising industry in Britain had learned to become efficient and competitive in an age of print advertising which saw its peak between the 1890s, when the first commercially viable half-penny papers came on the market, and the 1950s, when the circulation of the *News of the World* reached 8.4 million. This dominance of the printed paper as the most important advertising medium was aided by the relatively high production costs of posters and the taxation imposed on outdoor advertising sites. Moreover, the BBC's monopoly over broadcast radio since the 1920s ensured that only the very largest advertising agencies ventured into the field of producing radio commercials in the 1930/40s. These were broadcast to Britain from commercial stations in France, Ireland and Luxembourg. British advertising agencies knew how to compete for clients and audiences but had adapted to a media environment consisting almost entirely of print and outdoor advertising. Agencies thus made their economic decisions – in which new departments they had to invest, what kind of specialists they needed to employ, etc. – based on what they were good at. If members of an entire industry focus on one type of technology in order to compete more efficiently with competitors for rare resources and make economic decisions according to a limited set of parameters only, economists talk about a competitive 'lock-in'.

The evidence presented above suggests that the British advertising industry had become very comfortable in that position. In addition, the capital investment needed to equip television and sound studios was horrendous and, just ten years after the Second World War, most British agencies simply lacked the working capital to make such investments. It was not even clear whether the new medium would take off and prove popular with the audience. The capital flows surrounding the new medium were unclear too. While print advertising brought agencies a comfortable 15 per cent commission on every pound a client spent on advertising, no one had a clear idea about the returns from television commercials after layouts and production costs. Those agencies that made the decision to purchase recording studio equipment and employ sound and screen specialists faced sunk costs of a, potentially, enormous dimension. Nor could they be sure whether other advertising agencies and their clients were likely to follow the trend.

The impression of an industry largely unaware of the challenges they faced also emerges from the pages of contemporary trade journals, such as the *Advertiser's Weekly*. While strong in its support of the ideological case for 'independent' television, the journal also had to run a series of articles from 1953 which explained the basics of television advertising. In September 1953, a 'Glossary of advertising film jargon' appeared, which explained terms such as 'producer', 'director', 'focus puller', 'cutter', 'frame' and 'play back' to British advertising practitioners who could 'talk fluently enough about zincos, deep-etched half-tones, chromo-lithos, scraperboard and so on'.[12] Between articles hailing the back-bench Tory stance on commercial television, quite a large number of sceptical letters and articles appeared too. A survey conducted among fifty advertising agencies in September 1953, for example, showed that about 44 per cent of all agents were personally against the introduction of commercial television, and only 46 per cent thought it would benefit their clients. For some within the industry, these rather surprising figures repre-sented the opinion of a 'bunch of clamorous canutes', who simply did not want to work hard enough to equip themselves to provide TV advertising. For others, it was not altogether clear whether the public good was not more likely to suffer from the commercialization of the medium, and they argued that 'those agents who are not falling for the blandishments [of the new medium] may, in fact, be the true custodians of their clients' best interest'.[13]

Giving the masses what the few wanted

The evidence presented here begs the question who really wanted commercial advertising in the first place and who benefited from it? Historical research suggests that, by the mid-1950s, a large proportion of the population did indeed favour another television channel that provided more choice and more light entertainment. More crucially, and in spite of what I have argued thus far, there were a number of advertising, public relations and media people who were more optimistic about the profitability of commercial television. And at the top of the list of future profiteers came the associates and members of American advertising agencies operating in London, in particular J. Walter Thompson and its market research subsidiary BMRB. By the mid-1950s, this agency had become not only the largest advertising agency in the UK, but was ranked globally as the 'Number One' in advertising. The most vocal group of supporters of commercial television was led by JWT and comprised other American agencies operating in London, namely McCann-Erickson, Young & Rubicam, Erwin, Wasey Co. and Masius & Ferguson as well as the four largest British advertising agencies, London Press Exchange, S. H. Benson, Mather & Crowther and W. S. Crawford's. These agencies pushed the way towards commercial television. As the *Statistical Review of Independent TV Advertising* showed in 1955/56, of the twelve largest advertising agencies in the field of television, exactly six were American and six were British.

American agencies however clearly led the field where cumulative expenditure was concerned. By 1960, seven out of the top fifteen agencies in television advertising expenditure were American, and around 51 per cent of the television advertising money spent through the top fifteen agencies went through American agencies (*Statistical Review of Independent Television Advertising* 1956: 2; 1960: 24–40; Jenkins 1961: 21). However, the fact that most of these 'American' agencies in London had a British board of directors or had themselves been products of Anglo-American mergers should make readers suspicious of historical explanations that resort to the idea of 'Americanization' (Williams 1962: 21–24; Tunstall 1994; de Grazia 2005; Schröter 2005).

This said, the extent to which American agencies followed the agenda of their often multinational clients and profited more from the new medium should not be underestimated. Nor should the extent to which these agencies made television less attractive be underestimated. When commercial television started, the top ten advertisers on ITV consisted of petrol manufacturers, newspapers and the makers of beverages and foodstuffs. The variety of these products ensured that the advertising breaks in 1955 and 1956 gave consumers a relatively meaningful overview of what was available on the market. By 1959, the ten most heavily advertised products on television included seven detergents and soaps and only three foodstuffs (*Statistical Review of Independent Television Advertising* 1956: 2; Jenkins 1961: 22). This shows how monopolistic competition between the makers of virtually identical soap and detergent products crowded into one advertising medium, thereby effectively homogenizing the commercial break on British television for much of the late 1950s and throughout the 1960s. As there were only two channels available and both the BBC and ITV had to compete for the same audience, the effects of duopolistic competition between the two channels meant that similar types of programmes – drama, quiz show, movie, documentary, children's programme – tended to be placed into the same time slots on the same days so that viewers ended up with two channels but stereotyped, run-of-the-mill and prepackaged content (Mayhew 1959). All these effects are known to economists as forms of market failure that often provide constant returns on investment for the few but hardly more choice for the many. Although the television advertising top ten was populated by both British and American agencies, the J. Walter Thompson agency always came out as the number one. Not only did JWT spend more money on television advertising in absolute terms, it also spent more on television advertising per client than all other agencies.[14]

During 1954 and 1955, the JWT agency was also behind the advertising campaign for the Popular Television Association (PTA), which used advertising and public relations to convince the British of the advantages of commercial television. This campaign was later credited with turning around the public opinion polls in favour of commercial television (Pearson and Turner 1965: 181).[15] While the rest of the advertising industry and a great many

British manufacturers played time in the belief – or hope – that commercial television would not arrive or prove a 'nine days' wonder', American agencies were busy planning and preparing for the transition. As early as January 1953, the London office of Young & Rubicam was headed by a managing director who had twelve years of TV experience in the US.[16] Also, whereas most British agencies had difficulty finding enough trained specialists, the American McCann-Erickson agency offered an entire Board of TV Operations, consisting of directors, producers and screenwriters who had been with the BBC, Paramount, Warner Bros, NBC and Walt Disney.[17] Given the lack of experience, the best that most British agencies could come up with were uninspired short movies, animated versions of the familiar press advertisements. The low level of technical sophistication contributed to the bad press most of the first commercials received in the wake of ITV's launch night in September 1955, when popular newspapers described what they had seen as 'irksome', 'lacking sparkle and novelty' and 'bewildering rather than bewitching'.[18]

It is therefore more than questionable whether the British advertising industry did itself a great service by allowing commercial television to be introduced. Nor does evidence suggest that they did a great favour to British consumers. For example, the excessive costs of television advertising crowded out for example the Co-operative Wholesale Societies as suppliers of soaps and detergents as they saw themselves unable to match the high expenditure of Unilever and Procter & Gamble (Harris and Seldon 1962: 139–53; Burton 2005: 223–29; Gurney 2005). The market share of 'the Co-op' sank steadily from the mid-1950s even though their detergent powder brand offered a chemically identical product to housewives.

Yet, the first opinion polls that were conducted on the question of whether people actually liked the commercials they saw on television showed that the majority neither liked them nor did they approve of television advertising as such. In fact, when polled by Gallup in 1958 and 1959, over 60 per cent of the people surveyed were 'annoyed a lot' by commercials interrupting the programme, and some 70 per cent voiced support for Chris Mayhew's Bill to restrict advertisements on television.[19] In autumn 1961, the JWT agency found that only 35 per cent of the people they surveyed actually 'liked' televised advertising (compared with 63 per cent who said they 'liked' press advertising). Indeed, JWT found that detergent powder commercials, with their ceaseless promotional offers, their endless presentation of happy housewives, their tedious jingles and mind-numbingly simplistic dialogues, contributed most to the low esteem of television advertising.[20] Six years later, the British Market Research Bureau found in a laboratory-style opinion poll that more people actually 'liked' the commercials they had seen (65 per cent); but an even smaller minority of people (33 per cent) said they 'liked' and approved of television advertising as such (British Market Research Bureau 1967; Treasure 1967: 12–20).

These surveys also put a question mark behind the idea that the cultural battles over the introduction of commercial television were fought along the lines of left and right. The polls showed that the typical Tory voter and, on the whole, the cultivated middle classes objected to 'independent' television and TV commercials, whereas the typical Labour voter and the working classes tended to favour the new channel and its advertising. It was also found that regular viewers of ITV – women, the elderly, working class people and those who had not been educated beyond the age of fifteen – liked commercials more than men and members of the highly educated, high-earning middle classes (British Market Research Bureau 1967: 13). These findings of course supported the arguments of both the traditional right and the intellectual left that commercial television pandered to the feeble, the fickle and the fools.

Conclusions

From the evidence presented here, the British advertising industry emerges as overwhelmingly reluctant to embrace the potential of the new medium of commercial advertising. Technically unprepared, managerially incompetent and unwilling or incapable of making the necessary financial investments, a large number of British agencies failed to adapt to the new era early enough. The predominance of technical experience in the realms of craftsmanship and design for print advertising resulted in early British TV commercials often looking like press advertisements redone for television. Journalists and newspaper readers often found them drab, uninspiring and lacking the humorous, entertaining spark.

This case study also challenges the populist interpretation of media history, which sees people empowered as consumers in an increasingly 'independent' media world that replaced the allegedly repressive influence of the Edwardian cultivated elites by the cultural democracy of the market. This narrative is based on the misconception that markets are *per se* of a democratic nature and therefore better equipped to 'give people what they want'. The British historical experience, especially since the privatization waves of the 1980s, has shown that marketization is not the same as privatization and that markets can be distorted (imperfect) and they can harbour oligopolistic as well as duopolistic and monopolistic competition, none of which is necessarily beneficial to consumers. In short, the cultural interpretation of the marketization of the media in the twentieth century fails to understand that, in the battle over commercial television, some businesses emerged victorious, not 'the market', 'the people' or 'the consumer'.

Finally, the introduction of commercial television in the United Kingdom was not at all a moment in which the market won over politics and civil society, as it is often described by critical media historians. The evidence presented here shows that only a minority of 'the advertising interest' was actually keen on the new medium, while the majority of the advertising industry found itself overpowered by the political imperative represented by a certain section of the post-1951 Tory government. It was the Conservative Central Office, not the advertising industry, that gave out the slogan that 'commercial television will mark a moment of triumph in the history of the free mind'.[21] Many contemporary advertising agents and their clients would have rejected such claims. At the time, however, marketers were forced into adopting this new medium by the political imperatives of a new Tory elite which was bent on eliminating the legacies of Labour policies at all costs and in all areas of society.

Notes

1 'Bevan blasts advertising: an "evil service"', *Advertiser's Weekly*, 7 May 1953: 234.
2 *Advertiser's Weekly*, 1 January 1953: 29.
3 See also the Labour leader Herbert Morrison making the point publicly in the Commons, 'MPs' interests in television: advertising agencies', *The Times*, 15 December 1953: 2.
4 Minutes of the IPA Radio Committee, 17 July 1952, History of Advertising Trust Archive, IPA collection 16/2.
5 'Competitive TV: appeal for a commonsense plan', *Advertiser's Weekly*, 24 September 1953: 551.
6 Minutes of the IPA Radio Committee, 19 November 1953, History of Advertising Trust Archive, IPA collection 16/2.
7 Ibid., Meetings 28 October 1954, 16 December 1954, 20 January 1955, History of Advertising Trust Archive, IPA collection 16/2.
8 Meeting 1 December 1953, *Minutes of the Board Meetings, Samson Clark*, SAM 3/2 (Box C), History of Advertising Trust Archive.
9 Ibid., Meeting 21 July 1954.
10 Ibid., Meeting 11 August 1954.
11 Ibid., Meeting 15 September 1955.
12 *Advertiser's Weekly*, 10 September 1953: 452, 454.
13 *Advertiser's Weekly*, 17 September 1953: 522, 524; 27 September 1953: ii; 1 October 1953: ii; 8 October 1953: ii.
14 JWT Newsletter *Round the Square*, September 1956: 19; November 1956: 18.
15 Minutes of the IPA TV, Film and Radio Committee, 19 May 1955, History of Advertising Trust Archive, IPA collection 17/2; *Public Relations*, January 1956: 54. The PTA was also the playground of a number of Conservative party spin doctors and advertising agents, such as Toby O'Brien and Geoffrey Tucker: *The Observer*, 27 September 1959; Arthur Cain, 'Pictures in the home', *Public Relations*, October 1955: 7–8.
16 *Advertiser's Weekly*, 29 January 1953: 190; see also Young & Rubicam's Dan Ingman, 'Low cost message catches listeners when they are relaxing at home', *Advertiser's Weekly*, 16 April 1953: 110.
17 *Advertiser's Weekly*, 23 September 1955: 12 (commercial TV supplement).
18 *Advertiser's Weekly*, 30 September 1955: 6–7, 16.
19 'TV advertisers surprised by Gallup Poll findings', *Advertiser's Weekly*, 13 March 1959: 7.
20 See J. Walter Thompson, 'The Advertising Image' (a presentation made by JWT, 22 January 1962), History of Advertising Trust Archive, Advertising Agencies Collection, Box 'JWT'.
21 'Government determined on TV "a triumph" – Conservative Central Office', *Advertiser's Weekly*, 23 July 1953: 147, 187.

Chapter 7

The Pilkington Report
The triumph of paternalism?

Jeffrey Milland

The Pilkington Report on the Future of Broadcasting, commissioned in 1960 and published in 1962, has been little regarded by media historians. Somewhat typically, in a textbook for undergraduates, Andrew Crisell (1997: 112) called it 'politically, a dinosaur...no government of any colour would attempt radical reforms to a service as popular as ITV'.[1] This chapter will argue that, although Pilkington's main recommendations for the radical restructuring of ITV were rejected, it remains a classic and cogent attempt to embody in policy what James Curran (2002: 4) has recently styled 'the liberal narrative' of media history, even if in the last decades of the twentieth century it succumbed to Curran's 'populist' narrative. Broadcasting in Britain continued to be based on Pilkingtonian principles for forty years, establishing criteria for judging the performance of broadcasters which few challenged, at least until the 1980s. Pilkington's insistence on broadcasting's moral responsibility dominated the debate. The programmes that resulted were much praised, especially perhaps by programme-makers themselves. Furthermore, an analysis of the structure that Pilkington helped put in place supports Curran's insistence on the need for a synthesis of rival narratives to provide proper historical understanding. As he says, this should 'offer a...contingent view of ebb and flow, opening and closure, advances in some areas and reverses in others' (ibid.: 51). But by failing to examine the philosophical underpinnings of the terms in which Pilkington and its supporters made their case, and in scorning populist notions, in the end, the report carried little moral authority. Broadcasters were told they must not just give the audience what it wanted. But how was Pilkington's paternalist approach justified, and how was it to be sustained?

The system that operated from 1968 onwards (when the ITA awarded new contracts) left many discontented. Pre-Pilkington, people had been choosing in very large numbers to watch programmes such as *Take Your Pick*, *Double Your Money* and *Beat the Clock*. In 1962, a survey for the *Sunday Times* found that 60 per cent of the television audience believed that the general standard of television programmes was 'satisfactory' or better, despite having only two channels to choose from (Sawers 1962: 71). In 1985, post-Pilkington, the Peacock Committee was given evidence that, with four channels on offer, only 46 per cent of television viewers declared themselves 'very or fairly satisfied' with the quality of television as against 45 per cent who were 'very or fairly *dis*satisfied' (Peacock 1986: 198). In the post-Pilkington world, with the ITA having the power to vet schedules ahead of transmission, *Take Your Pick* and *Double Your Money* were taken off the air despite the undiminished size of their audiences. For decades, viewers were denied programmes they wanted to watch. David Cannadine (1998: 160) wrote of the 1970s that it was widely agreed then that there had been 'a collapse of deference'. But a society that was witnessing that collapse saw it continue to be enforced on television, where overwhelmingly working class viewers of all three channels and, later, even more so of a fourth channel, were expected willingly to defer, much of the time, to the tastes of the educated middle class.

Why was this? How, in a largely democratic society, did Conservative governments, torn between paternalism and populism, come to acquiesce in a broadcasting system that tried to marginalize the profit motive and regularly neglected popular taste?

It was in 1958 that television in the United Kingdom reached five million homes for the first time. That year, also for the first time, there were more combined radio and television licences issued than radio licences alone. With increasing affluence, television was on the point of genuinely becoming a mass medium, as had been noted by the celebrated anthropologist Geoffrey Gorer (1958), who was commissioned by the *Sunday Times* in 1958 to research and write a series of articles on the effect television was having on British life.

> Five years ago [in 1953] there was something near an absolute majority of middle-class ownership of TV sets, with the greatest amount of ownership in the upper middle class; even three years ago [in 1955] there was something not very far from a balance between middle-class and working-class viewers...[Now] there are approximately three owners of a [television] set from the working-classes for every two from the middle-classes; and if, as seems likely, this pattern continues over the next few years, the television audience will be at least two-thirds working-class.

A medium that had been almost entirely the preserve of the comfortably off was, through increasing affluence, becoming available to all. Its audience would be predominately working class, and likely therefore to reflect working class taste. For some, like Gorer himself, this was a disturbing prospect.

In that year also, the Conservative government was forced to confront the political problems caused by the medium's increasing penetration into British society. By now, audiences were dividing four to one in favour of ITV. A BBC executive explained to his Board of Governors in 1957 that the attraction of ITV was a schedule consisting of 'wiggle-dances, give-aways, panels and light entertainment' (Briggs 1995: 16). One result was the rancour-inducing profitability of the ITV companies, which, it has been calculated, were making an average profit of 130 per cent on capital per annum before tax (ibid.: 11). Scottish Television began operating in the autumn of 1957 and, shortly afterwards, its Canadian owner, Roy Thomson, is famously said to have told fellow guests at a social function that he held 'a licence to print money'. His biographer adds that his advisers, aware of the damage it might cause, 'begged him not to repeat this observation elsewhere' (Braddon 1965: 240). But Thomson, pleased with it, repeated the phrase to journalists in Canada. In government, the size of the contractors' profits was regarded as one of 'the most pressing current problems' in broadcasting policy; the other was the imminent feasibility of a third, and even a fourth, television channel, and the consequent need to make a decision as to whether any should be allowed, and who should operate them.[2]

The performance of ITV since it had gone on the air in 1955 had sharpened differences within the Conservative party, which included both those fervently committed to it and a minority equally opposed. In 1951, Selwyn Lloyd, then a Conservative back-bencher (later, of course, to become a senior minister) added his own Minority Report to that produced by the Labour government's Beveridge Committee. He called for a new television service to be funded entirely by advertising, leaving the BBC to broadcast only on radio. 'If people are to be trusted with the franchise', he argued, 'surely they should be able to decide for themselves whether they want to be educated or entertained in the evening' (Beveridge 1951: 201). In 1953, 'competitive television' was supported by a large majority at the Conservative party conference, its supporters having claimed that the vote symbolized their commitment to private enterprise (Ramsden 1995: 254). But others were bitterly opposed to the introduction of commercialism into any form of broadcasting. In a debate in the House of Lords in 1953, the newly ennobled Lord Hailsham compared those Conservatives in favour of commercial television with 'the ancient Israelites who applauded the erection of a golden calf in the Temple [in order to] provide [an] element of healthy competition'.[3] Later, he was to scorn 'the bulk of Conservatives…[who] in their almost inspissated ignorance of the issues…thought they were fighting for liberty and freedom of choice' (Hailsham 1990: 277). In 1975, he was still an opponent of ITV, writing that 'the introduction into the home of the most powerful advertising stimulant ever devised may have been an important contributory cause of…wage demands and inflation' (Hailsham 1975: 127).

In order to placate such opponents, the Act which Parliament passed in 1954 provided for an initial experiment lasting only ten years. As the decade's end approached, the government became uneasily aware that new legislation would be required to keep ITV in existence. Its disappearance from the screen was unthinkable, despite a Labour party pledge to abolish it. There were many Conservatives who wanted to use its popularity for electoral purposes. Lord Poole, the Party chairman and a senior figure close to Macmillan, called it 'the most important thing we have done' and argued in the committee preparing the party's manifesto for the 1959 election that it should figure prominently.[4] But he was replaced in the actual run-up to the election by Lord Hailsham, a more effective campaigner, whose opposition to ITV had not reduced his popularity in the party. In the end, no Conservative claim to the authorship of ITV was included in the manifesto. And by the time of the election, Hugh Gaitskell, recognizing that his Labour voters were also likely to be ITV viewers, had withdrawn the commitment to abolish it to the chagrin of many in his party.

On the left, the division was between, on the one hand, most of the intellectuals and others who had an instinctive dislike of advertising and 'hucksterism' and, on the other, the great bulk of Labour party voters who were inclined to accept consumerism and were ready to join 'the affluent society'. On the right, many Conservatives, especially those who recalled the BBC's role in wartime, wanted to ensure that its presence in the life of the nation would continue, unaffected by the values of the marketplace. Others insisted that, whether or not the BBC survived, the television industry should, in keeping with the ideology of the free market, be competitive, consumer led and market driven. In 1960, unable to agree on a policy of its own, the government set up a committee under the industrialist Sir Harry Pilkington to look into the issues and to recommend a future structure for British broadcasting.

Sir Harry was not the government's first choice. Files in the National Archive show clearly that many other names were considered before his. He was chairman of the family glass-making firm (which, in 1960, was establishing a monopoly in the supply of float glass), a believer in consensus, with a reputation as a paternalistic employer in Lancashire, where his company had been based since the 1820s. Apart from the footballer Billy Wright, the best known name on the committee was the entertainer Joyce Grenfell, who was clearly one of its most talkative and influential members. Others, such as a senior university administrator from Wales and a clergyman's wife from Edinburgh, shared either a distaste for commercialism or a partiality for the BBC, or both. Grenfell was to form a close alliance with another critic of ITV, Richard Hoggart, the second youngest member at 41. He was to write later that he believed that his nomination had come from civil servants in the Ministry of Education who had read his book *The Uses of Literacy*, which had sold widely on its publication in paperback in 1958 (Hoggart 1992: 60). More recently, he had won some tabloid newspaper notoriety in 1960 when he had given evidence for the defence in the *Lady Chatterley* trial. He certainly shared the distaste for television game shows and quiz programmes common to patricians and left-wing intellectuals. But probably the strongest influence on the committee was its secretary, Dennis Lawrence, a career civil servant in the Post Office (where he had risen through the ranks after joining at the age of 16), which shared with the BBC a belief in the ideal of a public service operated by a benign monopoly. The extent of his influence is best demonstrated by extracts from a paper he wrote for the committee at its second full meeting, an opinion that would reappear in the Report published nearly two years later:

> Such slogans as 'broadcasting should give the public what it wants and not what someone thinks is good for the public' invite us to believe that the issue is democracy versus paternalism, or the free society freely choosing versus the directed society having what it is given…these are two extremes…the issue is not one of either–or principle, but one of degree.[5]

Many more examples could be given. Although there was widespread expectation in politics and the media that a third channel would be advertising financed, the committee's deliberations show that from the start it believed that commercialism had little place in broadcasting. In fact, it argued, the need to satisfy advertisers prevented broadcasters from maintaining the 'constant and sensitive relationship with the moral condition of society' that was required of them. The sale of advertising needed to be physically wrenched away from programme making and a new role given to the Authority, which, freed from any desire to maximize audiences and with no interference from advertisers, would itself control the schedules. One committee member, Dr Elwyn Jones, a former geography lecturer and Secretary of the University of Wales, wrote to the chairman, as the Report was being completed, that he was looking forward to a future in which its recommendations would be implemented. Then, 'programme companies [would] compete to provide programmes of real merit and of regional and national relevance, and not of high TAM rating'. There would be an absence, he predicted, of 'mediocrity' and 'triviality', 'relief from violence and crime, more freedom of expression in religion and politics, the reasonable protection of the young and family, and the cultivation of wholesomeness'.[6]

Given the dominance of such opinion on the committee, it is unsurprising that it recommended that the third channel should go to the BBC, and that ITV should not be given a second channel until it was fundamentally reformed. Its programmes were not only overwhelmingly 'of poor quality', 'vapid' and 'puerile', but also had a tendency to encourage greed, immorality and violence. No weight was given to the judgements of the British public as measured by viewing figures, which were still showing 70 per cent of the audience regularly won for ITV's undemanding schedule of popular entertainment. The Authority was excoriated for failing to recognize what the committee saw as the immense power of television to damage British society. It was clear that the Report agreed very largely with the evidence given to it by the Association of Municipal Corporations, which claimed to speak for some 27 million people. It certainly spoke for ITV's critics. The Association shared, it said, a common criticism of some television programmes that they have been damaging in certain moral aspects, and that too many have featured sordid, unsavoury and violent themes. Wrong standards of behaviour and domestic life have been portrayed, such as regular and frequent drinking of alcoholic liquor and incessant smoking…the Association considers that popular appeal and financial considerations play too important a part in the selection of programmes.[7]

It can be seen that the criticism was thought to be strengthened by being called 'common', but 'popular appeal' was to be disregarded. Many other organizations such as teachers' unions, Women's Institutes and various local and national church bodies gave similar evidence. In fact, the BBC archives reveal that its senior executives were regularly in touch with a variety of organizations, including sporting bodies, in order to persuade them – in many cases successfully – to give evidence in support of the BBC. The General Secretary of the Association quoted above even wrote to the Director-General suggesting a meeting to discuss what form his oral evidence should take if he was required to give it.[8]

In some quarters, there was uproar. The *Daily Mirror* – which had a substantial shareholding in the largest ITV company, ATV – headlined its report PILKINGTON TELLS THE PUBLIC TO GO TO HELL in its thickest and biggest type. Conservative backbenchers were overwhelmingly opposed. Harold Macmillan recorded in his diary that 'the tone and temper of the Report [was] deplorable', accusing it of 'spleen' and 'bias'.[9] But by 1963, a settlement had been achieved on Pilkingtonian lines, not entirely by design, which would endure for decades. The BBC would remain the country's dominant broadcaster, with two channels, as Pilkington had recommended, while ITV – its structure admittedly left largely unchanged – was to be placed under the strict control of a newly strengthened Authority. Not until 1982 (although the frequency was available) was a second advertising-funded channel allowed, and that was Channel Four, constructed on strictly Pilkingtonian lines, with the sale of advertising totally quarantined from programme making and a carefully delineated public service remit. Some described the system that resulted as a 'benevolent duopoly', claiming that 'the excellence of British programmes [was] unmatched anywhere in the world' (Dunkley 1985: 83). Others called the duopoly cosy and campaigned for it to be cracked open. Overlapping with them were commercial interests who were waiting more or less patiently for the day when, in a metaphor once used by Macmillan, who had spoken in discussions on the 1959 manifesto of his fear of losing what he called 'the Malvolio vote', Sir Toby Belch's hedonism would overcome Malvolio's puritanism. Only then could *Take Your Pick* return to British screens in the guise of *Deal or No Deal*.

A clue to the reasons for the BBC's success in reasserting its authority is to be found in Macmillan's reference to the Malvolio vote. That can be seen as the vote of those who believed in decorum and moderation, and abhorred the pursuit of pleasure for its own sake, conservatives with a small 'c', more or less puritanical in spirit, convinced, many of them, that they knew what was best for others better than they knew themselves (even if the more austere and intellectual among them were often drawn to the Labour party). Many Malvolios did not watch television at all. But if they did, they watched the BBC. Politically, those in the Conservative party identified with ITV; socially, with the BBC. There were many Malvolios on the Pilkington Committee itself – as the BBC was relieved to discover through its well-organized network of spies and moles. And many were also to be found in the higher ranks of the Civil Service. Throughout the decision-making classes, there was an overwhelming consensus that the BBC's position in British life had to be safeguarded. And that *something* had to be done about the awfulness of ITV.

While waiting for Pilkington, officials in the Post Office, then the department responsible for broadcasting, had drawn up a basis for possible legislation on ITV which was barely less radical than that the committee was to recommend. Treasury officials, for their part, were anxious to derive as much revenue as they could from ITV, which led them to think of it as a welcome source of funds rather than a capitalist enterprise in need of support. Initially, officials had proposed an increased levy on profits, but had decided instead to impose a levy on the companies' revenues. That was after they had realized how many ingenious methods ITV companies would have of evading a profits tax, such as switching profits to subsidiary production companies. Some Conservative ministers were hopeful that this new tax on revenue, which would be very lucrative, could finance the BBC's second channel without an electorally damaging increase in the licence fee. That was successfully resisted by the BBC, which insisted on retaining the licence fee as a guarantee of its independence.

Meanwhile, ITV mounted a fierce campaign against the levy, in public, and in private contacts with their friends in the government. Often they made what seemed to Treasury officials hysterical claims that they would be driven out of business. The Deputy Chairman of ATV, for example, claimed that ITV would become 'a licence to lose money'. Enough support was available among Conservative leaders to force the civil servants to go over the figures they had produced, and time after time officials concluded not only that they were right on any reasonable prediction of advertising revenue – ITV *could* afford to pay the levy (as indeed it could) – but also that the figures produced by ITV were deliberately misleading. A flavour of the attitude inside government is given in a note from one Treasury official to another about the answer to an ITA request, on the companies' behalf, for a meeting with the Prime Minister to go over the figures again. 'We have already allowed' wrote the official 'an appeal to the Chief Secretary [over the head of the Postmaster-General, the responsible minister]; now we have an appeal to the PM. Are the ITA contemplating a petition to Her Majesty?'[10]

In the end, it was Reg Bevins, as Postmaster-General, who ensured the passage of the Act with the levy intact. That was in the face of opposition from several members of the Cabinet, itself distracted coincidentally by the Profumo affair, and a sustained back-bench campaign led by Selwyn Lloyd, now out of office again. The supporters of ITV were calling for the government to announce a timetable for a second commercial channel. This would have the effect of enabling the companies to make a fresh case for their inability to pay the levy and, once a second channel was in operation, could very likely be run in such a way as to reduce the audience for the BBC to insignificant levels. After threatening his own resignation, and with Opposition support, Bevins won a crucial vote only with a studiedly ambiguous response in the House of Commons to a demand for the government to make a specific commitment to a second ITV. It was just enough.

But the most significant factor in all of this had been spotted by the BBC's political correspondent, Hardiman Scott, at the time of the Report's publication. In one of his regular briefing notes for the Director-General, not intended for broadcast, he referred to

> the anxiety of [much of] the Conservative Party to present the image of responsible government...the Prime Minister has been developing the theme of a party with a sense of responsibility not only for material values but for spiritual values. So, when all the fuss has died down, there will be strong pressures within the party for the Government to do the right and honourable thing.[11]

Inside the BBC, as elsewhere among the governing classes, there was no doubt that 'the right and honourable thing' was to defend the BBC by defending the cause of paternalism in broadcasting. And by 1970, the ITA's leadership was also in paternalist hands.

Until then, its Director-General was an Australian former journalist, Sir Robert Fraser, of unorthodox views, with a background in the Labour party. He was described by a contemporary as 'believing in democratic choice, in contrast to the platonic ideals of the BBC' (Sampson 1962: 610). According to his deputy, he believed 'passionately' in the judgement and good sense of 'ordinary people' (Sendall 1982: 136). He approved of commercial television as 'people's television':

> If you decide to have a system of people's television then people's television you must expect it to be, and it will reflect their likes and dislikes, their tastes and aversions, what they can comprehend, and what is beyond them.
>
> Fraser quoted in Sampson (1962: 610)

His successor was to demonstrate very different attitudes. Brian Young, an Etonian and an affable former headmaster of Charterhouse, who was also later to be knighted, chose the title *The Paternal Tradition in British Broadcasting* for a lecture he gave to a university audience in 1983 following his retirement. He spoke of the 'commanding paternal role' played by the Authority, a role which was strengthened, he said, after it had been 'too indulgent with its children'. The reference, of course, was to the post-Pilkington increase in the Authority's powers. The context indicates that by 'children' Young meant the ITV companies, but he might well have meant the British people as a whole. Indeed, he said, he was happy to use the word 'paternal'; in broadcasting, and in television in particular, the state should act like 'a wise father' (Young 1983: 2). That meant regular opera from Glyndebourne (in peak time), two current affairs programmes a week, at least one 'main' weekday drama and one documentary and regular programmes on art and religion, all in peak time. And tight limits on the number and style of quiz shows. ITV became a channel many of whose programmes – *Brideshead Revisited*, *The World at War*, *News at Ten* – could be watched in middle class homes without a health warning.

Many in the educated classes – certainly on the left – were active in campaigns in the 1960s and 1970s against censorship in areas such as films, theatre and print. But, they argued, the freedom of expression they were demanding for artists in those areas – and the 'quality' of programmes – could only be guaranteed in television, along with freedom of choice for the viewer, if the industry continued to be closely regulated. If few would now argue that the cinema, the most influential art form of the twentieth century, would have benefited, or might still benefit, from closer government regulation, and so produce better films, Pilkington's central argument was that the interests of advertisers on advertising-funded channels would always work against the possibility of producing better television. Richard Hoggart has continued to make this case, most recently in a book published in 2004. The advertisers' almost constant need for the largest possible audience, he has argued

> more and more determines that populist programming wins, programmes which do not disturb or suggest wider horizons, which offer instant and repetitive gratifications, whose world is, except intermittently, closed to other considerations.
>
> Hoggart (2004: 112)

He also quotes approvingly Huw Wheldon's well-remembered aphorism about public service broadcasting: that it exists 'to make good programmes popular, and popular programmes good'.

> By 'good' programmes, Wheldon 'meant those made because the broadcaster thought them, though perhaps "difficult"', of great value and wished, without selling them by over-simplification, to make them widely available. By popular programmes, he meant those unlikely to appeal to and not designed specifically for a highly educated audience, but

which became 'good' because they too did not sell out by patronising, or secretly despising, their audience's taste, by talking down to them.

Hoggart (2004: 116)

In other words, it was the programme-makers themselves whose attitudes determined whether their programmes were 'good' or not. In an earlier article, he had offered a defence of the Report, in similar terms:

The Report said that light and serious programmes each had their place, that goodness or badness was not a matter of height of brow but had to do with the quality of the imagination and the response to life in any work, whatever its mood. It attacked…triviality.

Hoggart (1973: 192)

'Triviality', the Report had said, was 'a natural vice of television…where it prevails it operates to lower standards of enjoyment and understanding. It is, as we were reminded, 'more dangerous to the soul than wickedness' (Pilkington 1962: 34).[12] But who was to judge that standards were lower? By whose standards? And how would 'the quality of the imagination' in any particular programme be measured? Or its 'response to life'? What criteria were to be used other than those honed by life-long 'highbrows' in the course of successful 'highbrow' careers? And was 'triviality' really more dangerous than 'wickedness'?

This is not to argue that all judgements are of equal worth and validity. Some are more soundly based than others. But the evidence for a judgement has to be given, and an articulate case has to be made for it. And those who make it have to remember that they are only taking part in a debate, not issuing papal-like pronouncements. And it is not adequate to say that a television programme is 'good' because it was concerned with something the producer thought had 'great' value, or because of the 'quality' of the imagination at work in it, or because of its 'response to life'. All that is happening in these cases is that synonyms are being offered for 'good'.

A judgement as to whether a programme is 'good' or not, or 'trivial' or not, will always depend on who is making that judgement. As when the Pilkington Committee decided in their consideration of quiz shows, in the words of Joyce Grenfell (1980: 138), that 'the prizes should be trivial but the programmes shouldn't'. But what about those people who liked quiz shows the way they were, who *wanted* the questions to be 'trivial' and the prizes significant? Hoggart wrote, in an article attacking the Report's critics, of 'the difficulties of democratic debate' (Hoggart 1973: 183). Were those people not as entitled as anyone else to take part in a democratic debate? As has been said, many of their favourite programmes were not available to be watched in the decades after 1968. But there was little debate over whether there was a place for such 'triviality' on television. Nor about whether those who objected to it should have the right to deny it to those who *did* want it. It was to Pilkington's discredit – and indeed it is part of the historical significance of Pilkington – that it failed to encourage such a debate.

Despite the weaknesses in the paternalists' arguments, with their unmistakeable flavour of special pleading for the kind of programmes they liked (and that employed significant numbers of them), it is clearly the case that British television under paternalist control produced many programmes thought by people of cultivated taste to be 'good', and that many such programmes would have been unlikely to have been made under a regime determined to maximize audiences at all times.

That can be seen in the success of British television in international festivals, where in the seventies and eighties it did spectacularly well, although it is worth quoting the Peacock Report's point that 'the award of professional accolades…can only be at most an indirect guide to what will promote the interests of those for whom the system is ultimately designed' (Peacock 1986: 198), that is the audience. And the programmes that won prizes were seldom those most popular with audiences, which continued to prefer triviality to seriousness. It was harder for viewers to find all the triviality they liked on ITV – although easier than it had been on BBC1, which transferred much of its more serious programming to BBC2, leaving more room for triviality on BBC1. In contrast, the proportion of 'serious' programmes on ITV in peak time had risen in the 1970s at the expense of light entertainment, by up to 50 per cent, according to the company that operated one London franchise. As a consequence, ITV's share of top ten programmes fell from over half in 1972 to just a quarter in 1976 (Potter 1990: 227).

There was one area in which the authorities had found themselves obliged to give in to popular taste. That was radio. Pilkington had paid little attention to the campaign for commercial radio, and nor had the government. But the demand for more pop music was irrepressible, and enterprising businessmen could meet it. In 1964, Radio Caroline started broadcasting non-stop pop from a ship moored just outside territorial waters. Within a month, a BBC executive was complaining that 'most of our part of Suffolk is listening to Radio Caroline and, I am sorry to say, comparing it favourably with our own output' (Lance Thirkell to Frank Gillard, quoted in Briggs 1995: 512). Figures for Caroline and other pirate stations quickly reached two million. Here were mostly young people, in the spirit of the time, *not* prepared to defer to those who thought they should have something better to do than to listen to pop music. By 1967, the Labour government had passed legislation designed to prohibit the pirate operations. But only after the BBC had been forced to create Radio One to supply practically non-stop pop music and legal land-based private stations replaced the ships after 1972. Happily for the broadcasting authorities, pirate television ships were a technical impossibility.

That a change in society had taken place was not always recognized. On the night of ITV's debut in 1955, the then Sir Kenneth Clark, the ITA's first chairman, had spoken to 500 or so dinner-jacketed dignitaries and their ball-gowned wives in the City of London.

> This is a historic occasion...here is a means of communication which enters the homes of millions of our countrymen, and has an unrivalled power to persuade...hitherto it has been in the control of a single institution...[now] free television, like a free Press, will *not* be controlled by any council or committee, but by two factors, the television companies' sense of responsibility and the fundamental good sense and right feeling of the British people.[13]

Clark's faith in the companies' sense of responsibility did not long survive working with them. A BBC internal document reported him as saying privately in 1960 – after his early retirement from the ITA – that ITV programmes were 'awful'.[14] Equally, his faith in the 'right feeling' of the British people may have been short-lived. Seven years after ITV went on air, it had become clear to elite groups that they could *not* trust the people to choose for themselves what to watch on television. Pilkington was commissioned because there were influential concerns that 'free' television *had* to be controlled by councils and committees. In 1963, those concerns were enacted into legislation. The backlash, when it came with the availability of digital channels, was savage and sustained. Now, in the era of broadband and video-on-demand, the viability of ITV itself is threatened as it clamours to be set free from the last vestiges of the principles of public service broadcasting. The populist narrative, thus, is unchallenged. But far from its victory resulting from the particles of gold that Curran (2002: 44) discerns to be contained somewhere within it, it marks only how feeble and flabby have been the counterarguments of the cultural elite.

Notes

1 If Michael Tracey's (1998: 21) gloomy survey in 1998 of *The Decline and Fall of Public Service Broadcasting* recognized that the Report was 'the high-water mark of public and official acclaim for the notion of public service broadcasting', this was undercut by his failure to acknowledge the Report's authorship of a significantly original claim. 'By its nature', the Report declared, 'broadcasting must be in a constant and sensitive relationship with the moral condition of society'. Broadcasters, it insisted, 'are, and must be, involved; this gives them a responsibility they cannot evade' (Pilkington 1962: 15). Tracey has twice, in separate publications, misattributed these remarks to a pamphlet published privately a year after Pilkington, by Sir Arthur fforde, then chairman of the BBC (Tracey 1998: 19; 2003: 15).

2 Burke Trend to the Prime Minister, 29 July 1958: The National Archive, PREM 11/3669, Note on Broadcasting Policy.

3 House of Lords debates 1953: col. 1517.

4 Draft minutes of Conservative Steering Committee, 26 June 1959: Conservative Party Archive CRD 2/53/34.

5 Lawrence 1960: paper for the Pilkington Committee, BC/Sec/32, TNA HO244/4.
6 Elwyn Jones 1962: letter to Sir Harry Pilkington, TNA HO244/293.
7 Memorandum from the Association of Municipal Corporations 1961, Pilkington (b): 1157.
8 Sir Harold Banwell, letter to Hugh Greene, 26 May 1961: BBC Written Archive, R4/46/15.
9 The Diaries of Harold Macmillan, entry for 8 June 1962. I am grateful to Dr Peter Catterall for enabling me to see this material.
10 Note from John Littlewood: 30 April 1963: TNA T319/476.
11 Hardiman Scott to Hugh Greene, 28 June 1962: BBC Written Archive R4/51/1.
12 The quotation is from evidence submitted to the committee by the Workers' Educational Association, quoting an address at an unspecified date from their President, R. H. Tawney.
13 Clark 1955: Tate Gallery Archives: Clark Papers/8812.2.2.1021, quoted in Weight (2002: 249).
14 Note from Colin Shaw to Harman Grisewood, 7 November 1960: BBC Written Archive R4/46/2.

The libertarian narrative

Introduction

While the history of censorship dates back to ancient Greek and Roman times, in Britain, censorship – particularly moral regulation – is usually traced back to the puritan ideas of the sixteenth and seventeenth centuries, since when there have been endless attempts by the state, church and moralists to regulate what the public sees and hears in the belief that this will influence social and political conduct.

One of the earliest examples of modern-day censorship dates back to the 1857 Obscene Publication Act. The Act was passed in an effort to curb the Victorian underworld trade in pornography, particularly in London. While the act was only intended to censor porn, very soon it was also used to ban some now famous early twentieth-century works of literature which moralists then deemed to be offensive (e.g. James Joyce's *Ulysses* and Radcliffe Hall's lesbian novel, *Well of Loneliness*).

Early radio is yet another example of a medium that was subject to considerable moral regulation. What is clear from many interwar broadcasts and broadcasting policy is the extent to which the BBC undertook its wider civilizing mission with a religious zeal (see Bailey 2007b). That is to say, there was a direct link between religion and morality, on the one hand, and culture and self-improvement on the other. For just as Jesus told his disciples that the farmer goes out to sow his seed in order to yield a crop, so too did broadcasting sow the word of God through regular religious broadcasts in the hope that it would prevent any further decay of Christian morality.

Another heavily regulated medium during this period was cinema and film. Moral and social reformers were concerned about the influence of the new medium, particularly on young people. Consequently, under the 1909 Cinematograph Act, all cinemas had to be licensed by local authorities. Without a licence, a cinema could not exhibit films. Local authorities also decided what films could be screened. It was in response to increasing state intervention that the industry decided to set up the voluntary and self-financing British Board of Film Censors in 1913 [British Board of Film Classification

(BBFC) from 1985]. The idea was that the industry would regulate itself. In reality, although an independent body, the Board saw itself as the guardian of public morality and the protector of the status quo, and therefore worked closely with government to help maintain standards of taste and decency.

The possibility that newspapers might corrupt their readers with sensational and lurid content has caused anxiety for moralists since the earliest days of the press. From the mid-nineteenth century, however, these concerns became significantly more widespread as a commercially based popular press designed to entertain a mass audience gradually emerged. The people who were deemed to be most impressionable – the working classes, the ill-educated, the young – became regular newspaper readers, first of Sunday and, then, in the twentieth century, of daily papers. To many politicians, church leaders and traditionalists, the diet of court reports and scandal stories that the popular press served up to this audience seemed to be designed to undermine moral standards and social discipline. The volume of criticism varied over time, but Fleet Street was never able to quieten it completely and, at some points, it reached a deafening crescendo – in the mid-1920s, in the early 1950s, in the mid-1960s and in the late 1980s, for example – when there were numerous calls for the state to intervene to ensure a greater sense of responsibility among journalists.

It is with the above in mind that Adrian Bingham explores the various moralizing campaigns to regulate or reform the press, considering their achievements, analysing the assumptions of the protagonists and examining how journalists defended themselves. On the one hand, he argues that the critics of the press certainly made an impact. If popular newspapers were to protect their status as 'family publications', they could not afford to receive too much adverse publicity or alienate too many of their more traditional readers, and so editors made sure that their journalists did not cross certain moral boundaries. In spite of these pressures, Bingham's contribution shows that campaigners could not persuade parliament to establish a statutory body to monitor and regulate the press. Time and time again, governments shied away from taking on Fleet Street and encroaching on the hallowed 'freedom of the press'. The press were also able to weaken their critics by portraying them as 'old-fashioned', 'prudish' and 'elitist'. In short, the libertarians were ultimately able to outmanoeuvre the moralists and preserve a regime of self-regulation, a legacy that continues to this day.

Su Holmes' chapter explores similar issues with respect to questions of taste, ethics and regulation in British television in the 1950s, a subject that is often neglected in existing historical research, with the focus gravitating towards the following decade. For Holmes, this neglect is a major oversight, partly because the 1950s is possibly more interesting for the reason that – in a still new and developing medium – there appeared to be more uncertainty when it came to conceptualizing how television could (or 'should') be regulated. Holmes' chapter is all the more interesting because her narrative focuses on the micro history of an individual case study, the BBC's *This is Your Life*. Although the celebrity biography programme may appear to be a curious site upon which to explore issues of regulation and censorship, Holmes' analysis makes clear that *TIYL* was as controversial as it was popular. Widely perceived by critics as fronting the BBC's battle to beat commercial TV, the programme rapidly came to represent what the era of competition might mean for British television. Hence, *TIYL* was regarded as a deeply sensational and exploitative show that catered to questionable audience pleasures, evidenced in the repeated calls by the press to censor the programme. What emerges from Holmes' analysis is less a paternalistic and moralistic BBC (which was aiming to ignore the populist and commercial challenge of ITV) than a relatively daring exploration of permissible television material.

Further reading

Not surprisingly, much of the literature on the history of media effects and regulation tends to be in relation to film and video. Tom Dewe Mathews' (1994) *Censored* is widely regarded as the best introduction to cinema censorship in Britain, is nicely illustrated and covers some 100-odd years of film history. Richards (1997b) is remarkably concise and covers the basics, as does Carter and Weaver (2003). Former Secretary of the BBFC, John Trevelyan (1973), offers a fascinating account of what it is to be a film censor, as well as summarizing some of the key developments in the history of the BBFC. For more detailed analyses of specific historical periods, see Aldgate (1995), Black (1997), Hill (1986), Jacobs (1991), Johnson (1997), Kuhn (1988), Medhurst (1996), McGillivray (1992), Pronay and Croft (1983), Richards (1981) and Slide (1998), among others; see also a special issue of the *Journal of Popular British Cinema* (Conrich and Petley 2000).

Of the literature that looks at more recent cinematic case studies, Barker *et al.* (2001) provide an interesting analysis of the controversy surrounding David Cronenberg's *Crash* based on audience research. See also Barker (1984) for a passionate analysis of the debate surrounding video nasties in the 1980s, a debate that was to resurface in the immediate aftermath of the James Bulger murder case in the 1990s (cf. Barker and Petley 1997; Critcher 2003; Osgerby 2004). Readman (2005) and Falcon (1994) are invaluable teachers' guides to film censorship and contain useful suggestions for teaching materials, including a filmography.

For a general history of laws and morals in postwar Britain, see Newburn (1992). For a history of 'culture wars' over the last twenty-five years between representatives of different social and moral values, see Curran *et al.* (2005). Alan Travis' (2000) *Bound & Gagged* is one of the most recently published histories of censorship in Britain and covers a variety of case studies from the passing of the Obscene Publications Act (1857), the banning of 'offensive' literature (cf. Rolph 1969; Sutherland 1982; Morrison and Watkins 2006) and theatrical plays (cf. Findlater 1968; Shellard *et al.* 2004; Thomas *et al.* 2007) through to the regulation of the internet in the present day. Another useful introduction to the long and varied history of moral regulation, especially the influence of Puritanism in relation to sexual moralities, is Bocock (1997). For those interested in the history of queer sexualities, anything by Jeffrey Weeks (e.g. 1989, 2003) is essential.

For a related discussion about moral panics – historical and contemporary – surrounding the decline in social mores and falling cultural standards, see Cohen (1980), Critcher (2003), Pearson (1983) and Thompson (1998). Boyle (2005), Carter and Weaver (2003) and Trend (2007) provide excellent introductions to current thinking about media violence and its possible effects on the public in relation to a variety of different media contexts. Much recent debate and controversy has tended to focus on children and television violence: see, for example, Buckingham (1996, 2000), Gunter and Harrison (1998), Gunter and McAleer (1997), Livingstone (1998) and Singer and Singer (2001). Of course, the regulation and censorship of sexual imagery and pornography, in all its forms, remains as topical as ever: see Arthurs (2004), Bocock (1997), Bragg and Buckingham (2002), Buckingham and Bragg (2004), Dworkin (1981), Dyer (2002), Gunter (2002), McNair (1996, 2002), Shaw (1999), Watney (1987) and Williams (1999) for a full and frank discussion of the key issues and most current debates.

Chapter 8

'A stream of pollution through every part of the country?'

Morality, regulation and the modern popular press

Adrian Bingham

Fears about the corrupting powers of newspapers can be traced back to the beginnings of the press in the seventeenth century. Ever since there was a market for the printed word, journalists have been accused of peddling sensation, encouraging vice and eroding respect for religion and authority.[1] While newspapers were too expensive to be bought regularly by working class readers, these concerns remained limited in extent. From the mid-nineteenth century, however, there were rapid improvements in newspaper production and distribution processes, prices dropped, and a commercially based popular press designed to entertain a mass audience gradually emerged. As the habit of newspaper reading spread throughout society, so anxiety about the impact of the press intensified. A wide range of politicians, religious leaders, cultural commentators and campaigning organizations argued that in the competition for profits newspapers were ignoring their social responsibilities and exploiting the basest instincts of their readers. These critics were determined to ensure that public morality was not surrendered to the dictates of the market, and demanded that the press was reformed or regulated. Editors and journalists fought back, denying that their papers were immoral, claiming that their opponents were unrepresentative and out of touch with what the public wanted and declaring their intention to resist outside interference. While the moralists scored some short-term victories, ultimately they found it difficult to restrain the press from continuing to publish what they regarded as 'inappropriate' content. They could not secure parliamentary agreement for any form of regulation that would encroach too heavily on the 'freedom' of the press. Yet this was certainly not a straightforward victory for liberty and pluralism. Few popular newspaper editors and journalists were genuine libertarians: most were themselves highly moralistic and shared many of the underlying assumptions of their opponents. The 'libertarian' narrative, at least as it relates to the press, is a complex one involving competing moralities as well as different understandings of liberty.

This chapter begins by outlining the main arguments of those who wished to tighten the regulation of the press in order to prevent it damaging the moral fabric of society. These arguments changed in focus across the period, although there were several underlying continuities. There follows an exam-ination of the ways in which editors and journalists responded to such criti-cism. The second half of the chapter considers the progress of these contests over the twentieth century by examining three moments when the censure of the press reached a crescendo and methods of regulation were debated in parliament: the mid-1920s, when disquiet over the newspaper coverage of divorce trials resulted in legislation restricting court reporting; the early 1950s, when the newly established Press Council was forced to deal with a flurry of complaints about the treatment of sex and private life; and the late 1980s, when concern about salacious and intrusive tabloid journalism led to the demise of the Press Council and its replacement by the Press Complaints Commission. In each case, the press was forced onto the defensive and made concessions, but eventually managed to evade the comprehensive statutory regulation that it feared. Traditionalists could not prevent what they regarded as a disastrous undermining of standards of taste and decency. Nevertheless, there remained strict limits to the sorts of content editors would include in their papers, and they remained very conscious about the dangers of offending the moral sensibilities of the public.

Moral criticism of the press

At the root of all the attacks on the press was the belief that popular news-papers had a powerful impact on the attitudes and behaviour of their readers. This belief was based on a number of widely held assumptions about the nature of the 'mass society' that gradually emerged in Britain from the second half of the nineteenth century. It was clear that industrialization, urbanization and the transformation of transport and communications had disrupted tradi-tional patterns of life and structures of authority. At the same time, an educa-tion system had developed that gave working class children an elementary schooling, but offered few opportunities for further learning. Many com-mentators suggested that the producers of the new mass market newspapers were exploiting an audience educated enough to want simple reading matter, but intellectually unequipped to challenge or resist the ideas it conveyed. Disoriented by rapid social change, and no longer guided by the institutions and hierarchies that had previously brought stability, these working class readers, it was argued, were particularly susceptible to outside influences. The newspapers that began to circulate throughout the nation, building circulations in the millions, appeared to be one of the most potent of these influences (Williams 2003: 23–43).

The moralist critics of the press articulated three main concerns. First, they feared that the extensive reporting of crime, scandal and sexual transgression would weaken the moral sense of readers, particularly young readers, and might even encourage imitation and experimentation. They believed that the protagonists of major trials were unhealthily glamorized, and claimed that exposure to endless stories of criminal and unethical behaviour would inevitably dull the horror of such activity and gradually undermine social discipline. The second anxiety was that, by providing a superficially stimulating diet of sensation, gossip and human interest stories, the popular press prevented readers from developing an appetite for more nutritious fare which addressed the important political, social and cultural issues of the day. Newspapers entrenched a distorted scale of values in which questions of concern to the wider community were relegated behind trivia and titillation. Such content, it was suggested, encouraged a selfish, philistine and politically apathetic outlook among readers. This line of argument, it should be noted, was heavily influenced by the liberal narrative of the press, which suggested that the proper function of newspapers was to operate as an independent channel for conveying political information to the public. The popular press was accused of betraying its democratic role by amusing rather than educating its readers. The third criticism was that the press was too intrusive and undermined the respect for privacy that was an essential feature of British life. Journalists harassed public figures and pried into their private lives; ordinary people unexpectedly caught up in a newsworthy event were likewise treated with discourtesy. The press coarsened public life with this undignified behaviour and, in the endless competition for revelations, fed the prurience of its readers.

In the late nineteenth and early twentieth century, these three concerns were voiced by a wide range of commentators from across the political and social spectrum. Queen Victoria and her grandson George V both informed the Lord Chancellors of the day of their apprehension about the threat the press posed to public morals (Savage 1998: 514, 511). Notable Conservative politicians, including Lord Salisbury, Stanley Baldwin and Winston Churchill, launched stinging attacks on the sensationalism and triviality of the press, while Labour figures such as Keir Hardie and George Lansbury accused press barons of 'doping' the working classes (Koss 1981/1984; Richards 1997). Defenders of the cultural hierarchy, from Matthew Arnold to F. R. Leavis, argued that popular newspapers were undermining important social traditions and values, while progressive authors, such as Stephen Spender and C. Day Lewis, condemned the press for its crass commercialism and for pandering to base instincts (Carey 1992; Williams 1996; Bingham 2004: 244–48). Disapproval was so widespread that Lady Rhondda, the proprietor of the feminist periodical *Time and Tide*, could write in 1937 that 'everyone says almost every day' that the press 'constitute the gravest of our national perils, that they exploit mass fear and mass selfishness, that compared to them the devil himself is a clean-minded purveyor of the strict, honest and sober truth' (Haig 1937: 56). From the 1960s, these sweeping moral condemnations of the press became less common, and debate focused more narrowly on questions of privacy, accuracy and the stereotyping of particular groups in society. At the same time, the older moral concerns certainly did not lose all resonance, and they could often be found underlying different types of complaints about press content.

The press's defensive strategies

Fleet Street employed a variety of strategies to counter or defuse these criticisms. The first was self-censorship. It is important not to accept at face value the caricature that portrays newspaper producers as amoral individuals willing to include anything that would titillate readers and generate a profit. Editors and journalists were well aware that their publications would struggle in a mass market if they could not claim to be 'family newspapers' suitable for everyone: being too offensive was commercially counterproductive. They therefore tried to maintain a careful balance between sensation and sobriety, in the knowledge that they could withstand considerable amounts of censure as long as they did not print anything too outrageous (Bingham 2004: 154–58). Crime and scandal certainly featured prominently, but the reporting was euphemistic and precise details of indecent behaviour were not given. The technique of popular journalism was to suggest rather than to describe directly, making evasive references to 'vice', 'immoral activities' and 'indecent offences' rather than using more explicit language. In the first half of the twentieth century, newspapers remained very cautious about the use of sexual terminology – indeed, in 1943, a number of national papers refused to allow the inclusion of the phrase 'sex organs' in a government health advertisement warning of the danger of venereal diseases (Bingham 2005). There was an absolute prohibition on 'vulgarities' and swear words. Popular newspapers included photographs of 'bathing beauties' and glamorous film stars, but they were not overtly sexualized and there were few provocative poses. This self-restraint enabled editors to argue that their newspapers were entirely suitable for a family audience.

Some in Fleet Street went further, arguing that popular newspapers actually performed an important role in protecting public morality. Court reports, it was claimed, provided a valuable record of the administration of justice that informed readers about what society considered unacceptable. The producers of the *News of the World*, for example, protested that the paper covered not crime but punishment, and was in that respect little different from the Old Testament (Royal Commission on the Press 1948: 27). Others pointed to the moral crusades launched by newspapers against activities such as prostitution or the sale of pornography. There can be little doubt that the press's conspicuous moralizing was a useful defence mechanism against the criticism it received. Singling out and condemning 'perverts' and 'deviants' both underlined a paper's commitment to 'family values' and distracted attention away from its own faults (Cudlipp 1962: 317–24). Journalists were particularly keen to censure 'indecency' in other art forms, in the cinema, theatre, popular literature and, later, television: the effect of such denunciations was to suggest that any doubtful content provided by the press was insignificant compared with that found elsewhere.[2]

When these tactics did not deflect criticism, editors and journalists embraced more libertarian arguments, based on the 'freedom of the press' and the right of the public to read what it wanted. Readers were not forced to buy news-papers, and they had the choice of a wide range of alternative publications if they believed that one was offensive or inappropriate. The huge circulations of the most popular newspapers demonstrated, it was claimed, that they were fulfilling a genuine demand. Why should a small number of 'elitist' individuals be able to intervene and censor their content? (LeMahieu 1988: 7–55). In any case, how would regulation be administered? Any system of state regulation would be dangerous because it would open the door to abuse by a govern-ment with authoritarian instincts; yet who else had the authority and impar-tiality to monitor the national press? Some in Fleet Street conceded that the press was occasionally irresponsible, but argued that any form of censorship would be far more damaging to society than the evils it was trying to prevent.

These, in general terms, were the arguments used on either side of the debate about the moral content of the press. This was not a simple battle between 'moralists' and 'libertarians', but a broader contest about the role and responsibilities of the press in society. To what extent should newspapers be allowed to move away from their traditional function of providing informa-tion about the public sphere and instead give the public 'what it wanted'? Should newspapers be made to fulfil certain 'public service' requirements, as radio and television broadcasters were? What limitations could be placed on a newspaper's freedom to pursue its own commercial interest? We shall now examine how this debate progressed by considering some of the most promi-nent controversies about the moral content of the press.

1920s: divorce court reports

The divorce court, established in 1857, immediately became an important source for newspapers seeking human interest stories. To obtain a divorce, it was almost always necessary to prove adultery, so cases usually had consider-able potential to provide titillating copy, especially if high-profile individuals were involved. Within months of the court's foundation, there were com-plaints that the press coverage of its proceedings was dangerously salacious and posed a threat to public morality. A series of proposals to restrict the flow of sensitive material by conducting trials *in camera* were, however, defeated by MPs convinced that more people would break their marital vows if the threat of unwelcome newspaper publicity was removed (Savage 1998). But as newspaper circulation increased in the early years of the twentieth century, and more and more readers were exposed to details of marital breakdowns, concern mounted. These anxieties were exacerbated by the widespread belief that the turmoil of the First World War had disrupted family life and encouraged a weakening of moral standards. The result was the emergence in the early 1920s of a concerted parliamentary campaign, led by the Conservative MP Sir Evelyn Cecil, to restrict the reporting of divorce cases to brief details of the parties involved and the judge's summing up. The campaign was supported by a wide range of organizations, including the Mothers' Union, the National Council of Women, the National Union of Teachers and church societies representing each of the main Christian denominations.

Introducing his bill into the House of Commons, Cecil admitted that it was impossible to isolate particular sentences or phrases of divorce reports as being obscene: as we have seen, editors were careful to avoid such explicitness. 'The real truth of the matter', he argued, 'is that the whole thing is suggestive and revolting from beginning to end'. He claimed that the reports 'have a very deteriorating effect on public morals and cause an infinity of harm'.[3] The bill was taken to a select committee, which heard a number of testimonies from prominent legal and religious figures agreeing that the press coverage was indeed damaging. The Director of Public Prosecutions, Sir Archibald Bodkin, pointed out that 'newspaper space could be so much better occupied' than to give such publicity to conjugal infidelity, and suggested that 'familiarity with what ought to be avoided takes away half the horror of it'.[4] A consensus gradually emerged in political and religious circles that the relentless flow of such salacious reporting seriously harmed society. One Conservative MP told the House of Commons that newspapers were conveying 'a stream of pollution through every part of the country'.[5] But not only did divorce court coverage have a deleterious effect on the impressionable British public, it was claimed that it also damaged the reputation of the nation abroad. Major Kindersley, a Conservative back-bencher, told the Commons in 1926, for example, that 'the altogether disproportionate space' devoted to divorce cases gave foreign readers 'an entirely wrong impression of the social and domestic life of this country', and thereby caused 'infinite harm to our national prestige'.[6] A powerful case was made, both inside and outside parliament, that statutory regulation of divorce reports was essential to protect public morality and preserve national standing.

Popular newspapers denied that their coverage of divorce cases was irresponsible and indecent. Indeed, they protested that they exercised considerable restraint: the experienced court reporter Henry Fenn reminded readers 'that what is published in the leading newspapers regarding unsavoury matter is the merest bagatelle compared with the details which are eliminated' (Fenn 1910: 291). The press argued, furthermore, that prohibiting reports of divorce suits would have unwelcome legal and social consequences. The *Daily Mirror* contended that it would prevent decisions from being scrutinized by the public and therefore might encourage a 'grave legal scandal', while the *Daily Mail* claimed that it would produce 'a very considerable increase' in the number of suits as couples would no longer be deterred by the prospect of negative publicity.[7] Direct appeals to the 'freedom of the press' were less common, although the *Mirror* did suggest that newspapers were merely feeding natural human curiosity: 'We ask the average man to clear his mind of cant and say: Does he or does he not read these reports himself? Is there not in them a "human interest" that he cannot resist?'[8]

By 1926, however, newspapers were firmly on the defensive. In April, the second reading of Cecil's Regulation of Reports Bill passed by an over-whelming 222 votes to three. The strength of the campaign persuaded many in Fleet Street that it was unwise to try to resist too strongly, and the bill overcame its remaining parliamentary hurdles with ease. *Newspaper World*, the main trade publication, did not try to portray the new legislation as an unwarranted imposition by an authoritarian parliament, but accepted that 'The people demanded the measure. Things were being reported by some journals that made men and women shudder'.[9] The act was a symbol that parliament was prepared to encroach on the 'freedom of the press' in order to protect public morality. From another perspective, however, it was an illustration of the difficulty of controlling the content of the press. While divorce trials could no longer be built up into extended melodramas over several days, the judge's summing up – which MPs had agreed could still be reported – was enough to provide entertaining articles. As one later editor observed, 'some judges pro-vide fairly meaty reading when they get a contested case to review' (Wintour 1972: 139). Divorce court reports, therefore, continued to appear in both popular dailies and Sundays, and they continued to provoke complaints. More importantly, though, the legislation referred only to divorce suits and left plenty of other sorts of trial that could be used to provide titillating details of sexual transgression. *The Times* had predicted that 'the ingenuity which ran-sacks all the world for garbage is not likely to be cramped by the loss of this particular field', and it was proved correct.[10] Fleet Street could afford to con-cede on divorce cases, while at the same time turning its attention to similar material found elsewhere. The result was that complaints about salacious and unsuitable court reporting soon resurfaced and were expressed throughout the 1930s and 1940s. The moralists' victory in 1926 was, therefore, rather less impressive than it initially appeared. The Regulation of Reports Act ulti-mately did little to inhibit the development of a journalistic style based on human interest, sex and melodrama.

1950s: 'brothel journalism?'

Moral criticism of the press reached another crescendo in the early 1950s. The upheavals of another war had once again stimulated fears about morality and 'delinquency', and popular newspapers, reaching record circulations in this period, were identified by a number of politicians, religious leaders and social commentators as an obstacle to the reassertion of traditional standards (Murray 1972: 71–106). There was particular objection to the brasher, irreverent style of popular journalism that was being developed by a new generation of edi-tors, led by Hugh Cudlipp at the *Daily Mirror*, and aimed directly at a young working class readership (Cudlipp 1962). A central element of Cudlipp's strategy was the inclusion of bolder sexual content, in the form of pin-ups, advice columns, features about celebrities' private lives and investigations into 'vice'. His motives were undeniably commercial, but he also had a genuine conviction that the traditional evasiveness about sex was not just old-fashioned but socially harmful. The *Daily Mirror*'s campaign in 1942–43 to educate its readers about the dangers of venereal disease pushed back the boundaries of what was considered acceptable in the national press and, in the postwar years, the *Mirror* and its sister paper, the *Sunday Pictorial*, built on its success to open up other sexual topics for discussion (Bingham 2005). But critics argued that profit-making newspapers could not be trusted to provide balanced and restrained discussions of sex. On the contrary, they contended that the press's tendency to sensationalism and prurience encouraged an unhealthy pre-occupation with sex and made it more difficult for parents and teachers to inculcate responsible moral attitudes into young people.

The moralists' favoured solution in the 1950s was not legislation aimed at restricting a particular type of report, but a broader system of regulation. In 1949, the Royal Commission on the Press – established in 1947 as a response to concerns about the concentration of newspaper ownership and a related decline in the quality of journalism – recommended that the industry set up a General Council that would monitor newspaper output, work to improve standards and respond to complaints from the public (Royal Commission on the Press 1949). But most proprietors viewed even this limited form of self-regulation as a grave encroachment on their freedom and, three years after the Royal Commission's report, no action had been taken. At this stage, critics in parliament began to voice their disquiet. In November 1952, the Labour MP James Simmons presented a bill placing a statutory requirement on the industry to introduce a Press Council. Simmons was absolutely explicit about his concern for public morals. 'The ethical and moral standards of today are not as high as they were a generation ago', he observed, 'probably as the result of two world wars in one generation'. He believed that the press was 'the most powerful instrument capable of moulding public opinion and creating a worthwhile sense of values', but that it was abusing its position by playing down to base appetites; instead of giving readers an appreciation of 'good literature and current affairs', it regaled them with details of the 'love lives, usually sordid, of film stars or the experiences of spivs or drug addicts'. A Press Council, he argued, would help to raise the 'moral, ethical and technical standards of journalism'.[11] The Conservative MPs Ian Harvey and William Deedes led the opposition to the bill because they preferred to see a Press Council introduced by voluntary agreement, but they shared Simmons' opinions of the press's moral conduct. Deedes suggested that it 'would be a splendid thing if honourable Members on both sides said, "We may disagree about this Bill and many other things, but we do agree these sections of the Sunday Press are a disgrace"'.[12] The bill was narrowly defeated, but the threats of statutory intervention, and the widespread criticism of popular newspapers, gave a renewed momentum to the negotiations. In June 1953, a General Council of the Press was finally established.

Moralists hoped that the Press Council would, over time, foster a sense of responsibility and public service in Fleet Street. Many were encouraged when, at its first meeting, the Council condemned a *Daily Mirror* opinion poll asking readers whether Princess Margaret and Group Captain Peter Townsend – whose relationship at that stage was still an unconfirmed rumour – should marry as 'contrary to the best tradition of British journalism' (Press Council 1954: 22). The following month, the Council was forced to react when discontent about the increasingly frank coverage of sex was brought to a head by the reporting of Alfred Kinsey's scientific study, *Sexual Behaviour of the Human Female*. Some of the strongest criticism came from within Fleet Street. John Gordon, a veteran columnist writing in the *Sunday Express*, claimed the coverage given to the Kinsey Report was final confirmation that many newspapers were now purveying 'brothel journalism' and had become 'a menace of considerable gravity to the moral standards of the nation'.[13] The outrage felt by Gordon was widely shared. The Press Council received many complaints and resolutions from religious bodies and citizens' organizations, including the British Council of Churches, the National Women Citizens Association and the Public Morality Council. While 'defending the right of the Press in the contemporary world to deal in an adult manner with matters of sex', the Press Council declared that it was 'deeply concerned by the unwholesome exploitation of sex by certain newspapers and periodicals' and recorded its view that 'such treatment is calculated to injure public morals especially because newspapers and periodicals are seen and read by young persons' (Press Council 1954: 21). The strength of the moralist case was recognized by the industry's own regulatory body.

Yet while the Press Council's resolutions received considerable publicity, it had no means of punishing erring newspapers. With circulation reports revealing considerable public interest in both Princess Margaret's private life and the findings of the Kinsey Report, popular newspaper editors could simply ignore the Council's strictures. Hugh Cudlipp nevertheless believed that it was important to respond publicly to the charges laid against the press and devoted four pages of the *Mirror*, over three days, to outline his editorial policy on these sensitive matters. 'We make no bones about presenting life as it is', the paper argued, and that inevitably included the realities of sex and crime. If it did not, it would be giving a 'false picture' and misleading the public. 'We give plain meanings in plain words so that we all can understand them'. The coverage of sex merely reflected the changing attitudes of the younger generation, which had become much 'healthier' and much 'franker': 'But of course an attitude which seems perfectly normal to young people still shocks the elderly. And many critics are old fogies – well-meaning, no doubt, yet out of touch with modern trends and tastes'. To justify the extensive reporting of Kinsey's findings, the paper quoted the Methodist leader Dr Leslie Weatherhead that: 'The place where evil flourishes is in the shadows of ignorance, half-knowledge, false values, and distortion'. The *Mirror* admitted that it was 'a cheeky, daring, gay newspaper', but denied that it crossed the boundaries of acceptability: 'We have the biggest daily circulation on earth. No newspaper could keep such popularity with the British public if it followed a morally offensive policy'.[14]

The *Mirror's* response effectively illustrated some of the weaknesses of the moralist position. The press's critics were easily portrayed as old-fashioned and elitist, unnecessarily intervening to prevent ordinary people from being entertained and informed by the papers of their own choosing. It was somewhat disingenuous of the *Mirror* to claim that it merely presented 'life as it is' – reporting invariably involves various degrees of selection, simplification and packaging – but its argument that it had a responsibility to inform readers about all aspects of society, including sex, was a persuasive one. Moralists were, moreover, rather indiscriminate in their attacks on sexual content, tending to issue blanket condemnations rather than distinguishing between different forms of reporting. The *Mirror* could legitimately claim, for example, that the Kinsey Report was a serious study deserving of detailed press coverage; critics would have had a more valid argument had they focused on the alarmist and crudely sensational reporting of homosexuality or the intrusions into the private lives of celebrities.[15] So while the moralists scored a couple of early victories in obtaining critical resolutions from the Press Council, it soon became clear that the council was too weak to fulfil hopes that it would change the culture of journalism. Popular newspapers continued to be as 'irresponsible' as ever: indeed, faced with increasing competition from television, they pursued their agenda of sex, crime and human interest even more aggressively. In 1957, five years after Simmons' motion about the Press Council, there was another debate in the House of Commons about the state of the press, and the opinions voiced were very similar. As before, widespread agreement about the failings of the industry did not translate into a consensus about how to reform it.[16] Throughout the postwar period, concern about encroaching on the 'freedom of the press' ultimately outweighed the fears about public morality (O'Malley and Soley 2000: 51–70).

1980s: intrusion and inaccuracy

From the 1960s, the traditional moralist critique of the press became significantly less prominent. With the rise of television, moralists became far more concerned about the corrupting power of broadcasting than of newspapers. The moving visual images beamed directly into the home seemed to be more vivid and seductive – and hence potentially more dangerous – than the printed pages of the press. Mary Whitehouse's National Viewers and Listeners Association (originally established as the Clean-up TV campaign in 1964) was the most visible expression of these fears: the association fought tirelessly what it regarded as an unhealthy preoccupation with sex, bad language and crime on screen, and called on the BBC to commit itself to a defence of Christian morality (Newburn 1992: 17–48). More broadly, the ideas and outlook associated with the moralist position were marginalized and challenged by the erosion of the authority of the Christian churches, the increasing recognition of a pluralistic society and the emergence of more liberal ideas about the discussion and portrayal of sex. The assumptions made about an unstable 'mass society' seemed inappropriate in the affluent world of the 1960s: adults could be trusted to make their own moral decisions, so it was only children who needed to be protected from unsuitable media portrayals of sex and crime (Marwick 1998).

In the 1980s, therefore, critics of the press tended to focus on specific issues such as accuracy, stereotyping and privacy, rather than offer broader moral denunciations of 'immoral' content (O'Malley and Soley 2000: 71–96). A number of Labour party politicians and trade unionists complained about the conservative bias of the press and demanded a 'right of reply' to correct false statements made by newspapers. Feminists attacked the sexism of popular journalism, particularly its reliance on pin-up photography and the unsympathetic coverage of sex crimes and domestic violence (Davies et al. 1987). The hostile and prejudiced reporting of ethnic minorities was likewise condemned (Institute of Race Relations 1989). Conservative commentators, in contrast, tended to be more concerned about intrusions into privacy and the lack of respect accorded to public figures such as the royal family. Underlying these complaints, however, it was frequently possible to discern residues of the older moralist critiques. Clare Short's attempt in 1986 to prohibit the publication in newspapers of 'pictures of naked or partially naked women in sexually provocative poses' was, for example, motivated primarily by feminist opposition to the sexual objectification of women. At the same time, she also exhibited a moral distaste for the tabloid press: 'future generations', she observed, 'will see those pictures as symbolic of our decadent society' (Short 1991: xvi). Fears that an irresponsible, crassly commercial press was undermining public morality retained some of their power.

The volume of criticism reached a peak in the late 1980s. The breaking of the power of the print unions and the move out of Fleet Street transformed the finances of the press, increasing editorial self-confidence and stimulating competition. Led by Kelvin MacKenzie's *Sun*, tabloid newspapers became even more aggressive and sensational. Ever more daring claims were made about the private lives of public figures, usually secured by the liberal use of the editorial chequebook and often illustrated with long-lens photography (Snoddy 1993). In parliament, there were several efforts to introduce bills guaranteeing a 'right of reply' or establishing a privacy law, but all were defeated or talked out. There were signs outside parliament, however, that the press could not continue to push back the boundaries without generating a backlash. In autumn 1987, for example, the *Star*'s attempt to outdo the *Sun* with a new strategy of 'bonk journalism' and soft-porn pictures backfired spectacularly. There was a series of staff resignations and numerous protests from MPs and the public; the experiment came to an abrupt end when Tesco cancelled a £400,000 advertising contract and other advertisers, including the Co-op, made clear that they did not want to be associated with such a disreputable paper (Engel 1997: 285–91). In courtrooms, too, jurors expressed their distaste for the excesses of tabloid journalism by awarding punitive damages in libel cases. The *Sun*'s payment of £1 million to Elton John in an out-of-court libel settlement in 1988 was a dramatic illustration of the paper's fear of facing the juries' wrath. The *Sun*'s crass and grossly inaccurate reporting of the Hillsborough tragedy in April 1989, meanwhile, led to a widespread and longstanding boycott of the paper in Liverpool (Chippindale and Horrie 1999: 331–53, 405–11).

As in the past, however, it proved difficult for critics of the press to translate short-term successes into longer term solutions. Recognizing the extent of public concern, the Conservative government in June 1989 established a committee of inquiry, chaired by David Calcutt, QC, to examine the privacy laws and the regulation of the press. The Calcutt committee recommended the introduction of three new criminal laws to counter journalistic intrusion, and called for the discredited Press Council to be replaced by a tougher and more focused self-regulatory body, the Press Complaints Commission (PCC) (Calcutt Committee 1990). Following the pattern of the 1920s and the 1950s, the industry made limited concessions while obstructing more fundamental changes. It established a new Commission and produced a code of conduct – but the code was not particularly restrictive, and the PCC had no powers to punish newspapers that transgressed it. Reviewing the new regime in January 1993, Sir David Calcutt argued that the PCC was not an effective regulator, was not sufficiently independent and operated a code that was 'over-favourable' to the industry. He recommended that a statutory tribunal replace the PCC (Calcutt 1993: 44). The Major government, which was in a weak political position and wary of challenging the press, shied away from implementing Calcutt's recommendations (Bingham 2007). The report was shelved, the PCC survived, and the new criminal offences were not introduced.

In subsequent years, the PCC would claim that it had gradually altered the culture of British journalism, but such protestations failed to convince the press's many critics, who continued to warn that newspapers were coarsening society. Yet despite occasional eruptions – such as in September 1997 when Princess Diana died in a car crash after a chase with paparazzi photographers – the controversy about the effects of the popular press had become notably less intense by the end of the century, as the circulations and cultural prominence of newspapers steadily declined in the face of the rise of multichannel television and the internet. The fierce debates about the press in the 1920s, the 1950s and even the 1980s belong to another media era. Moralists will continue to raise concerns about unsuitable media content, but it is unlikely that many will consider newspapers, as was so fashionable in the interwar period, to be the 'gravest of our national perils'.

Conclusion

Throughout the century, the view that the popular press posed a moral threat to society won widespread support. Ultimately, however, the moralists were unable to develop a realistic solution that did not encroach too severely on two highly prized freedoms, the freedom of the press and the freedom of the market. Small-scale prohibitions and restrictions, such as that imposed on divorce reports in 1926, were insufficient to change the culture of the press, but politicians repeatedly recoiled from more substantial forms of statutory regulation. The compromise solution was a system of self-regulation, first introduced in 1953, but even after various reforms the self-regulatory regime was not tough enough to prevent Fleet Street from persisting with the aggressive, sensational and populist journalism that so many commentators despised. Editors could always point to the circulation figures and protest that they were simply providing what the public wanted. Most editors also knew, however, that it was dangerous to ignore the moralists entirely or to transgress the boundaries of public taste too often or too flagrantly. The press found that the most profitable strategy was not to rely solely on libertarian defences of its content, but to exercise some restraint and to emphasize its own moral recti-tude. In this way, the press did just enough to avoid handing their critics enough political capital to build a consensus in favour of statutory regulation.

Notes

1 On the early press, see Conboy (2004) and Cranfield (1978).
2 James Douglas' infamous *Sunday Express* article in August 1928 condemning Radclyffe Hall's novel *The Well of Loneliness* is a good example of this (Bingham 2004: 178–79).
3 Matrimonial Causes (Regulation of Reports) Bill, 15 May 1923, 164 H.C. Debs, 5s, col. 249–51.
4 Parliamentary Papers, 1923, VII, Select Committee on the Matrimonial Causes (Regulation of Reports) Bill, *Minutes of Evidence*, pp. 23–24.
5 200 H.C. Debs, 5s., Judicial Proceedings (Regulations of Reports) Bill, 10 December 1926, col. 2443.
6 194 H.C. Debs, 5s., Judicial Proceedings (Regulation of Reports) Bill, 16 April 1926, col. 744.
7 *Daily Mirror*, 26 March 1925, p. 6; *Daily Mail*, 13 December 1926, p. 7.
8 *Daily Mirror*, 26 March 1925, p. 6.
9 *Newspaper World*, 11 December 1926, p. 7.
10 *The Times*, 15 April 1926, p. 15.
11 508 H.C. Debs. 5s., Press Council Bill, Second Reading, 28 November 1952, col. 962–72.
12 Ibid., col. 994.
13 *Sunday Express*, 23 August 1953, p. 4.
14 *Daily Mirror*, 12–14 November 1953.
15 On the *Mirror*'s coverage of homosexuality in the 1950s, see Higgins (1996: 267–305).
16 570 H.C. Debs, 5s, State of the Press, 17 May 1957.

Chapter 9

'Outrageously bad taste'

The BBC and the controversy over *This is Your Life* in the 1950s

Su Holmes

In 1955, critics reviewed a new programme on BBC television, *This is Your Life* (hereafter *TIYL*).[1] The programme saw the subject of the show surprised by the presenter, with the narrative of their life then retold through the testimonies of friends, family and colleagues. After its opening episode, one critic describes being 'repelled but fascinated' by the show, and he recalls a 'morbid but compulsive' form of engagement.[2] Another critic brings out the uncomfortable nature of the viewing experience, and how *TIYL* left him:

> [F]eeling much embarrassed with a sense of acute discomfort verging on nausea. I bought a TV set, not a key-hole, and the screen is no place to present a person's very personal life for the sake of so-called entertainment. To say that this is outrageously bad taste is an understatement.[3]

Cut to the year 2000, and terms such as 'compulsively compelling' and 'morbidly fascinating' pervade the critical reception of Reality TV. More specifically, and as part of the flurry of comment which greeted the first UK *Big Brother*, Kathryn Flett (*The Observer*) pondered how her viewing experience had led to a 'soul-searching' form of engagement: 'Was this pain or pleasure?...I watched the Friday night show [thinking] "this is horrible. Horrible. I hate this". But we remained glued, because there's no doubt this show brings out the car crash voyeur in us all' (Flett 2000: 12). Given that Reality TV is often held up as a *new* form of programming, epitomising what many critics perceive as the social ills of television *in the moment*, it is intriguing that these comments were written 45 years apart. They offer very similar descriptions of how the desire to look is attended or circumscribed by notions of ethics, guilt and, most crucially, questions of 'taste'.

This historical example becomes doubly interesting when situated within another taste culture at this time – the institution of the BBC. Discourses of 'taste' have historically been central to conceptions of public service: we only need to consider Lord Reith's famous mission to 'uplift the nation's taste'. While the BBC is understood to have been progressively shaped by a popularizing imperative from the late 1930s onwards (Scannell and Cardiff 1991), its image in the 1950s, *especially* when set against the populist newcomer of ITV, retains paternalistic and conservative associations. How, then, might this be reconciled with their decision to adopt and promote a format which critics unanimously insisted should be *banned*? *TIYL* became a site through which fears and concerns over the very status of television (its social, ethical and political role) were articulated and debated with vigour. More than simply a controversial series, *TIYL* was apparently a 'social problem' and a 'social menace' to which the BBC should 'give immediate and critical attention'.[4] While it may now be best remembered for its reverential treatment of celebrities and its ceremonious presentation of the 'Big Red Book' ('This is Your Life!'), in the 1950s, it was a deeply controversial programme, perceived as 'an unpardonable intrusion into personal privacy'.[5] This is a field that remains neglected in the contours of the libertarian narrative of media history recently identified by James Curran (2002a). From the perspective of the libertarian narrative, television only becomes significant in the 1960s – a time when it was seen to chafe at restriction in new and exciting ways. Television, the BBC and the 1950s are all left in the corner, seen as epitomising consensus, conformity and conservatism.

Drawing on archival research based on existing programmes, scripts, press reviews and the internal documentation of the BBC, this chapter uses *TIYL* as a way of interrogating the construction of British television history in the 1950s. In relation to this, I want to use *TIYL* as a way of considering wider critical and methodological issues in the field. How do we come to 'narrate' media history, and what approaches and sources are used in this task? How and why are some narratives privileged over others, and what is at stake in their articulation? This makes this chapter not so much a detailed textual analysis of *TIYL*,[6] as it is a consideration of the institutional, aesthetic and cultural circumstances that surrounded its inception.

The libertarian narrative and 1950s television

Curran's (2002a) bid to map different narratives of media history is the product of a self-reflexive historical gaze: it speaks to the scholarly emphasis on history as an act of construction, a fundamentally interpretative project. Part of Curran's project here was to foreground the benefits of a cross-media history that ranged beyond the boundaries of a single media form. Nevertheless, the idea of assessing and returning to broader historical narratives has a particular relevance to the historical study of television at this time. The growing interest in television history has prompted a renewed reflection on the status of television as a 'researchable entity' (Corner 2003: 275), a particular historical object that is explored through various historiographic practices. This framework includes the need to address the relationship between the 'macro-overview of broadcasting history' and the more local analyses of specific genres or texts (Jacobs 2000: 9). The wider institutional narratives of broadcast history pre-existed archival interest in programme forms, and this has encouraged their appropriation as a backdrop which can help to contextualize studies of programmes, genres and audiences. This is in many ways a practical necessity but, as the dichotomous constructions of the BBC and ITV in the 1950s suggest (the BBC is often constructed as elitist and paternalistic, while ITV is aligned with a 'brash', energetic populism), such 'macro-overviews' paint their stories in very broad strokes, often relying on 'common sense' assumptions rather than detailed historical research. Thus, despite the increasingly self-reflexive attitude that shapes the construction of media history, the potentially *complex* relationship at work between macro and micro narratives has witnessed little debate.

In relation to the writing of media history, it is worth noting that the role and significance of the case study also has an ambiguous position in Curran's historical map. While his intention was deliberately to merge media histories in order to bring out broader developments, Curran's discussion later nods to the importance of examining how micro examples come to shape these broader frameworks. For example, in relation to the populist media narrative and the issue as to why a particular media product might be popular, Curran observes that 'carefully argued, [and] textually examination…is the absent centre of most populist media history' (2002a: 42). But what appears to be left unexplored here is how the case study may (or may not) fit the thrust of the broader contours in which the narratives are drawn. The case study is necessarily limited in its scope, but it is also precisely for this reason that it raises interesting historical and methodological issues with respect to the broader project of this book.

The libertarian narrative of media history describes 'how traditionalists and liberals fought each other both through the media and over its control' (Curran 2002a: 26), although the overriding thrust of the narrative pivots on the gradual liberalization of media representation and regulation. Ideas about censorship and regulation are inevitably shaped by the internal historical trajectories of different media forms and, especially in the 1950s and 1960s, the comparative relations between them. Film and, to a degree, theatre and literature were partly defined *against* the emerging competition of television, effectively offering what its 'tame', domestic and familial screen could not. Ideas about conservatism are further framed by the perceived historical contrasts between the BBC and commercial television in the 1950s, reinforced by the image of 'the energetic…showbiz visionaries [of ITV] elbowing aside the complacent bureaucrats of the BBC' (Black 1972: 109). This perspective largely maps contrasts at the level of the popular, and its relationship with commercialism and mass appeal. But it also contributes to a pervasive image of class elitism where the BBC is concerned, which in turn fosters an image of moral traditionalism. Indeed, the underlying sense here is that, when it came to the BBC, the 'moral traditionalists' of which Curran speaks were residing *within* television at this time.

This is at least the case with regard to the 1950s, which makes sense from the perspective of the libertarian narrative which is of course 'the signature tune' of the 1960s (Curran 2002a: 26). However, in terms of censorship and regulation, very little is written about the years of television prior to the 1960s, when television was only just developing as a mass medium. Furthermore, it is worth noting the fact that media censorship relaxes as the importance of that medium declines – a factor that contributed to the British Board of Film Censors' (BBFC) increasing liberalism in the 1960s when the cinema was moving away from its status as the most popular mass medium. It follows, then, that just as the earliest years of cinema were free from stringent censorship, so the early years of television were characterized by a less cohesive and institutionalized form of regulation – strategies and rules were still being formed. For example, in a study of the popular genre of the TV cinema programme, I have elsewhere discussed the extraordinary spectacle of the BBC introducing excerpts of the X-rated *La Ronde* (1950) and *Rashomon* (1951) in the early 1950s – much to the shock of critics, viewers and the BBFC (Holmes 2005). While this could simply be viewed as a strange lapse of judgement on the part of the BBC (the *Rashomon* excerpt focused on the rape scene and went out at 8:15 pm), it is more productive to suggest that it points to the unpredictable and often precarious process of *forming* ideas about regulation, and their relationship with social responsibility and potential audience response.

'The revolting emetic': *TIYL* is bad for you

TIYL was originally a radio format in the US, and the fact that it had not attracted substantial controversy on radio supports the centrality of the visual here. Hosted by Ralph Edwards, it began on US radio in 1948, then transferred to network television in 1952. In 1955, the BBC agreed to take out a two-year option on the format, and with Irishman Eamon Andrews as the host (already well-known from his role as a sport's anchor on radio and as the chairman on the BBC's popular panel game *What's My Line?*), it began on British television on 29 July 1955. According to BBC Audience Research, the programme regularly attracted audiences of 13 million,[7] and critics perceived that *TIYL* had emerged as 'part of the BBC's battle to beat commercial TV'.[8] The show was invoked as the epitome of commercial fare and as a regrettable example of what the era of competition might mean for British television. This context is also significant in suggesting how, certainly from the perspective of moral traditionalists, the bid to transgress traditional moral values and to exploit 'questionable' audience pleasures is intimately intertwined with discourses of commercialization, or what Curran (2002a: 26) identifies as the rise of the populist narrative of media culture.

Although the popular image of the 1950s pivots on perceptions of affluence and suburbanization, with television itself imagined as a catalyst for an increasingly home-centred lifestyle, the medium – with its new images and experiences – also played a crucial role in exploring and renegotiating the boundaries between public and private. *TIYL* quickly became a privileged site for the exploration of these discourses on a number of different levels.

In terms of the press reception of *TIYL*, there were firstly vehement objections to the *ethics* of the programme, and discussion circled around two key features: a concern over the ambushing of the guest and its subsequent invasion of their privacy. The following review offers a typical response:

> [*TIYL*] now heavily underlines a problem to which I urge the BBC to give immediate and critical attention…To what extent is television justified in poking into the private life of a person who has not given his or her permission to appear in a 'live' programme to be transmitted into millions of homes throughout the country?[9]

This concern led to claims of torture and victimization. The popular parlance used to describe the subject of the show was always that of the 'victim' (even within the BBC), and critics routinely ran such headlines as 'This is Torture by TV'.[10]

The primary subjects of *TIYL* at this time were not always celebrities, whether these emerged from cinema, theatre, sport or literature. In the first decade of its existence, guests could just as often be an 'ordinary' person, and the BBC saw this as an important aspect of the show with regard to public service. As Stuart Hood, then the BBC's Deputy Editor of News and Current Affairs, argued:

> A great deal of our output…is concerned with international tensions, racial antagonism, political intrigue and industrial strife. It is not often that we demonstrate that…people are doing good deeds in a naughty world. This…is the function and justification of *This is Your Life*.[11]

The 'ordinary' subject was to be honoured as really 'extraordinary', and (with a philanthropist bent) they ranged from doctors and nurses who had won medals of bravery during the war, heroic military personnel and charity fund-raisers to people who had contributed to their community in other ways (see also Desjardins 2002). Some critics felt that the use of 'ordinary' subjects was evidence of the programme's *ultimate* intrusion. Critics recalled an example of an unsuspecting vicar who was 'tricked and deceived' and 'then dragged' to the studio – unwillingly finding himself thrust into the limelight.[12] At the same time, most reviews made no distinction between 'ordinary' and famous subjects when it came to their critique of the show: *nobody* was safe.

Structuring such concern was also urgent discussion about the relationship fostered between programme and viewer. There was often an emphasis on the complicity of the audience and the worrying pursuit of questionable pleasures and desires. *TIYL* was variously described as 'gobbled up and gloated over', as catering to an 'insatiable addiction to shockers and shocks' and as 'the best-devised show yet for the mass exploitation of morbid curiosity'.[13] In comparison, critics reported physical symptoms of nausea, and a prevalent perception of *TIYL* positioned it as an unbearable mixture of emotion, sentimentality and flattery. If it wasn't 'a revolting emetic',[14] it was a 'great gooey meringue'[15] or a 'saccharine encrusted process of personal exposure'.[16] Lastly, and intersecting with all of the above, there was the perception that *TIYL* was 'utterly UnBritish'.[17] Various assertions regarding the national character were advanced, but these primarily circled around the suggestion that Britain was a 'private, self-derogatory, shy, modest and honest nation… [composed of] people of the grunt and understatement'.[18] Although the majority of discussions about the programme adopted a note of earnest concern, one critic at least approached the 'UnBritish' nature of the format with a sense of playful humour. In doing so, he makes the contours of the debate here more explicit:

> The English are reputed to show no emotion, they hate Peeping Toms; and their home is their castle. Obviously, however, while they resent one single prying look on the part of their neighbour, they *welcome* a chance of crying in public, weeping before an audience, or discussing their emotions, religion and sex-life within sight and earshot of 12 million neighbours.[19]

Although (in terms of Curran's populist narrative of media history), the BBC often emerges as an elitist institution (2002a: 17), it is the Corporation's relations *with* the popular which irritate taste cultures here. Furthermore, not only was *TIYL* outrageously popular, but its popularity coincided with, and was enabled by, the development of the mass television audience. The debate surrounding *TIYL* most clearly parallels the concerns that surrounded the emergence of ITV – the primary, but not only, site for the exploration of 'commercial' television in Britain. In this regard, the programme becomes discussed through discourses that have long expressed an elitist distaste for 'mass culture' in the populist narrative of media history. Indeed, *TIYL* is positioned as the epitome of 'vulgarity, sentimentality, emotional corruption, and a remorseless cultural descent to the lowest common denominator' (Curran 2000: 16). In fact, BBC audience research indicated in 1958 that *TIYL* was particularly popular with the working classes and women[20] – the two groups significantly imagined as the most 'vulnerable' to the persuasions of popular culture and the primary targets of its address. Yet in connection with the expression of disgust at the public's lack of discernment and 'taste' (if the latter is conceived as legitimating class distinctions and hierarchies) (Bourdieu 1986), it seems precisely the point that the working class constituted the *majority* of the television audience by this time. It is also no surprise to see the popular aligned with the American here. The postwar period is more widely recognized as a time when fears about the Americanization of British life and culture were particularly apparent. Britain's status as a declining world power and its substantial war debt created a dependency on American finance for postwar reconstruction. This fostered (or accelerated) the feeling that British values, histories and forms of culture were under threat. Furthermore, and with respect to television, fears surrounding 'Americanization' had been high on the agenda in the run up to the launch of ITV.

The descriptions of the programme are also quite recognizable to us today. With an emphasis on the personal, and the distaste for sensationalism, emotionalism and immediacy, the debate surrounding *TIYL* prefigures debates about the tabloidization of television (see Turner 1999). Feminists have argued that television forms such as soap opera, talk shows and Reality TV are derided and controversial because they challenge the traditional masculine and bourgeois hegemony of public/private spheres (e.g. Van Zoonen 2004). Furthermore, and from a historical point of view, feminists have drawn attention to how the discourses surrounding the development of television (technology, viewing and programme culture) are in many ways marked by 'the troublesome concept of "the feminine"' (Thumim 2004: 11; cf. Spigel 1992a,b). It does not take much probing to see that the reaction to *TIYL*'s mixture of emotion, subjectivity and its perceived intrusion into the 'private' realm is troubled by discourses of feminization.

'Not sordid or embarrassing in anyway': censoring the life narrative

The BBC were aware when they purchased the format that it had attracted some controversy in America. In their planning of the programme, the US version constantly functioned as the undesirable 'Other' – something that should be adapted to accommodate a different television system and national sensibility. The Controller of Television Programmes outlined how:

> The Television Service knew of this programme from its inception [in the US] and for a long time considered it could not be transmitted by the BBC. Study of kinescopes, however, made us change our opinion. We came to the conclusion that provided the people, the type of story (success not failure) and the incidents (not sordid or embarrassing in any way) were carefully selected, we could avoid the obvious dangers, except the criticism of intruding into the life of a private individual.[21]

It is clear from this quote that the Corporation's precautions operated as a form of both repression and censorship, aiming to police the boundaries between the 'private' and 'public' self. If after 'four weeks of intensive research, matters are disclosed which might prove embarrassing to the subject, they are either eliminated from the life story or…the whole project is dropped'.[22] Just what the BBC considered embarrassing matters are not defined and the term scandal is never used, although it remains implicit.

Yet the recurrent complaint that *TIYL* exposed the private *lives* of its subjects would seem to imply that critics were nevertheless concerned about the knowledge produced by the show. The script for the edition featuring Norman Wisdom, although shaped by the specific inflections of his star persona, can serve as a case study in this respect. It begins with Andrews hiding in the wings of the stage, and Wisdom thinks he has been invited to the studio to perform. Andrews then springs out with the cry 'Norman Wisdom – this is your life!' as the stage is illuminated and the studio audience revealed. Andrews then introduces the story thus:

> This is the story of a poor cockney boy who drew on the hard, struggling experiences of life and turned them to his advantage, and who today stands at the top of his profession. And to his credit he still takes the same size in hats.[23]

Wisdom's mother then speaks of his 'determination to succeed' as Andrews recounts how 'your story starts in the grimy streets of Paddington. Frail and small even for your years, you're still pugnacious and always trying to emulate your brother Fred'. Along comes Fred to recount childhood pranks, followed by a school friend who tells stories of a shy Wisdom, bullied and vulnerable at school. We then hear of his job in a grocer's and his difficulty riding the tricycle. But according to his old boss, he was a 'wonderful worker, on the go from 8 every morning to 7 at night…although he did pinch the cheese from the shop next door'. We cut back to Andrews' narration as we move closer towards Wisdom's acting aspirations, but he finds that the 'streets of London are not paved with gold'. We are told how his first act 'dies the death' at a music hall in Islington, but how 'fate and the kindness of a fellow-artiste then takes a hand, as well as, of course, your irrepressible talent'. We then hear testimonies from film colleagues, which give Andrews the opportunity to stress how Norman 'is clearly still the same kid from Paddington', and we end on contributions from Norman's children who are so proud of 'his journey to success'.

The programme drew on the 'success myth', a longstanding trope in star construction (Dyer 1998), in which a combination of talent, 'ordinariness', hard work, setbacks and lucky breaks functions to catapult the subject to celebrity status. No matter what the class background or profession of the subject, they were also constructed as remaining essentially *unchanged* by their fame (Vera Lynn is still 'the same unspoiled girl who sang around the house at number 3, Thackery Rd…'). Although it might be suggested that there was rather a difference in 'achievement' between 'rescuing dying and injured from a train accident' (Edith Powell), saving 'many from the ravages of leprosy' (Dr

Philip Clayton) and the success of a 'glittering film career' (Anna Neagle), the emphasis on hard work and determination prevailed in all spheres. But what is important here is that – as the Wisdom narrative makes clear – there was actually an emphasis on a seamless *continuity* between 'personal' and 'professional' self.

'The great dramatic moment': caught on camera

Despite the emphasis on the divulging of private *lives*, the key issue here is not the discourse of the programme, operating at the level of knowledge or information. Rather, it responds to the medium's emerging ability to produce and visualize the self. This demands some consideration of the aesthetic and cultural meanings that surrounded the development of the television close-up. As Jason Jacobs (2000) has explained, emergent debates about aesthetics in television drama stressed the significance of intimacy and closeness, with respect to both the literal positioning of the camera, as well as subject matter and performance style. Intimacy was discussed with respect to observation, with the television close-up imagined as a penetrating 'microscope'. As one reviewer commented:

> In the close-ups the cameras seem to penetrate into the very minds of the characters, so much so that one had the feeling that what they were photographing was not the faces of the characters but their innermost thoughts.
>
> Cited in Jacobs (2000: 122)

Given the general philosophical view that positions the human face as the ultimate communicative and expressive agency (Jacobs 2000), the development of the cinematic close-up was unsurprisingly discussed through similar discourses (see Dyer 1998: 15). But as Jacobs expands, the televisual close-up was not discussed in terms of identification (seduction) but observation: television's agency was less to visualize 'motives and emotions' than to 'observe or monitor' how they are interpreted – up close (ibid.: 120). What comes across strongly in the quotes is the insistence on the *realism* of the television close-up. Yet once we bring non-fiction programming into view, we begin to see that this epistemological claim had its limits. While the quotes describe observation of the ability to become someone else (to act), a key problem with *TIYL* was that its images were only *too real*.

The 'frisson' of excitement generated by the live and the 'real' here was imagined as being central to the pleasures of *TIYL*. When it first began, the Controller of Television Programmes emphasized that there is no doubt that 'the success of *This is Your Life* is due to "shock" and "stunt value"',[24] and it was later agreed that the confrontation between host and subject 'was the great dramatic moment' of the programme.[25] On one level, *TIYL* was an extensively planned and crafted arena (after weeks of research, the host and witnesses rehearsed twice before the live broadcast), with an appeal to the unscripted and the unpredictable at its core. Given that, until 1961, the programme was broadcast live, this charged appeal should not be underestimated. Perhaps not dissimilar to Reality TV today, *TIYL* orchestrated a space to *produce and then capture* 'the real'. This investment is implicit in the BBC's initial description of the programme, which confirmed that 'as a *documentary method* it is strikingly dramatic' [my italics].[26] The reference to a 'documentary method' signalled less a generic relationship with documentary than an appeal to the 'real'.

TIYL was in fact a curious generic hybrid, combining aspects of the celebrity biography, the award ceremony, with the 'ambushing' set-up of the game show.[27] It was not an interview at all and, as such, it offered a uniquely passive position to its subject. Although the subject responded to the experience in a range of different ways, their role was essentially to *react to* the narrative. In the words of one critic, they were 'trapped into having [their]…past life *unrolled before them* like a trail of scented glue' [my italics].[28] The camera aimed to capture the initial shock and surprise of the event, and then the succession of reactions as the narrative was told. The introduction of each person by voice specifically enabled the camera to dwell on the subject's face as it expressed a mixture of anticipation and uncertainty. The subject was always required to verify the authenticity of the surprise ('Did you have the slightest idea?'), although one of the key differences from today is that, while the television appearances of celebrities and 'ordinary' people alike are now understood as performances within which moments of 'authenticity' might be glimpsed (see Hill 2005), doubt about the authenticity of *TIYL* rarely featured in the debate.

But this also suggests that the programme's appeal *pivoted* on a claim to authenticity, especially where the representation of the famous was concerned. *TIYL* aimed to visibly catch its subjects *off-guard* – a desire that now has a staunch place in the tabloid rhetoric of paparazzi photographs (*heat* magazine initially promised to capture celebrities 'off-guard, unkempt, unready, unsanitized') (Llewellyn-Smith 2001: 120). The intention of *TIYL* was less aggressive or boisterous: after all, it clearly aimed to revere its subjects, and the media construction of celebrity culture has changed *substantially* since this time. But it *does* share the visual desire to penetrate the more polished nature of the public façade. Indeed, the BBC wanted *TIYL* to offer an insight into what they called another 'side' to the person, and they would privately complain if the subject was unresponsive when confronted with the carefully planned surprise.

While evocative of the 'unauthorized' paparazzi snap, these images also unfolded in real time, within the co-present intimacy of live transmission. Critics were appalled at the sight of men and women, celebrities and ordinary people, weeping before the camera's gaze, and the most controversial edition here featured the British film star, Anna Neagle. With headlines such as 'Anna Neagle Weeps Before TV Millions',[29] critics talked for days of the:

> [U]nnecessary spectacle of an adult, mature woman being moved to tears, trying to hide her face from the relentless cameras which…would not spare her the discomfort of being exposed…and us the sensation of being made into impertinent snoopers.[30]

Janet Thumim's comment that 'images could not always be contained by the narrative structures within which they were located' (2004: 20) seems applicable here. The BBC had concentrated on policing and 'censoring' the verbal discourse of the show, but the images spilled over from the narrative trajectory which aimed to anchor them. This possibility had not escaped the BBC's attention. One of the Corporation's precautions in adapting the format from America concerned the use of the close-up or, as the producer T. Leslie Jackson explained, the British *TIYL* is more 'tactful and sober…I never use a close-up on a face that is obviously overcome with emotion if I can avoid it. Sensationalism doesn't pay'.[31] Those critical of the programme did not always agree, and the BBC's conception of *TIYL* suggests a competing struggle between what, on the one hand, they perceived would make 'good TV' and, on the other, questions of taste, ethics and integrity.

There is the sense here that this subject matter, and especially its aesthetic framework, offended the prevailing taste cultures of the time – particularly discourses of a middle class (and masculine) restraint. This also fostered a palpable concern with the potential viewing pleasures of the programme. It is not difficult to see that the discussion surrounding *TIYL* was saturated with sexual connotations – whether we point to the references to 'exposure', 'peep shows' or the cultivation of 'gutter-like curiosities' and 'base and reprehensible desires'. As even the most popular Freudian reading would suggest, what is repressed in the text (the censoring of all those 'sordid or embarrassing' incidents) may emerge elsewhere. Indeed, unusual for approaching the programme with a sense of humour, one critic imagined a scenario in which a 'friend' would appear as a witness to the 'Life', only to quickly turn on the subject with malicious revelations:

> Remember Harry? Of course I remember Harry, a rat. A lousy slimy rat. This man stole my wife and sent me her laundry bills. He has deserted his children and his mother has broken more lives than a public executioner.[32]

The critic's imagining of an uncomfortable spectacle of on-screen embarrassment returns us to where we began: the conception of 'car crash TV' as a way of describing the oscillating viewing experience of Reality TV. At the very least, this suggests that mapping a history of change with respect to the controversial and the offensive (and indeed the daring or the 'new') is a more complex business than it first appears.

Conclusion

While this chapter has concentrated mainly on the libertarian narrative, it has also aimed to raise broader questions about the construction of media (and here primarily television) history, particularly in terms of the conceptual and historical value of the case study. Furthermore, while my attempt to 'reconstruct' the early circulation and reception of *TIYL* is necessarily partial, the programme makes momentarily visible the deeply intertwined relationship between different 'narratives' of media culture: discourses from the populist narrative (commercialization), the feminist narrative (gender) and the libertarian narrative (regulation and censorship) intersect in a dynamic movement here. Indeed, *TIYL* has a less direct relationship with discourses of censorship in any conventional sense. Although critics constantly lobbied the BBC to axe, drop or indeed 'ban' the programme – which clearly indicates the strength of the feelings roused and the language used – its historical interest lies more in negotiating the more elusive boundaries of good (television) 'taste'. The programme does not fit into the conventional textual field when it comes to the study of censorship, controversy and regulation on television, which has more often focused on drama, news, documentary or feature films. In other words, *TIYL* emphasizes how the idea of what is controversial in television, and how we might conceive of the practices of regulation and 'censorship', cannot be approached in simple terms. Nor, from a historical point of view, should we expect these texts to fall into our laps. Case studies are not always obvious, neatly conforming to our expectations of taste cultures and social/cultural mores from 'the past'. At the same time, while there is the problem of forcing an 'undue proximity' and similarity between then and now, we should also be wary of an 'over-distanced approach (the past as very much "another country")' (Corner 2003: 277). The cultural debate which surrounded the advent of talk shows and Reality TV is *not* radically dissimilar to the critiques surrounding *TIYL*, and a wider historical lineage here is worth some thought. While it may be the case that, much like the live close-up, 'the past can be seized only as an image which flashes up at the instant when it can be recognised' (Benjamin 1970/1973: 257), there are clearly many more moments to seize and explore.

Notes

1 BBC, 1955–64, ITV, 1969–93, BBC, 1993–2003.
2 Peter Black, *Daily Mail* 30 July 1955, BBC press cuttings Box 771, BBC Written Archive Centre (WAC).
3 Untitled press report, 30 July 1955. BBC press cuttings Box 712 (WAC)

4 Untitled press view, 18 November 1958. BBC press cuttings Box 663 (WAC).

5 Untitled press review, 18 November 1958. BBC press cuttings Box 663 (WAC).

6 The extent of existing audio-visual material would in any case make this difficult. A compilation of extended excerpts from the 1950s and early 1960s remains accessible in the public domain.

7 'The Future of This is Your Life', 27 February 1961. C. Tel to D. Tel, T16/590.

8 *Daily Express*, 19 February 1958. BBC press cuttings Box 663 (WAC).

9 Untitled press review, 18 November 1958. BBC press cuttings Box 663 (WAC).

10 *The Western Mail*, 25 March 1958. BBC press cuttings Box 663 (WAC).

11 'Policy', Stuart Hood to D. Tel. B, 9 March 1961, T16/590.

12 *The Daily Telegraph*, 18 January 1957. BBC press cuttings Box 663 (WAC).

13 *Stage*, 4 December 1958. BBC press cuttings Box 663 (WAC).

14 *Daily Mirror*, 6 January 1959. BBC press cuttings Box 670 (WAC).

15 *Daily Mirror*, 18 February 1960. BBC press cuttings Box 670 (WAC).

16 *Daily Mirror*, 7 January 1959. BBC press cuttings Box 670 (WAC).

17 *Daily Mail*, 30 July 1955. BBC press cuttings Box 771 (WAC).

18 *Sunday Telegraph*, 14 May 1961. BBC press cuttings Box 670 (WAC).

19 Ibid.

20 Viewer Research Report, 'The Audience for This is Your Life', Autumn 1958. VR/59/2.

21 21 November 1955. CTP to D. Tel. B, T12/522/1.

22 Assistant H.L.E. to D. Tel. B, 'Policy', 12 June 1960, T16/590.

23 *This is Your Life* script, Norman Wisdom.

24 C.P.T to H.L.E, 29 November 1955, T12/522/1.

25 Michael Mills to H.L.E, 20 January 1965, T12/1,302/1.

26 C.T.P to D. Tel. B, 21 November 1955, T12/522/1

27 The US import *People are Funny* was the most famous example of this in the 1950s. Significantly, it too was seen to offend public taste and was taken off ITV shortly after its emergence.

28 *Daily Mirror*, 19 February 1958. BBC press cuttings Box 663 (WAC).

29 *Daily Express*, 18 February 1958. BBC press cuttings Box 663 (WAC).

30 *Manchester City News*, 4 April 1958. BBC press cuttings Box 663 (WAC).

31 *Sunday Dispatch*, 11 May 1958. BBC press cuttings Box 663 (WAC).

32 Untitled press review, 15 October 1958. BBC press cuttings Box 663 (WAC).

The anthropological narrative

Introduction

Following the political and economic union of England and Wales with Scotland in 1707 and the legislative union of Britain and Ireland in 1801, the media have been crucial in trying to harmonize what has, for the most part, been a quarrelsome union of four nations, each with their own national history and culture, not to mention regional nationalisms. In the context of narrating media history, the anthropological narrative looks at the various ways in which the media have sought to unite the British public around a nucleus of cultural values and practices that have helped to foster a sense of national citizenship, identity and sense of belonging.

The study of nationalism as a cultural construct has received considerable scholarly attention, of which Benedict Anderson's *Imagined Communities* (2006 [1983]) is undoubtedly the most widely read and oft cited. What is particularly instructive about Anderson's comparative study of national communities is his analysis of 'print capitalism' in the aftermath of the Reformation in the sixteenth century. One of the principal effects of the development of 'print-as-commodity' was the proliferation of vernacular languages. Vernaculars were then pulled together through the further development of print capitalism to establish 'print languages' in an effort to create national markets for the consumption of mass-produced literature, made possible following the invention of the Gutenberg press. All of this had the effect of replacing imagined sacred communities with imagined national communities that began to identify more closely with a national secular consciousness expressed in and through their own territorialized language.

The standardization of language was crucial for the emergence and development of a national British identity. Although the home Celtic nations maintained their own languages – albeit to varying degrees of success – the lingua franca that became increasingly common throughout Britain from the sixteenth century onwards was 'Modern English', itself a hybrid of Anglo-Saxon, Norman French, German and Latin. Notwithstanding the continuation of regional differences of pronunciation, the ascendancy of British English was more or less complete by the late eighteenth century, by which time London had established itself as the main city around which much of the printing press was centred. Attempts by grammarians and printers to fix the English language, an enterprise that culminated in the publication of the first English dictionary by Samuel Johnson in 1755, more or less guaranteed the use of standard English.

Empire building also provided an opportunity for uniting the British public: it made ordinary people feel that they belonged to a superior nation steeped in historical traditions and military glory. National social and political institutions were created or reinvented to legitimize and augment this new imperial identity. Royal occasions (e.g. weddings, funerals, coronations, trooping the colour) were imbued with a new symbolism that represented Britain's imperial greatness. Similarly, ceremonial festivals (e.g. the Great Exhibition of 1851) exhibited exotic foreign objects in an image of Britain's making, thus encouraging visitors to believe that everything they saw belonged to them. Household commodities (e.g. crockery, food and tobacco packaging) helped to domesticate the Empire by commemorating national heroes and famous colonial conquests. The British public were encouraged to take up patriotic flag-waving, a tradition that still endures to this day, especially during national sporting events and the national proms, both of which are also occasions for the nostalgic celebration of national anthems (e.g. 'God Save the Queen', 'Land of Hope and Glory', 'Rule Britannia') that date back to Victorian Britain.

The main vehicle for popular, British nationalism, however, has been the national media which first emerged with the national press in the early nineteenth century, subsequently evolving through advertising, the network of Victorian music halls and the arrival of cinema and broadcasting in the early twentieth century. Of these, broadcasting has been foremost in the mediazation of a national identity, not least because of its widespread use by the British public. Broadcasting was particularly suited to extending, renewing and re-embedding traditions in temporal and spatial contexts on a scale that was previously unimaginable. This was especially so in the early days of broadcasting when the BBC became an abstract embodiment of the nation; a new source of cultural authority quite literally licensed to broadcast to and represent the nation (Hall 1986; Bailey 2007c). BBC English was one of the most salient features of this major effort of social unification and standardization. Many in the BBC thought that making the public more speech conscious would result in the nation speaking with one voice, thus mitigating 'parochial patriotism' and 'petty nationalisms'.

Interestingly, both chapters in this section are historical analyses of the complex relationship between broadcasting – radio and television – and national identity. Furthermore, they both pay particular attention to the ways in which UK broadcasters have had to reimagine British nationalism by catering for the regional nationalisms associated with Scotland and Wales.

Jamie Medhurst concentrates on the history of television in Wales from the 1950s onwards, a period when Welsh cultural politics was becoming increasingly intertwined with nationalist pressure groups, such as Plaid Cymru and Undeb Cymru Fydd. As well as analysing the ebbing and flowing of the various provisions for an all-Wales television service, Medhurst also considers the role such services have played in fostering a sense of Welsh identity, not least the preservation of the Welsh language, as opposed to English. What is especially interesting about Medhurst's analysis is that the history of Welsh television is located within a much wider historiography of Wales. In other words, the importance of broadcasting in Wales features in a number of histories of Wales, not just histories of Welsh broadcasting. It would seem that media history is not as neglected in a nation that has struggled – and continues to struggle – to maintain a sense of its national consciousness and cultural identity.

Daniel Day's contribution looks at the changing articulation between the English centrism of the early BBC and its efforts to represent the multiple identities associated with Britain's 'Celtic fringe' – Scotland in particular – from the late 1960s through to the 1980s. Like Medhurst, he demonstrates that postwar Britain was an era of evolving and often transient identities in which a growing number of its citizens no longer saw themselves as first and foremost British, but began to develop or reinvent often submerged hybrid identities. Consequently, institutions such as the BBC were forced to reassess and adapt their roles in the light of the changing mentalities of the publics they served. More crucially, Day argues that the BBC embraced this change more positively than has hitherto been acknowledged by media historians. Instead of homogenizing British culture, he suggests ways in which the BBC has reflected and enriched British cultural diversity.

Notwithstanding the subtle differences in interpretation and historical emphasis, both chapters are timely in terms of recent developments concerning political devolution in Scotland and Wales. They also raise questions – albeit implicitly – concerning more recent cultural struggles and the mediazation of Britain's ever multiplying multicultural publics. Future anthropological narratives will have to take this into account. They will also have to reflect on the paradoxical revival of religion as a supranational imagined community, contrary to what secularists and nationalists would have us believe. Meanwhile, we would do well to heed the words of John Donne – a seventeenth-century English poet – on the interconnectedness of human experience, and to remember that, although Britain may be an island, it has never existed in splendid isolation, nor been entirely free from 'foreign' cultural influences. Rather, Britain is a rich collective of nations and nationalities, and it belongs to an increasingly globalized world. We are all 'a part of the main' and therefore involved, whether we realize it or not, in the material and spiritual well-being of humankind in its entirety, not just 'our own kind'. Only history will tell what part the media will play in facilitating or hindering a more tolerant and multicultural Britain in the twenty-first century.

Further reading

There are numerous comparative studies of the historical origins of nation-states and the spread of nationalism; apart from Anderson (2006), see also Gellner (1983), Hobsbawn (1990) and Smith (1983). For historical accounts of the formation of the modern British state and the complexities of Anglo-British national identities, see Colley (1992), Colls (2002), Kearney (1989), Kumar (2003), Nairn (2003), Pittock (1999), Robbins (1997), Samuel (1989, 1998), Schama (2002), Ward (2004) and Weight (2002).

Some of the earliest unifying mediations of Britain were representations of British imperialism in the nineteenth century. Potter (2003, 2004) and Kaul (2003) are excellent analyses of the relationship between the British Empire and the press. McClintock (1995) and Richards (1990) chronicle the evolution of racist advertising and the domestication of empire through the consumption of household commodities, including commodity spectacles. Humphries (1989) offers a succinct, illustrated analysis of how the magic lantern was used to promote jingoism and British patriotism. Similarly, Peter and Olivia Bailey (1986, 2002) demonstrate how Victorian music was assimilated for imperialist reasons of state.

Moving into the twentieth century, there is an abundance of literature on British cinema, national identity and the related 'condition of England' question: see, for example, Aldgate and Richards (1994, 1999), Chapman (1998, 2005b), Higson (1996, 1997), Richards (1983, 1997a) and Street (1997). For similar accounts of early broadcasting, Cardiff and Scannell (1987) and Scannell and Cardiff (1991) are exemplary; Camporesi (1990a,b) provides a fascinating, comparative analysis of broadcasting in the UK and the US; Harvey and Robins (1993) present a useful historical overview of the changing relationship between the BBC and its regions. Medhurst (2007) considers how English comedy – from the music hall to contemporary sitcoms – has played a role in the construction of the English national identity. Although an analysis of contemporary British newspaper journalism, Martin Conboy's (2006) recently published, *Tabloid Britain*, is an excellent exemplification of this particular narrative; see also Louw (2005) for a useful summary of national identity and communication generally.

Bocock (1974), Chaney (1986), Dayan and Katz (1992), Pimlott (1998) and Thompson (1995), offer superb historical–sociological analyses of the mediation of civic rituals and the remooring of British traditions in and through the media generally; Couldry (2003) provides a useful summary of these works, as well as presenting new insights of his own.

Histories of Celtic national media are steadily increasing. See the two chapters by Medhurst and Day for a comprehensive listing of Welsh and Scottish media-related literature. For analyses of the complex relationship between Irish media, history and national identity, see Barton (2004), Hill (2007), Horgan (2001), Legg (1999) and Pettitt (2008).

For those interested in the contemporary history of post-colonial, British multiculturalism, there is wealth of critical literature: for analyses of black Britain, identity and/or racism, see Baker *et al.* (1996), CCCS (1982), Dabyden *et al.* (2007), Fryer (1984), Gilroy (2002, 2004, 2007), Hall (1987) and Philips and Philips (1998); recent studies of Muslims in Britain and Islamophobia include Abbas (2005), Ansari (2004), Modood (2005, 2007) and Poole (2002). For a history of Indians in Britain, see Visram (2002). Parekh (2000) was commissioned by the Runnymede Trust and provides an important commentary on the current state of multiethnic Britain and covers most of its diasporic communities, as does Hesse (2000). Ever in search of 'A New England', Bragg (2006) offers a passionate exposition of what it is to be a progressive patriot in twenty-first-century Britain. Finally, Harvey (2006) is a timely collection of essays that explores a variety of contemporary and historical case studies that relate to national and local cultures in the context of transnational film and television.

Chapter 10

Television in Wales, c. 1950–70

Jamie Medhurst

The aims of this chapter are threefold: to provide a narrative account of the history of television in Wales in its formative years; to consider the relationship between the broadcast media and Welsh identity and cultural politics; to locate historical writing on television in Wales within the context of Curran's anthropological narrative of media history. What emerges is a picture of the complex relationship between broadcasting and national identity, in particular the specific linguistic and cultural tensions that exist in Wales.

Overview of television in Wales, 1950–70

Following the closedown of the BBC's television service during the Second World War, the BBC resumed television broadcasts on 7 June 1946 from Alexandra Palace in north London. At the time, the service was available to only 15,000 households in the London area, but it soon spread as transmitters were opened across the UK – in the West Midlands in 1949, in Manchester in 1951 and in 1952 in Scotland and south Wales (Crisell 1997/2002: 79). However, as Kevin Williams (1998: 151) notes, '[it] struggled to establish itself in a hostile environment'. There was a deep suspicion among many senior executives at the BBC as to the value of television, and the medium remained relatively underfunded and underdeveloped during the immediate postwar period. In 1947–48, television accounted for only one-tenth of the BBC's total expenditure and, even by 1950, the budget for television was only half of that of BBC Radio's Home Service (Crisell 1997/2002: 80).

Television first came to Wales when the Postmaster-General, the Earl de la Warr, opened the BBC's Wenvoe transmitter in Glamorganshire on 15 August 1952. The transmitter carried the BBC's television service to viewers in Wales and the west of England – and therein lay a problem. A degree of broadcasting autonomy had been granted to Wales in 1937 following a con-certed campaign for a measure of broadcasting independence led by, among others, the University of Wales and Welsh local authorities. The establishment of the 'Welsh Region' provided Wales with its own radio service separate from that of the west of England (much to the approval of listeners on both sides of the Bristol Channel), but this was brought to an abrupt halt with the outbreak of war in 1939. When television was established in Wales in 1952, once again, the fabled 'Kingdom of Arthur' was resurrected, and the BBC in Wales was again tied to the west of England.

Nevertheless, the early 1950s saw the advent of the 'opt out' system whereby a 'national region' such as Wales could opt out of the national (British) network and broadcast programmes of 'regional' interest. However, broadcasting Welsh language programmes during this opt out period would have deprived the English language majority of programmes in English. Consequently, programmes in Welsh were broadcast at off peak, often very unsociable hours, such as Sunday lunchtime, weekday afternoons and late evenings.

The debates over television between 1952 and 1956, from a Welsh perspective, focused on the perceived damage that would be inflicted on the language and culture of Wales from two sources: first, from the requirement placed upon the BBC to deliver a television service to a Welsh-speaking and English-speaking population (on both sides of the Bristol Channel) within one region; second, from the proposed new market-driven, commercial television service. These debates, however, appear to be confined to parliament as, during this period, there is little evidence in contemporary newspapers and journals to suggest that the population at large in Wales was overly concerned with developments in television. This was to change with the advent of commercial television in September 1955 and the Independent Television Authority's (ITA) announcement of a licence area for south Wales and the west of England in 1956.

On 26 October 1956, the ITA announced that the television company Television Wales and the West (TWW) had been granted the licence to provide independent television programmes for south Wales and the west of England. The mix of directors with business acumen and experience together with Welsh cultural figures who were experienced and well respected stood the company in good stead for the dual region it was to serve. The ITA, in creating a new dual licence area for this part of the UK, was driven by technical and economic considerations (location of transmitters and economic viability for advertisers respectively). Charles Hill, former Postmaster-General and later chairman of the ITA, referred to Wales as an 'awkward area' in his broadcasting memoirs (Hill 1974: 48). The reason for this, he stated, was that TWW, like the BBC, had to serve Wales and England in both the Welsh and English languages.

1958 signalled an increase in activity in a number of key areas of broadcasting in Wales. After a number of setbacks, TWW finally broadcast for the first time on 14 January 1958. The initial reaction to TWW was positive. A January 1958 editorial in the Welsh language weekly newspaper, *Y Cymro*, hoped that the coming of ITV would mean competition for the BBC and a resulting improvement in the quality of the fare on offer. The editorial also touched on another issue, that of the timing of programmes. It was hoped that Welsh programmes would be transmitted during the early evenings at peak time in addition to the afternoons in order that the working audience might be allowed access to the programmes.

The period between 1959 and 1961 witnessed a heightened level of activity in the demand for a separate all-Wales television service. Driven initially by Plaid Cymru, and subsequently by the cultural nationalist pressure group Undeb Cymru Fydd (the New Wales Union), a National Television Conference was called and held in Cardiff on 18 September 1959. A representative gathering from all walks of Welsh life debated the future of television in Wales and agreed on a resolution that charged a small group to continue with the work of pressing the government and broadcasting bodies for a separate television service for Wales.

Meanwhile, in August 1960, the ITA announced that it would soon be inviting applications from companies to operate an ITV service in the west Wales area. In April 1961, the invitation to apply for the west and north Wales licence was released by the ITA and, in June 1961, the licence was awarded to the 'Wales Television Association'. However, the Association, which eventually operated as Wales (West and North) Television (or Teledu Cymru in Welsh) was short-lived. Transmissions began in September 1962 but, by May 1963, the company had folded, becoming the only regional ITV company to fail on financial grounds. The reasons for the failure were numerous: a company founded on clear cultural aims was doomed to fail within the competitive commercial environment of ITV. Yet there were other factors such as the late opening of transmitters, a lack of audiences (and hence advertising revenue) and internal tensions between staff and directors (for a detailed account of the demise of the company, see Medhurst 2005).

During the mid-1960s, two significant changes took place which shaped the future of television broadcasting in Wales. In 1964, a 'freeing up' of frequencies allowed the BBC to launch its BBC Wales region, creating for the first time a unified BBC television service for Wales, separate from England. The following year, the ITA was granted permission by the government to split the Welsh and English services of TWW (who had taken over the Teledu Cymru region in 1964). This allowed for an all-Wales ITV service and gave TWW the opportunity to provide a specific service to viewers in the west of England. For many, the new regional structures of the BBC and the ITA acknowledged the existence of Wales as an identifiable entity in broadcasting terms. Yet the status quo was to be shaken in 1967 when TWW lost its contract to a new, dynamic consortium, Harlech Television. Headed by the enigmatic Lord Harlech, the new company promised to deliver more responsive and regionally based programmes. Given that the board of directors included the likes of Richard Burton, (Sir) Geraint Evans and Harry Secombe, the consortium was bound to create a stir at the ITA interview round. Harlech began operating in March 1968 and immediately created an impact on Welsh homes, becoming synonymous with high-quality 'regional' (or, in the case of Wales, national) programming.

The broadcast media and Welsh identity

Before discussing the way in which television has featured in the histories of Wales and Welsh media, it is worth considering the relationship between the broadcast media and Welsh national identity. This will serve to set a framework for the section that follows.

In his history of the BBC in Wales, John Davies quotes Asa Briggs who stated that to write the history of broadcasting was to write the history of everything else. 'This is particularly true of Wales', Davies (1994: ix) argues, 'where, to a greater extent than perhaps in any other country in Europe, broadcasting has played a central role, both positive and negative, in the development of the concept of a national community'. This view has taken root in Welsh historiography. As Aled Jones (1993: 3) states: 'The belief that forms of communication materially affect both social consciousness and behaviour remains deeply rooted in the political culture as well as in the historiography of Wales'. He goes on to argue that the mobilization of opinion which led to the establishment of S4C (the Welsh language channel launched in November 1982) 'rested on a collectively held assumption that a medium of communication...could play a major part in rescuing the Welsh language from its precipitous decline'.

It is clear from the cultural, political and educational groups and institutions that engaged in broadcasting politics in the 1950s and 1960s that the shared assumption was that television was an influential medium. This can be seen in the evidence submitted to the two key committees of enquiry appointed to consider the future of broadcasting in the UK in 1949 (Beveridge Committee) and 1960 (Pilkington Committee) (Medhurst 2004). The main line of argument was that, in order for the Welsh language and culture to survive, a television service for Wales would be a prerequisite. For example, the memorandum submitted by Undeb Cymru Fydd to the Beveridge Committee was unequivocal in its aim and was headed 'Statement in favour of an independent broadcasting corporation of Wales'. The submission underlined the perceived deleterious effects of broadcasting on the life of the Welsh nation and noted with grave concern that 'the general effect of broadcasting in Wales as now organised by the Corporation is to undermine both the language and culture of the Welsh people, and indeed their whole way of life' (Report of the Broadcasting Committee 1949: 423). During the Pilkington Committee's gathering of evidence, one of the strongest statements relating to the relationship between television and national identity was that from the University of Wales (which had played an instrumental role in the 1930s campaign for a separate Welsh Home Service). Having established its role in Wales as one of conserving, interpreting and promoting a range of activities, thought and modes of expression of Welshness, the University went on to state that:

The few years that have elapsed since the introduction of television have made it abundantly clear that the grievously inadequate space and time given to programmes of a Welsh character, whether in Welsh or in English, under the existing unsatisfactory arrangements must have disastrous consequences for the future survival of the national culture and for the distinctive contributions that Wales can make to the common stock. This view may perhaps seem exaggerated to those whose language and culture are completely secure, but we who are concerned with the survival of a separate culture…are only too convinced of its truth…[M]any of the most vigorous elements in contemporary Welsh culture lie under a grave threat of extinction.

Report of the Committee on Broadcasting (1960: 959)

The fact is that radio and television were politicized from the outset. Both media were caught up in issues of language, culture and identity. The reason for this is that, from the perspective of the Welsh language – and the fiercest debate in Wales has been over issues of the Welsh language and culture – radio and television have been considered both a threat and an opportunity. From the 1930s onwards, Welsh journals and newspapers resonate with concerns over the influx of Anglo-centric and English language programmes into Welsh homes. Writing in the Plaid Cymru newsletter, *Y Ddraig Goch* ('The Red Dragon'), at the time, one author stated: 'The majority of the material broadcast is alien to our traditions, damaging to our culture, and is a grave danger to everything special in our civilization'.[1] Pressure was placed upon the BBC to recognize Wales as a nation with its own unique linguistic and cultural heritage. At the same time, the *opportunity* which the media provided resonated with other aspects of Welsh activity in the spheres of educational and cultural activity such as publishing. As Ned Thomas (1995: 176) has noted:

Territorial linguistic minorities…experience the erosion on their territory of a life that was normal in that language; they tend to regard media and an education system in their own languages not just as cultural support for individuals but as ways of re-establishing linguistic normality…

Thomas goes on to argue that a language that does not have access to the media is 'doomed, as the media are an extension of people speaking to each other' (Thomas 1995: 179). It is for this reason, for example, that the first Welsh language daily newspaper, *Y Byd* ('The World'), is being launched in March 2008. Likewise, Michelle Ryan (1986: 185) argued that the driving force behind the campaign to establish a Welsh language television channel in the 1970s was an awareness that the key to the survival of the Welsh language and culture was a communications network that would provide a more cohesive identity to the language.

Similarities may, of course, be drawn with other nations. The history of broadcasting in Ireland bears a number of similarities to the Welsh situation. Given that identity is an artefact and not a natural phenomenon, the broadcast media of both nations have played (and continue to play) a role in the formation and maintenance of a collective sense of belonging. Indeed, John Davies has gone so far as to state that Wales is an artefact created by the broadcast media. Both nations have faced the issue of linguistic and cultural tensions of bilingualism, although the Welsh language has, for a number of years, been in a much stronger position than its Irish counterpart. The major difference is that Ireland is a nation-state while Wales is a stateless nation, its native language and culture being dependent on the support of the British state (even in an increasing age of political devolution).

Writing on television in Wales

This section considers the discussion of the development of television in Wales within a selection of histories of Wales, broadcasting histories and histories of the Welsh media. In particular, the history of the failed Teledu Cymru venture will act as a focal point.

Kenneth O. Morgan's detailed volume on the history of Wales between 1880 and 1980, *Rebirth of a Nation*, locates broadcasting in Wales within a tradition of perceived threat. He described the growth of sound broadcasting in Wales (tied as it was to the west of England) as a 'source for concern' (Morgan 1981: 251). He also argued that pressure from the University of Wales Committee on Broadcasting eventually resulted in a separate service for Wales and that, by the time of the Second World War, 'the influence of sound broadcasting as a medium for injecting new life into the Welsh language world was being more widely recognized' (Morgan 1981: 251). Morgan locates debates over broadcasting within a framework of cultural and linguistic tensions and issues relating to a wider Welsh identity at this time.

John Davies' *Hanes Cymru: A History of Wales in Welsh*, published in 1990, locates broadcasting (and the BBC in particular) clearly within a tradition of linguistic and cultural conflict with London, a theme that he developed four years later in his study of the history of the BBC in Wales. He refers to the reaction to the declaration in 1927 of the Cardiff station director, E. R. Appleton – that to foist the Welsh language upon listeners would be to yield to the demands of the extremists – as 'one of the most important battles in the history of the language' (Davies 1990: 542). Debates over broadcasting are also placed in a wider context of linguistic and cultural decline and, at the same time, there is a clear view that broadcasting has a role to play in the formation of a national identity for Wales. For example, the establishment of the Welsh region of the BBC on 4 July 1937 is portrayed as an important concession to nationalist sentiment on a par with the disestablishment of the Church of Wales in 1920 and the formation of the Council for Wales and

Monmouthshire in 1948 (Davies 1990: 567). The advent of commercial television in Wales is set firmly within a context of the rise of affluence and mass consumerism. Although there is a reference to the impact of television on the traditional pastimes of rural Wales (drama clubs, whist drives, choral activities, *eisteddfodau*), Davies (1990: 612) also warns against oversentimentality, noting that there is evidence to suggest that such activities did in fact witness a 'comeback' once the initial enthusiasm for ITV had waned.

Dai Smith's account of Welsh history which, according to his 1999 work on the culture and politics of the country, has 'a History that has gone pear-shaped' (Smith 1999: 9), does feature broadcasting although he takes a stance which is opposite to that taken by Davies. Whereas the emphasis in Davies' work on the history of Wales places broadcasting within the framework of linguistic struggle, Smith (1999: 35) argues that '[B]roadcasting in Wales will increasingly have to stress the achievements and tradition of the majority experience in twentieth-century Wales in the language of that majority, the English tongue that has become our principal Welsh means of communication'. Referring to Plaid Cymru sentiment in the 1960s, he writes that the notion of regaining a 'lost world' was central to the whole cultural nationalist project of the time:

[T]he Anglicisation of Wales was an avoidable disaster, the industrialisation of Wales had deracinated the native Welsh, mixed them into an anonymous conglomerate of 'half people' and effectively dehumanised them. They, and Wales, could only be saved by the restoration of 'Welsh' values through the vehicle of the language

Smith (1999: 44)

It was this belief that underlay the project that was Teledu Cymru, although it clearly was not a venture driven solely by Plaid Cymru, but by other cultural groups such as Undeb Cymru Fydd (the New Wales Union) and Urdd Gobaith Cymru (the Welsh League of Youth) and supported by the Welsh language press. In relation to the language, Smith (1999: 46) denigrates those historians whose 'insistence on a culture-based politics…saw language not merely as a mode of communication but as the essential underpinning of a social order'.

In one of the most recent works on Welsh history, Gareth Evans' *A History of Wales 1906–2000*, broadcasting is, again, treated within a broad context of national identity. The author notes that, until the establishment of BBC Wales in 1964, 'television output in Wales was largely similar to England's' (Evans 2000: 276). However, although the BBC certainly increased its hours in terms of Welsh language and Welsh-interest programming, Evans does not take into account the new and relatively innovative programmes pioneered by TWW that were aimed at the Welsh audience, for example Myfanwy Howells in the magazine programme *Amser Te* and the Welsh language game shows hosted by Wyn Roberts.

In terms of *television* history, the work of Asa Briggs is noted (Briggs 1961–95). The five-volume history of British broadcasting has been the cornerstone of historical research in this area for many years. Indeed, John Davies' history of the BBC in Wales follows much the same pattern in stylistic terms and in many respects can be considered a sister volume of the larger work. In the context of this chapter, the fourth and fifth volumes are the most relevant. Briggs clearly demonstrates an understanding of the complexity of the relationship between broadcasting and the cultural politics in Wales (and indeed Scotland). Wales is not positioned so much as a 'problem' but as an issue to be addressed with needs that required answers. There is an awareness that broadcasting *mattered* to the BBC in Wales and Briggs' judgements are based on meticulous archival research, although the level of detail from the Welsh perspective comes more to the fore in Davies' later work on the BBC in Wales. There is no mention of ITV in Wales or Teledu Cymru in Briggs, despite the fact that the BBC and Teledu Cymru were in discussion on several occasions over the possible sharing of transmitters and programmes.[2]

In 1982, Bernard Sendall published the first of what was to become six volumes covering the history of independent television in the UK. The first volume focused on the origin and foundations of ITV between 1946 and 1962, while the second volume, published in 1983, covered the period 1958–68, a period defined by the author as 'expansion and change' (Sendall 1983). What emerges from Sendall's history of the first decade of ITV is first an indication of the willingness on the part of the Authority to address the specific linguistic and cultural needs of Wales and, second, an awareness within the Authority of the complexity (in political, linguistic, cultural and geographical terms) of achieving this. 'The rightness of establishing national companies outside England was…even more patent in the case of Wales with its live spoken language and cultural tradition' notes Sendall. 'Yet nature had made the job much more difficult' (Sendall 1983: 70). Sendall's work on Teledu Cymru locates the company firmly within a framework of a cultural project that was hit by a series of setbacks and disappointments.

In 1998, Kevin Williams published his account of the historical development of the mass media in the UK. It offers a broad historical sweep from the beginning of the printed word through to the development of the new media. Given Williams' background as an academic at Cardiff University and, more recently, as Professor of Media Studies at Swansea University, Wales is afforded a more prominent position in his work than in the work of others. Williams' interpretation differs from that of Sendall as he argues that, while the ITV regions may have made economic sense, they did not make cultural sense. As such, Williams notes, the commitment to cultural identity in the establishing of the ITV network was limited. Williams goes on to explain the failure of the company by citing the fact that Granada was already broadcasting to North Wales and that the TWW area covered part of the

Teledu Cymru south-west Wales area. He also points to 'technical problems' that hampered progress (Williams 1998: 163). Although these go some way to explain why Teledu Cymru failed and, in this respect, reflect the explanation offered by Sendall, they are only two of a number of complex factors.

The most detailed work on Welsh broadcasting to emerge in recent times was that by John Davies, *Broadcasting and the BBC in Wales*, in 1994. The focus of the work was the BBC, with commercial television companies in Wales taking a minor or supporting role. This, of course, is understandable. The BBC is one of the largest and most recognized broadcasters worldwide and has been broadcasting on a regular basis since 1922, first via radio, then from 1936 through the medium of television and, more recently, online. Commercial television, on the other hand, is a relative newcomer, with the first station broadcasting in September 1955. Its growth was slower than that of the BBC, and it took until 1962 to complete the network across the UK. Once it had arrived, however, its impact was considerable.

Davies clearly locates himself in the tradition that sees broadcasting (and television in particular) as being central to the creation of a national consciousness and identity. In this respect, he echoes Aneirin Talfan Davies' argument that broadcasting in Wales needs to be seen as a 'battle for the nation's rights' (Davies 1972) and Michelle Ryan's (1986: 185) assertion that '[t]elevision in Wales has been defined as one of the key areas in the struggle for a national identity'. Television (in particular public service television) is seen by Davies as a key site for the creation of a Welsh identity, and so his work sits alongside the work undertaken on Ireland (see, for example, Barbrook 1992). ITV in Wales is given consideration in the chapter on the period 1952–64, which deals with the era of the fourth BBC charter (1952–64). Possibly because Davies did not consult ITA primary source material (relying solely on the BBC Wales Record Centre and the BBC's Written Archives at Caversham), ITV is examined solely in the light of the impact on the BBC in Wales.

The only major piece of academic work on Teledu Cymru is that by Ifan Gwynfil Evans (Evans 1997a). His thesis argues in favour of the centrality of television to the cultural politics of Wales during the 1950s and 1960s and follows in the steps of historians such as Davies, politicians such as Gwynfor Evans and cultural commentators such as Emyr Humphreys in arguing that television has played a dominant role in the formation and alteration of the national culture.

The strength of Evans' thesis is his attention to historical contextualization of the company and the framing of its history within the political, social and cultural life of Wales in the 1950 and 1960s. It is a detailed historical study matched by rigorous attention to the sources consulted. The central conclusion of the thesis is that Teledu Cymru failed because of financial difficulties – from the outset, it was never a viable proposition. The reason for the financial failure is laid clearly at the feet of the Board of Directors and the Chairman of the Board, Haydn Williams, in particular. 'He was…the most determinedly optimistic member of the Board of Directors, in which capacity he continually failed to predict the difficulties which would face his company, and consistently overestimated advertising revenues' (Evans 1997a: 28). He also criticizes the directors as a whole for their idealism and 'an optimism born of an almost complete ignorance of the realities of independent television broadcasting' (ibid.).

One of the main issues arising out of Evans' thesis is the nature of the sources used. The main secondary sources consulted – Sendall, Briggs, Davies and Butt Philip – have provided him with a sound foundation, as have the contemporary newspaper and journal sources. In terms of primary sources, the papers of Jac L. Williams in the National Library of Wales (for papers on the National Television Conferences) and Emrys Roberts in the National Library (which contain the minutes of the Teledu Cymru Board of Directors) were used, as was the archive of Plaid Cymru. By his own admission, however, Evans (for reasons outside his control) was unable to consult the Undeb Cymru Fydd archive at the National Library of Wales. Furthermore, Evans did not consult the BBC's archival material or ITA material held at the Independent Television Commission. As such, the study is restricted in its ability to create a full picture; the intricacies of debates are illuminated when access has been made possible to a wide range of sources. Despite these gaps, Evans' thesis is a detailed historical account of the company. It draws on a range of sources and relates the company to wider issues surrounding nationalism, identity and contemporary politics.

Those who have written on the history of broadcasting in Wales have tended to see the rise and fall of Teledu Cymru as being essentially a failed nationalist enterprise and stress the role of nationalist (political and cultural) pressure groups in the formation and demise of the company. Butt Philip (1975) and Evans (1997b) both stress the nationalist pressure group influence on the project, although Evans is the only writer to provide any detail on the exact roles played. John Davies points to the failings of this form of nationalism to encompass south Wales (Davies 1994: 230), while Dai Smith (1999: 44, 46) underlines the failings of the rural language-based model which excludes the industrial south-east. Sendall (1983: 76) also accounts for the failure of Teledu Cymru in terms of the 'impetuous excess of zeal…common to men who are convinced of the rightness of their cause'. These writers, therefore, express the foundation and failure of the company in terms of the nationalist politics of the period, but all, apart from Evans, fail to provide empirical support for their arguments.

Conclusions

The histories of television in Wales fall within what Curran calls the 'anthropological narrative' of media history, and this, I would argue, for four reasons.

First, in his assessment of the anthropological narrative, Curran (2002a: 26) draws upon Benedict Anderson's notions of the nation and national identity. Two key arguments are highlighted: the nation as a cultural construct and the role of the media in the construction of national identity. The historiography of the broadcast media – and television in particular – has highlighted the centrality of these media in the creation and maintenance of a Welsh national consciousness and identity. As Aled Jones (1993: 237–38) has noted:

> ...some of the general assumptions regarding the functions of media in society and political life were also carried over from nineteenth-century newspapers to twentieth-century broadcasting. Among them was the idea that, if employed in the right way, forms of communication could help maintain a sense of nationhood and protect the integrity of the Welsh language.

Second, the anthropological narrative tends to present a British identity as a construct and yet, argues Curran (2002a: 32), it should not be inferred that the rival Celtic nations were any more organic or unified. Indeed, what is often overlooked in narratives of Welsh media history is the lack of consensus and unity in Wales with regard to media development. There are several factors for this, not least the divide that existed (and continues to exist) between north and south Wales and between the predominantly Anglicized areas of the east relative to the Welsh-speaking areas of the west. These divisions came to the fore in the history of Teledu Cymru where many north Walians affiliated themselves more closely with Manchester than with Cardiff for historical economic and geographical reasons (e.g. trade and transport links) and therefore had little time for a separate Welsh television service.

Third, Curran (2002a: 30) argues that, by the 1960s, Britain was in a period of 'newness and modernity'. What emerges from the historiography of television in Wales is that this newness and modernity resulted in the Welsh cultural elite adopting a dual stance in relation to the medium. This reflected not only a desire to withstand 'alien' influences that would perceivably damage the so-called 'Welsh way of life' but also a realization that the new medium of television should be 'harnessed' for the good of the nation.

Finally, Curran (2002a: 33) argues that the anthropological narrative 'unmasks the ideologies of nationalism'. Certainly, from the historical writing on Teledu Cymru, this can be verified. My own work has shown that viewing the venture through a narrow nationalist prism gave a distorted picture, and the wider complexities of interactions with the British state and the broadcasting regulatory bodies had to be factored into the account of the company's demise (Medhurst 2005). Furthermore, television, from the outset, has been one of the key focal points for debates surrounding national identity and national consciousness in the 'awkward area' of Wales. In an age of increasing globalization, the arguments are unlikely to abate.

Notes

1 'Gorchfygwn y BBC', *Y Ddraig Goch*, February 1932, p. 2.
2 See, for example, BBC W(ritten) A(rchive) C(entre) R34/1144 – 'Should the BBC share a transmitter with W.W.N.', 1 October 1962.

Chapter 11

'Nation shall speak peace unto nation'

The BBC and the projection of a new Britain, 1967–82

Daniel Day

Introduction

The crest of the British Broadcasting Corporation bears the motto 'Nation shall speak peace unto nation'. Inscribed not only upon its coat of arms but also above the entrance doors of Bush House in central London, the headquarters of the World Service, the inscription stands as an enduring reminder of the potential of mass communication in acting as a forum to facilitate international co-operation and understanding. Yet the phrase, first devised in 1927 by Dr Montague Rendell, one of the Corporation's first governors, had by the late 1960s come to take on a quite different connotation when applied to the BBC's domestic broadcasting. No longer simply an expression of BBC internationalism, the maxim became an effective rhetorical device, used in irony by a range of journalists, organizations and pressure groups who believed the BBC was failing in its duty to provide representative programming to all parts of the United Kingdom. It seemed to many that, within the British broadcasting system, the English voice and, more specifically, a London-centric one was being heard loud and clear. In contrast, Scotland and Wales appeared to have all but lost theirs.

A cartoon published in the Welsh journal *Planet* in October 1970 summed up this sense of grievance neatly. Standing in front of a range of hills atop of which were situated transmitters beaming broadcasts into the valley below, one perplexed looking Welshman turned to another to ask 'What do you mean "Nation shall Speak unto Nation?" That's what we've got isn't it?' The cartoon was emblematic of a recurring criticism made of the corporation throughout the twentieth century, namely that, despite its public service ethos, the BBC had a poor record in representing Britain's cultural diversities and minority tastes. More recently, Glen Creeber has argued that, throughout its history, the BBC has presented a very narrow view of the nation, based on a limited range of values and attitudes. As a consequence, it is 'responsible for producing a form of cultural hegemony that has helped to dictate and form British public opinion and social attitudes' (Creeber 2004a: 28–29). Indeed, such was the culturally conforming power of the Corporation, he contends, that the BBC brand, or '*Publicservicization*', should be allied with the concepts of *Coca-Colonization* and *McDonaldization* because of its culturally homogenizing force.

This chapter takes a different approach. It seeks to show that, far from simply acting as a catalyst for a common culture, the BBC also played a significant role in maintaining and fostering distinct identities in what the historian Hugh Kearney has labelled as 'Outer Britain'. By presenting an overview of various key developments in Scottish broadcasting, as well as reference to Wales, I want to demonstrate how, from the late 1960s onwards, the BBC sought to reconceive its role as the 'national' broadcaster, making a concerted effort for the first time since the 1920s to develop and expand upon a range of programmes and services designed to appeal specifically to audiences at a 'regional' and local level, thus offering a much more plural 'projection of Britain'. In doing so, it seeks to move beyond narrow 'culturally imperialist' accounts that privilege a narrative of the BBC as imposing 'English' culture on an unwilling audience in Britain's 'Celtic fringe'. Not only were audience responses invariably much more complex, but this approach belittles the significant contribution made by the Corporation to Scottish and Welsh culture, especially in the decades after the Second World War. From this vantage point, the BBC can be seen to have played a significant role in sustaining identities at multiple levels across the United Kingdom rather than simply moulding a homogeneous Britishness. Neither Britishness nor the BBC's projection of it, as we shall see, remained static across the decades.

The BBC and Britishness

Since its establishment as the British Broadcasting Corporation in 1927, the history of broadcasting, as John Tulloch (1990: 141) notes, 'has essentially been the history of a debate about the composition and maintenance of the British nation state'. Over the course of the twentieth century, this debate has taken on a variety of forms as the BBC has been forced to reinvent itself in the light of often rapid social, political and cultural change. Innovative programming of the 1960s, such as 'kitchen sink' dramas like *Cathy Come Home* or the groundbreaking satire of *That Was the Week That Was*, are frequently cited as exemplifying a time when the Corporation was at the forefront of societal trends (Tulloch 1990; Weight 2002; Creeber 2004b; Sandbrook 2005) On the other hand, however, the longevity of *The Black and White Minstrel Show*, a programme in which performers 'blacked up' to sing and dance in stereotypical portrayals of black people, is alluded to as evidence of the BBC's failure to engage changing notions of Britishness. As one historian put it, the programme, like much of British popular culture of the period, 'reflected a country which had not accepted the physical portrayal of black people, never mind come to terms with the need to alter its national identity' (Weight 2002: 428). Indeed, in this instance, the BBC can be seen as simply reflecting societal prejudices rather than challenging them. Although the programme eventually became an anathema in an ever more multiracial society and was finally taken off the air in 1978, the fact that it attracted an audience of up to 18 million viewers, as well as hundreds of protest letters on its demise, exemplified the difficulties faced by the broadcaster when mediating between the values of different sections of society (Briggs 1995: 433–34; BBC WAC R78/1921).

Despite such differences, however, the BBC has been central to constructing a unified notion of Britishness throughout the twentieth century. Krishnan Kumar (2003: 237) labels the Corporation as being 'surely the most pervasive force' shaping British identity in this period, while as Monroe Price (1995: 16) reminds us, 'dominant broadcasters like dominant religions set forth the framework of national identity...supporting it with a set of moral precepts, providing a history and vision for the future'. This vision was articulated most forcefully in the philosophy of the BBC's first Director-General John Reith. Imbued with a strong sense of religiosity and moral purpose, Reith viewed broadcasting as a means of bettering society through a process of cultural and spiritual uplift. From 1930 when the National programme was first established, the listening public were afforded a single service that bound them together as a common audience in a process both more intimate and immediate than that of the mass newspaper reading publics of the early twentieth century.

Early radio broadcasting was imbued with the principles of democratizing culture, of bringing what was deemed to be the best of metropolitan life, through live programming of, among other things, theatre and music, as well as the production of a range of talks and actualities, to a previously excluded public. In doing so, it aimed to 'raise the level of taste, information and understanding and so make all members of society more actively responsive to and more responsible for, the nation's culture and politics' (Cardiff and Scannell 1987: 158). To make, as Reith put it in an oft-quoted phrase, 'the nation as one man'. As an institutional mindset, it was a philosophy that would dominate the ethos of the Corporation for at least a generation after his departure as Director-General in 1938. As Tom Burns' (1977: 42) seminal sociological study of the BBC in the 1960s and 1970s put it:

> The BBC was developed under Reith into a kind of domestic diplomatic service, representing the British, or what he saw as the best of the British – to the British. BBC culture like BBC standard English, was not peculiar to itself but an intellectual ambience composed out of the values, standards and beliefs of the professional middle class, especially that part educated at Oxford and Cambridge. Sports, popular music and entertainment that appealed to the lower classes were included in large measure; but the manner in which they were purveyed, the context and the presentation, remained indomitably middle class.

'Representing the best of the British' also included the relaying of the great occasions of nation and state. Despite initial reluctance from Buckingham

Palace, royal occasions were closely followed, with the speech by George V at the opening of the Wembley Empire Exhibition in 1924 the first to be broadcast. From then on, the BBC became a 'vigorous promoter of the state ceremonial' (Samuel 1998: 183). It acted, with the start of outside broadcasting in 1927, as a witness to national events such as the State opening of parliament and Remembrance Sunday, as commentator on sporting occasions such as Wimbledon, the FA Cup Final, the Boat Race and the Grand National, a celebrator of Christmas, Easter and other religious festivals as well as an instigator, as with the monarch's Christmas message, of annual broadcast traditions. As Scannell and Cardiff (1987) note, the 'programmes of national identity' were 'set apart' from the rest. Not only were they imbued with a 'sacred' dimension, but their 'ritualistic regularity' brought a sense of order to the randomness of the early schedules.

Yet within this homogenizing role, there also existed a diversity of sorts with the gradual implementation of a 'Regional programme' from 1930 onwards. Although the function of radio remained fundamentally that of a national medium, the development of the 'Regional scheme' allowed for a distinct, if albeit limited, arena in which to reflect the country's cultural diversities. This was not, however, the scheme's original purpose. Rather, its origins lay in Reith's overall policy of the centralization and standardization of broadcasting structures and with its enactment came the elimination of the nineteen localized stations that had operated under the auspices of the British Broadcasting Company in its embryonic years (see Briggs 1965; Scannell 1993). Indeed, as Briggs notes, in England at least, the regions were not developed along recognized historic, geographical or cultural delineations but rather were divided into the three huge regions of North, Midland and West based on 'engineering practicalities' (Briggs 1995: 623). Hence, Wales was joined in a rather unhappy 'marriage of convenience' with the West region until 1937 in what the Region's director E. R. Appelton rather improbably claimed was an attempt to reunite 'the Kingdom of Arthur after centuries of separation by the Bristol Channel' (*BBC Yearbook 1934*: 189).

The establishment of six regional stations, including those that covered Scotland, Wales and Northern Ireland, laid the initial foundations for the development of the BBC's regional services across the twentieth century. In the interwar years, they contributed both to the limited diversity that existed within BBC broadcasting as well as to its unifying impulses, with their programming often playing a central role in many of the great ceremonies of state. Take for example the 'Coronation week' leading up to the investiture of George VI in 1937 when Wales, Scotland and Northern Ireland all produced special celebratory programmes to mark the occasion. Northern Ireland relayed an 'all British variety show' from Belfast; a children's programme in Wales elided the greatness of the future King with Bendigeidvran, a hero of Welsh folklore; while programming in Scotland included a talk on the Scottish roots of the new Queen (Hajkowski 2005).

Although regional broadcasting did enjoy something of a renaissance in the late 1930s, the outbreak of the Second World War resulted in the closure of the Regional scheme until the end of hostilities. The development of television from the early 1950s followed similar centralizing tendencies to those of prewar radio, although there were gradual concessions to the regionalist cause with the establishment of television centres across the country ostensibly for news and current affairs. In addition, the opening of Network Production Centres in Bristol, Manchester and Birmingham initiated a broader decentralizing tendency away from London – a process continuing intermittently to the present day. In part, these developments can be seen as a response to the Beveridge Report of 1949 which, among other things, criticized the excessive 'Londonization' of the Corporation. Indeed, a direct consequence was the establishment in 1952 of National Broadcasting Councils for Scotland and Wales, which were granted responsibility for the policy and content of programmes produced in their respective areas. The arrival of ITV in 1955 also played its part. Its federal structures stood in marked contrast to the highly centralized BBC, although the extent to which this directly impacted upon the balance of national and regional programming produced by the Corporation is difficult to assess (see Turnock 2005).

It was changing political dynamics, however, that acted as the major catalyst for change. From the mid-1960s onwards, the rise of previously latent political nationalisms in both Scotland and Wales not only threatened to undermine the postwar political consensus but also presented a fundamental challenge to the BBC. Although cultural nationalist groups such as the Saltire Society and Cwm Deri had as far back as the 1920s campaigned for better programming, the electoral success of the Scottish National Party (SNP), first in a by-election in 1967, and then at the general elections of 1970 and 1974, transformed the political paradigm.[1] Although the nationalists never gained a majority in either Scotland or Wales, their presence shifted the parameters of debate and, throughout the 1970s, broadcasting officials conducted their work in anticipation, at the very least, of a new Scottish Assembly in Edinburgh and the devolution of power and responsibility that would entail.

Thus, with the growth of Celtic nationalisms and the prospect of a new constitutional settlement, there was much soul searching about the 'regional' nature of the BBC. In January 1965 in a BBC *Lunchtime Lecture*, the then Head of Programmes Wales, Hywel Davies, had outlined his vision of the role of the regions in British broadcasting. 'The things we are broadly concerned with', he stated, 'are the frustration, the satisfaction and resentment, the inspiration and vanity of those who are not at the seeming heart of things. We are concerned with the joys and tribulations of being off-centre' (Davies 1965: 3). It was in many ways a surprisingly metropolitan view and one that, within a decade, had become somewhat obsolete. Scotland and Wales were no longer content with being 'off centre'. They were now firmly centre stage.

Scottishness on screen

In an article published in 1970 entitled *The Backwardness of Scottish Television*, Stuart Hood, a former BBC programme controller, offered a forthright critique of the nature of programming produced in Scotland. A Scot himself, his criticism was not so much focused on the structures of broadcasting but more on the insular vision of those who had previously worked for the BBC in Queen Margaret Drive in Glasgow[2] and, in particular, their subservience to Scotland's political and religious elite. As a consequence, they were often ill-equipped to deal with the broader changes taking place in Scottish society. As the Annan Committee reported in 1977:

> Something is wrong with the image of Scotland which television projects to the rest of the United Kingdom. The national culture is reflected too much by hackneyed symbols, and too little importance is given to the new opportunities and hopes, the shifts in pattern of industry and occu-pation, as well as the dour problems and grim realities of life in some parts of Scotland today.
>
> Annan Committee (1977: 409)

The first steps in reshaping the output of BBC Scotland had been taken ten years earlier with the appointment of Alasdair Milne as Controller in 1967. His predecessor, Andrew Stewart, had first joined the BBC in 1926, which meant that, when compared with Milne, he was not simply from a different generation but from a different broadcasting era all together. With most of his experience gained in the radio age, there was reluctance from many executives in London to substantially expand the scope of BBC Scotland's television output. A substantial outlay of resources on the new and expensive medium needed a Controller who enjoyed the confidence of the centre. Stewart was not that man. Thus, Milne's appointment represented more than simply a break with the past; his arrival brought brand new horizons to the Scottish broadcasting landscape, something unthinkable when compared with the 'puritanical parochialism' that had effectively become the Corporation's insti-tutional mindset north of the border (Harvie 1982: 128).

At the age of just thirty-eight, Milne became the youngest Regional Controller in the history of the BBC. But with him he brought experience unparalleled on the Scottish scene, especially in television production. Although he may not quite have been the 'tiger at the gates', as the *Glasgow Herald* described him, he was certainly a very different type of Controller compared with those who had preceded him. Indeed, it would not be unfair to state that a certain degree of paralysis in terms of broadcast/programme innovation had been reached before his arrival. Milne's entrance heralded a very different way of doing things, bringing with it a new culture of pro-fessionalism and a new mindset that sought to modernize the dominant Reithian image that was still very much in the ascendancy. Having worked previously in London on the groundbreaking current affairs programme *Tonight* as well as on *That Was The Week That Was*, he brought with him expertise in the latest television techniques as well as a proven track record of working on some of the Corporation's most cutting edge programmes. It was during his tenure that Scottish television developed for the first time into a truly professional service and engaged with subjects, most notably Scottish nationalism, which had previously only been addressed in a very peripheral manner. Indeed, one of his first actions – the decision to add the word Scotland to the letters BBC that were adorned upon the side of the Corporation's headquarters in Glasgow – although superficial, was also symbolic of a broader desire to highlight the fact that the BBC was not simply broadcasting to Scotland but was itself part and parcel of Scottish life.[3]

This was to be reflected in BBC Scotland's two central remits. The first was to produce programming about Scotland to a Scottish audience, with the second to reflect Scottish distinctiveness in network programming, i.e. on BBC One, BBC Two as well as Radio 4, which were transmitted across the whole of the United Kingdom. Reflecting Scotland both to itself and to a broader British audience were on the face of it complimentary goals, yet the latter was dependent both upon the outlook of controllers in London and on their willingness to finance and commission any substantial projects with funding drawn in large part from their own network budgets. Indeed, according to Tony Whitby, the perspectives of London-based staff often struggled to reach beyond the Watford Gap. As he noted in a memo, 'it is notorious that most producers and programme executives are more familiar with the Costa Brava than with Birmingham and Manchester, let alone Cardiff and Glasgow' (quoted in Hendy 2007: 120). Having worked in London in the formative years of his career, Milne was in a strong position to negotiate programmes for the network, but it was a process that was fundamentally dependent upon a strong individual rapport between Regional and Network Controller and one that necessitated Scottish culture to be viewed through a London-centric, or at the very least British-oriented, perspective.

In many ways, this was the root cause of the Annan Committee's criticism cited earlier. Throughout the 1960s and well into the 1970s, a central function of networked Scottish programming was, according to one former BBC executive I interviewed, to provide 'Light Entertainment for Britain'.[4] Programmes such as *The White Heather Club* and *The Kilt is My Delight* typified the tartan-clad imagery and music hall tradition of many of the most popular Scottish-originated series transmitted throughout the UK. With the addition of programmes such as *Dr Finlay's Casebook*, which remained on air until 1970 and presented a romanticized view of the work of an interwar rural medical surgery, these programmes provided the staple fare of Scottish-orientated output produced for the networks. As one columnist writing for *The Scotsman* in 1976 noted, the association of this particular version of Scottishness with the BBC proved difficult to shake off in both its Scottish and British-oriented productions.

> In the past week we have had several doses of the Kenneth McKellar brand of 'folk song', sheep dog trials, and 'Matter of Opinion' courtesy of the Women's rural institute of Ballater…The result is a programme better suited to expatriates in need of gentle reminders of the old country, than a changing, challenging Scotland…Considering the severe economic restrictions imposed on the BBC it seems bad budgeting to spend so much of Scotland's broadcasting time on music and a limited, repetitive diet at that. Can you imagine 'BBC England' cheerfully grinding away at 'Hearts of Oak' and 'Land of Hope and Glory?' BBC Scotland often seems not much more than the BBC with tartan frills.[5]

Yet though there were many shortcomings, it would be unfair to label the output of BBC Scotland in the 1970s as simply being that of the BBC with 'tartan frills'. From the controllership of Milne onwards, there were a number of important innovations that, combined with constant internal and external political pressures, resulted in ever more diverse representations of Scottish life. Indeed, in addition to an expanding news and current affairs service, programmes such as *Who are the SNP?* and *Lilybank*, an undercover exposé of the extent of poverty in Glasgow's East End, were some of the most prominent television documentaries dealing with contemporary Scottish issues. This was an area of output that expanded greatly in the latter half of the 1970s, most markedly under the guidance of Alastair Hetherington who became Scottish Controller in December 1975. Having worked as editor of *The Guardian* for more than twenty years, his appointment to what was in effect a middle-ranking BBC post was not simply testament to a desire on his part to return to Scotland, but also to the importance the BBC placed on finding an appropriate figurehead for Scottish broadcasting in an era of great political uncertainty.

Drama production also offered a greater diversity of representation. Although tending more towards the adaptation of literary classics rather than contemporary works, the groundbreaking production of *Sunset Song* in 1971, for example, showed that gritty realism, in this instance in the hardship of life in an early twentieth-century crofting community, was not prone to romanticism. This is not to say that television shied away from controversial contemporary issues, but much of the most groundbreaking work of the period about Scotland was edited in London rather than Glasgow. Most prominent among these was *Just Another Saturday* about Protestantism and Orange order marches in Glasgow and *The Cheviot, The Stag and The Black, Black Oil* by John McGrath, which followed in the tradition of a long line of radical plays that featured in the BBC's *Play for Today*. Focusing upon English 'exploitation' of the Highlands, from the Highland clearances to the discovery of North Sea Oil, *The Cheviot, The Stag and The Black, Black Oil* was adapted from a successful touring production by the 7:84 Theatre Company. As Les Cooke (2003: 110) argues, it was 'unique within the history of British television drama…politically, with its radical socialist agenda, it is a product of its time, a period when such an "extreme" play could not only get made within the BBC but could be screened at primetime on BBC One'. The audience may not have cared that it was produced in London rather than Glasgow but, to those within the Corporation who called for greater devolution of responsibility, it was a prime example of a programme that should have been made by BBC Scotland (Hetherington 1992).

An additional point to note in the production of Scottish programmes, however, was that a combined lack of resources and the problem of scheduling programmes for a Scottish audience, which in television could only be provided at the expense of rather than in addition to network programmes, often raised considerable tensions about what should be shown and when (McDowell 1992: 212–13). Although the situation was by no means as severe as that in Wales, where schedulers had to deal with the problem of a linguistic divide, the response of the Scottish audience showed that a significant number of viewers would be happy to forgo Scottish 'opt outs' altogether. Indeed, a survey conducted in 1976 concluded that the public thought programming produced by BBC Scotland was 'less professional, less experimental and less controversial' than that broadcast across the rest of Britain (ibid.: 213). Thus, somewhat paradoxically, although the rhetoric for more Scottish-oriented programming increased sharply in these years, large sections of the audience remained happy with the status quo.

It was radio, however, that presented the greatest opportunity for providing a truly distinctive Scottish service. Unlike in television, where programmes formed part of a broader UK-wide schedule, the decision to launch separate radio stations for Scotland, Wales and Northern Ireland in November 1978 presented for the first time the opportunity to move beyond simply producing individual programmes. As John Gray, the chief assistant of radio in Scotland noted, this meant 'the freedom to plan a service, to place (programmes) at times and durations determined solely by policy and editorial decisions made in Scotland for a Scottish audience'. He continued, 'this is more important than the actual quantity of origination. A service operating as an "opt out" from another channel, however sympathetic and understanding the planners of that channel may be, and however autonomous in the use of its resource Scotland may be, can never become a Scottish service' (BBC WAC SC1/71/1).

Yet Radio Scotland was a service that the listening public by and large failed to fully engage with. Despite attempting to offer a mix of genres to appeal to as broad an audience as possible, listening figures showed that the station struggled to maintain a 10 per cent share in its early years, often falling to just over 5 per cent in the mid-1980s, in part because it was operating in competition with both local commercial radio and the BBC's main networked stations (BBC WAC SC1/71/1). Indeed, audience reaction to Radio Scotland's initial programmes was especially illuminating on two counts. Not only did it mirror beliefs expressed in relation to television that anything produced in Scotland was inferior to material emanating from London, it also pointed to a regional divide within Scotland itself. As one survey respondent from Aberdeen noted, there was 'too much Glasgow…You'd think there was a gate at Dundee and we're in the North Pole' (BBC WAC SC1/63). The expansion of Radio Scotland to include a range of community and area stations for the north and west of the country undoubtedly helped to placate some of these critiques. However, the allegation that BBC Scotland remained too focused on the Glasgow–Edinburgh central belt was one that reverberated across the decades and at times was every bit as potent as the charge of London centrism levelled at the BBC as a whole.

In programming terms, however, Radio Scotland in the early 1980s in particular witnessed a greater degree of innovation and experimentation, especially around non-music-based shows. Central to this was the success of programmes such as *Naked Radio* – a comedy sketch show – which, as its risqué logo of a dekilted Scotsman baring his backside indicated, was a very deliberate attempt to move beyond tartanry clichés. Other programmes had more practical purposes. *Kilbreck*, for example, a weekday ten-minute soap often likened to a Scottish *Archers* was first broadcast in 1981 and was conceived as a way of improving the health and well-being of the Scottish public. Financed in association with the Scottish Health and Education Group (SHEG), the programme, set in a fictional Scottish new town, strove to deal directly with a range of personal and community health issues. Although it attracted a considerable audience of about 300,000 listeners a week, it also provoked the ire of some religious leaders for its promotion of premarital sex and advice on contraception. As Charles Renfrew, Auxiliary Bishop in Glasgow and clearly more of an *Archers* fan, wrote in a letter of complaint, 'I would, if this sort of thing continues, be tempted to burn down the little village and return to Ambridge forever' (BBC WAC SC1/40/30/2). Although *Kilbreck* would run for less than three years, its brevity did not detract from the fact that it was the first daily soap opera to be produced by BBC Scotland. And while it may not quite have attained the same status as *The McFlannels* a generation earlier, *Kilbreck* was certainly much more attuned to the sensibilities of contemporary Scotland and central to the changing representations of Scottishness produced by the BBC.

Conclusions

Writing in 2001 about British cinema in the 'Celtic fringe', Martin McCloone highlighted the 'reimagining' and 'reworking of national or regional tropes and stereotypes' that was taking place. He noted, 'if many of these are inventions of the metropolitan centre, nevertheless their reinterpretation impacts upon a concept of Britishness, which is already under pressure…the peripherality has moved towards the cutting edge of contemporary debate' (quoted in Blandford 2007: 11). McCloone was writing in the aftermath of political devolution in Scotland and Wales in 1999, yet in reality Britishness had been under pressure for at least three decades, and its reimagining was something that was not solely confined to the first years of the twenty-first century. As we have seen, despite often justified criticism of its London centrism and centralized bureaucracy, the BBC played a central role in this reimaging thirty years earlier. With no 'national' theatres in either Scotland or Wales, let alone film industries, the BBC was undoubtedly the major institutional patron of Scottish and Welsh cultural life. Although there were undoubtedly many shortcomings, not least in the amount of programmes produced outside London, the changes in the 1970s were emblematic of the Corporation's response to broader societal change. As Jean Seaton (2007: 42–43) notes, the BBC,

> has repeatedly metabolised Britishness. The Corporation, in competition with other public service programme makers has reflected the mutating condition of the nation. This is the bedrock of everything it has achieved. Yet it has also added something to the reflection. The spectacle of being British that public service broadcasting has provided has, at its best, added careful thoughtfulness to the image, and an empathy with the audience that is like the responsiveness of a market, yet driven by other values. The BBC has done this as an institution, with principals and habits of working and things it fears to get wrong, standards that it applies to British life, ambitions and a worrying away at problems, not just as a 'broadcaster'.

What in effect this chapter has highlighted is one aspect of the continuing debates about the Britishness of the British Broadcasting Corporation. Although such debates have again been accentuated by the success of the SNP in the 2007 Scottish Parliamentary elections and, for example, by the decision of the BBC to relocate production facilities away from London to Salford, as we have seen, their genesis can be traced back at least forty years. Indeed, although the idea of a homogeneous British culture has quite rightly long been considered problematic by academics, the role of the BBC in simply reinforcing a common culture has not. It is perhaps time that greater attention was paid to the Corporation's considerable role in reflecting the diversity of British life, not simply its role in homogenizing it.

Notes

1 At the October 1974 General Election, the Scottish National Party returned eleven MPs to Westminster.
2 The headquarters of the BBC in Scotland until 2007.
3 Alasdair Milne, interview with author, 19 May 2006.
4 Christopher Irwin, interview with author, 11 March 2006.
5 BBC WAC Governors Press Cuttings 6.12.1975–1.6.1978, Fay Young, *The Scotsman*, 8 March 1976.

The radical narrative

Introduction

Of all the narratives identified by Curran, the radical one is perhaps both nearest and furthest from where we started with liberal histories of the media. Nearest, in the sense that representatives of the two traditions have been in dialogue with one another for the past thirty-odd years. However, in spite of efforts to facilitate an intermediary position, there is still much that divides these two varieties of history, and ink continues to be spilled, with radicals typically accusing liberals of papering over the cracks and flabby pluralism, while liberals have tended to respond with charges of radical functionalism and vulgar Marxism. To put it simply, if a little crudely, the two narratives are to each other like a red rag is to a bull, an intellectual provocation that can sometimes result in angry polemic as much as it does a fruitful exchange of ideas.

This difference of opinion is partly to do with the way in which liberals and radicals conceive power, at least in the context of Western democracies. On the one hand, liberals do not think there to be any one enduring source of power. Instead, there is a multiplicity of power relationships that are forever changing and widely diffused among many competing groups of interests. Radicals, on the other hand, favour a more pessimistic interpretation of social relations and processes. Drawing on the intellectual traditions associated with Western Marxism and political economy, a classic radical perspective would argue that power serves the interests of capitalism, a relatively recent mode of production that is characterized by the ascendancy of market economics where labour is bought and sold in exchange for wages. More than this, the capitalist forces/relations of economic production result in a conflict of interests between labour and the working class, on the one hand, and the state, its functionaries and those who own the means of economic production, the bourgeoisie, on the other. This is because the latter seek to monopolize the means of economic production so that they can exploit the proletariat's labour in order to make excess profit.

The significance of a Marxist view of society is that it has a direct bearing upon how we think about media history. Whereas liberal media historians would argue that the media functions with a certain degree of autonomy and indifference, both from other social institutions and, more importantly, from the state, a Marxist viewpoint would argue that the media tends to operate as an adjunct to a centralized nexus of power in the form of the state and a ruling political elite by reflecting hegemonic interests and thus legitimizing the socio-political status quo. One of the ways in which the media have done this is by monopolizing 'the production and distribution of ideas', which has nearly always coincided with the ideas of the ruling class as they tend to own the material means of media production. Indeed, the increase in the concentration of media ownership since the late nineteenth century has effectively resulted in the media becoming an oligopoly of sorts, owned and managed by an elite of enterprising capitalists whose main interest is the accumulation of capital and renewing the social conditions necessary to the reproduction of capitalist social relations of economic production. In short, where liberals see political censorship and talk of market competition, radicals see market censorship and talk instead of concentration of capitalism.

Both chapters in this section are closely aligned with radical perspectives on media history and offer critical overviews of the ways in which media technologies have shaped and been shaped by the aims and objectives of the modern liberal state and industrial capitalism. Graham Murdock and Michael Pickering's chapter opens up alternative ways of looking at the mediated alterations of temporal and spatial distance generated in the process of becoming modern, with all its accompanying contradictions. Taking two key technologies, photography and telegraphy, as their main objects for analysis, the authors begin their historical narrative by challenging the postmodern 'discovery' of time/space compression by tracing the roots and course of the debate from the mid-nineteenth century onwards, and by attending more closely to the *longue durée* of technological change, rather than just focusing on moments of innovation and historical breaks. They also argue that, contrary to technological determinist accounts of media development or liberal narratives of progress, technological innovations do not always facilitate social betterment or more expansive solidarities. Instead, they consider how the aforementioned media technologies were simultaneously deployed as capitalist technologies of subjectification and objectification, as a means of classifying and individualizing populations, problematizing certain social relations and valorizing others. The chapter concludes by redressing the privileging of space in the time–space couplet by looking more closely at the changing experiences of time and temporality set in motion by new communications technologies, and the implications of these changes for our understanding of the relationship between past and present.

Julian Petley provides another fine example of a radical narrative by critically interrogating the idea of the press as the 'fourth estate'. Drawing on the work of Curran and like-minded press historians, Petley claims that the press have frequently acted in a manner so critical of liberal opinion that it verges on the censorious. He also argues that most of the British press has consistently acted as a particularly significant and influential source of Establishment opinion, and is itself an extremely powerful corporate actor. Such a stance makes it extremely difficult to consider the British press as a fourth estate, that is to say, an essentially liberal institution that acts in the interests of the public as a watchdog over state and corporate power. Instead, Petley makes a pressing case for rethinking the press as a fourth-rate estate that has essentially failed the public in terms of its civic duty. His narrative finishes with what has been characterized as a 'period of shame', a reference to Rupert Murdoch's special relationship with the British government since the 1970s, especially the Thatcher and Blair governments. Coupled with the incontrovertible ascendancy of neo-liberalism, continuing media deregulation and the lack of an effective left political opposition, Petley's conclusions are disquieting and reminiscent of George Orwell's *Animal Farm* – a world in which it is no longer possible to differentiate between pigs and farmers, and the principles of 'animalism' are but a distant memory.

Further reading

The classic study of radical media history in Britain is Jurgen Habermas' (1989) account of what he famously called the 'refeudalisation of the public sphere'. E. P. Thompson's (1991 [1968]) seminal re-creation of working class life in late eighteenth- and early nineteenth-century Britain provides a magisterial analysis of British radicalism, including the unstamped press. Equally important is the edited collection by Boyce *et al.* (1978). Other historical analyses of the rise and fall of radical newspapers and periodicals include Conboy (2004), Curran (1977, 1978a), Gilmartin (1996), Hall (1986), Harrison (1974), Hollis (1970), Johnson (1979), Lee (1974), Wiener (1969), Williams (1998) and Williams (1970; cf. 1961); see also Boston (1970), Curran (1978b) and *The People & the Media* (1974), which were among the first publications to challenge the traditional view of press freedom and offer concrete proposals for press reform in the interests of pluralism and the renewal of democratic politics; cf. Baistow (1985), Bingham (2007), Curran (1995, 2000a, 2002a: 217–47), Curran and Seaton (2003: 346–62), Hutchinson (1999), O'Malley and Soley (2000) and Snoddy (1992).

The aforementioned should be read alongside various historical studies of working class literacy and popular literature: see, for example, Altick (1957), James (1976), Rose (2001), Shattock and Wolff (1982), Shepard (1973), Vincent (1993), Vinicus (1974) and Webb (1955). Of these, Jonathan Rose's account of *The Intellectual Life of the British Working Classes* is simply staggering in terms of its scholarship and fastidious attention to detail. Although more 'top-down' in terms of method and sources, John Carey (1992) provides a fascinating account of the various ways in which the literary intelligentsia sought to exclude the masses from modern culture by producing literature that was only accessible to an avant-garde elite.

In terms of broadcasting history, Raphael Samuel (1998) offers a compelling critique of Asa Brigg's official history of the BBC. Tom Burns' (1977) study of BBC managerialism in the 1960s and 1970s is a superb example of radical historical sociology. Although more gradualist in his method, the idea of public service – as opposed to working class solidarity – and the controversies surrounding broadcasting technologies as a means of social integration and control have been discussed at length by Raymond Williams (1962, 1966, 1974). Stuart Hall's (1986) analysis of early broadcasting history is an eloquent and sophisticated exemplar of 'the turn to Gramsci' that characterized a lot of media and cultural studies in the 1980s. A subtly different radical perspective is offered by Michael Bailey (2007a,c), who argues that the early BBC and its public service ethos is better reconsidered as a civilizing mission whose political rationality was to render the listening public more amenable to techniques of cultural governance.

Like most of the narratives discussed so far, it is necessary to look beyond narrowly focused media history texts if one wants to acquire a fuller understanding of the ways in which the media might be understood as – in the context of the radical narrative at least – an extension of late capitalism and as an instrument for monopolizing the cultural production and circulation of ideas. One of the earliest and most enduring influences in this field of study is the Marxist critique of the 'cultural industry' and the attendant rise of 'instrumental reason' as theorized by the Frankfurt school (e.g. Adorno 2001; Adorno and Horkheimer (1986 [1944]); Marcuse 1964). Critical evaluations of the now seminal 'Dialectic of Enlightenment' narrative include Garnham (1983; cf. 2000), Keane (1991) and Thompson (1990, 1995), among others. Hall (1977, 1988, 1997) provides a commanding survey of the some of the key works within Marxist and post-Marxist traditions of media studies, especially in relation to media representations and ideology (cf. Fairclough 1995 on media discourse). Work by the Glasgow University Media Group is widely regarded as crucial reading for anybody interested in radical media sociology (see, for example, 1976, 1980, 1982). Edwards and Cromwell (2005) provide a riveting exposé of the myth of liberal media based on a variety of empirical case studies; cf. Herman and Chomsky's (1988) path-breaking book on manufacturing consent and media propaganda. For a critical analysis of media political economy, from both a UK and a US perspective, see Calabrese and Sparks (2004), Curran (2000b), Garnham (1990, 2000), Golding and Murdock (1991), Herman and McChesney (1997), McChesney (1999), Mosco (1996), Murdock (1988, 1990), Murdock and Golding (1977) and Wasko (2001); see also Doyle (2002a,b), Hesmondhalgh (2007) and Williams (2003) for a useful overview of key debates in relation to media economics and the cultural industries. Of the most recent publications that best exemplify the radical tradition, Wayne (2003) provides an excellent guide to key Marxist concepts and their relevance for understanding the contemporary media landscape.

Finally, although the radical press is not what it used to be in terms of readership and political influence, there is nevertheless a thriving radical media that continues to disseminate alternative communication to a variety of counterpublics. For a contemporary history of alternative and activist media, see Atton (2002), Bailey *et al.* (2007), Downing (2000, 2008), Fountain *et al.* (2007), Hamilton and Atton (2001) and Waltz (2005), among others.

Chapter 12

The birth of distance

Communications and changing conceptions of elsewhere

Graham Murdock and Michael Pickering

Reading recently a batch of rather shallowly optimistic 'progressive' books, I was struck by the automatic way people go on repeating certain phrases which were fashionable before 1914. Two great favourites are the 'abolition of distance' and the 'disappearance of frontiers'.

George Orwell (1944)

Proximity and paradox

For many commentators, the development of modern communications is defined by the increasing ability to compress time and space and offer instantaneous and undistorted connections between places and people. This chapter subjects the easy assumptions behind arguments for the 'death of distance' and the emergence of a 'borderless world' to critical scrutiny taking two key technologies, the telegraph and photography, as illustrations. The telegraph laid the foundations for the spatial networks that provide the essential infrastructure for organizing global commerce and security. By seeming to offer democratic and objective access to events, landscapes and faces, photography altered popular experience of biographical and historical time. The frozen moment of the photographic image became the basic unit of personal and collective memory, summing up experience like a proverb but with the exactitude of a quotation from reality. Our personal mental stocks of 'hundreds of photographs, subject to instant recall' came to operate as a vernacular archive that never closed and could always be added to (Sontag 2003: 22).

From the mid-nineteenth century onwards, the increasing potential to see and contact distant others has been greeted as the basis for new national and transnational settlements based on empathy and solidarity. Many observers of the telegraph's erosion of spatial distance shared the hope, expressed by one contemporary enthusiast, that because 'the different nations and races will stand, as it were, in the presence of one another' they will get to 'know one another better [and] may be moved by common sympathies' (quoted in Standage 1998: 98). This optimistic reading of the impact of modern media has been reproduced with each successive innovation, from the legend 'Nation Shall Speak Peace Unto Nation' engraved above the entrance to Broadcasting House, the hub of the BBC's radio services, through McLuhan's vision of the 'global village' inspired by the early days of television satellite relay to contemporary claims for the borderless commons of the internet. These assertions embrace an ideology of progress that casts technological innovations as instruments of increasing betterment. They prevent us from grasping the paradoxes generated by time–space compression.

In this chapter, we focus on two of these paradoxes. First, we want to suggest that the increasing centrality of photographic images in organizing accounts of personal and national change over time renders the construction of historical understanding more not less problematic. Second, we want to argue that the collapse of geographical distance has been accompanied by the expansion of psychological estrangement rooted in a 'culture of distance' that objectifies people and reduces them to data entries and typologies (Williams 1990: 36). In pursuing these particular lines of interpretation, our position is obviously at variance with the affirmative, at times Panglossian drift of much media history which James Curran (2002a: 3–54) has outlined with admirable clarity. Along with him, we are also hostile to the many accounts which argue that media (and social) development is determined by changes in technology (see also Williams 1974: 9–14). In particular, we oppose the view that telegraphy and photography necessarily facilitated better communication or led to improved forms of understanding.

For the two communications technologies on which we focus, we can argue quite the opposite case. From its inception, the telegraph was assimilated to commercial and security interests and employed as a weapon of control in which the powerless were seen not as potential participants in an enlarged communicative sphere but as workers, natives, enemies or threats to social order to be contained and disciplined. Photography too was deployed as an instrument of objectification playing a key role in anchoring new systems of classification and separation. To understand why this obvious point has so often been missed, we need to look more closely at prevailing accounts of innovations in media technology.

Innovation and application

Much talk about technology centres on 'invention (the creation of a new idea) and innovation (the first use of a new idea)' (Edgerton 2006: ix), and looks for a defining moment that ushers in a new 'age'. London in 1839 suggests itself as just such a turning point. In July, the first commercial electric telegraph system, based on Charles Wheatstone's needle system, opened for business. It ran for 13.5 miles along the Great Western Railway line out of Paddington Station. Earlier that year, Henry Fox-Talbot, spurred on by Louis Daguerre's unveiling of his rival system at the French Academy of Sciences, had demonstrated his photographic process to the Royal Institution. Daguerre's images were sharper, but Fox-Talbot's offer of multiple rather than single copies proved the more attractive option and laid the foundation for the positive–negative process that dominated photography until the arrival of digital technologies. In telegraphy too, being first proved not to be decisive. It was the process developed by Samuel Morse, based on his code of dashes and dots, launched in 1844 with a 40-mile link between Washington and Baltimore, that became the international standard. These narratives of ingenuity, persistence and rivalry have proved deeply attractive. Analytically, they present major problems.

First, by focusing attention on breaks rather than continuities, they oversimplify the process of change. In an influential essay, James Carey (1989: 203–4) argues that, by permitting 'for the first time the effective separation of communication from transportation', the electric telegraph freed communication 'from the constraints of geography'. Although Carey does not mention him, this proposition was first outlined by Charles Cooley in 1894. Remembered now as a founding figure in American sociology, he had, at the time, just completed stints in government service, first at the Interstate Commerce Commission, of which his father, a distinguished Supreme Court justice, was the first Chair, and later at the Bureau of the Census. Originally trained as an engineer, he had gravitated towards the study of political economy and become interested in transport issues. Following an initial article on urban transit systems (Cooley 1891), he produced a major synoptic essay on 'The Theory of Transportation', in which the divorce of communication from transportation, made possible by the electric telegraph, is pivotal to the argument:

> [S]ince the introduction of the telegraph it may almost be said that there are no space relations. Space – distance – as an obstacle to communication has so nearly been overcome that it is hardly worth considering. In the transportation of material goods and persons such a result is inconceivable, and in this field the 'annihilation of space' must remain a figure of speech.
>
> Cooley (1894: 292)

By presenting the telegraph as an unprecedented innovation, Cooley and those who have taken up his argument offer a history of events rather than unfolding processes. A longer view reveals a complex interplay between innovations and general developments in modern state and commercial formations. The idea of flows of information moving independently of physical transportation had first been operationalized in 1794, with the completion of an optical telegraph between Paris and Lille using rotating arms to send semaphore signals along a line of towers. This technique, which was widely seen as aiding Napoleon's efforts to co-ordinate his military and administrative ambitions, was extensively imitated and, by 1830, European governments were operating 1,000 towers (Starr 2004: 157). The system lasted for another fifty years with the last semaphore link, in Sweden, ceasing service in 1880. In economic relations, we can trace the separation of physical goods transportation from the records of transactions back to the development of double entry bookkeeping in the late fifteenth century (Peters 2006: 147; and see Postma and van der Helm 2000). This ability to do business on paper was central to securing the stability and reach of capitalist relations. It was grounded in a fundamental shift in world views, from fate to risk. Faith in the new calculus of probability replaced belief in the arbitrary occurrence of natural calamities and the intervention of vengeful deities. It relegated 'acts of God' to the small print in insurance contracts (see Hacking 1984; Gigerenzer *et al.* 1990). The statistical taming of chance made it feasible to invest in the future and in commodities accumulated from around the globe: sugar, spices, tea and slaves. Communication networks were the circuits around which flowed calculations and projections of likely profits from these investments, and possible threats to them (see Mattelart 1996, 2000).

If a broader historical perspective is obscured, claims of the annihilation of distance are exaggerated. The electric telegraph never freed itself entirely from the constraints of physical movement. As the Indian strike of 1908 demonstrated all too clearly, if the messenger 'boys', who delivered telegrams to clients in their homes and offices, withdrew their labour, the system ground to a halt (see Choudhury 2003). To avoid this, various efforts were made to mechanize delivery. In 1853, for example, a 'pneumatic' link was opened between the London Stock Exchange and the City's main telegraph office, using pressurized air tubes to send messages. Other cities built extensive pneumatic postal networks. In Berlin, for example, the system stretched for a total of 400 kilometres. Opened in 1865, it finally closed in 1976. The conventional postal system also expanded. In 1894, the British Post Office relinquished its monopoly control over post cards, allowing private publishers into the market. The introduction of picture cards in 1902, coupled with same day or overnight delivery, created a message system that was cheap and popular and operated as the forerunner of e-mail as a way of keeping in touch and making appointments. It also accelerated the mass distribution of photographic images.

As the continuing vitality of the postal system alongside the expansion of the electric telegraph illustrates, innovations need to be understood in terms of superimposition rather than displacement. The introduction of a novel technology does not necessarily cancel out or replace existing systems. Rather it modifies the prevailing ecology of communications, setting in motion a series of collisions between the potentialities it offers and the requirements of various social interests. As Paul Starr (2004: 155) argues, nineteenth-century media technologies created 'divergent possibilities. They could expand social connections, increasing the possibilities of association, exchange, and diffusion of information, but they also created new means of controlling communication that the state or private monopolies might use for their own purposes'. Examining how technologies impact on prevailing relations of power, and how these relations might be contested, is the central concern of a critical perspective.

The 'long' nineteenth century, which stretched to the end of the First World War, saw the cementation of the three central institutional formations of capitalist modernity: industrial capitalism, nation-states and colonial empires. Each was fragile and needed to be continually secured. As Marx had famously pointed out, by bringing workers together in factories and high-density urban neighbourhoods, capitalism had created the ideal conditions for popular mobilizations against economic exploitation and social inequality. The stability of nation-states was threatened by the spectre of civil war, by secessionist movements and by imbalances and antagonisms between metropoles and provinces. Colonial empires were subject to insurrections and continually contested as the major Western powers vied for geopolitical supremacy, a process culminating in the 'scramble for Africa' and the advent of 'total wars' involving civil populations alongside military combatants. Against this background, power holders at every level found themselves continually struggling to impose order. This required two kinds of resources. First, robust systems of classification that identified possible threats and gave faces and physiognomies to potentially 'dangerous' elements. Second, workable systems of extended communication that supported the exercise of command and control over complex processes of manufacture, administration and warfare, occupying increasingly dispersed geographical arenas.

Classification and co-ordination

From an early point in its development, photography was mobilized to construct visual records of those passing through institutions of order: prisons, asylums, police stations and consulting rooms. The resulting images, showing the sitters fully illuminated, often holding up boards with their name and/or number, confirmed the unbridgeable gulf between the 'power and privilege of producing and possessing' and the burden of being an object of scrutiny (Tagg 1988: 6). These myriad impressions formed the raw materials for new forms of social classification designed to identify threats and dangers, so laying the foundations of contemporary surveillance systems. As David Lyon has argued, surveillance 'sorts people into categories, assigning worth or risk, in ways that affects their life-chances. Deep discrimination occurs' (Lyon 2003: 1). Although mostly confined to bureaucratic files, the typologies these records generated also found their way into popular circulation through caricatures, cartoons and photographic post cards. In a situation where the majority of encounters in the new urban centres were with strangers, images played a key role in mediating sociality. With no other knowledge to go on, appearances assumed increasing importance. Narrow typifications offered a handy resource. The resulting stereotypes were further amplified by much early documentary photography. Observers set off for the slums of the great cities in much the same spirit as they embarked for the interior of Africa. Their photographic capture of the exotic working class species inhabiting the urban jungles of the industrialized world was embedded in the same discourse of imperial exploration. The evolutionary temporalizing of a primitive 'then' and 'there' as opposed to a civilized 'now' and 'here' became mapped onto the modern urban landscape, with entrepreneurial acumen and the seat of Empire co-existing with low-life degeneration and iniquity. As an early technology of surveillance, the photography of social investigation and documentation appeared to provide stark evidence of this as it was viewed across the distance of the class divide. More broadly, every photographic portrait was implicitly placed within this social hierarchy, as noted by Sekula (1989: 347): 'The private moment of sentimental individuation, the look at the frozen gaze-of-the-loved-one, was shadowed by two other more public looks: a look up, at one's "betters", and a look down, at one's "inferiors"' (see also Sekula 1984).

In colonial administration and early visual anthropology too, photography was co-opted into ideological constructions of 'natives' and 'savages' who, compared with modern civilized Europeans, occupied a far distant temporal elsewhere. Through mass-produced post cards, images of the exotic 'Other' provided by photography were widely considered to reveal racial backwardness. In this way, photography was used to support evolutionist ideas of social development and eugenicist claims about racial difference. Spatial distance became temporal distance as images of 'primitive' peoples were perceived as representing a living early stage of human society long surpassed by the leading imperialist nations: 'savage and barbarous tribes often more or less fairly represent stages of culture through which our own ancestors passed long ago' (Tylor 1913: 388). Culture became temporally coded in anthropology's 'denial of coevalness' or temporal co-presence to its referent (Fabian 1983: 26, 31). In modernizing nations, photographs of the primitivized 'Other' were viewed in contradistinction to industrial and technological advance, with photography itself considered as clear proof of that advance.

Photography's claim to offer a complete and disinterested capture of the world as it appeared in front of the lens provided a general metaphor for objective observation that was taken up by journalists and early social scientists eager to demonstrate their professional credentials. By claiming to be human cameras, manufacturing evidence untainted by personal values or commitments, these new social investigators presented themselves as servants of science rather than ideology. But objectivity all too easily became objectification, stripping those observed of their agency and subjectivity and repositioning them as problems to be worked on. The physical proximity entailed in photography all too often produced images that validated a new kind of psychological distance based on stereotypes of danger and destitution. This in turn opened the way for forms of administration and intervention that approached populations as raw data for risk calculations.

Electricity was widely regarded by nineteenth-century observers as a force capable of clearing blocked neural pathways. Medical and mental health patients were subjected to 'Faradization', named after Michael Faraday, the discoverer of electromagnetic induction, the basis for electric motors and generators. The electric telegraph was seen likewise as an agency capable of regenerating the global body politic. As Ezra Gannett noted in 1858: 'The world will be made...a great assembly, where every one will see and hear everyone else' producing 'a practical unity of the human race' (quoted in Sconce 2000: 22). Seventy years later, Henry Ford, witnessing the rise of cinema and radio, could still argue that, because technologies of communication 'pass over the dotted lines on the map without heed or hindrance', they were 'binding the world together in a way no other system can [and] will soon bring the world to a complete understanding' (quoted in Edgerton 2006: 113–14). It is particularly ironic that this pious hope should appear in *My Philosophy of Industry*, his apologia for the rationalization of industrial production that he, more than anyone, had helped bring about. The reorganization of the factory system depended crucially on the new systems of command, control and communication based on transnational communication networks that extended and intensified connections between geographically dispersed people, places, suppliers and markets. The same systems that Ford celebrated as the basis for enhanced connection and understanding were deployed as instruments of economic management and social control. From the outset, however, there were tensions between the requirements of commerce and the dictates of security.

While Britain opted initially for a commercially funded and operated telegraph system, elsewhere in Europe, governments concurred with the opinion expressed by the French Minister of the Interior in 1847 that 'telegraphy should be a political instrument, and not a commercial instrument' (quoted in Starr 2004: 159). Its potential value in co-ordinating troops was demonstrated by the cable laid across the Black Sea employed in the Crimean War (1854–56), although it did not prevent the logistical incompetence that dogged the campaign. The Crimea also saw the deployment of photography as a weapon. While Roger Fenton, armed with a letter of introduction from Prince Albert, was taking his carefully orchestrated shots of military leaders and camp life for public distribution, two serving officers were pioneering photointelligence by compiling a dossier for the military files. It was during the Indian Mutiny of 1857 that telegraphy first proved its worth as an infrastructural resource for military command, control and communication. Between 1853 and 1855, William Brooke O'Shaughnessy had overseen the construction of an Indian network covering 3,500 miles, and it was this resource that was later credited with 'saving' India for the English (Hills 2002: 5). The Military Field Telegraph established in 1857 continued to operate as an integral element in British campaigns alongside a civil branch dominated by traffic generated by government and international business interests (see Choudhury 2003: 49–53).

By 1875, India, as the main overland link between the West and the Far East and Australia, had assumed a pivotal role within the imperial and global trading systems. As the French discovered in Africa, another major arena of imperial conflict, rapid telegraph links bestowed considerable political and diplomatic advantages. When Lord Kitchener's expeditionary force, bent on establishing control over East Africa, encountered Major Marchand's rival army in the Sudanese village of Fashoda in 1898, it was Kitchener's access to the British-controlled Egyptian telegraph network and the link onwards to London that proved decisive in securing an advantageous settlement (see Standage 1998: 149–50).

It was in Africa too that the intelligence potential of the telegraph was realized. During the Boer War, the British state established a special unit, Section H, devoted to 'monitoring all traffic using the two main submarine cables connecting South Africa to Portugal and Aden' and 'maintaining strict control over the civil land line cables' (West 1986: 11). In 1906, its activities, which had continued after the end of the war, were taken over by the War Office's military intelligence division, which later became MI5, Britain's major internal security agency.

By the turn of the twentieth century then, the telegraph and photography had become integral to the emerging apparatuses of state surveillance and security. The telegraph in particular had demonstrated the indispensability of networked systems capable of co-ordinating activities across dispersed sites of military and commercial activity, but both these media were used in ways that distanced different peoples and cultures from each other, rather than binding them together and bringing the world 'to a complete understanding'. They were integral to increasing social control, objectification and stereotyping. New forms of distance were born out of the drastic reduction in spatial distance. These are easily overlooked by histories of communications technologies, which concentrate on invention and innovation, rather than longer term interrelations of old and new technologies and their spatio-temporal patterns of social use. In this respect, time–space compression is a technocentric concept.

Time and distance

There are further problems associated with the concept. They begin with the question of how time contributes to it. Although time seems to share equal weighting, it is space that is privileged. The temporal dimension is largely confined to a specifically space-oriented conception where the emphasis is on how time is compressed as messages cross space. Temporal compression is considered primarily in relation to the speed with which spatial barriers are broken down. New forms of communication are seen as enabling the crossing of space in less and less time than in previous historical epochs. What counts most is the rapid traversal of space, not temporal reduction. Instantaneity comes to mean the disappearance of time or the 'timeless time' that Manuel Castells (1996: 429–68) claims as characteristic of the network society. This privileging of space characterizes cultural theory more generally, as in Edward Soja's (1989: 61) indicative claim that 'space rather than time hides things from us...the demystification of spatiality and its veiled instrumentality of power is the key to making practical, political, and theoretical sense of the contemporary era'.

It may be one key, but it is not the master key. Contrary to this, we argue for a conception of 'elsewhere' as multidimensional, as not only a spatial conception, but also a temporal one, encompassing experiential senses of time and raising the question of how we relate to the notion of historical time or, in any given present, to the evidence of other times. If the past is a foreign country, how do we respond to its foreignness? As stay-at-home xenophobes, as package tourists or as watchful itinerants?

In this section, we want to redress the privileging of space in the concept of time–space compression by attending to changing experiences of the temporal elsewhere. Photography demonstrates very clearly that the spatially oriented annihilation of temporal distance is only one aspect of how new communications technologies from the later nineteenth century onwards are linked to changing experiences of time and temporality. These involve different ways of considering and engaging with time and the temporal elsewhere in ways that can again be said to involve not so much the death as the birth of distance, with the photograph involving the peculiar experience of some fragment of the past being both here and not here at one and the same time.

Before we consider this in more detail, it is important to outline at least three major consequences of playing down or ignoring the temporal dimension when considering new communication technologies in their social and cultural usages.

First of all, the emphasis on volatility, ephemerality and the collapse of time horizons in the time–space couplet means that our sense of long-term continuities diminishes and we become increasingly present focused, ruled by the 'tyranny of the moment' (Eriksen 2001). Time horizons 'shorten to the point where the present is all there is' and 'past experience gets compressed into some overwhelming present' (Harvey 1991: 240, 291). Past images may be drawn on, but only for their contribution to an ahistorical collage of remediated elements of the past, primarily in the interests of ratings and revenue. This is part of the paradoxical condition of being surrounded with historical detritus while becoming increasingly dissociated from the past in its contemporary inheritance. The concept of time–space compression reinforces cultural presentism of this kind because of its emphasis on temporal speed at the increasingly ascendant point of 'now', so deflecting attention away from how technologies of recording and retrieval have over time contributed to shifts in the economy of perception and memory, and alterations in our sense of temporal location, movement and distance.

A second consequence of the privileging of space in time–space compression is that the relation of time to place is overlooked. While place exists in space, it is contrary to undifferentiated, levelled out, global space in the ways in which it serves as a site for memory and belonging. Biographically and in relation to broader historical processes, the social experience of time becomes meaningful through place rather than space. The mystique of place is only a far extreme of what is otherwise a common feeling of attachment to particular towns, streets and landscapes. This can be reactionary and inward looking, or exploited as fake heritage and historical façadism, but it can co-exist with a more expansive outlook and may be a positive response to deracinated forms of cosmopolitanism. Time helps to configure place into a source of personal and collective identity and so becomes more significant the more people feel the world continually shifting around them. Developing such identity means turning space into place and investing place with a sense of temporal continuity. Photographs are used personally as a particular way of doing this in that they closely associate place with a continuous sense of self that runs counter to the experience of modernity's relentless change and disruption. Personal photos in albums or frames are associated with a sense of lived time and place. The paradox here is that time and place are always cross-cut by other times and places, either materially in the consumption of commodities and services originating at a distance or symbolically through the media representation of distant places and peoples. Individual, family and community uses of photography are not necessarily a defensive reflex in the face of this paradox. They are used in remembering as a way of helping to moor us in time, even if they also seem in this way to 'guard against the ravages of time–space compression' (Harvey 1991: 292).

The third consequence we want to highlight is the conventional model of linear time that is invoked in the sense of either temporal speed across spatial distance or temporal movement forwards in ever increasing acceleration. It is at one with a sense of history as a continuous sequence of cause and effects leading ever onward from then to now. The relentless march of time proceeds under the liberal banner of progress. Walter Benjamin contrasts this way of constructing historical narrative with another mode of engaging with the past that involves bringing historical moments or periods into alignment with the present and seeking elective affinities with the past. 'The true picture of the past flits by. The past can be seized only as an image which flashes up at the instant when it can be recognized and is never seen again' (Benjamin 1970: 257). This alternative mode of historical narration is opposed to recreating the past as 'the way it really was'. It is an illusion that we can know the past in this way and so recreate it. It homogenizes time and empties it out by ignoring historical difference and historicity, change and the consequences of change. Instead, for Benjamin, to articulate the past means seizing hold of a memory 'as it flashes up in a moment of danger' (ibid.).

Conceiving of history as in a continual state of emergency clearly made sense in 1940, while Benjamin was in flight from Nazism, but the past is remembered, experienced and understood in many different ways. What is more significant than Benjamin's conjunction of memory and alarm is his use of the language of photography to address the question of how we connect with and articulate the past. This was deployed in opposition to historicism and positivism which Benjamin understood 'as so many versions of a realism that establishes its truth by evoking the authority of so-called facts' (Cadava 1997: 3). The irony here is that photography can be seen as closely aligned with empiricist realism, seeming to collapse temporal distance and bring a past event or scene starkly into the present, with all its so-called factual evidence. During the later nineteenth and early twentieth centuries, photography seemed a vast improvement on human memory, infallible and flawless in what it recorded and reproduced. Its power lay in preserving something that was previously evanescent and carrying this forward over time with a claim to greater accuracy of representation than writing, painting or statuary. As well as altering the relation of images to time and temporal movement, photography freed visual signs from the human body, overcame the blindness of writing and appeared to offer precise copies rather than an idealized version of the original. Despite the advent of digitally manipulated images, photographic realism continues to provide a key criterion of representational precision. What does this mean for our relationship to the photographic image over the distance of time? If we now look at a photograph of a street scene, or an individual portrait, from the late nineteenth century, have we in fact been brought psychologically close up to the past? Telegraphy and telephony produced simultaneity across spatial distances, but can we say that photography provides simultaneity across temporal distances?

While few people believe that the camera never lies, it is still widely felt that photographs maintain a strict fidelity to what they show. But even when not consciously stylized, what does a historical photograph actually show, and what does it convey across distance in time? There are various ways to address these questions. Personal photographs, as we have mentioned, relate to our own memories and speak to our own experiences of place, time and the passage of time, whereas most historical photographs we encounter bear little if any relation to our own experiences and memories. What we negotiate is the image alone or the image with reference to other images. It is when other associations are stripped away that we may become especially prone to the ultra-naturalist seduction of the photograph, seeing its capture of an event or group of people in one temporal fragment and taking its apparent indexical veracity as the cue for wanting passionately to know what led to and from the event, who these people were and what happened to them. There are cases when we do not and cannot know. The photograph seems to be a direct imprint of a past event or scene, but it remains silent, locked inside its historical otherness. This increases our awareness of distance across time and the impossibility of travelling back to the moment when these people were alive, standing there in this setting or when this event was fixed and flung up out of a lost sequence and range, becoming ever more attenuated in meaning as it moves across time. Photography monumentalizes temporal fragments and tells us nothing of how to conceive of duration or how to negotiate the irreducible distance between then and now.

This does not mean that photographs are of no worth as historical evidence. Our point is that what seems most obvious about them as evidence is actually what is most problematic. Their stark claim to provide indexical links to the past – their emphatic quality of 'as it really was' – should make us suspicious of what exactly they seem to represent and communicate, while the distance between then and now that is concealed by this claim should be the very starting point of our interpretation of them.

As we saw earlier with the relations between mechanically recorded images, colonial administration and urban documentation, temporal distance has not always been concealed by photographic realism. The influence of ideological values on photographic evidence is perhaps easier to see with the benefit of historical hindsight, as we try to dissociate how we see an image now from how it may have been seen in the past. That move should remind us of the provisional and partial nature of all interpretation, and especially of evidence which seems to deny the need for interpretation. It is this apparent denial that underwrites the pathos of expecting any communications medium to produce definitive contact, whether across time or space.

John Durham Peters makes the point that new media of the late nineteenth/early twentieth centuries, 'claiming to bring us closer, only made communication seem much more impossible' (Peters 2000: 143). The two new media of this period that we have focused on show that just as much as abolishing spatial distance, they were intimately bound up with the development of a new culture of distance associated with objectification, classification and containment as means of maintaining social and imperial order. This has formed the basis of modern systems of command and control, security and surveillance. The psychological estrangement intrinsic to this culture of distance is arguably of much greater historical significance than the spatial compression generated by new media. Such media have also been associated with changing experiences of temporality and the possibilities of communication across time. Photography may seem to foster and enhance these possibilities, but a photograph on its own confounds communication precisely because it gives an image without a story, an instant without a duration. Its apparent technological fidelity to its referent seems to immortalize what it represents and so transcend temporal distance and historical difference. We do not and cannot commune with the past in this way. Distance remains an insuperable barrier. In this sense, new media of this period increased recognition of a key aspect of hermeneutics, which is that the historicity of experience means that communication always occurs in and through distance (ibid.: 150). Media communications are inherently distantiated communications. The time–space separation that is a built-in feature of the disjunctions between media production and consumption is exacerbated by the reproduction of media images from the past, across the distance between then and now. Once more, communications technologies were pivotal to the modern birth, rather than the death of distance, and this has made the hermeneutic problem of negotiating the distance separating different historical horizons ever more insistent. It is only through such negotiation that understanding the past is possible.

Chapter 13

What fourth estate?

Julian Petley

> The English Press, instead of enlightening, does, so far as it has any Power, keep the People in Ignorance. Instead of cherishing Notions of Liberty, it tends to the making of the people Slaves; instead of being their Guardian, it is the most efficient Instrument in the Hands of all those who oppress or wish to oppress Them.
>
> William Cobbett (1807)

Introduction

The idea of the press as a 'fourth estate' came to prominence during the nineteenth century. Its origin is unclear, but Robert Carlyle, writing in 1841, stated that 'Burke said there were Three Estates in parliament; but in the Reporters' Gallery yonder, there sat a *Fourth Estate* more important far than they all'; and his own 1837 work *The French Revolution: A History* referred to 'A Fourth Estate of Noble Editors'. In 1855, *The Times* leader writer Henry Reeve wrote that 'journalism is now truly an estate of the realm; more powerful than any of the other estates' (quoted in Boyce 1978: 23); and the idea was satirized as arrogant and self-important by Trollope the same year in his novel *The Warden*.

In this essentially liberal view of the press, journalism is seen as a central component of democracy and, in particular, as a crucial check on the power of the state. Liberal theory holds that the right and duty of the press is to:

> serve as an extralegal check on government...to keep officers of the state from abusing or exceeding their authority...to be the watchdog over the workings of democracy, ever vigilant to spot and expose any arbitrary or authoritarian practice...[and] to be completely free from control or domination by those elements it was to guard against.
>
> Siebert *et al.* (1963: 56)

This is a position associated with figures as varied as David Hume, Tom Paine, Thomas Jefferson and James Mill, *inter alia*, and which still underpins much thinking about journalism today. The fourth estate view of journalism is a seductive one (not least for journalists themselves), but it is also highly questionable – in particular, its tendency to assume that it is the state that is today the greatest enemy of press freedom. Equally problematic is the fact that it is frequently (albeit implicitly) underpinned by a form of free market theory which assumes that, as long as the press is not shackled by state restrictions, the market will ensure that it reflects a wide range of views and interests. Newspapers that reflect readers' interests will survive, because there is a market for them, and those that don't, won't. Newspapers submit themselves to the public judgement every day that they go on sale, unlike politicians who stand for election only occasionally. Thus, newspapers are actually more representative of the people than are MPs. However, as James Curran points out:

> Concealed beneath the folds of these arguments, often well out of sight, is a contentious premise. Liberal theory assumes tacitly that press freedom is a property right exercised by publishers on behalf of society. According to this approach, publishers should be free to direct personally their newspapers, or delegate authority to others, as they see fit. What they do is consistent, ultimately, with the public interest since their actions are regulated by the free market. This ensures, in liberal theory, that the press is free, diverse and representative.
>
> Curran and Seaton (2003: 346–47)

This view was clearly evident in the report of the final Royal Commission on the Press, which approvingly quoted Justice Wendell Holmes' famous 1919 judgement that 'the best test of truth is the power of the thought to get itself accepted in the competition of the market' (1977: 109). The Commission itself stated that:

> In the case of the press, with certain limited exceptions, no legal restriction is placed on the right to buy or launch a newspaper. The justification is that this freedom produces a sufficiently diverse press to satisfy the public interest by ensuring a broad spectrum of views, and at the same time meets the individual interest by enabling virtually anyone with a distinctive opinion to find somewhere to express it. Consequently, there is no specific obligation on editors or proprietors to have regard, in what they publish, to the need to meet either the public or the individual interest, since the invisible hand of the market is expected to fulfil both.
>
> Royal Commission on the Press (1977: 9)

This view of the press, and specifically of press freedom and accountability, is still very much the dominant one in press and official circles in contemporary Britain. But it is possible to take a very different view, in which the British daily and Sunday national press, far from being a watchdog over the establishment, is actually a crucial part of it, and where market forces, far from being the guarantor of press freedom, are at least as great a threat to it as are controls and restrictions emanating directly from the state. Such a view of the press would be an example of what Curran (2002a) calls the 'radical narrative' of media history. And the purpose of this chapter is to resume that narrative – mostly through Curran's own accounts of British press history and those of like-minded press historians – and then to suggest its continuing relevance to recent British press history.

A police of safety and a sentinel of public morals

In order to illustrate this narrative, Curran (2002a: 34) focuses on Habermas' *The Structural Transformation of the Public Sphere*, which shows how 'modern media fell under the sway of public relations, advertising and big business... encouraged consumer apathy, presented politics as a spectacle, and provided pre-packaged, convenience thought. The media, in short, managed the public rather than expressed the public will'. Organized commercial interests and an expanded state, often acting in concert, increasingly circumscribed the realm of the public; in political terms, straightforward control or patronage of the press by political parties was replaced by the modern machinery of media management, and politicians and media owners increasingly struck mutually beneficial deals in which the public interest counted for little or nothing. The press may have been liberated from direct political controls in the nineteenth century, but the market to which it was delivered would rapidly reveal itself to be a 'system of control rather than an engine of freedom' (ibid.: 35) in which power was exercised by wealthy, and frequently conservative-minded, individuals and corporations, while the market itself was constituted in such a way as to make it either inherently inimical or downright hostile to left/liberal values.

Indeed, many of those who argued for the abolition of the Stamp Duty and other 'taxes on knowledge' that fettered the press in the first half of the nineteenth century did so because they thought that a commercially successful press firmly in capitalist hands would serve as the best possible antidote to the radical press and so could help to preserve and spread values that were supportive of the status quo. As the Lord Chancellor put it in 1834: 'the only question to answer, and the only problem to solve, is how they [the people] shall read in the best manner; how they shall be instructed politically, and have political habits formed the most safe for the constitution of the country' (quoted in Curran and Seaton 2003: 18). Or as Bulwer-Lytton argued in 1832: 'we have made a long and fruitless experiment of the gibbet and the hulks. Is it not time to consider whether the printer and his types may not provide better for the peace and honour of a free state, than the gaoler and the hangman. Whether, in one word, cheap knowledge may not be a better political agent than costly punishment (quoted in Curran 1978: 55). He also claimed that the Tolpuddle martyrs would probably never have been created if the Stamp Duty had been repealed; in his view, 'instruction, not the strong arm of the law, was the only effective instrument to put them [the unions] down' (ibid.). Likewise, the MP George Grote argued that not only 'the evil of the unions' but also 'a great deal of the bad feeling that was at present abroad amongst the labouring classes' was due to the 'want of proper instruction, and correct information as to their real interests' (ibid.) caused by the economic restraints upon the press. As Curran himself puts it, for these parliamentarians, 'the cause of a free market press was synonymous with the suppression of trade unionism: the dream for which they fought was an unfettered capitalist press that would police the capitalist system' (ibid.: 56) and secure the loyalty of the working class to the social order.

So, for example, Thomas Milner-Gibson, the president of the Association for the Repeal of the Taxes on Knowledge, argued in 1850 that repeal would create 'a cheap press in the hands of men of good moral character, of respectability, and of capital' and would 'give to men of capital and respectability the power of gaining access by newspapers, by faithful record of the facts, to the minds of the working classes' (Curran 1978: 60). In 1854, Palmerston argued that: 'the larger we open the field of general instruction, the firmer the foundation on which the order, the loyalty and good conduct of the lower classes will rest' (ibid.: 58). The Irish MP John Francis Maguire proclaimed that, with the repeal of the taxes on knowledge, 'you render the people better citizens, more obedient to the laws, more faithful and loyal subjects, and more determined to stand up for the honour of the country' (ibid.). Meanwhile, Gladstone declared that 'the freedom of the press was not merely to be permitted and tolerated, but to be highly prized, for it tended to bring closer together all the national interests and preserve the institutions of the country' (ibid.). And in 1859, Alexander Andrews, the editor of the first journalists' trade magazine, wrote in *The History of British Journalism to 1855* that the great mission of the press was to 'educate and enlighten those classes whose political knowledge has been hitherto so little, and by consequence so dangerous' (ibid.: 60). He continued: 'the list of our public journals is a proud and noble list – the roll call of an army of liberty, with a rallying point in every town. It is a police of safety, and a sentinel of public morals' (ibid.). The cause of freeing the press from the taxes on knowledge was thus, in certain highly influential circles, inextricably intertwined with the notion that educating (read indoctrinating) the working class with the 'right' ideas was the best way of warding off social unrest and maintaining the capitalist system.

Giving the public what it wanted

With powerful capitalist forces entering the newspaper market, considerable technological innovation and development followed. Increasingly, a craft system of newspaper production was replaced by an industrial one. This had the result of significantly increasing both running costs and fixed capital costs in the newspaper sector, making it difficult for those with more limited funds to remain in, let alone break into, the marketplace. On the other hand, the major operators could benefit from economies of scale, offering attractive products while still keeping cover prices low. This combination of rising expenditure and lower cover prices forced up the circulation levels that newspapers needed to reach in order to become profitable, which meant that it was difficult for newcomers to enter the marketplace, especially if they were undercapitalized and not aimed at a mass audience.

Equally significant in marginalizing (and ultimately destroying) the radical press was the rise of advertising as a means of funding newspapers after the abolition of the advertisement duty in 1853. The influx of advertising revenue meant that newspapers could halve their cover prices, and then halve them again, in subsequent decades. But it also meant that they became heavily dependent on advertising, as their net cover prices no longer covered their costs. As Curran puts it: 'advertisers thus acquired a *de facto* licensing power because, without their support, newspapers ceased to be economically viable' (Curran and Seaton 2003: 30). Radical newspapers were unattractive to many advertisers for two reasons – their politics and the nature of their readership. Regarding the latter point, the head of a well-known advertising agency wrote in 1856: 'some of the most widely circulated journals in the Empire are the worst possible to advertise in. Their readers are not purchasers, and any money thrown upon them is so much thrown away'; while in 1921 an advertising handbook warned: 'you cannot afford to place your advertisements in a paper which is read by the down-at-heels who buy it to see the "Situations Vacant" column' (both quoted in ibid.: 31). Radical papers were left with two options – either to move upmarket in an effort to attract the kind of readers attractive to advertisers or to remain minority publications with manageable losses that could be offset by donations from readers. What they could not do, without incurring crippling losses, was to move into the mass market and sell themselves, without advertising, as cheaply as competitors effectively subsidised by the advertisers.

As George Boyce (1978: 25) points out, the opportunities provided by the press in the second half of the nineteenth century 'attracted people whose interest lay, not primarily in enlightening or informing public opinion, nor in criticising public policy, but in making money by giving the public what it wanted – or, at least, what it was supposed by the entrepreneur to want'. Equally, the politics of these papers were those that would sell – especially to the increasingly prosperous and literate lower middle classes – which meant appealing to popular prejudices and an essentially conservative, 'common sense' view of the world. Here, the archetypal paper was the *Daily Mail*, which was launched on 4 May 1896, and the archetypal proprietor was its owner, Lord Northcliffe, who knew exactly how to market his journalism to readers and his readers to advertisers. He also understood perfectly how to address people both as readers to be informed and as consumers ready and eager to spend their money on goods and services. Ideology and economics were inextricably bound together, as the paper, determined not to alienate its readers, confirmed them in what they thought they already knew as opposed to trying to provide a challenging or alternative view of the social order. Thus the jingoism and xenophobia of its coverage of foreign affairs (the Boer War in particular) was as much commercial as ideological in origin, as it precisely reflected the views of the paper's predominantly lower middle class readership. By 1900, its circulation had almost reached the million mark, and henceforth other popular papers had to compete with Northcliffe on his own terms.

An extension of the political system

In 1903, Northcliffe proclaimed: 'every extension of the franchise renders more powerful the newspaper and less powerful the politician' (quoted in Smith 1979: 169). However, it would be an extremely grave mistake to underestimate the profound links between politicians and the press from the last third of the nineteenth century onwards. By the 1870s, governments had come to realize that carrots rather than sticks represented the more effective way of getting and keeping the press onside. As Alan J. Lee (1976: 205) puts it: 'the most successful way of doing this was by the provision of information, and by making certain journalists feel at home within the "governing classes", and even within the political system'. Lord Palmerston had already established a close relationship with the *Morning Post* between 1838 and 1864, and various political grandees followed suit with successive editors of *The Times* (see Boyce 1978: 26). In this respect, Boyce's analysis of the *Morning Post*'s relationship with leading politicians between 1911 and 1937 is singularly revealing (ibid.: 29–31). And if journalists could be seduced by information, the honours system could have the same effect on proprietors – thus giving new meaning to the term 'press baron' (see Lee 1976: 205–8). Lee also estimates that by 1885 there were no less than twenty-two MPs who were press proprietors and concludes that 'there can have been few large newspaper companies who lacked a parliamentary representative, and to this extent the newspaper industry resembled other successful Victorian industries, and like those other industries the press had to a considerable degree become integrated into the political system by such a process' (ibid.: 209).

Close financial links between newspapers and political parties remained firmly in place until well into the twentieth century. For example, Boyce (1978: 28–29) reveals how substantial funds from the Unionist Central Office were channelled to the *Standard*, *Globe*, *Observer* and *Pall Mall Gazette* between 1911 and 1915. The *Morning Post* was bought by a Conservative syndicate headed by the Duke of Northumberland in 1924, while Lloyd George engineered the purchase of the *Daily News* in 1901 by the Cadbury family in the Liberal interest (not least in whipping up support for the Boer War) and arranged the purchase of the *Daily Chronicle* in 1918 with monies accumulated through the sale of honours. Boyce (1978: 29) thus concludes that 'the press was an extension of the political system, not a check or balance to Parliament and Executive, but inextricably mixed up with these institutions. Government was not "government by journalism"…but government by politicians, with journalists acting as go-betweens, advisers, and, occasionally, opponents of the practising politicians'.

The worst aspects of the capitalist world

What is so striking about this particular narrative of press history is that it demonstrates how most of the salient features of today's press were well in place by the end of the nineteenth century. In the years that followed, the press continued to develop along the same lines and, as Boyce (1978: 36) puts it, 'the newspaper world appeared more and more to be a mirror of the worst aspects of the capitalist world, with its transformation into a major enterprise, and the consequent emergence of the commercial corporation'. Most newspapers were, and remained, decidedly right wing, but even when they were not lending their support explicitly to the Conservatives, they radiated an illiberal, authoritarian–populist world view that blatantly appealed to popular prejudices and folk wisdom and was resolutely hostile to progressive opinion of all kinds. Jingoism, xenophobia and an increasingly shrill nationalism were crucial ingredients of this unappetising ideological brew, in which the creation of folk-devils of one kind or another (early examples being the 'Red Menace' and Jewish immigrants) played a key role in creating the 'imagined community' of the British (increasingly the English) to and for which the press presumed to speak.

On the economic front, concentration of ownership became the order of the day; thirty newspapers closed between 1921 and 1936, although the total sales of newspapers doubled in the same period. The result was an even greater narrowing of the range of political and ideological viewpoints available in the daily and Sunday national press. Between the two world wars, newspapers had to cope with radio as a rival news medium and, in the 1950s, television. After the war, readership began to decline and, in the 1950s, production costs began to rise steeply. Advertisers thus became an even more important source of revenue than they had been hitherto, further accentuating the process whereby, as Anthony Smith (1979: 147) puts it, 'newspapers came to look upon their potential readers as segments of consumerdom'. Newspapers increasingly tailored their content to what would appeal to advertisers – which also meant avoiding content that threatened to puncture the 'buying mood'. At the same time, however, the popular press remained more dependent on readers than on advertisers as its main source of revenue. Competition for readers thus became ever more intense. As a result of all these factors, journalism became ever more market driven, first in the popular papers and then in the so-called 'qualities', which many accused of becoming tabloid not simply in format but in terms of their content as well. Martin Conboy's (2004: 181) definition of tabloidization as 'an increase in news about celebrities, entertainment, lifestyle features, personal issues, an increase in sensationalism, in the use of pictures and sloganized headlines, vulgar language and a decrease in international news, public affairs news including politics, the reduction in the length of words in a story and the reduction of complexity of language, and also a convergence with agendas of popular and in particular television culture' is not only usefully inclusive but also serves to remind us of all the various processes that have been developing within British journalism ever since the latter part of the nineteenth century.

In the twin processes of concentration and commercialization, the minority left-liberal tradition was decisively the loser, with the *News Chronicle* closing in 1960, the *Daily Herald* being transformed in 1964 into the *Sun* (which was sold to Murdoch in 1969, who turned it first of all into a tabloid and then into a raucous cheerleader for Thatcher) and the *Sunday Citizen* (formerly *Reynolds' News*) closing in 1967. The fate of the *Herald* and *Chronicle* illustrates all too clearly the truth of Conboy's (2004: 179) observation that 'the demands of advertisers for specific target groups meant that newspapers increasingly restricted their appeal to particular groups based on income as well as social class'. The *Daily Herald* in particular was hit by loss of advertising, not because it was left wing but because its readership was disproportionately working class, male and ageing. When it closed, it had a circulation five times greater than that of *The Times*; similarly, when the *News Chronicle* closed, its circulation was roughly the same as that of *The Daily Telegraph*.

A period of shame

From the mid-1970s until the end of the Thatcher era, the vast majority of the press became even more stridently partisan towards the Conservatives and bitterly hostile to Labour than it had been hitherto. Conservative newspapers played an absolutely key ideological role in paving the way for the Thatcher regime which, once in power, found no more vociferous supporter than the British press. Indeed, the *Kulturkampf* that was Thatcherism was fought out largely in the columns of illiberal British newspapers, both tabloid and otherwise, in a fashion that makes one wonder whether their authors had read Gramsci. In Thatcher, British newspapers had at last found a leader in their own image, and they not only backed her to the hilt and cheered her every excess but excoriated any criticism of their heroine as akin to treachery. As Tim Gopsill and Greg Neale (2007: 251) put it in their history of the National Union of Journalists (NUJ): 'this was a period of shame for the British press: rarely before or since – even in wartime – had they been so close to government. Most papers were besotted with Margaret Thatcher'.

Newspapers are, of course, entitled to their own (or rather their proprie-tors') views, but what needs to be emphasized here is that the Thatcher gov-ernment, the most ideologically driven and extreme that Britain experienced in the twentieth century, came to power determined to rip up the political consensus and rule solely in the interests of those who elected it. Furthermore, it faced a desperately weak opposition in the shape of a Labour party bitterly divided against itself and then, additionally, fatally split between Labour and the SDP. Never, therefore, had there been a greater need for a press that would act as a check and watchdog on overweening state power, in other words as a genuine fourth estate. However, the vast bulk of the British daily press, with the honourable exceptions of the *Guardian*, *Financial Times*, *Independent* and *Mirror* (the only mass circulation paper of the four), chose instead to act as *Pravda* to Thatcher's Brezhnev and, in so doing, forfeited the last vestiges of any residual claims that they might have had to be a fourth estate in any meaningful sense of the term.

In the 1970s and 1980s, Trafalgar House (which owned the *Express*, *Sunday Express* and *Star* from 1977 to 1985) made substantial donations to the Tories. While Thatcher was in power, its owner, Lord Matthews, delivered himself of the view that 'I would find myself in a dilemma about whether to report a British Watergate affair because of the national harm. I believe in batting for Britain' (quoted in Curran and Seaton 2003: 71). And on the eve of the Thatcher government's first budget, he prevented the editor of the *Star* from writing a leader critical of it, informing him that 'there aren't any poor. You can take my word for it. There are no poor in this country' (ibid.: 72). The group's next owner, United Newspapers, was headed by Lord Stevens, who stated that 'I think it would be very unlikely that I would have a newspaper that would support the socialist [sic] party. That isn't what some people would call press freedom, but why should I want a product I didn't approve of? I believe it is in the best interests of United Newspapers in terms of its profits and shareholders to support the Conservatives' (quoted in Snoddy 1993: 133). Sir Nicholas Lloyd and Sir John Junor, editors of the *Daily* and *Sunday Express* respectively, both received their knighthoods during the Thatcher regime, as did Sir Larry Lamb (*Sun*) and Sir David English (*Mail*) in what can only be considered as rewards for services to the Conservative party as opposed to journalism.

The phantom prime minister

The classic Tory-supporting proprietor was of course Rupert Murdoch. The oleaginous *Journals of Woodrow Wyatt* are full of evidence of the unhealthily close relationship between Thatcher and Murdoch. For example, in the first volume, we find, on the occasion of the US bombing raid on Libya from British bases: 'Rupert has been magnificent. I told her [Thatcher] that he had rung saying how much he admired what she had done. She commented on *The Times* and the *Sun* giving "wonderful support"' (Wyatt 1999: 125). And in *Press Gang*, Roy Greenslade (2003: 384) quotes *Times* editor Charles Douglas-Home thus: 'Rupert and Mrs Thatcher consult regularly on every important matter of policy, especially as they relate to his economic and political interests. Around here he's jokingly referred to as "Mr Prime Minister", except that it's no longer much of a joke. In many respects he is the phantom prime minister of the country'.

As already noted, at the *Sun*, Murdoch changed the paper's allegiance from muted Labour to strident Tory. *News of the World* editor Barry Askew complained that, in the early Thatcher years, Murdoch 'would come into the office and literally re-write leaders which were not supporting the hard Thatcher monetarist line. That were not, in fact, supporting – slavishly – the Tory government' (quoted in Hollingsworth 1986: 18–19). Having acquired *The Times* and *The Sunday Times* in 1981 in a deal that should have been referred to the Monopolies and Mergers Commission but wasn't, thanks to the Faustian pact that he had struck with Margaret Thatcher, he proceeded to make his hostility to the latter's liberal editor, Frank Giles, abundantly clear. According to Giles, he would spread the paper out before him and demand '"what do you want to print rubbish like that for?" or, pointing to a particular by-line, snarl "that man's a commie"' (quoted in Curran and Seaton 2003: 70).

Nor was dissent from the Thatcherite line to be tolerated outside the Murdoch empire. Thus, when during the Falklands War the BBC's Peter Snow had the gall to question the government's veracity, the *Guardian* printed a mildly critical cartoon and the *Mirror* took a stand against the whole enterprise, the *Sun* responded, on 7 May 1982, with an extraordinary editorial headed 'Dare call it treason', which alleged that 'there are traitors in our midst' and went on to remark of the *Mirror*: 'what is but treason for this timorous, whining publication to plead day after day for appeasing the Argentine dictators because they do not believe the British people have the stomach for a fight, and are instead prepared to trade peace for honour?' Similarly, a few years later, the once-liberal *Sunday Times* embarked on a sustained and overt campaign of liberal baiting reminiscent of those American papers that supported the McCarthyite witch hunts of the 1950s. Thus, for example, an editorial of 20 September 1987 entitled 'Britain's breed apart' lamented that 'rarely have the ideals of the country's intellectual elite been so out of kilter with the aspirations of plain folk'. And battle was joined again by Brian Walden in his column on 29 November. According to him, 'the preoccupations of many intellectuals in our society are divorced from popular sentiment…Eventually the bulk of the population will be confronted by an elitist culture which shares few of its values'. Further on, we discover that 'the frightening truth is that any anti-capitalist, anti-Western, anti-Israeli material is meat and drink to many intellectuals. They swallow it uncritically'. As a consequence, Walden argues, 'there is already a widespread view, faithfully reflected in the tabloid press, that our cultural and intellectual elites are inherently treacherous. They are seen as the enemies of what most people want and the friends of those who want to destroy Western values'.

The end result of this 'treachery', it is claimed, is 'a severance of much of the intellectual community from the rest of society'.

No wonder, then, that Sir Ian Gilmour (1993: 2) claimed that, in the Thatcher era, the press 'could scarcely have been more fawning if it had been state controlled'. Nor that the Tory MP Richard Shepherd called it the 'hallelujah chorus' (quoted in Gilmour 1993: 8). Similarly, the former *Sunday Times* investigative journalist Bruce Page (2003: 393) condemned it as 'grossly servile'. And interviewed for a BBC2 *Open Space* programme on the so-called 'Loony Left' transmitted on 14 March 1978, the veteran Fleet Street political editor Anthony Bevins stated:

> You don't really have to differentiate between certain newspapers and the Conservative Party. Certain newspapers, from where I stand as an independent journalist, are the Tory Party. They go out and they get the press release, they go back to their offices, they write the press release as if it was some great feat of investigative journalism. They go to Bernard Ingham at 10 Downing Street, to hear what he says, then they go away and they regurgitate it. It is all part and parcel of Conservatism. What's the difference between Conservative Central Office and some of the newspapers in Fleet Street? I can't distinguish between the two. If I want to know what the Conservative Party is thinking, I'll read the *Daily Telegraph* and get the dirt first hand.

A dance of death for democracy

However, the collusion between the majority of the press and the Thatcher government cannot be explained simply in terms of ideological affinities. With the Thatcher era came media deregulation, in particular allowing the press into areas of the media hitherto denied to it by cross-media ownership restrictions. The relaxing of such regulations speeded up the process whereby press barons were mutating into media barons who, whatever their personal political preferences, were willing to bestow their favours (namely their newspapers) on whichever party would best serve their own corporate interests and ambitions. As Steven Barnett and Ivor Gaber (2001: 6) argue, from this there followed

> a growing interdependence of media entrepreneurs and political parties for their own respective self-advancements. Senior politicians have become more and more convinced (whether rightly or not) of the power of the media and have therefore sought to create harmonious relationships with a few elite owners. Simultaneously, electronic and market developments in the media have raised important legislative issues (for example, on cross-ownership and pay-TV access) which have made it more imperative for owners seeking government favours to ensure productive relationships with ruling parties.

Again, the Thatcher–Murdoch axis provides a particularly acute example of such a mutually productive relationship: Thatcher twisted the rules to allow Murdoch to buy *The Times* and *The Sunday Times*, to operate Sky as a purely commercial enterprise largely exempt from the public service obligations of his terrestrial competitors and effectively to take over his satellite TV rival BSB. In return, Murdoch's papers lauded Thatcher as 'Britannia come to life' (the *Sun*'s words) and ceaselessly excoriated her critics – including, of course, the minority liberal press.

Subsequently, the Murdoch press, along with other Conservative newspapers, turned against John Major. This was partly because they could never forgive him for being the beneficiary of what they regarded as the Thatcher *Dolchstoss*. However, in the case of the Murdoch press, the attack was intensified because Major was seen as being insufficiently supportive of – if not hostile to – the further expansion of the Murdoch media empire. This becomes abundantly clear in the third volume of the Wyatt journals (the relevant entries of which are quoted in Page 2003: 424–25). And subsequent history has demonstrated all too clearly that Murdoch has been prepared to offer support to New Labour – albeit far more qualified and conditional support than was offered to Thatcher – to the extent that Tony Blair will support Murdoch's business interests.

Murdoch's relationships with the Thatcher and Blair governments (as well as with governments in Australia, the USA and China) lead one inescapably to the conclusion that, to quote Bruce Page (2003: 372), 'political journalism consists of maintaining sympathetic relations with authority'. In this, however, Murdoch is hardly alone in the modern British press, and nor, as we have seen, is what Page calls this 'politico-business' model of press/government relations a particularly new one. Murdoch's papers, and in particular their extraordinarily close relationship with the Thatcher government, are but the most recent products of tendencies which, as the radical narrative of British newspaper history demonstrates, have had a long gestation within the British press. These may have brought considerable benefits to politicians and press proprietors but, as Page puts it (2003: 479), they also involve politicians and journalists in 'a dance of folly which has at least the potential to be a dance of death for democracy'. The spectacle of Murdoch pimping his papers to whichever party he thinks will best serve his business interests, while titles such as the *Telegraph*, *Mail*, *Express* and *Star* insist on treating Labour as usurpers who have somehow ousted the 'natural' party of government, is one that is entirely inimical to the idea of the press as a fourth estate. Of course, we still have a minority liberal press, in the shape of the *Guardian*, *Observer*, *Independent*, *Financial Times* and, on a good day, *Mirror* and *Sunday Mirror*, but so illiberal has New Labour become (partly, of course, in order to placate the Conservative press) that, bizarrely, it now regards these last remaining bastions of what's left of the fourth estate as far more poisonous than its traditional Conservative foes.

The technological determinist narrative

Introduction

While there is a great deal of variance in interpretation and emphasis, much of the work associated with this particular narrative has its origins in the Toronto school of media theory. Perhaps the best known advocacy for technological determinism is to be found in the work of Marshall McLuhan. Writing over forty years ago now, it was McLuhan (1964) who famously declared, 'the medium is the message'. By this, McLuhan meant the essence of communication is less to do with content than it is the medium itself. Indeed, he notes that the content of any medium is always another medium: the content of writing is speech, the written word is the content of print, print is the content of the telegraph, and so on. Other luminaries include Harold Innis, Elisabeth Eisenstein and Walter Ong, among others. Between them, they painstakingly map out what are generally regarded as the major landmarks in the development of communication technologies – ranging from prehistoric oral cultures, innovations in the printing press, through to more recent advancements in electronic media – apropos their impact on the circulation of ideas, sensory experiences, interpersonal relations and socio-cultural change generally.

In its most extreme form, technological determinism is the grandest of all master narratives, which is why it is subject to special criticism in Curran's original essay. Echoing concerns first expressed by Raymond Williams (1974) over thirty years ago now, Curran argues that technological determinism is intellectually flawed because it pays too much attention to the technology of communications and too little attention to their content and the socio-historical processes in which they are located. That is to say, communication technologies are nearly always developed in the context of solving particular social needs that are historically specific (cf. Winston 1986). More crucially, such accounts tend to overlook the ways in which people themselves make history, assuming instead that technology is the primary agent of historical change.

Both chapters in this section are fine exemplars of technological determinist narratives that are historically informed and sensitive to the intricacies surrounding media technologies. Thus, Paddy Scannell begins his account by arguing that, contrary to Curran's criticisms, the question of technology is at the heart of mediated communication. Unlike many of the forefathers of British cultural studies (e.g. the Frankfurt School, F. R. Leavis, Georg Lukacs, George Orwell), who tended to be extremely critical of technology on the grounds that it was part of the impersonal economic logic of capitalism, Scannell argues that the technical/communicative infrastructure that was gradually put in place in most Western democracies from the nineteenth century onwards was crucial to the long historic process of world modernization and, at the same time, served to make this process visible. He also suggests that technologies both embody and facilitate historical change, that is to say, a society's desire for and commitment to change. One such change has been the desire for greater interconnectivity, social interaction and a sense of togetherness. Hence the increasingly communicative character of technologies in the latter half of the twentieth century. Such technologies not only affirm McLuhan's 'global village', they are also what Scannell calls, 'life enhancing technologies of communication'. In other words, technology need not always be for immoral ends. It can also be a gift of freedom from hardship and toil, a remedy for anguish and poverty, assuming it is put to good use.

Menahem Blondheim's narrative makes an equally persuasive case for taking seriously the history of media technologies as technologies. Drawing on a variety of case studies, he illustrates how the technology of mediated communication is ever present, being integral to the process and active in it: a *telephone* conversation, reading a *book* or watching *television* are activities that are inextricable from the technologies that support them. Even naming or describing these activities entails mention of the technology. This is precisely because communication is the process by which all constitutive elements, sender, message, coding, receiver and channel – the locus of technology – become connected as active, integral parts. On the other hand, Blondheim also raises interesting and important questions about the complex ways in which technologies are mobilized, shaped, modified and reinvented in the process of their application and diffusion. By introducing social–constructivist interpretations of media technology that focus on historical explanations charting the rise and fall of electric media, his chapter is also an exercise in demystifying the role technology has been assumed to play in shaping media and in communication generally.

Further reading

The key studies that make up this narrative include Carey (1989), Eisenstein (1979), Innis (1951, 1952), Meyrowitz (1985), McLuhan (1962, 1964) and Ong (1982); see Kroker (1984) and Watson and Blondheim (2007) for a detailed analysis of the Toronto school and its continuing influence. Not surprisingly, there is a wealth of literature that focuses on the effects on new media technologies – not least the internet – and the so-called 'information society': see, for example, Evans and Wurster (2000), Levinson (2001), Negroponte (1996) and Rheingold (2000, 2002). Castells' (1996, 1997, 1998) three-volume *magnum opus* is widely regarded as the most significant attempt to explain the information age as we enter the twenty-first century. Bell and Kennedy (2000) and Trend (2001) are both edited collections and provide comprehensive guides to the most recent research and public debates. *Wired* magazine is essential reading for those interested in current debates surrounding the latest technological innovations.

The development of new communication technologies is also central to claims made about postmodernity. Echoing the 'medium is the message' determinism of McLuhan, Baudrillard (1988) is undoubtedly the most important exponent of this postmodern sensibility, arguing that mediated representations and reality are one and the same, giving rise to a playful state of 'hyperreality' [cf. Virilio (2000) on the 'acceleration of reality'; see also Jameson (1991) and Harvey (1991) for an altogether more sophisticated and meaningful discussion about the 'compression of time and space' and its implications for 'the social']; see Merrin (2002, 2005) for a critical analysis of Baudrillard's development of McLuhan's work and a sympathetic rendering of Baudrillard's *oeuvre* in relation to the contemporary media landscape.

Not all analyses of new media technologies necessarily adopt a determinist or postmodernist position. Indeed, there are a growing number of books that take a more sceptical view towards such matters and are distinctly less celebratory in their conclusions. Among them, May (2002) subjects many of the aforementioned works to a detailed critique; similarly, Mattelart (2003) looks at how technological determinist accounts surf 'over society and history'; Sarikaskis and Thussu (2006) raise some interesting questions about the ideological struggles over who controls the internet and it social uses, as do Hassan (2004) and Webster (2001); Bennett (2005) offers a radical, culturalist reading of technological determinist accounts in relation to 'the media sensorium'. More forthright criticisms of technological determinism include Raymond Williams' (1974) groundbreaking, *Television: Technology, and Cultural Form*, and Brian Winston's (1986; cf. 1998, 1999) seminal polemic, *Misunderstanding Media*.

Chapter 14

The question of technology

Paddy Scannell

I

In James Curran's provoking account of seven types of media history, the last – communication as technology – is also the least (Curran 2002a: 51–54). It is however what roused him into writing his rival narratives of media history. Media history is, he claims, the neglected grandparent of media studies. Today, it is isolated, ignored and rarely visited by its offspring. By way of proof, an American textbook is cited whose chapter on 'Narratives of media history' makes no reference even in passing to any conventional historical study of the media. It focuses instead on Marshall McLuhan and Jean Baudrillard. Both are returned to in the epilogue to the chapter, which deals with 'technological determinist accounts of the media's transformative influence'. It is not clear that these in fact *are* historical accounts – some of the authors cited are clearly historians (Innis and Eisenstein), some have made gestures in that direction (McLuhan's *Gutenberg Galaxy* is *kind of* historical), and some are not concerned with history at all (Meyrowitz, Castells and Baudrillard). In short, a disparate body of authors whom Curran has read are lumped together and called a 'tradition' but, if it is a tradition, it has not much to do with media histories (conventional or otherwise) and more to do with what Meyrowitz has called 'medium theory', a label that has achieved some degree of recognition in the last fifteen years or so (Meyrowitz 1994).

But let that pass, and also the absence in the narrative of any reference to much good and interesting historical work, in Europe and North America, on media and communication technologies.[1] I am more interested in Curran's bafflement as to 'why this tradition [as so defined by him] should be invested with such authority'. His objection to it, which he takes to be fatal, is that it is overdeterministic. It treats technology as a monocausal, explanatory factor of historical change and ignores all those other factors (economic, political and cultural) in the play of history. This is not exactly a new argument. It was made rather more fully and thoughtfully over thirty years ago by Raymond Williams in *Television: Technology and Cultural Form*, a book that made an important contribution to thinking historically about technologies of communication (Williams 1974). As such, it surely merited at least a mention in James Curran's 'seventh narrative'. Williams, as we will see, took the question of technology seriously. Curran does not, and that is fatal, if it is the case, as I wish to argue, that the question concerning technology is (or should be) at the heart of *any* serious effort to think about the question of mediated communication or, in short, the media.

II

What follows then from raising the question of technology? It has two dimensions to it: the question of technology *as such* and the question of this or that technology. The first asks 'what is technology in general?', while the second asks 'what are the implications of particular technologies?' Both questions are crucial to understanding media, but I will focus on the first one in this chapter. It will readily be granted, I hope, that the question of technology has been a matter of abiding concern throughout the modern era, however defined. Technological innovation is one defining characteristic of modernity. What was the industrial revolution if not a revolution in the means of production, a transformation in the relationship between human beings and machines? Older technologies depended on human input and energy; they were hand powered. The new technologies that brought in the era of mass production had energy inputs from non-human sources (fire, steam, electrical and atomic power) that far surpassed the labour power of human hands and had the effect of inverting the relationship between human beings and their creations. Hitherto, human beings controlled the machines they made. From the nineteenth century onwards, it seemed to be the other way around. It was as if the awesome power of modern technologies produced human beings as their servo-mechanisms, mere cogs in their complex industrial machinery. In the popular imagination of the early twentieth century, human beings were themselves transmogrifying into machines in a machine civilization.

Modern power technologies right through the nineteenth and the first half of the twentieth century were a constant source of anxiety in literature and the arts, in academia and the popular culture of the so-called advanced industrial societies of Europe and North America. It is not necessary here to sketch in the details. I will simply note, by way of illustration, how the question of technology was thought of in the early twentieth century by some of the intellectual ancestors of late twentieth-century cultural and media studies. It was a central concern of critical theory. Technical efficiency, scientific management in the workplace, was developed in America by the industrial psychologist, Frederick Taylor, in the early years of the twentieth century and applied to the automobile industry by Henry Ford. Taylorism and Fordism became bywords, in Western Marxism, for the ruthless exploitation of industrial labour. A critique of Taylorism was at the heart of Georg Lukacs' famous essay, written in 1923, on 'History and class-consciousness'. For Lukacs, the application of scientific methods to the achievement of technical efficiency in the workplace was the mark of the definitive reification of modern consciousness. It confirmed Max Weber's melancholy conclusion that instrumental (means-oriented) rationality prevailed over substantive (ends-oriented) rationality in the iron cage of modernity. It was proof of the rationality of the parts and the irrationality of the whole. The world as a whole was no longer accessible to modern thought.[2]

Lukacs' synthesis of Marx and Weber was absorbed into the bloodstream of the Frankfurt School's thinking. The critique of the culture industries developed by Max Horkheimer and Theodor Adorno, exiles from Germany in America from the mid-1930s, was premised on the penetration of culture by industrial methods. The technological process itself was at the heart of their critique – mass production was an anonymous, machine-dominated process whose uniform, standardized products eliminated individuality and difference. The inhuman technologies of mass production dehumanized the workers, their products and their consumers. This, although elegantly put, was a commonplace argument. In England at exactly the same time, F. R. Leavis (the perhaps unlikely 'grandfather' of British cultural studies) was developing a critique of what he variously called machine or mass civilization along the same lines but without the theoretical sophistication (cf. Leavis and Thompson 1932). And both cases were part of a much wider general societal concern with technology as part of an overall logic of domination that threatened to overwhelm vulnerable, isolated individuals. If this now seems somewhat apocalyptic, it should not be forgotten that the apocalypse was indeed nigh. The destructive powers of modern technologies were unleashed on land, sea and air in a six-year global war at the end of which over 50 million people had perished and large parts of urban Europe had been reduced to rubble. The annihilation of Hiroshima and Nagasaki by the atomic bomb, which ended the Japanese–American war immediately, was final awesome proof of the power of modern scientific technologies and ushered in a new era of global politics.

This brief historical sketch of the technological question in the era of high modernity, from the early nineteenth to the mid-twentieth century, although hopelessly condensed, is not, I hope, inaccurate. The dominant perception of technology, for more than a century, throughout the industrial world and in all sectors of society was fraught with anxiety and for good reasons. Technological innovation drove the economy on all fronts and, in the emerging industrial–military–political complexes of the conflict-ridden countries of the world, weapons of mass destruction were stockpiled and at last put to their mass destructive use in a war which was, for Horkheimer, the end of reason. It was the end of reason in a double sense: the final end or outcome of modern secular rationality and, at the same time, its termination. 'The dictators were rational enough to build tanks. Others should be rational enough to submit to them' (Horkheimer 1978 [1946]: 28).

III

Is technology then no more than a curse? How might it be a blessing? To put it this way is to raise its question as a dialectics, a morality, of power – a power for human good and ill. That is how it was raised, on the cusp of the mid-twentieth century, in a hugely influential essay whose title has echoed through my text thus far: 'The question concerning technology', by Martin Heidegger (1949/1978). The philosophy of technology is a recent and fast-growing subdivision of intellectual labour in that field of academic enquiry, and Heidegger's essay is a key text. In the view of the editors of the *Philosophy of Technology*, it 'is probably the single most influential – though by no means the most popular – position in the field' (Scharff and Dusek 2003: x. See pp. 265–338 for various responses to Heidegger). Here, I am less concerned with the substance of Heidegger's essay and more with its historical significance, as a response to the experience of the world at that time. The substance of Heidegger's essay does not strike me as particularly original beyond the important fact that he raised the question of technology as a proper concern of philosophy. His views on that question echo fairly commonplace attitudes at the time. When Heidegger thinks of technology, he thinks of then ultra-modern things in the late 1940s – jet aircraft, radar and (characteristically) the hydro-electric plant on the river Rhine (Heidegger 1978: 312). These very new things are then contrasted with very old hand-made things, craft products, a silver chalice for instance, whose making he discusses in some detail. Heidegger does not of course discuss the making of a jet plane for that he simply could not imagine.

For someone like Heidegger, writing in the late 1940s at the age of sixty, there were memories from childhood of an older pre-industrial way of life – of rural, village life, rooted in the landscape and quietly adjusted to the order of nature and natural time. That was Heidegger's heritage in the small town of Messkirch in Southern Germany where he was born and grew up. There is much irony in the rediscovery (reinvention) of Heidegger as the precursor of postmodern thought, for he was in just about every conceivable way a pre-modern thinker. An illuminating recent monograph by Adam Sharr on *Heidegger's Hut* confirms this point. The hut was built in 1922 as a retreat for thinking – a retreat from the urban life of a university professor in the town below to a little three-roomed cabin built into the hillside of a sloping meadow with no other buildings around it. It had no electricity or running water (which was fetched by bucket from a nearby well) and looked out across a valley to the mountains in the distance. For the next fifty years and more, Heidegger escaped to *die Hütte* whenever he could. It was where he thought and wrote. Its simplicity gave him tranquillity for thinking and kept the busy modern world below at bay. Heidegger resisted modern technologies in the hut for many years but finally acknowledged the usefulness of electric lighting and a telephone which were installed some time in the 1950s (Sharr

2006: 104). It was from his hut that Heidegger contemplated the question of modern technology.

Heidegger came from a generation for whom there was still a lingering real memory of a pre-technological world. That nostalgia shows up equally in the thinking of his exact English counterpart who resembles him in many ways, F. R. Leavis, who taught English Literature at Cambridge University. Leavis, like Heidegger, looked back to a pre-industrial, rural era and grieved for its passing. Like so many intellectuals in the early to mid-twentieth century, they both experienced and thought of technology as a malignant, alien power. Their prevalent response was one of repulsion at The Wasteland of modern urban life and aesthetic disgust with the ugliness of modern technologies – the blight, say, cast on the traditional landscape by the march of electricity pylons across the fields in the 1930s. There was moral indignation at the plight of the masses, victims in both the workplace and their homes, of the forces of mass production. There was existential anxiety about the alienated conditions of modern metropolitan life and fear of the destructive potential of high-technology weapons of mass destruction made horribly plain for all to see in the aerial bombing of Madrid in the Spanish Civil War. The dialectics of technological power are plain enough in all of this, and the fears and anxieties of those times cannot be dismissed as the products of fevered intellectual imaginations. They were real and widespread and justified.

IV

But we also see the emergence in the early twentieth century of something else that Raymond Williams saw so passionately: the industrial revolution, driven by technology, was a long revolution for the good – 'not just mechanical, external progress, but a real service of life'.

> For one thing I knew this: at home we were glad of the Industrial Revolution, and of its consequent social and political change. True, we lived in a beautiful farming valley, and the valleys beyond the limestone we could see were all ugly. But there was one gift that was overriding, one gift which at any price we would take, the gift of power that is everything to men who have worked with their hands. It was slow in coming to us, in all its effects, but steam power, the petrol engine, electricity, these and their host of products in commodities and services we took as quickly as we could get them and were glad. I have seen all these things being used, and I have seen the things they replaced. I will not listen to any acid listing of them – you know the sneer you can get into plumbing, baby Austins,[3] aspirin, contraceptives, canned food. But I say to these Pharisees: dirty water, an earth bucket, a four mile walk each way to work, headaches, broken women, hunger and monotony of diet. The working people, in town and country alike, will not listen (and I support

them) to any account of our society which supposes that these things are not progress: not just mechanical, external progress, but a real service of life. Moreover, in these new conditions, there is more real freedom to dispose of our lives, more real personal grasp where it matters, more real say. Any account of our culture which implicitly or explicitly denies the value of an industrial society is really irrelevant; not in a million years would you make us give up this power.

Williams (1989 [1958a]: 10)

The industrial revolution offered 'the masses' a priceless gift, 'the gift of power that is everything to men who have worked with their hands' and they will not, in a million years, give it up. The power of technology – 'steam power, the petrol engine, electricity, these and their host of products in commodities' – is the gift of freedom. Negatively, it is a liberation from toil, suffering and hardship; positively, it is the freedom of control over one's life and circumstance – 'more real personal grasp where it matters, more real say'. And who are the Pharisees who would deny this with their easy sneers?

Williams is almost certainly thinking of George Orwell and this passage from *The Road to Wigan Pier*:

Whole sections of the working class who have been plundered of all they really need are being compensated, in part, by cheap luxuries which mitigate the surface of life. It is quite likely that fish-and-chips, art-silk stockings, tinned salmon, cut-price chocolate, the movies, the radio, strong tea and the foot-ball pools have between them averted revolution.

Orwell (1965 [1937]: 90–91)[4]

We should note the easy presumption (so characteristic of bourgeois intellectuals then) of knowing what the masses 'really need' and what they really don't. What they really needed, in Orwell's considered opinion, was a revolution (such as he had just fought in) and not an array of cheap luxuries that mitigated the surface of life but failed, presumably, to plumb its depths. In Williams' carefully thought out list of things, each is a remedy to an ill: indoor plumbing [running water, a bathroom and water closet (WC)] replaces dirty water and an outdoor earth closet, a small car alleviates a four-mile walk each way to work, aspirin relieves headache, contraceptives prevent women from being broken, in body and spirit, by endless unwanted pregnancies, canned food mitigates hunger and monotony of diet. Williams knows what (and who) he is talking about. Does Orwell? Yet his was the prevalent view of the masses at the time among the European progressive intelligentsia, for whom the revolutionary potential of the urban proletariat had been undone by the soft deceptions of mass culture. That was the whole point of Horkheimer and Adorno's critique of the new culture industries and Marcuse' influential concept of 'affirmative culture' (Adorno and Horkheimer 1986 [1944]; Marcuse

1968 [1937]): the masses were 'bought off' and made safe for capitalism by the ground-bait of cheap luxuries.

Williams' postwar thinking is radically different from that of prewar intellectuals, and a key reason for this is that the postwar world of the 1950s to which he was responding had changed profoundly from the prewar world in Europe and North America with which Adorno, Horkheimer, Orwell, Heidegger, Leavis and their generation had engaged. I have suggested elsewhere that the global war of the 1940s was the historical hinge of the last century (Scannell 2007: 260–93). The world going into it and the world coming out of it was different. And this was due, I argued, to a long-term shift in the world economy, in train well before the war but only decisively established in its aftermath, as it moved from an economy of scarcity to an economy of abundance. The life circumstances of individuals were changing from prewar work-defined patterns of existence to new postwar leisure-defined ways of living. The coercive time of work and the workplace no longer dominated individual life and experience which were now oriented towards free time. The pendulum was swinging from production to consumption. It was a decisive change of gear in the long, still continuing world historical process of societal modernization in which subsistence economies and the forms of life developed in adjustment to them gave way to unprecedented surplus economies of abundance and new forms of life defined, for the time, by economic choice and freedom.

This structural transformation of the world economy, taking place in the mid-twentieth century, marked the passing of the time of the masses and the emergence of the time of everyday life. The time of the masses was defined by the politics of poverty which erupted into historical life in the French Revolution when the Parisian masses rose in the name of bread and freedom. Poverty at that moment ceased to be a natural fact and became social fact and a central, unavoidable political issue. The question of the masses, from the late eighteenth century to the end of the Second World War, was the defining economic and political issue in North America and Europe: mass production, mass politics, mass society, mass culture and, in the end, mass slaughter through weapons of mass destruction. This was the era of modernity, the era in which the secular politics of European enlightenment were worked through in continuous response to the new mode of production, factory capitalism and its mass-produced commodities, themselves the products of the appliance of science and new power technologies.

V

Technologies are not superimposed on history from above by the invisible hand of God or the market, but are rather the material means through which history is made, key instruments of historical change in a double sense – the expression of changes taking place in the world and the means whereby that change is sought for and realized.[5] Williams (1974) emphasized that technologies are always meant and intended as solutions to current economic, political and social concerns – the kinds of technologies a society produces and puts to use tell you something essential about that society, not merely its level of material 'development', but also the character of its social relations, where it puts its energies, its concerns and commitments. The essence of technology is nothing technological, as Heidegger pointed out. Technologies, the products of human thought, imagination and knowledge, are world disclosing: in their conceptualization, application and use, they reveal something central about the historical human world that has produced them as the material means to human ends.

As a small historical thought experiment to explore this a little further, the core theme of this chapter, we might try to identify what we think of as *the* world-defining technologies of today and compare them with those of sixty years ago. Why that particular moment in the past? Because I take it that our world, the world on the cusp of the twenty-first century, is in almost every way the product of the world that emerged from the end of the Second World War. The war was an end and a beginning. The emergent world of the late 1940s has begun to surpass the era of high modernity whose boundaries were defined by revolution at the start and war in the end. 1945 marks the passage from modernity to postmodernity. We can 'read' the essential character of this transformation through structural differences in the world-defining technologies of sixty years ago and now. What were they then, what are they now? I have already mentioned what I take as the world-defining technology of the late 1940s – the atomic bomb. As for today, I think the internet and (or) the cell phone would be pretty safe bets, but either will do for they are closely connected.

No technology has a stand-alone existence. The atomic bomb stands alongside all the other technologies of mass destruction – the planes, tanks, battleships, guns and munitions – that had long been invented, manufactured and stockpiled for killing purposes in Europe and North America. And likewise many technologies of communication converge in the application and use of the internet and the cell phone. The atomic bomb still exists today, just as the telephone existed sixty years ago. But the bomb was then a world-dominating technology (and the telephone was not), whereas today their positions have reversed with the telephone in the foreground of daily life everywhere and the bomb as a background threat in global politics, no longer the defining issue in world politics today as it was in the cold war era. The bomb and the cell phone, then: one a technology of mass destruction, the other a technology of interpersonal communication. I take this difference, which I will explore in a little detail, as pointing to the essence of the transformation from the world of modernity to our postmodern world.

The classic 'moment' in which this change first clearly showed up was the 1950s – the pivotal decade of the last sixty years in which the decisive transition to an economy of abundance made its impact felt in all aspects of contemporary life. The decade of the 1950s is the historical key to an understanding of the world we inhabit today. In those years, for the first time, the majority of people in North America and Northern Europe began to enjoy a life of modest affluence: in Britain, the Tories won an election in 1959 with the slogan 'You've never had it so good!' and, in the United States, its most distinguished economist, J. K. Galbraith, wrote a bestselling book called *The Affluent Society*. The majority of people – and this was Williams' core perception in the passage quoted above, published in 1958 – now had a marginal surplus of disposable time and money. The hungry thirties, as they were known in both countries, became a vanishing memory as most people, no longer governed by necessity, began to enjoy a measure of freedom and control in the disposition of their lives.

And this change depended, as Williams saw so clearly, on the technological transformation of everyday life then taking place. When Heidegger thought about the question of technology he thought of radar, jet planes and a hydro-electric plant and contrasted them with pre-industrial craft instruments and technologies. Such thinking was typical of an older generation at that time. What he failed to attend to was the emergence, at that moment, of quite new technologies that we are all now familiar with as *white goods* or *domestic appliances*. The wired home of today, with its host of electrical appliances, was decisively established through *all* sectors of societies only fifty or so years ago. Electric clothes and dishwashers, vacuum cleaners, fridges and freezers took the toil out of domestic labour and saved time. In the thirties, the family wash would take a working class woman four days: on Mondays, clothes were washed and wrung dry by hand. On Tuesdays and Wednesdays, they hung out to dry. On Thursdays, they were ironed. Before fridges and freezers, shopping was a daily necessity and involved trips on foot to different shops for different things: to fetch and carry from the grocer, the baker, the butcher, the greengrocer, the fishmonger. Today, the family shop is done by car once a week in one large convenience store or supermarket.

The new domestic appliances that came into general use in the 1950s were labour- and time-saving innovations that freed people from hitherto unavoidable and necessary domestic toil and from time-consuming daily tasks. That was the negative freedom they offered. And what did people do with their new-found free time? They continued to enjoy the services of the prewar culture industries (radio, cinema and the record industry), widely condemned by the prewar intelligentsia. They began, in millions, to watch television. And they talked to each other. 'Talk' was, in various ways, one of the great academic discoveries across a range of disciplines in North America and Europe in the 1950s (Scannell 2007: 171–97). The disappearance of 'the masses' in the 1950s was accompanied by the discovery of people – ordinary people talking to each other in the mundane situations and circumstances of daily life. If it is true that sex began in the 1960s, then conversation began in the 1950s – or at the very least it came to the notice of academics in that decade as part of their discovery of 'everyday life'.

This is not to say that talk and everyday life did not exist before the second half of the last century, but it is to draw attention to the fact that hitherto they were beneath history and below the radar of sociology for instance. In the 1950s, the mundane world of daily life and its universal medium of communication, talk, were both historicized by the then very new medium of television: not *just* by television, of course, but by television as a significant index of world transformation taking place in the 1950s and certainly by television as the emerging new medium of everyday life itself, in which the mundane and the ordinary now began to achieve a universal visibility that it had never before possessed. Television was the key electrical, domestic appliance that contributed to the historicization of the hitherto unhistorical mundane world of ordinary, everyday existence.

It did not appear in the 1950s by happenstance. The general conditions of its possibility did not exist before then; that is, the possibility of its wholesale uptake and use across all sectors of society. More than its precursor, radio, television is pre-eminently a technology whose purchase and use presupposes societies in which the majority of people have marginal surpluses of disposable money and time for its enjoyment. Television was, from the start and has remained to this day, an everyday social medium enjoyed by its viewers in their free time as a leisure activity, primarily as a source of entertainment and (to a lesser extent) as a source of information, a 'window on the world'. The technology of the TV set, the apparatus that must be acquired in order to access the viewing world, is one of those domestic apparatuses discussed above that contributed to the unobtrusive transformation of daily life in the postwar world. The condition of television's possibility presupposes a world oriented to domesticity; a way of life centred on households, the sphere of privacy, home and family, whose members were free from domestic necessity, from such time-consuming and onerous chores as daily fire-lighting (cleaning the ashes from the grate, chopping wood, fetching coal, laying the new fire – as I did, in my childhood), shopping for food, cooking, washing and so forth.... The new domestic technologies of the 1950s gave the conditions of domestic leisure which television fulfilled so spectacularly: freedom *from* toil and necessity, freedom *for* relaxation and leisure.[6] Ever since then, in European and North American households, watching television has remained the preferred daily leisure activity of whole populations across all classes, for women and men, young and old.

VI

What are we to make of this – what does television-as-an-appliance (as a domestic technology, a household good, a consumer durable) tell us about the kind of society that created it and the kind of world that it complements and enhances? Let me tie this question in with the little thought experiment I proposed above. I'll put it summarily. The atomic bomb is a formal indication of a world defined by struggle, conflict and war. The internet and cell phones are formal indications of a world defined by communicative sociability. In short, the fundamental underlying transformation of the world, driven by continuing technological innovation in the last sixty years, was perfectly and presciently anticipated by the late Winston Churchill as a change from 'war war to jaw jaw': from global conflict (Second World War) to global conversation (the cell phone) and, hence, the crucial significance of the role of television in the historicization of talk and the mundane world (and their academic discovery at the same time) in the 1950s. The technological turn in the postwar world was away from technologies of mass destruction (no new weapon has been developed in the last sixty years that in fact surpasses the destructive power of the now old technologies of the atomic and hydrogen bombs) and towards technologies of communication; a field that has seen massive, continuing innovation in every decade with new technologies sometimes displacing and sometimes combining with older ones. The increasing interconnection of communication technologies old and new, their convergence in the internet, is a formal indication of the single, globally interconnected world that we inhabit now at the start of the twenty-first century. At the start of the 1950s, the natural horizon of experience for most people was defined by where they lived and worked. In the course of the fifties and sixties, their horizons were extended by nationwide broadcast services. And in the last thirty years or so, continuing technical innovation in all aspects of telecommunications has produced the whole world as the common and natural horizon of all individual experience, a development anticipated by Marshall McLuhan well before it actually happened.

I began by emphasizing the prevailing attitude to technology throughout the classic era of industrial modernization as one of high anxiety – and not without good reason for coal- and steam-powered technologies were large, dirty, dangerous and unhealthy, often positively life-threatening, not just for coal-miners, say, but for the whole of society. But more than that, what drove science and technology in the conflict-ridden Europe of the first half of the last century was the pursuit of bigger and better weapons of mass destruction. The technological sublime of modernity, one might say, was oriented to destruction and death and realized in its ultimate achievement, the 'ultimate weapon' of the atom bomb. This is not to argue for the atom bomb as the *cause* of anything: it is simply to take it as a formal indication of a world whose defining realities were, in the end, conflict, war and mass destruction. The technologies that a society produces are real and true indications of its fundamental concerns and commitments. The atomic bomb is a significant index (and indictment) of the whole international economic, military and political power structure of that era. It serves as a metonym for the logic of domination so clearly articulated in the critical tradition that ran from Marx, Weber and Lukacs through to Adorno, Horkheimer and other members of the Institute for Social Research at Frankfurt.

Now of course, in the era of high modernity (the interwar period), another technological formation was 'working through' those years as the world economy began to turn towards the mass production of domestic goods and of entertainment for the masses. The full working through of that development took off in the defining postwar decade of the 1950s when conditions of modest affluence were finally secured through all sectors of society in the countries of North America and Northern Europe. The key new technologies of the second half of the last century, through to the present, are all to do with communication: television, the internet and the cell phone – surely the three now interconnected, world-defining, world-disclosing technologies of today.

How utterly different they are from the world-defining technology of sixty years ago. The cell phone is as small as the atom bomb was huge. The new technologies are clean and safe. They are durable and reliable. They are non-malevolent, manifestly non-hostile to human life and human interests. They are people oriented, not people threatening. They are user friendly. They have what I have called a 'for-anyone-as-someone' structure (Scannell 2001): they are designed in such ways that anyone can use them for their own and particular purposes. PCs (personal computers) and cell phones are personal and interpersonal technologies of communication. The communicative turn is a crucial, defining feature of the postwar world. Talk is an intrinsically sociable and co-operative interaction that requires of all participants that they speak *and* listen to each other. To refuse to talk to someone is an intrinsically hostile act, a termination of friendship and a declaration of war (as when children say 'I'm not talking to you any more!'). The increasingly communicative character of the postwar world is disclosive of two things: it is not merely the antithesis of the dominant anti-communicative ethos of the prewar world, it is its solution and resolution.[7] War is the negation of communication and communication is the negation of war – as shown recently in the decision of the parties in Northern Ireland at last to stop killing each other and start talking to each other instead. Technologies in themselves neither create nor resolve conflict but, in either case, they are expressive of a prevailing ethos, a disposition one way or the other. As such, they are the material realization of general societal concerns, intentions and purposes, the means whereby they are valorized for good or ill. The take-off into the material world of modernity was brought about by the harnessing and exploitation of the power of natural energy sources. The question of power is at the heart of the question of technology and it is a moral question – the application of power for worldly purposes of good or ill. Life-threatening technologies of mass destruction on the one hand, for instance; life-enhancing technologies of communication on the other.

Notes

1 To take just a notable sample: Douglas (USA) 1987; Marvin (USA) 1990; Blondheim (Israel) 1994; Flichy (France) 1995; Kittler (Germany) 1999.

2 The *Principles of Scientific Management* was published by Frederick Winslow Taylor in 1911. For a review of Lukacs, Horkheimer and Adorno's critique of Taylorism and the industrialisation of culture, see Scannell (2007: 31–51).

3 One of the first British mass manufactured small and affordable family cars.

4 For a mordant critique of this facile rhetorical style in Orwell's writings, see Williams (1962 [1958b]: 278–79).

5 For a classic, nuanced defence of the claim that machines *do* make history, see Heilbroner (1967/2003).

6 The classic study of television, domestic life and leisure in the USA in the 1950s is Spigel (1992). In the UK, David Morley's work on television as a domestic technology that exists in situ with other domestic electrical appliances is exemplary (Morley 2007).

7 I have in mind the key distinction, made by David Riesman, between the 'modern' inner- and 'postmodern' other-directed individual. The former strong, silent, uncommunicative and unsociable type is taken to be the ideal–typical (Weberian) character in nineteenth- and early twentieth-century America. The latter – oriented to others, sociable and chatty – is, in Riesman's view, a very new phenomenon that is becoming visible in the immediate postwar era (Riesman 1950/1976). The gendered character of these two types is striking: the inner-directed individual is 'masculine' while the other-directed individual is 'feminine'.

Chapter 15

Narrating the history of media technologies

Pitfalls and prospects

Menahem Blondheim

I

Communications may have preceded history; after all, in the beginning, many believe, there was the word. Nevertheless, the notion of communications as a distinct and significant aspect of the human lifeworld, worthy of historical investigation, has come very late in the history of history. Media history is one of Clio's youngest offsprings and, as this volume makes amply clear, it is still in the process of trying to define and establish itself alongside its mature siblings such as economic and military, social and political history.

This late coming of media history is all the more curious when considering that it narrates such a ubiquitous aspect of life as communications. But precisely the ubiquity of communication may have, paradoxically, concealed it as an aspect of history, delaying the emergence of media history as an agenda for historical research. In fact, and surprising as it may seem, 'communication' as we use it today is a remarkably young concept, and a relatively new category to the systematic analysis of social life. To illustrate, my university library does not hold a single book published before the Second World War that includes the word 'communication' – in the sense of the field of human interaction – in its title or subtitle.

As it appears, only the emergence of electrical communications in the mid-nineteenth century paved the way for recognizing communications as a thing unto itself. By divorcing communication from transportation and 'annihilating time and space', electric communications shook up conventional notions. Common sense could now isolate the communicative process from the physicality of transportation, on the one hand, and the amorphous nature of message contents, on the other. Now one could think of the process of linking people by the transference of information independently and abstractly. This was one of the ways in which electric media had, according to an 1844 observer, 'originated in the mind an entirely new class of ideas, a new species of consciousness'.[1]

If communications, as a concept, was a new idea midwifed by technology, only the distinct 'species of consciousness' generated by the era of mass electric broadcast, in the second quarter of the twentieth century, turned communications into a field of academic research. The emergence of broadcast as a dominant player in political and cultural life and, moreover, a supposedly uniquely powerful one, directed scholarly attention to communications, ultimately turning its study into an academic discipline (Park and Pooley 2008). In other words, both the rise of the concept of communication and the onset of its systematic investigation were associated with breakthroughs in communication technology. Little wonder, therefore, that technology was an aspect of communication seized on in early pioneering works on the history of communication and on communication in history.

Moreover, at the time communication studies were taking shape, after the mid-twentieth century, structural functionalism had considerable influence on notions of historical development. From a functionalist perspective, communications, like other social arrangements, served the stability of the system. The stasis would be disturbed only by the injection of new inputs from outside the system, launching change that would reverberate throughout it. As the source of change, technology was an ideal suspect. Understood as the child of ideas developed in a supposedly autonomous sphere of scholarly and scientific speculation, technology could infiltrate society, imbalance it and cause a chain reaction of change. Once historians – the students of change – became mindful of communication, technology presented itself as a prime venue for exploring the difference communication really made.

For different reasons, a new generation of historians has also been lured by, perhaps driven to, this field. Scholars who have experienced the dramatic change wrought by new information and communications technology (ICT) – the personal computer (PC), cell phone, internet – inevitably read their experience of change back into history. After all, in no previous era in history has technological change affecting the workaday been concentrated in a single aspect of life as it has been focused on communication in the past generation. The dramatic diffusion of new technologies in the 1920s, for example, included the refrigerator, automobile, washing machine, radio, improved prophylactics, gas ranges, skyscrapers, talkies – one could go on. In the past generation, however, except for the microwave oven and the snow/foliage blower, all new gadgetry entering the household was ICT related (cf. Leuchtenberg 1958 with Van den Bulte 2000).

But even given these circumstances, the lure that technological aspects seem to have in the study of media history would still appear exceptional. Lynn White's (1962) proposition that the introduction of the stirrup in effect brought about feudal society has remained marginal, something of a curiosity, in medieval historiography. Similarly, one seldom hears scholars in gender research discussing the invention of the washing machine and Pampers (a brand of babies' nappies) as the master key to understanding the transformation of gender relations, and consequently the world. Yet the works of Innis and McLuhan, Eisenstein and Ong, and a host of others, focusing as they do on communication technology, remain staples in the study of media history.

The source of this unique emphasis on technology in understanding communications appears to be rooted in some of the most fundamental aspects of communication as a human practice. Communication, by its nature, constitutes an end-to-end process, in which all components and their relationship are active and integral. Communication is essentially the circuit closing-like process of linking minds through the transference of information. Inevitably, the conduit for this connection – the channel through which minds are linked – is integral to the process and active in it. As in all mediated communicative acts there is a technology at work, it is necessarily transparent, being elemental to the act itself – the closing of the communication circuit. Thus, a telephone conversation encapsulates speakers, messages and a relationship, but it always features a telephone machine too, just as a book, a technological artefact, is that which establishes a relationship between an author and a reader. Even naming or describing these communicative activities entails mention of the technologies that are inextricable from them: hence, watching television, videoconferencing, sending an email, reading a book. This is not necessarily the case with other technologies, as for instance when one eats a food which was produced by ploughs, combine harvesters, genetic engineering or other sophisticated technologies. For these crucial technologies are completely absent from our experience of eating or thoughts about it. Thus, communication technologies tend to be transparent; they receive constant attention and eminence in any thinking about communications.

But not only are the workings of technology in processes of communication transparent to their users, the difference they make tends to be constantly refreshed. Communication is a most prevalent activity, and individuals constantly engage in unmediated, face-to-face exchanges, in parallel to using technological tools for communicating. With unmediated communications as an ever-present standard, the wonders worked by communication technologies are constantly underscored, and hence they become salient. With each new application of technology to the act of communicating, the fundamental face-to-face experience is re-evoked as a benchmark. People still respond to an overseas phone call by exclaiming 'but you sound so near!'.

Given the transparency and salience of technologies in communication, it is not surprising that some of the most powerful technologies ever developed pervaded public consciousness through their application to the process of communication and transportation. Possibly beginning with the wheel and then the steam engine as put to use in transportation, subsequently electric technologies, electronics and transistors, satellites and digital processing, all made their first appearance to the large public as ingredients of communication machines. This, in turn, would strengthen the association of dramatic technological breakthroughs with communication, enhancing the salience of the technology in communications.

Moreover, because of their transparency, the application of basic technological innovations to communication may short circuit the process of their diffusion. Diffusion of innovations is fundamentally a two-step process: first, the diffusion of knowledge about an innovation, then its adoption. In communication, the two steps may converge; receiving knowledge about the innovation and its application can become a single step, as in reading a printed book, hearing a loudspeaker or a radio or receiving a telegram. Furthermore, given the networking capacity of many electric media, their diffusion curves tend to be particularly steep. This telescoping of the diffusion process and the consequent notion of abrupt and sudden emergence makes the technology stand out, adds to its striking nature and may lead to great expectations for change.[2]

A further fundamental attribute of communications fortifies the transparency and salience of technology in enabling communications, but also goes far beyond it. The commodity exchanged in the process of communications is knowledge: information, sentiments, ideas. This of course implies that communicating is a conscious, mindful activity, further ensuring that attention is paid to the process, to which technologies, as noted, are central. But beyond that, ideas are perceived as the origins and agent of all action. A universal bias, articulated at least since Plato, is that ideas and thoughts wield action and direct action, that mind controls matter. As the commodity communications process is thought, changes in the media of its recording, dissemination and reception are expected to affect other aspects of life too, inevitably and profoundly. This bias contributes to the great transformative potential that new ICT is thought to have on individuals and society.[3]

Finally, and most generally, the generation and diffusion of knowledge are commonly considered the most elevated human activity, and communicating as one of the most powerful human drives. The ultimate function of communication is to overcome human separateness and link people.[4] The paramount social and psychological importance of this function tends to make any change in the means of achieving it of great consequence. Such change is perceived to be capable of revolutionizing social relations, serving as a launch-pad for dramatic change in the human condition.[5]

II

The transparency and salience of innovations in media technology and the great expectations they raise for revolutionary change has led to an extensive debate on the role of technology in understanding media. Media historians share in that debate but, in many cases, fail to bring to it their two greatest assets: broad context and hindsight. All too often technological media, new to their times, bow into historical narratives in the role of sharp swords cutting through the Gordian knot-like complexity of historical development. The orientation of these narratives tends to be from the technology onward: upon encountering a new ICT, minds seem to enter a fast-forward mode and evaluate their potential impact as agents of change, not its culmination.

And indeed, in both historical and general discourse, the introduction of communication technologies tends to launch a project of technological assessment (hereafter TA) (e.g. Schumacher 1973; Schot and Rip 1997). While the assessment of intricate developments in nanotechnology and materials, biotechnology and energy, has tended to remain in institutional settings, subject to formal TA, the assessment of media technologies[6] has developed into a popular pastime, performed in the public sphere. Given the unique nature of communication technologies as discussed above – their transparency and salience, their unusually rapid diffusion and the expectations for major social and existential consequences built into them – their launching captures the public imagination and becomes the topic of popular discourse. Concepts such as the information society and the digital age, the communication revolution and the digital divide, have become household words, and insights such as 'the medium is the message' or the world shrinking into a 'global village' can be heard in any respectable cocktail party.

The discourse of new communication technologies has been led, in past decades, by characteristic types of commentators, who have assumed the mission of interpreting the thoroughgoing change in the communication environment to a fascinated public. Modelled to an extent on the first specimen of the type – Marshall McLuhan – the new media gurus explain and give meaning to our transformed media experience and forecast its consequences, for public consumption.[7] These eloquent, often brilliant, commentators, the likes of Alvin Toffler, Howard Rheingold, Nicholas Negroponte, George Gilder, Esther Dyson, John Perry Barlow – one could go on and on – are understood as commercially and politically disinterested players, whose mission is to do the thinking and to make sense of a storm of change on behalf of a bewildered public.

Four overlapping elements appear to characterize the media technology gospel according to its popular apostles. First, and much like the TA approach, the point of departure in these analyses tends to be scientific and technological know-how, which can be harnessed to shape new and improved media. Holding technology in sharp focus, adjacent factors lurking in the broader context, such as state policy, law, the business environment, even other media technologies, tend to be discounted, let alone less tangible aspects of the environment such as ideology and cultural patterns. Related to this bias towards the autonomy of technology is a second common element: the tendency to consider media technologies as lucid and unambiguous, and to interpret them on their own terms. This what-you-see-is-what-you-get approach tends to overlook the mutability of technologies, their potential adaptation, transformation and reinvention in the course of their diffusion and use. A third characteristic of future-oriented discussions of communication technology is their particular construction of the chain of causes and effects. With new technologies as the point of departure and with the future open ended, technology necessarily plays cause, the future its effect. Such an orientation is necessarily blind to the view of technologies as consequences of historical change, and to their role as mere elements of a much broader front of change.

Revolution is the trope of the gurus' commentary. To draw attention and be heard, the rhetoric of the communication technology mavens commonly predicts that the launching of new media will yield striking and prodigious, usually benign, effects patterned as a revolution, 'third wave' style. Conversely, it is those commentators who present a world revolutionized by communications that have drawn a massive following.

At its worst, media history echoes the clap-trap of the guru-type deterministic discourse, albeit looking at technology backwards rather than forwards. As James Curran (2002a) has noted, much writing in the field has been based on premises that are 'intellectually flawed' (see also Briggs and Burke 2002). Histories of media technologies, Curran observes, tend to overemphasize technology and view it as an 'autonomous cause of change'. They stand in danger of overlooking 'the ways in which the development and application of…technology was influenced by the wider context of society'. And above all, argues Curran, they may exaggerate 'the impact of new communications by downplaying non-media influences'. 'The technological deterministic tradition', he concludes, 'is seductive, stimulating but ultimately simplistic'.

But at its best, narrating the history of media technologies can be more than stimulating. It has the potential of serving as a much needed corrective to popular and professional biases in understanding the development path of media technologies. After all, history is the uncovering of the past in all its richness and all its complexity. Not only does history provide a wide-angled view, allowing broad-ranging, multicausal analysis, it wields the ultimate weapon for untangling cause-and-effect chains – hindsight.

The balance of this chapter will provide a scattering of examples to illustrate the ways in which media history can serve as a corrective to the common pitfalls in understanding new media. These illustrations follow the three, somewhat overlapping categories of challenge to the responsible study of media technologies just discussed. As the present chapter is about the study of media history, rather than a study of media history, the examples are merely suggestive. They are brief, eclectic and thoroughly unrepresentative glimpses of media history. Coming from a variety of times and places, they are culled, unsystematically, from a variety of types of research into the history of media technology. Nevertheless, they may suggest the potential usefulness of a historical approach to understanding the dynamics of media development, and further afield, of the role of media technologies in social development.

III

The bias of autonomy

The fundamental strategy of the TA approach in projecting the impact of new media technologies is a sharp focus on the technology at hand, drawing inferences as to its communicative affordances and projecting their impact. At its root, this approach is congruent with the veteran notion mentioned above, of technology as an autonomous player that has the potential of transforming the status quo. But the notion of autonomous emergence and play of technology, however attractive, is beset with problems from its very first step – the process of technological innovation – and on.[8]

Consider the standard model of the technological innovation process, presented in Figure 15.1. The model demonstrates quite strikingly that technological innovation is a to-and-fro process, applying technical know-how to perceived and real social needs. And such needs, of course, directly reflect the particular conditions of their specific historical time and place. On its own, the upper trajectory of the innovation process – the 'state of technical knowledge' – cannot explain the sources, development, or diffusion patterns of a medium, nor its subsequent modifications and reinventions.

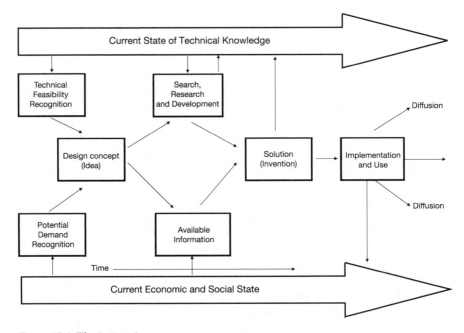

Figure 15.1 The innovation process.
Source: Brown (1981: 4). Cf. Winston (1986: 18) and Winston (1999: 786–815).

The model, however, fails to account for a preliminary phase in the innovation process: identifying the instigator of the consultative process that leads to an operative technology. That culprit, today, may be found in garages in Silicon Valley and New Delhi, and lofts in London and Moscow, where vision- and need-driven amateurs translate their dreams into ICQs, Disc-on-keys and YouTubes, later to be seized on and perfected by the Microsofts and Intels of the world (themselves the outgrowths of wild-eyed beginnings). Engineering handbooks and international standard specs simply do not qualify as mothers of invention.

This dynamic has a long and celebrated lineage. Gutenberg, an unassuming artisan recently voted man of the previous millennium, can well serve as its prototype, and Alexander Graham Bell as a fine representative. Bell was the son and husband of deaf women, and his father was an expert on elocution. Bell was a teacher to the deaf, an amateur ventriloquist and had all the advantages of 'not being an expert' (Hounshell 1975; Bruce 1990; Gray 2006). Samuel F. B. Morse, a painter, was traumatized by the death of his wife, who fell ill in Connecticut while he was sojourning in Washington. She died alone while giving birth to their fourth child, her desperate messages to summon Morse simply did not arrive in time (Blondheim 1994). In the process of translating their vision into innovation, Morse and Bell – the non-experts – embodied the innovation process model (Figure 15.1). Both consulted with eminent American scientist Joseph Henry at the Smithsonian on finding ways in which electricity could be bridled to make the telegraph tick and the telephone talk.

Nor would it be far-fetched to link David Sarnoff's ingenious weaving of wireless technology, programming, operating system and financing in making mass broadcast radio happen to a life-changing experience. That experience was his frantic mediation between the dim radio signals he was receiving from the Northern Atlantic as a telegraph operator and throngs of excited journalists acting for an anxious nation that besieged him, as the Titanic's maiden voyage was nearing its end. Sarnoff's subsequent career was dedicated to linking radio, then television, signals to the mass audience direct, disintermediating professionals such as the telegrapher he had been (Barnouw 1966: 43, 76–77). These personal glimpses may serve as a parable for a more general proposition (which by now is almost universally accepted): rather than viewing technology as an independent variable generating dependent effects, a better approach may be to scrutinize historical conditions – personal experiences among them – as the independent variable, with technology as the dependent one.

But not only individuals and their life experiences determine the emergence and nature of media technologies; the development process has other partners too. The state, for instance, has compiled a venerable track record of shaping the media environment, promoting, retarding and designing communication technologies. States can make technologies happen or not happen, appear or disappear. The fictional state-made communication environment drawn by

George Orwell in *1984* or the story of the Soviet regime's promotion of voice recognition technologies imagined by Solzhenitsyn in *The Cancer Ward* resonate the state's role in generating media technologies. In the real world and in contrast, contingencies of the cold war led the American defence establishment to develop a decentralized alternative to conventional trunk-and-branch communication networks. Perhaps it was America's unique ethos that helped to ensure that the defence established would later share its breakthrough in asynchronous networking with the academic community and, ultimately, in the form of the new and improved internet, with the public at large, the world over. State intervention is at least as effective on the desist side. Consider the resident of the former Soviet Union who had made their acquaintance with the photocopier only after Glasnost, or numerous states whose citizens can gain access to the internet only once their governments decide that the time and the content are right.

Israel in the late 1970s provides perhaps the most grotesque, and (literally) colourful, example for the role of the powers that be in both retarding and promoting communication technology, in this case via a single policy. The Israeli government, wary of 'the people of the book' becoming addicts of sitcoms and westerns, grudgingly allowed TV to be broadcast only in 1968, in black and white. By the late 1970s, however, Israel TV acquired new PAL production equipment, by then available only in colour, and some of its productions, along with foreign programmes, were broadcast in colour. The country's treasury department, witnessing soaring imports of colour TV sets, and threatened by a major dent in the country's balance of payments, got the broadcast authority to implement a 'colour killer' modulating technology that eradicated the relevant colour codes from its broadcast signal. In response, Israeli radiofrequency (RF) experts developed an immensely popular descrambling device, known as the 'anti-erasure' that subversively re-enabled colour reception. The immense popularity of the device ultimately led to full broadcast in colour, not before the 'anti-erasure' enterprise yielded windfall profits.[9]

States, and by now, coalitions of states (such as the European Community) do not only make or break media technologies: a voluminous literature documents the far-reaching implications of government regulation of both broadcast and telecommunication media on the communication technology sector. But the state is not the only player regulating media and thus charting the development path of communication technologies. The legal system can play a very similar role. A striking example links the mid-nineteenth century with the mid-twentieth, via telex and fax technology. In 1846, two years after Morse's telegraph went into operation, both Alexander Bain and Royal E. House introduced their alternatives to the Morse telegraph system. Bain had invented the functional equivalent of the fax, House had invented the prototelex. Bain and House lines were already in operation when American courts ruled that they infringed on Morse's patent (Blondheim 1994). The legal system thus retarded the diffusion of telex and fax by a century – one example of the ways in which premodern patent and copyright law has handicapped technological (and intellectual) progress in Western society.

A vast literature has documented the historical role of the corporate and business environment in promoting and retarding, shaping and reshaping, media technologies.[10] Much less has been done in uncovering the key role of non-institutional factors in shaping technological innovation, diffusion and use. Consider the start-up structure, responsible for many of the most spectacularly successful media technologies developed since the 1970s. The start-up structure, fuelled by venture capital, is characteristic of the Silicon Valley and Israel's high-tech sector. In contrast, innovative media technologies in Scandinavia, Japan, Korea and other European and Far Eastern countries tend to be developed within the context of large corporations such as Nokia and Ericsson, Matsushita and Samsung. It has been suggested that the origins of this curious difference are cultural. The relative 'newness' of the west coast and of Israel, their frontier and pioneering heritage, stark individualism and non-conformist traditions, may have conditioned the ambitious, improvised, competitive start-up mentality. The more communitarian, co-operational, self-restraining and hierarchical social traditions of Europe and Asia favoured controlled innovation within large units. Much more needs to be done to establish this kind of cultural heuristic of technological development. A technological deterministic outlook would hardly be conducive to such an exploration; a historical perspective would.

The prospects of studying the cultural underpinnings of media technology are just as high on the adoption side. An intriguing case in point is the phenomenal success of cellular telephony in Finland and Israel, two small countries that shared between them, early on, most of the world records for cellular use, to include diffusion curves, call and air time rate per subscriber, etc. An analysis of the success of the cell phone in Finland has suggested that the great distances and sparse density of population, language barriers, weak social ties and the loneliness, boredom and general untalkativeness of people were responsible for the high diffusion rates. While no equivalent study has been conducted in Israel (which now features 9 million handsets to serve its population of 7 million), it would be reasonable to attribute the skyrocketing rates of cellular use there to the compact and dense geography of the country, its elaborate and close-knit social networks, tension and intensity of life, and the talkativeness of its people. As the outlandish nature of this pair of observations may indicate, our tools for understanding the social dynamics of the use of technological media are meagre. This weakness may explain the common resort to the technological heuristic; or conversely, the fascination with technology-centred interpretations may have retarded the development of theoretical tools and methodologies that are soundly grounded in cultural and historical perspectives.

The larger moral of these stories and of many others that can be found in detailed media histories is as simple as it is challenging. Media technologies, in and of themselves, have no autonomous or inevitable origin, development path, role or impact. It is only the interaction of technology with the adjacent regulatory, legal, business, institutions and with other media, let alone with personal and social attitudes, norms, ideologies and cultural traditions, that can explain the emergence, uses, misuses and effects of ICTs. Thus, however appealing, the use of technology as a compass for tracing the development of communications is misleading; the alternative tack of understanding media in their historical context would appear more promising. Even more importantly, the accumulation of detailed and responsible studies of media technology in its historical context may provide the basis for developing theory of a higher order, to include the uncovering of general patterns in the relation of technological development to social and cultural change.

The bias of lucidity

Elements of communication technology systems have a material presence. They can be seen, touched and thought about concretely and in isolation. These tools can be counted on to perform their specific task in a prescribed way, and do so repeatedly and invariably. As has been noted above, upon encountering new ICT, minds tend to race forward and evaluate their meaning and potential impact. All too often, this is done on the basis of analysing the nature of the concrete device at hand. This bias underlies the philosophy of TA and the *modus operandi* of media gurus. Yet the history of media technologies suggests emphatically otherwise – that the technical functioning of a medium means little in itself. Rather, the hermeneutics of technological artefacts is akin to the interpretation of a polysemic text. It follows that inferring from the affordances of a communication technology to the actual role it will assume is at best speculative. Historically, this would imply that the differential between potential to actual application may provide illuminating insight into the vision and purpose of the society putting the technology to work for it.

The ambiguity of supposedly lucid communication technologies may be best illustrated by a transcript and a caricature. The transcript records an important turning point in the development of American and world telegraphy: the connecting of the pioneer lines in New York, leading to the city's becoming 'the one grand centre' of the first dense national network. The inauguration of the New York line began with Morse, in Washington, calling his operator in Baltimore:

Washington: Baltimore, are you in connection with Philadelphia?
Baltimore: Yes
Washington: Put me in connection with Philadelphia

Baltimore:	Aye aye sir! Wait a minute…Go ahead, you can now talk to Philadelphia.
Washington:	How do you do, Philadelphia?
Philadelphia:	Pretty well. Is that you Washington?
Washington:	Aye aye, are you connected with New York?

It was, but in the process of adjusting New York's electromagnets so as to receive Washington, the cacophony began:

Philadelphia:	I have been hard at work all day – I feel like bricks – had no supper – I have had a stiff evening's work, there has been so many messages to write…I want to go.
Washington:	Wait a little.
Baltimore:	Go it ye cripples.
Philadelphia:	Who is writing?
Washington:	Don't talk all at once.
Baltimore:	Mary Rogers are a case. So are Sally Thompsing. Gen. Jackson are a hoss. And so are Col. Johnsing.
Philadelphia:	Who is that? I will discuss that point.
Washington:	Baltimore, keep quiet.[11]

This kind of exchange, referred to in the press of the day by the unknowingly anachronistic 'general CHAT by telegraph',[12] demonstrated that the telegraph could be the medium of live, multipoint interaction, as in our contemporary chat rooms. However, the telegraph could also be used, and was used early on, for live two-way exchanges – described at the time as 'correspondence, in one instance' – like a present-day telephone conversation in writing. The telegraph could also be used for asynchronous messaging, like our contemporary email or SMS. But as it turned out, the killer application of the telegraph was none of the above. The telegraph was used mainly for broadcasting: for single messages to be 'scattered broadcasts over the country', as when a wire news report was sent to all American newspapers instantaneously, or when a market quotation was delivered, at once, to numerous commercial subscribers, or horse race results to bookies.

Clearly, there was nothing in telegraphic technology that determined the nature of its use; the technology was thoroughly mutable. Only its promoters, investors, regulators and users could determine whether it would be a synchronous or asynchronous, telecommunication or broadcast, medium; and consequently, what aspects of life it would impact and how. Nor was there anything in telephonic technology that could clue analysts or pundits on how it would be applied. Telephone technology came to be applied mainly for synchronous dyadic conversations. But it could be applied for voice broadcasting – as it was in a Bell demonstration carrying the voice of a singer in Salem to a hall in Boston, or in a later commercial telephone broadcast service in Hungary – namely, as what we now recognize as radio. Quite simply, there was nothing in telephone technology that determined that it would end up as a medium of telecommunications rather than broadcast. The internet provides the ultimate illustration for the openness of technology to serve social needs. A mere platform for asynchronous digital communications featuring a unique network structure, it has no obvious 'killer application'. The internet and its applications are constantly shaped and reshaped to serve new and imaginative communicative applications.

Understanding media technologies as murky and mutable has considerable implications for the interpretation of the causal relation of ICT development and social change – discussed in the following section.

The bias of causality

The preceding critical discussion of the notions of autonomy and lucidity of technologies would seem to highlight the role of society in shaping its communication environment. They suggest that, fundamentally, the causal arrow should be drawn from society to technology. However, this does not preclude an ergo arrow stretching back from technology to society. There of course remains the distinct possibility that these arrows, jointly, chart a continuing, cyclical dynamic in which society generates and shapes technologies, which in turn have a profound influence on society and on its course in developing, implementing and adapting subsequent technologies. Or as those tending to technological determinism would suggest, the cycle may work in the opposite direction.

The TA approach, as amplified by its popular apostles, would lead us to believe that new media are capable of doing just that. Seizing on new technologies, it conjectures about their future impact. As cause precedes effect, technology in this plan is necessarily the cause of social change, as a stone thrown into a lake is responsible for the ripples. But historians have a privileged position *vis-à-vis* other practitioners of TA. Hindsight allows them to observe the playing out of the causal chain. Particularly if not fixed on technological innovation as a point of origin, they can view it as a stage or a factor in the unfolding of the larger canvas of history.

Taking this agenda to the edge, the following is, to say the least, an ambitious exercise in viewing changes in ICT in relation to changes in the social organization of Western society from the onset of history to the present. Applying the work of Harold Innis (e.g. 1952; and see Blondheim 2004), it is an experiment in media cartography as well. It charts a single aspect of media – their reach in terms of geographical and demographic scope – and traces fluctuations on this dimension from the archaic to the present. Change in the scope of dominant media is juxtaposed to a no less ambitious schema of overall change in the scale of social organization in the West throughout history – surely overgeneralized and schematic, but possibly valid in a general sense. This exercise is intended to try and synchronize vicissitudes in the scope of media and the scale of social organizations, in quest of verifying the determinist argument of communication as cause, and more generally trying to understand the relation between media and society.

The technology aspect of Figure 15.2 starts with a primordial state of unmediated, oral communications. Once writing entered the scene, communications developed in two tracks. Literacy enabled the expansion of the audience of a message through its transport in space and resilience in time. Printing would later considerably expand that footprint. The scope of oral messages remained limited by the short reach of the human voice in space. Once electric communications entered history, it developed on two opposite trajectories with regard to the scope of communications. The telegraph was the starting point of both these orientations. Its dominant application was broadcasting messages to a national field, simultaneously, but it also left room for exchanges of messages between individuals, a mode of communication that would be significantly reinforced by telephone and wireless. Broadcast radio, in turn, would improve the telegraph's broadcast capacity, and that to expanding audiences. Television, and later yet its transmission by satellite, further expanded the scope of broadcast to worldwide audiences. On the opposite trajectory, stand-alone technologies enabled the targeting of smaller audiences with voice and video communications, as by the audio and video cassette, followed by still interpersonal and group communications by satellite.

With the satellite symbolically marking the great contrast between worldwide broadcast, on the one hand (vide CNN), and V–Sat phone and video interactive communications, on the other, digital took over. Its minimal band requirements enabled the breaking down of broadcast streams to smaller audiences, at the same time that it enabled group communications, as in web pages and lists. New interactive media, still in the process of development and diffusion, further enable the ultimate merging of the two historical trajectories on the meso-level. World broadcast is breaking down and being tailored to the time, taste and interest spans of individuals (e.g. Tivo), and individuals have scalable access to broadcasting themselves (e.g. YouTube).

The social organization aspect of Figure 15.2 shows major transformations of social organization in the West over the ages, in a nutshell. Characteristic of the archaic and ancient world were two overlapping social universes – the local community and the vast empire. While the former was oral, the latter controlled vast expanses via written communications and advanced transportations, ranging from horse relays to pigeon post. By the middle ages of Western civilization, long-haul communications crumbled, as did empires. Political entities were splintered, with the Catholic Church providing no more than a veneer of unity. Gradually, however, with the revival of cities, city-states and principalities, social organization expanded until the state came to dominate social affiliation, its scale intermediate between empire and local community, and its dominant medium first the printing press, then broadcast.

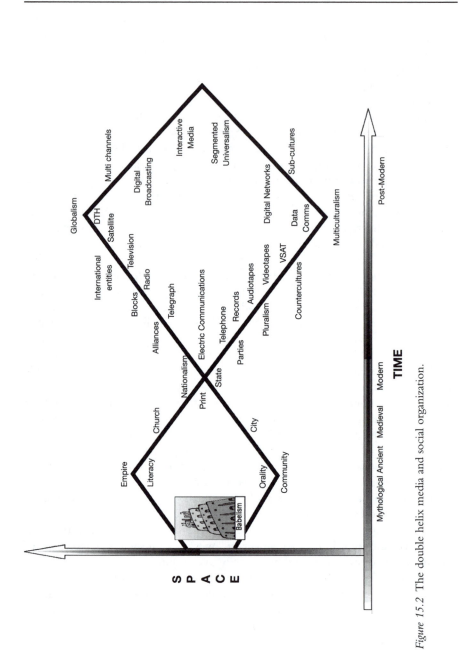

Figure 15.2 The double helix media and social organization.

The state dominated social organization into late modernity, with its potential scale expanding through imperialism and international alliances. At the same time, its internal cohesion and its monopoly of power were diminished by the emergence and legitimacy of political, ethnic and cultural division. By late modernity, social, cultural and political fragmentation went deeper, until the nation was no longer the main determinant of identity. In parallel, on the international level, states became part of large coalitions and blocks, as they gradually lost power to international organizations, interstate communities and world hegemons. By the turn of the second millennium, with globalization on the one hand and internal splintering along ethnic, religious and cultural lines on the other, the state of the world represents a type of segmented universalism. Non-state identities unite masses of people scattered over the globe, just as they divide humanity into new, and regrettably antagonistic, elements.

The point of this exercise in bird's-eye mapping is the convergence of the media reach and scale of social organization aspects of the graph. Should one happen to consider temporal priority to be a good indicator of cause and effect relations, this exploration may show that technology does not, in fact, precede social change, and presumably bring it about. Yet the general synchronicity of change in these two key realms of the human experience – communication media and social organization – exhibited throughout history remains striking. It suggests the overall reciprocity of media development and social and political change: minds, hearts and their media travel in time hand in hand.

This notion may have some power, dwarfing the entire project of determining exact cause and effect relationships between media development and social change. By pointing out the congruence of the nature of society and the contours of its media, it suggests that the two are inseparable, communications being the DNA of human society. As John Dewey (1916) famously averred, 'Society exists not only by transmission, by communication, but it may fairly be said to exist in transmission, in communication'. Medieval theologians held similarly at the individual level. In their explorations into the essence of humanity, people were tagged 'the speakers', just as the world they inhabited was supposedly created by the word that had preceded it. Humankind and its communications – contents, networks, media – are one and the same.

Notes

1 *New York Herald*, 30 May 1844.
2 These particular aspects of diffusion have not received the attention they deserve even in studies of diffusion in the communication studies tradition (e.g. Rogers 2003).
3 Marshall McLuhan (e.g. 1964) is identified with developing this thrust of media studies. Paul Levinson (2001) represents an important extension and updating of this thrust.
4 Broadminded discussions of this aspect include Peters (1999) and Pinchevski (2005).
5 The leading exponent of this proposition was Harold Adams Innis (e.g. 1951). For a variety of perspectives on the approach see Watson and Blondheim (2007).

6 According to Lievrouw and Livingstone's (2002) definition of media as 'information and communication technologies and their associated social contexts', this usage may be redundant. Nevertheless, it was used throughout alongside 'communication technology'.
7 This aspect of McLuhan's career is illuminated in Philip Marchand (1998).
8 There is a vast literature on the problem of technological vs. social and cultural determinism. Good starting points are Bijker (1986) and essays in Smith and Marx (1994). When it comes to the role of technology in communication, good summaries include Fischer (1992) and Boczkowski (2004).
9 http://www.he.wikipedia.org. One of Israel's leading poets, Natan Zach, published a volume of poetry entitled *Anti-Erasure* (Tel Aviv: haKibutz haMeuchad, 1984).
10 In the communication technology field, see Chandler and Cortada (2000); Spar (2003).
11 *Philadelphia Public Leger*, 11 June 1846.
12 Emphasis mine; unidentified newspaper clipping, reel 9, Morse papers, Library of Congress.

Bibliography

'A Journalist' (1937) *Foreign Journalists Under Franco's Terror*, London: United Editorial.

Abbas, T. (2005) *Muslim Britain: Communities under Pressure*, London: Zed Books.

Abbate, J. (2000) *Inventing the Internet*, Cambridge, MA: MIT Press.

Abrams, P. (1982) *Historical Sociology*, Shepton Mallet: Open Books.

Ackelsberg, M. (2005) *Free Women of Spain: Anarchism and the Struggle for the Emancipation of Women*, Oakland, CA: AK Press.

Adorno, T. (2001) *The Culture Industry*, London: Routledge.

—— and Horkheimer, M. (1986 [1944]) *Dialectic of Enlightenment*, London: Verso.

Advertiser's Annual (1937) London.

Aldgate, A. (1995) *Censorship and the Permissive Society: British Cinema and Theatre: 1955–65*, Oxford: Clarendon.

Aldgate, A. and Richards, J. (1994) *Britain Can Take It: The British Cinema in the Second World War*, Edinburgh: Edinburgh University Press.

—— (1999) *Best of British: Cinema and Society from the 1930s to the Present*, London: I. B. Tauris.

Allen, J. and Rushton, O. (eds) (2005) *Papers for the People*, London: Merlin.

Altick, R. D. (1957) *The English Common Reader. A Social History of the Mass Reading Public 1800–1900*, London: Phoenix.

Anderson, B. (2006 [1983]) *Imagined Communities. Reflections on the Origin and Spread of Nationalism*, London: Verso.

Anderson, C. (2006) *The Long Tail*, London: Random House Business Books.

Angell, N. (1922) *The Press and the Organisation of Society*, London: The Labour Publishing Company.

Annan Committee (1977) *Report of the Committee on the Future of Broadcasting* (Annan Report), Cmnd 6735, London: HMSO.

Ansari, H. (2004) *The Infidel Within: The History of Muslims in Britain, 1800 to the Present*, London: C. Hurst & Co. Publishers.

Arthurs, J. (2004) *Television and Sexuality: Regulation and the Politics of Taste*, Maidenhead: Open University Press.

Aspinall, A. (1973) *Politics and the Press, c.1780–1850*, Brighton: Harvester Press.

Atton, C. (2002) *Alternative Media*, London: Sage.

Baehr, H. (1980) 'The "Liberated Woman" in Television Drama', in Baehr, H. (ed.), *Women and Media*, pp. 29–40, Oxford: Pergamon Press.

—— and Ryan, M. (1984) *Shut Up and Listen! Women and Local Radio*, London: Comedia.

Bailey, M. (2007a) 'Broadcasting and the Problem of Enforced Leisure During the 1930s', *Leisure Studies*, 26(4): 463–78.

—— (2007b) '"He who has ears to hear, let him hear": Christian Pedagogy and Religious Broadcasting during the Inter-War Period', *Westminster Papers in Communications and Culture*, 4(1): 4–25.

—— (2007c) 'Rethinking Public Service Broadcasting: the Historical Limits to Publicness', in Butsch, R. (ed.), *The Media and the Public Sphere*, pp. 96–108, Basingstoke: Palgrave-Macmillan.

Bailey, O. (2002) *Empire of the Song: Victorian Songs and Music*, London: Caxton Editions.

——, Cammaerts, B. and Carpentier, N. (2007) *Understanding Alternative Media*, Milton Keynes: Open University Press.

Bailey, P. (ed.) (1986) *Music Hall: the Business of Pleasure*, Milton Keynes: Open University Press.

Baistow, T. (1985) *Fourth-Rate Estate*, London: Comedia.

Baker, H., Diawara, M. and Lindeborg, R. (1996) *Black British Cultural Studies*, Chicago, IL: Chicago University Press.

Bakewell, J. and Garnham, N. (1970) *The New Priesthood: British Television Today*, London: Allen Lane.

Barbrook, R. (1992) 'Broadcasting and National Identity in Ireland', *Media, Culture & Society*, 14: 203–27.

Barker, H. (1998) *Newspapers, Politics, and Public Opinion in Late Eighteenth Century England*, Oxford: Oxford University Press.

—— (2000) *Newspapers, Politics and English Society, 1695–1855*, Edinburgh: Longman.

Barker, M. (1984) *The Video Nasties: Freedom & Censorship in the Media*, London: Pluto.

—— and Petley, J. (eds) (1997) *Ill Effects: the Media/Violence Debate*, London: Routledge.

——, Arthurs, J. and Harindranath, R. (2001) *The Crash Controversy: The Censorship Campaigns and Film Reception*, London: Wallflower Press.

Barlow, D. Mitchell, P. and O'Malley, T. (2005) *The Media in Wales: Voices of a Small Nation*, Cardiff: University of Wales Press.

Barnett, S. and Curry, A. (1994) *The Battle for the BBC*, London: Aurum.

—— and Gaber, I. (2001) *Westminster Tales: The Twenty-First-Century Crisis in Political Journalism*, London and New York: Continuum.

Barnouw, E. (1966) *A Tower in Babel: A History of Broadcasting in the United States to 1833*, New York: Oxford University Press.

Barton, R. (2004) *Irish National Cinema*, London: Routledge.

Baudrillard, J. (1988). *Jean Baudrillard: Selected Writings*, Poster, M. (ed.), Cambridge: Polity Press.

—— (1998) *The Consumer Society*, London: Sage.

Bauman, Z. (1988) *Freedom*, Milton Keynes: Open University Press.

BBC Handbook (1955), London: BBC.

BBC (1965) Lunchtime Lecture Third Series, London: BBC.

BBC (W)ritten (A)rchives (C)entre Governors Press Cuttings 6.12.1975–1.6.1978.

—— R/78/2969/1 Controller Scotland.

—— R4/09/1 BBC Memorandum The BBC and Regional Broadcasting.

—— R4/112/1 Memorandum from the Broadcasting Council for Wales.

—— R6/219 Advisory Committees. Women's Advisory Committee. 1924–25.

—— R44/86/1 Publicity: Conferences, 1933, 1936.

—— R51/239 Talks: Household Talks, Files 1 and 2, 1928–47.

—— R51/646 Talks: Women's Programmes, 1936–38.

—— R78/1921 The Black and White Minstrel Show.

—— SC1/40/30/2 Kilbreck.

—— SC1/63 – Radio Scotland.

—— SC1/71/1 – Broadcasting Council for Scotland Papers.

Beaumont, J. (2000) 'The Times at War, 1899–1902', in Lowry, D. (ed.), *The South African War Reappraised*, Manchester: Manchester University Press.

Beetham, M. (1996) *A Magazine of her Own: Domesticity and Desire in the Woman's Magazine, 1800–1914*, London: Routledge.

Bell, D. and Kennedy, B. M. (eds) (2000) *The Cybercultures Reader*, London: Routledge.

Beniger, J. R. and Gusek, J. A. (1995) 'The Cognitive Revolution in Public Opinion and Communication Research', in Glasser, T. L. and Salmon, C. T. (eds), *Public Opinion and the Communication of Consent*, pp. 217–48, New York: Guilford Press.

Benjamin, W. (1970/1973) *Illuminations*, London: Jonathan Cape.

Bennett, J. (2007) *History Matters: Patriarchy and the Challenge of Feminism*, Philadelphia, PA: University of Pennsylvania Press.

Bennett, T. (2005) 'The Media Sensorium: Cultural Technologies, the Senses and Society', in Gillespie, M. (ed.), *Media Audiences*, pp. 51–96, Maidenhead: Open University Press.

Berkman, D. (1987) 'The Development of Television as an Advertiser-supported Medium: as seen by the Contemporary American Press', *European Journal of Marketing*, 21: 14–26.

Bermingham, A. and Brewer, J. (1995) *The Consumption of Culture 1600–1800*, London: Routledge.

Beveridge (1951) *Report of the Committee on Broadcasting*, Cmnd. 8116, London: HMSO.

Bevins, R. (1965) *The Greasy Pole*, London: Hodder and Stoughton.

Bijker, W. E. (1986) *Of Bicycles, Bakalites, and Bulbs: Toward a Theory of Sociotechnical Change*, Cambridge, MA: Harvard University Press.

Bingham, A. (2004) *Gender, Modernity and the Popular Press in Inter-War Britain*, Oxford: Clarendon Press.

—— (2005) 'The British Popular Press and Venereal Disease during the Second World War', *Historical Journal*, 48: 1055–76.

—— (2007) '"Drinking in the Last Chance Saloon": The British Press and the Crisis of Self-regulation, 1989–95', *Media History*, 13(1): 79–92.

Black, G. D. (1997) *The Catholic Crusade Against the Movies, 1940–1975*, Cambridge: Cambridge University Press.

Black, J. (2001) *The English Press 1621–1861*, Stroud: Sutton.

—— (2002) 'The Press and Politics in the Eighteenth Century', *Media History*, 8(2).

Black, L. (2001), '"Sheep may safely gaze": Socialists, Television and the People in Britain, 1949–64', in. Black, L. (ed.), *Consensus or Coercion? The State, the People and Social Cohesion in Post-war Britain*, pp. 28–48, Gretton: New Clarion Press.

—— (2003) *The Political Culture of the Left in Affluent Britain, 1951–64: Old Labour, New Britain?* Houndsmills: Palgrave.

Black, P. (1972) *The Biggest Aspidistra in the World*, London: BBC.

—— (1972) *The Mirror in the Corner: People's Television*, London: Hutchinson.

Blackman, L. (2006) '"Inventing the Psychological": Lifestyle Magazines and the Fiction of Autonomous Selfhood' in Curran, J. and Morley, D. (eds), *Media and Cultural Theory*, pp. 209–20, London: Routledge.

Blandford, S. (2007) *Film, Drama and the Break Up of Britain*, Bristol: Intellect.

Blondheim, M (1994) *News Over the Wires. The Telegraph and the Flow of Public Information in America, 1844–1897*, Cambridge, MA: Harvard University Press.

—— (2004) 'Discovering "the Significance of Communication": Harold Innis as Social Constructivist', *Canadian Journal of Communication*, 29(2): 119–43.

Blumler, J. G. and Katz, E. (eds) (1974) *Uses of Mass Communication*, Beverley Hills, CA: Sage.

Bocock, R. (1974) *Ritual in Industrial Society*, London: George Allen & Unwin.

— (1997) 'Choice and Regulation: Sexual Moralities', in Thompson, K. (ed.), *Media and Cultural Regulation*, pp. 69–104, London: Sage.

Boczkowski, P. J. (2004) *Digitizing the News*, Cambridge, MA: The MIT Press.

Boston, R. (ed.) (1970) *The Press We Deserve*, London: Routledge & Kegan Paul.

—— (1988) 'W. T. Stead and Democracy by Journalism', in Wiener, J. (ed.), *Papers for the Millions*, New York: Greenwood Press.

Bourdieu, P. (1986) *Distinction: A Social Critique of the Judgement of Taste*, London: Routledge.

Boyce, D. G. (1978) 'The Fourth Estate: the Reappraisal of a Concept', in Boyce, G., Curran, J. and Wingate, P. (eds), *Newspaper History: From the 17th Century to the Present Day*, London: Constable.

——, Curran, J. and Wingate, P. (eds) (1978) *Newspaper History: From the 17th Century to the Present Day*, London: Constable.

Boyle, K. (2005a) 'Feminism without Men: Feminist Media Studies in a Post-feminist Age', in Curran, J. and Gurevitch, M. (eds), *Mass Media and Society*, London: Hodder Arnold.

—— (2005b) *Media and Violence: Gendering the Debates*, London: Sage.

Braddon, R. (1965) *Roy Thomson of Fleet*, London: Collins.

Bragg, B. (2006) *The Progressive Patriot. A Search for Belonging*, London: Bantam Press.

Bragg, S. and Buckingham, D. (2002) *Young People and Sexual Content on Television*, London: Broadcasting Standards Commission.

Braithwaite, B. (1995) *Women's Magazines*, London: Peter Owen.

Brett, P. (1997) 'Early Nineteenth Century Reform Newspapers in the Provinces: the *Newcastle Chronicle* and *Bristol Mercury*', in Harris, M. and O'Malley, T. (eds), *Newspaper and Periodical Annual 1995*, Westport, CT: Greenwood.

Brewer, J. (1976) *Party Ideology and Popular Politics at the Accession of George III*, Cambridge: Cambridge University Press.

—— (1997) *The Pleasures of the Imagination*, London: Harper Collins.

Brewer, J. and Porter, R. (1993) *Consumption and the World of Goods*, London: Routledge.

Bridson, D. G. (1971) *Prospero and Ariel: The Rise and Fall of Radio*, London: Gollancz.

Briggs, A. (1961–95 [2000 reprint]) *The History of British Broadcasting in the United Kingdom*, Volumes I–V, Oxford: Oxford University Press.

—— (1979) *Governing the BBC*, London: BBC.

—— and Burke, P. (2002/2005) *A Social History of the Media: From Gutenberg to the Internet*, Cambridge: Polity.

Briggs, S. (1981) *Those Radio Times*, London: Weidenfeld & Nicolson.

British Market Research Bureau (1967) *Attitudes to Television Advertising*, London: IPA.

Bromley, M. (1991) 'Was It the Mirror Wot Won It? The Development of the Tabloid Press During the Second World War', in Hayes, N. and Hill, J. (eds) *Millions Like Us?* Liverpool: Liverpool University Press.

—— (1998a) 'The "Tabloiding" of Britain: "Quality" Newspapers in the 1990s', in Stephenson, H. and Bromley, M. (eds), *Sex, Lies and Democracy: the Press and the Public*, London: Longman.

—— (1998b) '"Watching the Watchdogs"? The Role of Readers' Letters in calling the Press to Account', in Stephenson, H. and Bromley, M. (eds), *Sex, Lies and Democracy: the Press and the Public*, London: Longman.

—— and O'Malley, T. (1997) *A Journalism Reader*, London: Routledge.

Brown, L. A. (1981) *Innovation Diffusion: A New Perspective*, London: Methuen.

Bruce, R. V. (1990) *Bell: Alexander Bell and the Conquest of Solitude*, Ithaca: Cornell University Press.

Brunsdon, C. (2000) *The Feminist, the Housewife, and the Soap Opera*, Oxford: Clarendon Press.

——, D'Acci, J. and Spigel L. (eds) (1997) *Feminist Television Criticism: A Reader*, Oxford: Clarendon Press.

Buckingham, D. (1996) *Moving Images: Understanding Children's Emotional Responses to Television*, Manchester: Manchester University Press.

—— (2000) *After the Death of Childhood*, Cambridge: Polity.

Buckingham, D. and Bragg, S. (2004) *Young People, Sex and the Media: The Facts of Life?* Basingstoke: Palgrave Macmillan.

Buckley, H. (1940) *The Life and Death of the Spanish Republic*, London: Hamish Hamilton.

Burke, P. (1980) *Sociology and History*, London: George Allen & Unwin.

Burns, T. (1977) *The BBC: Public Institution and Private World*, London: Macmillan.

Burton, A. G. (2005) *The British Consumer Co-operative Movement and Film, 1890s–1960s*, Manchester: Manchester University Press.

Buscombe, E. (2000) *British Television: A Reader*, Oxford: Clarendon.

Butsch, R. (1998) 'Crystal Sets and Scarf-pin Radios: Gender, Technology and the Construction of American Radio Listening in the 1920s', *Media, Culture & Society*, 20(4): 557–72.

Butt Philip, A. (1975) *The Welsh Question: Nationalism and Welsh Politics 1945–1970*, Cardiff: University of Wales Press.

Cadava, E. (1997) *Words of Light*, Princeton, NJ: Princeton University Press.

Cadman, E., Chester, G. and Pivot, A. (1981) *Rolling Our Own: Women as Printers, Publishers and Distributors*, London: Minority Press Group.

Caine, B. (1997) *English Feminism 1780–1980*, Oxford: Oxford University Press.

Calabrese, A. and Sparks, C. (eds) (2004) *Toward a Political Economy of Culture: Capitalism and Communication in the Twenty-First Century*, Lanham, MD: Rowman & Littlefield.

Calcutt Committee (1990) *Report of the Committee on Privacy and Related Matters*, Cmd. 1102, London: HMSO.

Calcutt, D. (1993) *Review of Press Self-Regulation*, Cmd. 2135, London: HMSO.

Callinicos, A. (2007) *Social Theory: A Historical Introduction*, Cambridge: Polity.

Camporesi, V. (1990a) '"We talk a Different Language". The Impact of US Broadcasting in Britain, 1922–27', *Historical Journal of Film, Radio and Television*, 10(3): 257–74.

—— (1990b) 'The BBC and American Broadcasting, 1922–55', *Media, Culture & Society*, 16: 625–39.

Cannadine, D. (1998) *Class in Britain*, London: Penguin.

—— (2000) *History in Our Time*, London: Penguin.

—— (2004) *History and the Media*, Basingstoke: Palgrave Macmillan.

Cardiff, D. (1980) 'The Serious and the Popular: Aspects of the Evolution of Style in the Radio Talk, 1928–39', *Media, Culture and Society*, 2: 29–47.

—— (1987) 'Broadcasting and National Unity', in Curran, J., Smith, A. and Wingate, P. (eds) *Impacts and Influences: Essays on Media Power in the Twentieth Century*, pp. 157–73, London: Methuen.

—— and Scannell, P (1986) '"Good Luck War Workers!" Class, Politics and Entertainment in Wartime Broadcasting', in Bennett, T., Mercer, C. and Woollacott, J. (eds), *Popular Culture and Social Relations*, pp. 93–116, Milton Keyes: Open University Press.

Cardozo, H. (1937) *The March of a Nation*, London: Right Book Club.

Carey, J. (1992) *The Intellectuals and the Masses: Pride and Prejudice Among the Literary Intelligentsia, 1880–1939*, London: Faber.

Carey, J. W. (1989) *Communication as Culture: Essays on Media and Society*, London: Unwin Hyman.

Carr, E. H. (2001 [1961]) *What is History?* Basingstoke: Palgrave.

Carter, C. and Weaver C. K. (2003) *Violence and the Media*, Buckingham: Open University Press.

——, Branston, G. and Allan, S. (eds) (1998) *News, Gender and Power*, London: Routledge.

Castells, M. (1996) *The Information Age – Economy, Society and Culture: The Rise of the Network Society*, Vol. 1, Oxford: Blackwell.

—— (1997) *The Information Age – Economy, Society and Culture: The Rise of Identity*, Vol. 2, Oxford: Blackwell.

—— (1998) *The Information Age – Economy, Society and Culture: End of Millennium*, Vol. 3, Oxford: Blackwell.

CCCS (1982) *The Empire Strikes Back, Race and Racism in 70s Britain*, London: Routledge.

Chalaby, J. K. (1998) *The Invention of Journalism*, Houndmills: Macmillan.

Chambers, D., Steiner, L. and Fleming, C. (2004) *Women and Journalism*, London: Routledge.

Champion, J. (2003) 'Seeing the Past: Simon Schama's "A History of Britain" and Public History', *History Workshop Journal*, 56: 153–74.

Chandler, A. D. and Cortada, J. W. (2000) *A Nation Transformed by Communication: How Information Shaped the United States from Colonial Times to the Present*, New York: Oxford University Press.

Chaney, D. (1986) 'A Symbolic Mirror of Ourselves: Civic Ritual in Mass Society', in Collins, R., Curran, J. Garnham, N., Scannell, P., Schlesinger, P. and Sparks, C. (eds), *Media, Culture & Society: A Critical Reader*, pp. 247–63, London: Sage.

Chapman, Jane (2005a) *Comparative Media History*, Cambridge: Polity.

Chapman, James (1998) *The British at War: Cinema, State and Propaganda, 1939–1945*, London: I. B. Tauris.

—— (2005b) *Past and Present: National Identity and The British Historical Film*, London: I. B. Tauris.

Chapman, R. (1992) *Selling the Sixties: the Pirates and Pop Music Radio*, London: Routledge.

Chippindale, P. and Horrie, C. (1999) *Stick it up Your Punter!* London: Pocket Books.

Chisholm, A. (1979) *Nancy Cunard*, London: Penguin.

Choudhury, D. K. L. (2003) 'India's First Virtual Community and the Telegraph General Strike of 1908', *International Review of Social History*, 48, Suppl.: 45–71.

Clark, J. C. D. (1985) *English Society 1688–1832*, Cambridge: Cambridge University Press.

Cockett, R. (1989) *Twilight of Truth: Chamberlain, Appeasement and the Manipulation of the Press*, New York: St. Martin's Press.

—— (1995) *Thinking the Unthinkable: Think-Tanks and the Economic Counter-Revolution, 1931–1983*, London: Fontana Press.

Cohen, S. (1980) *Folk Devils and Moral Panics*, 2nd edn, Oxford: Martin Robertson.

Colley, L. (1992) *Britons: Forging the Nation, 1707–1837*, London: Pimlico.

Colls, R. (2002) *Identity of England*, Oxford: Oxford University Press.

Conboy, M. (2002) *The Press and Popular Culture*, London: Sage.

—— (2004) *Journalism. A Critical History*, London: Sage.

—— (2006) *Tabloid Britain: Constructing a Community through Language*, London: Routledge.

Conrich, I. and Petley, J. (eds) (2000) 'Forbidden British Cinema', *Journal of Popular British Cinema*, Issue 3.

Cooke, L. (2003) *British Television Drama: A History*, London: British Film Institute.

Cooley, C. H. (1891) 'The Social Significance of Street Railways', *Publications of the American Economic Association*, VI: 71–73.

—— (1894) 'The Theory of Transportation', *Publications of the American Economic Association*, IX(3): 221–370.

Copeland, D. A. (2006) *The Idea of a Free Press: The Enlightenment and its Unruly Legacy*, Evanston, IL: Northwestern University Press.

Corner, J. (2003) 'Finding Data, Reading Patterns, Telling Stories: Issues in the Historiography of Television', *Media, Culture and Society*, 25: 273–80.

Couldry, N. (2003) *Media Rituals: A Critical Approach*, London: Routledge.

Cowles, V. (1941) *Looking for Trouble*, New York and London: Harper and Brothers.

Cox, G. (1999) *Eyewitness: A Memoir of Europe in the 1930s*, Otago: University of Otago Press.

Cranfield, G. (1978) *The Press and Society: From Caxton to Northcliffe*, London: Longman.

Creeber, G. (2004a) 'Hideously White – British Television, Glocalization and National Identity', *Television and New Media*, 5(1): 27–39.

—— (2004b) *Serial Television*, London: British Film Institute.

Crisell, A. (1997/2002) *An Introductory History of British Broadcasting*, London: Routledge.

Critcher, C. (2003) *Moral Panics and the Media*, Buckingham: Open University Press.

Cudlipp, H. (1962) *At Your Peril*, London: Weidenfeld & Nicholson.

Curran, J. (1977) 'Capitalism and Control of Press, 1800–1975', in Curran, J., Gurevitch, M. and Woollacott, J. (eds), *Mass Communication and Society*, pp. 195–230, London: Edward Arnold.

—— (1978a) 'The Press as an Agency of Social Control: An Historical Perspective', in Boyce, G., Curran, J. and Wingate, P. (eds), *Newspaper History*, London: Constable.

—— (ed.) (1978b) *The British Press: A Manifesto*, London: Macmillan.

—— (1991) 'Rethinking the Media as a Public Sphere', in Dahlgren, P. and Sparks, C. (eds), Communication and Citizenship: Journalism and the Public Sphere in the New Media Age, pp. 27–57, London: Routledge.

—— (1995) *Policy for the Press*, London: IPPR.

—— (2000a) 'Press Reformism 1918–98: A Study of Failure', in Tumber, H. (ed.), *Media Power, Professionals and Policies*, London: Routledge.

—— (ed.) (2000b) *Media Organisations in Society*, London: Arnold.

—— (2002a) *Media and Power*, London: Routledge.

—— (2002b) 'Media and the Making of British Society, c. 1700–2000', *Media History*, 8(2): 135–54.

—— (2004) 'Rise of the Westminster School', in Calabrese, A. and Sparks, C. (eds), *Toward a Political Economy of Culture: Capitalism and Communication in the Twenty-First Century*, pp. 13–40, Lanham, MD: Rowman & Littlefield.

—— (2008) 'Communication and History' in Zelizer, B. (ed.), *Back to the Future*, forthcoming.

—— and Seaton, J. (1981 [2003]) *Power Without Responsibility: Broadcasting and the Press in Britain*, 6th edn, London: Routledge.

——, Gaber, I. and Petley, J. (2005) *Culture Wars*, Edinburgh: Edinburgh University Press.

——, Smith, A. and Wingate, P. (eds) (1987) *Impacts and Influences: Essays on Media Power in the Twentieth Century*, London: Methuen.

Dabyden, D., Gilmore, J. and Jones, C. (2007) *The Oxford Companion to Black British History*, Oxford: Oxford University Press.

Davies, A. T. (1972) *Darlledu a'r Genedl*, London: BBC.

Davies, J. (1990) *Hanes Cymru: A History of Wales in Welsh*, London: Penguin.

—— (1994) *Broadcasting and the BBC in Wales*, Cardiff: University of Wales Press.

Davies, K., Dickey, J. and Stratford, T. (eds) (1987), *Out of Focus: Writings on Women and the Media*, London: Women's Press.

Davis, A. (2002) *Public Relations Democracy: Public Relations, Politics and the Mass Media in Britain*, Manchester: Manchester University Press.

Davis, F. (1940) *My Shadow in the Sun*, New York: Carrick and Evans.

—— (1981) *A Fearful Innocence*, Kent, OH: Kent State University Press.

Davis, H. (1965) 'The role of the regions in British Broadasting' in *BBC Lunchtime Lecture Third Series*, 3–15, BBC: London

Dayan, D. and Katz, E. (1992) *Media Events: The Live Broadcasting of History*, Cambridge, MA: Harvard University Press.

de Cordova, R. (1990) *Picture Personalities: The Emergence of the Star System in America*, Urbana and Chicago, IL: University of Illinois Press.

de Grazia, V. (2005) *Irresistible Empire: America's Advance through Twentieth-century Europe*, Cambridge, MA: Belknap.

de la Mora, C. (1939) *In Place of Splendour*, London: Michael. Joseph.

Deacon, D. (2009, forthcoming) *The Spanish Civil War and the British News Media: Tomorrow May be Too Late*, Edinburgh: Edinburgh University Press.

Delaprée, L. (1937) *The Martyrdom of Madrid: Inedited Witnesses*, No named publisher.

Desjardins, M. (2002) 'Maureen O'Hara's "Confidential" Life': Recycling Stars Through Gossip and Moral Biography', in Thumim, J. (ed.), *Small Screen, Big Ideas: Television in the 1950s*, pp. 118–30, London: I. B. Tauris.

Dewe Mathews, T. (1994) *Censored: The Story of Film Censorship in Britain*, London: Chatto and Windus.

Dewey, J. (1916) *Democracy and Education*, New York: Macmillan.

Dicenzo, M. (2000) 'Militant Distribution: Voices for Women and the Public Sphere', *Media History*, 6(2): 115–28.

—— (2003) 'Gutter Politics: Women Newsies and the Suffrage Press', *Women's History Review*, 12: 15–34.

—— (2004) 'Feminist Media and History: A Response to James Curran', *Media History*, 10 (1): 43–49.

Dickason, R. (2000) *British Television Advertising: Cultural Identity and Communication*, Luton: University of Luton Press.

Doane, M. A. (1987) *The Desire to Desire: The Woman's Film of the 1940s*, Bloomington, IN: Indiana University Press.

Donzelot, J. (1980) *The Policing of Families*, London: Hutchinson & Co.

Doughan, D. and Sanchez, D. (1987) *Feminist Periodicals, 1855–1984*, Brighton: Harvester Press.

Douglas, M. and Isherwood, B. (1996) *The World of Goods: Towards an Anthropology of Consumption*, London: Routledge.

Douglas, S. (1987) *Inventing American Broadcasting, 1899–1922*, Baltimore, MD: Johns Hopkins University Press.

Downing, J. (2000) *Radical Media: Rebellious Communication and Social Movements*, London: Sage.

—— (2008) *Encyclopaedia of Radical Media*, London: Sage.

Doyle, G. (2002a) *Understanding Media Economics*, London: Sage.

—— (2002b) *Media Ownership: the Economics and Politics of Convergence and Concentration in the UK and European Media*, London: Sage.

Dugaw, D. (1989) *Warrior Women and Popular Balladry, 1650–1850*, Cambridge: Cambridge University Press.

Dunkley, C. (1985) *Television Today and Tomorrow*, London: Penguin.

Dworkin, A. (1981) *Pornography: Men Possessing Women*, London: Women's Press.

Dyer, R. (1998) *Stars*, London: BFI.

—— (2002) *The Culture of Queers*, London: Routledge

Dyhouse, C. (1981) *Girls Growing Up in Late Victorian and Edwardian England*, London: Routledge.

—— (1989) *Feminism and the Family in England, 1880–1939*, Oxford: Basil Blackwell.

Edgerton, D. (2006) *The Shock of the Old: Technology and Global History since 1900*, London: Profile Books.

Edwards, D. and Cromwell, D. (2005) *Guardians of Power: The Myth of the Liberal Media*, London: Pluto Press.

Eisenstein, E. (1979) *The Printing Press as an Agent of Change*, 2 vols, Cambridge: Cambridge University Press.

Eldridge, J., Kitzinger, J. and Williams, K. (1997) *The Mass Media and Power in Modern Britain*, Oxford: Oxford University Press.

Engel, M. (1997) *Tickle the Public: One Hundred Years of the Popular Press*, London: Indigo.

Eriksen, T. H. (2001) *Tyranny of the Moment*, London: Pluto Press.

Evans, D. G. (2000) *A History of Wales 1906–2000*, Cardiff: University of Wales Press.

Evans, H. (1994) *Good Times, Bad Times*, London: Phoenix.

Evans, I. G. (1997a) 'Drunk on Hopes and Ideals: the Failure of Wales Television, 1959–63', *Llafur: Journal of Welsh Labour History*, 7(2): 81–93.

—— (1997b) 'Teledu Cymru: an Independent Television Service for Wales? (1959–63)', unpublished MA thesis, University of Wales.

Evans, P. and Wurster, T. (2000) *Blown to Bits*, Boston, MA: Harvard University Press.

Fabian, J. (1983) *Time and the Other: How Anthropology Makes its Object*, New York: Columbia University Press.

Fairclough, N. (1995) *Media Discourse*, London: Arnold.

Falcon, R. (1994) *Classified!* London: BFI and BBFC.

Featherstone, M. (1991) *Consumer Culture and Postmodernism*, London: Sage.

Fenn, H. (1910) *Thirty-Five Years in the Divorce Courts*, London: T. Werner Laurie.

Findlater, R. (1968) *Banned! Theatrical Censorship in Britain*, London: Panther.

Fine, B. and Leopold, E. (1993) *The World of Consumption*, London.

Fischer, C. S. (1992) *America Calling: A Social History of the Telephone to 1940*, Berkeley, CA: University of California Press.

Fischer, L. (1941) *Men and Politics*, London: Jonathan Cape.

Fiske, J. (1989a) *Reading the Popular*, Boston, MA: Unwin Hyman.

—— (1989b) *Understanding Popular Culture*, Boston, MA: Unwin Hyman.

Flanders, J. (2006) *Consuming Passions: Leisure and Pleasure in Victorian Britain*, London: Harper Press.

Flett, K. (2000) 'Television', *The Observer*, 29 August 2000, p. 12.

Flichy, P. (1995) *Dynamics of Modern Communication. The Shaping and Impact of New Communication Technologies*, London: Sage.

—— (2002) 'New Media History' in Lievrouw, L. and Livingstone, S. (eds), *The Handbook of New Media*, London: Sage.

Foster, A. (1990) 'The British Press and the Coming of the Cold War', in Deighton, A. (ed.), *Britain and the First Cold War*, New York: St. Martin's Press.

Foucault, M. (1991) *Discipline and Punish: The Birth of the Prison*, London: Penguin Books.

Fountain, A., Dowmunt, T. and Coyer, K. (2007) *The Alternative Media Handbook*, London: Routledge.

Fraser, D. (1982) *The Evolution of the British Welfare State: A History of Social Policy Since the Industrial Revolution*, London: Macmillan.

Fraser, N. (1993) 'Rethinking the Public Sphere: A Contribution to the Critique of Actually Existing Democracy', in Calhoun, C. (ed.), *Habermas and the Public Sphere*, pp. 109–42, Cambridge, MA: MIT Press.

Freeden, M. (2005) *Liberal Languages: Ideological Imaginations and Twentieth Century Progressive Thought*, Princeton, NJ: Princeton University Press.

Freedman, D. (2003) *Television Politics of the Labour Party 1951–2001*, London: Cass.

Frith, S. (1983) 'The Pleasures of the Hearth: The Making of BBC Light Entertainment, in Bennett, T. (ed.), *Formation of Pleasures*, pp. 101–23, London: Routledge & Kegan Paul.

Fryer, P. (1984) *Staying Power: The History of Black People in Britain*, Pluto Press.

Galbraith, J. K. (1958) *The Affluent Society*, Harmondsworth: Penguin.

Gannon, F. R. (1971) *The British Press and Germany, 1936–1939*, Oxford: Clarendon Press.

Garnham, N. (1983) 'Public Service versus the Market', *Screen*, 24(1).

—— (1990) *Capitalism and Communication*, London: Sage.

—— (1998) 'Political Economy and Cultural Studies: Reconciliation or Divorce?', in Storey, J. (ed.), *Cultural Theory and Popular Culture: A Reader*, pp. 600–612, Harlow: Prentice Hall.

—— (2000) *Emancipation, the Media, and Modernity: Arguments About the Media and Social Theory*, Oxford: Oxford University Press.

Gellner, E. (1983) *Nations and Nationalism*, Oxford: Blackwell.

Geraghty, C. (2000) *British Cinema in the Fifties: Gender, Genre and the 'New Look'*, London: Routledge.

Gerahty, C. (1937) *The Road to Madrid*, London: Hutchinson.

Gerbner, G., Gross, L., Morgan, M., Signorielli, N. and Shanahan, J. (2002) 'Growing up with Television: Cultivation Processes', in Bryant, J. and Zillmann, D. (eds), *Media Effects: Advances in Theory and Research*, pp. 43–67, Mahwah, NJ: Lawrence Erlbaum.

Giddens, A. (1991) *Modernity and Self-Identity*, Cambridge: Polity Press.

Gigerenzer, G., Swijtink, Z., Porter, T., Daston, L., Beatty, J. and Kruger L. (1990) *The Empire of Chance: How Probability Changed Science and Everyday Life*, Cambridge: Cambridge University Press.

Giles, J. (1995) *Women, Identity and Private Life in Britain 1900–50*, New York: St. Martin's Press.

—— (2004) *The Parlour and The Suburb: Domestic Identities, Class, Femininity and Modernity*, Oxford: Berg.

Gill, R. (2006) *Gender and the Media*, Cambridge: Polity Press.

Gilligan, C. (1982) *In a Different Voice: Psychological Theory and Women's Development*, London: Harvard University Press.

Gilmartin, K. (1996) *Print Politics: the Press and Radical Opposition in Early Nineteenth Century England*, Cambridge: Cambridge University Press.

Gilmour, I. (1993) *Dancing with Dogma: Britain Under Thatcherism*, London: Simon and Schuster.

Gilroy, P. (2002 [1987]) *There Ain't No Black in the Union Jack: The Cultural Politics of Race and Nation*, London: Routledge.

—— (2004) *After Empire: Multiculture or Postcolonial Melancholia*, London: Routledge.

—— (2007) *Black Britain: A Photographic History*, London: Saqi Books.

Glasgow University Media Group (1976) *Bad News*, London: Routledge & Kegan Paul.

—— (1980) *More Bad News*, London: Routledge & Kegan Paul.

—— (1982) *Really Bad News*, London: Writers and Readers.

Gledhill, C. (ed.) (1987) *Home is Where the Heart Is: Studies in Melodrama and the Woman's Film*, London: BFI.

—— and Swanson, G. (eds) (1996) *Nationalising Femininity: Culture, Sexuality and British Cinema in the Second World War*, Manchester: Manchester University Press.

Gleeber, G. (2004) *Serial Television*, London: British Film Institute.

Golby, J. and Purdue, A. W. (1984) *Civilisation of the Crowd: Popular Culture in England, 1750–1900*, London: B. T. Batsford.

Golding, P. and Middleton, S. (1982) *Images of Welfare*, Oxford: Martin Robertson.

—— and Murdock, G. (1991) 'Culture, Communications, and Political Economy', in Curran, J. and Gurevitch, M. (eds), *Mass Media and Society*, pp. 15–32, London: Edward Arnold.

Goodwin, P. (1998) *Television Under the Tories*, London: British Film Institute.

Gopsill, T. and Neale, G. (2007) *Journalists: 100 Years of the NUJ*, London: Profile Books.

Gorer, G. (1958) 'Television has Altered the Way of Life of Millions of People. Is this for Good or Evil?', *The Sunday Times*, 13 April–4 May 1958.

Gorham, D. (1982) *The Victorian Girl and the Feminine Ideal*, London: Croom Helm.

Grant Duff, S. (1976) 'A Very Brief Visit', in Toynbee, P. (ed.) *The Distant Drum: Reflections on the Spanish Civil War*, London: Sidgwick and Jackson.

—— (1982) *The Parting of Ways*, London: Peter Owen.

Gray, C. (2006) *Reluctant Genius: Alexander Graham Bell and the Passion for Invention*, New York: Arcade Publishing.

Greenslade, R. (2003) *Press Gang: How Newspapers Make Profit From Propaganda*, London: Macmillan.

Grenfell, J. (1980) *In Pleasant Places*, London: Macdonald.

Groombridge, B. (1972) *Television and the People: a Programme for Democratic Participation*, Harmondsworth: Penguin.

Grossberg, L., Wartella, E. and Whitney, D. (1998) *MediaMaking*, Thousand Oaks, CA: Sage.

Gunter, B. (2002) *Media Sex: What are the Issues?* Mahwah, NJ: Lawrence Erlbaum Associates.

—— and Harrison, J. (1998) *Violence on Television*, London: Routledge.

—— and McAleer, J. (1997) *Children and Television*, 4th edn, London: Routledge.

Gurney, P. (2005) 'The Battle of the Consumer in Postwar Britain', *Journal of Modern History*, 77: 956–87.

Habermas, J. (1989) *The Structural Transformation of the Public Sphere*, Cambridge: Polity.

—— (1992) 'Concluding Remarks' in Calhoun, C. (ed.) *Habermas and the Public Sphere*, Cambridge, MA: Massachusetts Institute of Technology Press.

Hacking I. (1984) *The Emergence of Probability: A Philosophical Study of Early Ideas About Probability, Induction and Statistical Inference*, Cambridge: Cambridge University Press.

Haig, M. [Lady Rhondda] (1937) *Notes on the Way*, London: Macmillan.

Hailsham, Lord (1975) *The Door Wherein I Went*, London: Collins.

—— (1990) *A Sparrow's Flight: Memoirs*, London: Collins.

Hajkowski, T. (2005) *The BBC and National Identity in Britain 1922–1953*, unpublished PhD thesis, Northwestern University.

Hall, S. (1977) 'Culture, the Media and the "Ideological Effect"', in Curran, J., Gurevitch, M. and Woollacott, J. (eds), *Mass Communication and Society*, pp. 315–48, London: Edward Arnold in association with The Open University.

—— (1981) 'Notes on Deconstructing the "Popular"', in Samuel, R. (ed.), *People's History and Socialist Theory*, London: Routledge & Kegan Paul.

—— (1986) 'Popular Power and the State', in Bennett, T., Mercer, C. and Woollacott, J. (eds) *Popular Culture and Social Relations*, pp. 22–49, Milton Keynes: Open University Press.

—— (1987) 'Minimal Selves', in Appignanesi, L. (ed.), *Identity*, London: ICA.

—— (1988) 'The Rediscovery of "Ideology": Return of the Repressed in Media Studies', in Gurevitch, M., Bennett, T., Curran, J. and Woollacot, J. (eds), *Culture, Society and the Media*, pp. 56–90, London: Routledge.

—— (1997) 'The Work of Representation', in Hall, S. (ed.), *Representation: Cultural Representations and Signifying Practices*, pp. 13–74, London: Sage.

—— (1998) *The Hard Road to Renewal*, London: Verso.

—— and Whannel, P. (1964) *The Popular Arts*, London: Hutchinson Educational.

——, Critcher, C., Jefferson, T., Clarke, J. and Roberts, B. (1978) *Policing the Crisis: Mugging, the State, and Law and Order*, London: Macmillan.

——, Hobson, D., Lowe, A. and Willis, P. (1992 [1980]) *Culture, Media, Language*, London: Routledge.

Hallin, D. (1989) *The 'Uncensored War': The Media and Vietnam*, Berkeley and Los Angeles: University of California Press.

—— and Mancini, P. (2004) *Comparing Media Systems: Three Models of Media and Politics*, Cambridge: Cambridge University Press.

Hamilton, J. and Atton, C. (2001) 'Theorising Anglo-American Alternative Media: Toward a Contextual History and Analysis of US and UK Scholarship', *Media History*, 7(2): 119–35.

Hampton, M. (2001) 'The Press, Patriotism, and Public Discussion: C. P. Scott, the *Manchester Guardian*, and the Boer War, 1899–1902', *The Historical Journal*, 44: 177–97.

—— (2004) *Visions of the Press in Britain, 1850–1950*, Urbana and Chicago, IL: University of Illinois Press.

—— (2005) 'Media Studies and the Mainstreaming of Media History', *Media History*, 11(3): 239–46.

——, O'Malley, T., Potter, S. and Wiener, J. (2006) 'Roundtable: Visions of the Press in Britain, 1850–1950', *Media History*, 12(1).

Hannington, W. (1936) *The Problems of Distressed Areas*, London: Gollancz.

Harris, B. (1996) *Politics and the Rise of the Press: Britain and France 1620–1800*, London: Routledge.

Harris, R. and Seldon, A. (1959) *Advertising in a Free Society*, London: Institute of Economic Affairs.

—— (1962) *Advertising in Action*, London: Hutchinson.

Harrison, B. (1982) 'Press and Pressure Group in Modern Britain', in Shattock, J. and Wolff, M. (eds), *The Victorian Periodical Press: Samplings and Soundings*, pp. 261–96, Leicester: Leicester University Press.

Harrison, S. (1974) *Poor Men's Guardians: A Survey of the Struggles for a Democratic Newspaper Press 1763–1973*, London: Lawrence & Wishart.

Harvey, D. (1991) *The Condition of Postmodernity*, Cambridge, MA and Oxford: Blackwell.

Harvey, S. (2006) *Trading Culture: Global Traffic and Local Cultures in Film and Television*, Eastleigh: John Libbey Publishing.

—— and Robins K. (eds) (1993) *The Regions, the Nations and the BBC*, London: BFI.

Harvie, C. (1982) *No Gods and Precious Few Heroes*, London: Penguin.

—— (2000) 'The Moment of British Nationalism, 1939–70', *Political Quarterly*, 71: 328–40.

Hassan, R. (2004) *Media, Politics and the Network Society*, Maidenhead: Open University Press.

Hebdige, D. (1979) *Subculture. The Meaning of Style*, London: Methuen.

—— (1988) *Hiding in the Light: on Images and Things*, London: Comedia.

Heidegger, M. (1978) 'The Question concerning Technology', in Heidegger, M. (ed.), *Basic Writings*, pp. 307–42. London: Routledge

Heilbroner, R. (1967/2003) 'Do Machines make History?', in Scharff, R. and Dusek, V. (eds), *Philosophy of Technology*, pp. 398–404, Oxford: Blackwell.

Helly, D. O. and Callaway, H. (2000) 'Journalism as Active Politics: Flora Shaw, *The Times* and South Africa', in Lowry, D. (ed.), *The South African War Reappraised*, Manchester: Manchester University Press.

Hendy, D. (2007) *Life on Air: A History of Radio Four 1967–2007*, Oxford: Oxford University Press.

Hennessy, P. (2006) *Having it so Good: Britain in the Fifties*, London: Allen Lane.

Henry, A. (2004) 'Orgasms and Empowerment: Sex and the City and the Third Wave Feminism , in Akass, K. and McCabe, J. (eds), *Reading Sex and the City*, London: I. B. Tauris.

Henry, B. (ed.) (1986) *British Television Advertising: the First Thirty Years*, London: Century Benham.

Herbst, J. (1991) *The Starched Blue Sky of Spain*, New York: Harper Perennial.

Herman, E. and Chomsky, N. (1988) *Manufacturing Consent: The Political Economy of the Mass Media*, New York: Pantheon Books.

—— and McChesney, R. (1997) *Global Media: The New Missionaries of Corporate Capitalism*, London: Continuum.

Hesmondhalgh, D. (2007) *The Cultural Industries*, London: Sage.

Hesse, B. (ed.) (2000) *Un/settled Multiculturalisms, Diaspora, Entanglements, Transruptions*, London: Zed Books.

Hetherington, A. (1992) *Inside BBC Scotland 1975–1980*, Aberdeen: Whitewater.

Hewison, R. (1995) *Culture and Consensus: England, Art and Politics Since 1940*, London: Methuen.

Heywood, P. (2007) *Political Ideologies: An Introduction*, Basingstoke: Palgrave Macmillan.

Higgins, P. (1996) *Heterosexual Dictatorship: Male Homosexuality in Postwar Britain*, London: Fourth Estate.

Higson, A. (ed.) (1996) *Dissolving Views: Key Writings on British Cinema*, London: Cassell.

—— (1997) *Waving the Flag: Constructing A National Cinema in Britain*, Oxford: Clarendon Press.

Hill, A. (2005) *Reality TV: Audiences and Popular Factual Television*, London: Routledge.

Hill, C. (1974) *Behind the Screen: the Broadcasting Memoirs of Lord Hill of Luton*, London: Sidgwick & Jackson.

Hill, J. (1986) *Sex, Class and Realism: British Cinema, 1956–1963*, London: BFI.

—— (2007) *Cinema and Northern Ireland*, London: BFI.

Hills, J. (2002) *The Struggle for Control of Global Communication: The Formative Century*, Urbana, IL: University of Illinois Press.

Hills, M. (2005) 'Who Wants to be a Fan of *Who Wants to be a Millionaire*?' in Johnson, C. and Turrock, R. (eds), *ITV Cultures*, pp. 177–95, Maidenhead: Open University Press.

Hilmes, M. (2007) 'Front Line Family: "Women's Culture Comes to the BBC"', *Media, Culture & Society*, 29(1): 5–30.

Hobsbawn, E. J. (1990) *Nations and Nationalism since 1780*, Cambridge: Cambridge University Press.

Hoggart, R. (1958) *The Uses of Literacy*, Harmondsworth: Pelican.

—— (1973) 'The Difficulties of Democratic Debate', in Hoggart, R. (ed.), *Speaking to Each Other*, Vol. 1, Harmondsworth: Penguin.

—— (1992) *An Imagined Life: Life and Times 1959–1991*, London: Chatto and Windus.

—— (2004) *Mass Media in a Mass Society*, London: Continuum.

Holland, P. (1998) 'The Politics of the Smile: "Soft News" and the Sexualisation of the Popular Press', in Carter, C., Branston, G. and Allan, S. (eds), *News, Gender and Power*, pp. 17–32, London: Routledge.

—— (2006) *The Angry Buzz*, London: I. B. Tauris.

Hollingsworth, M. (1986) *The Press and Political Dissent: A Question of Censorship*, London: Pluto Press.

Hollis, P. (1970) *The Pauper Press*, Oxford: Oxford University Press.

Hollows, J. and Moseley, R. (eds) (2006) *Feminism in Popular Culture*, Oxford: Berg.

Holmes, S. (2005) *British Television and Film Culture in the 1950s: Coming to a TV Near You!* Bristol: Intellect Books.

—— (2008) *Entertaining TV: The BBC and Popular Programme Culture in the 1950s*, Manchester: Manchester University Press.

Hopkin, D. (1978) 'The Socialist Press in Britain, 1890–1910', in Boyce, D. G., Curran, J. and Wingate, P. (eds), *Newspaper History: From the 17th Century to the Present Day*, London: Constable.

Horgan J. (2001) *Irish Media: A Critical History*, London: Routledge.

Horkheimer, M. (1978 [1946]) 'The End of Reason', in Arato, A. and Gebhardt, E. (eds), *The Essential Frankfurt School Reader*, pp. 26–48, Oxford: Blackwell.

Hounshell, D. A. (1975) 'Elisha Gray and the Telephone: On the Disadvantages of Being an Expert', *Technology and Culture*, 16(2): 133–61.

Hubble, N. (2005) *Mass Observation and Everyday Life: Culture, History, Theory*, Basingstoke: Palgrave.

Humphries, S. (1989) *Victorian Britain Through the Magic Lantern*, London: Sidgwick & Jackson.

Hutchinson, D. (1999) *Media Policy: An Introduction*, Oxford: Blackwell.

Innis, H. (1951) *The Bias of Communication*, Toronto: Toronto University Press.

—— (1952) *Empire and Communication*, Toronto: University of Toronto Press.

Institute of Race Relations (1989) *Racism and the Press in Thatcher's Britain*, London: IRR.

Jackson, A. (2002) *British Women and the Spanish Civil War*, London: Routledge.

Jacobs, J. (2000) *The Intimate Screen: Early British Television Drama*, Oxford: Clarendon Press.

Jacobs, L. (1991) *The Wages of Sin: Censorship and the Fallen Woman Film, 1928–1942*, Madison, WI: University of Wisconsin Press.

James, L. (1976) *Print and the People, 1819–1851*, London: Allen Lane.

Jameson, F. (1991) *Postmodernism, or the Cultural Logic of Late Capitalism*, London: Verso.

Jenkins, C. (1961) *Power Behind the Screen: Ownership Control and Motivation in British Commercial Television*, London: MacGibbon & Kee.

Jenks, J. (2006) *British Propaganda and News Media in the Cold War*, Edinburgh: Edinburgh University Press.

Jennings, H. and Gill, W. (1939) *Broadcasting in Everyday Life: A Survey of the Social Effects of the Coming of Broadcasting*, London: BBC.

Johnson, L. (1981) 'Radio and Everyday Life: the Early Years of Broadcasting in Australia, 1922–45', *Media, Culture & Society*, 3(2): 167–78.

Johnson, M. J. (2007) *Third Wave Feminism and Television: Jane Puts it in a Box*, London: I. B. Tauris.

Johnson, R. (1979) 'Really Useful Knowledge: Radical Education and Working Class Culture', in Clarke, J., Critcher, C. and Johnson, R. (eds), *Working Class Culture: Studies in History and Theory*, pp. 75–102, London: Hutchinson.

Johnson, T. (1997) *Censored Screams: The British Ban on Hollywood Horror in the Thirties*, Jefferson, NC, London: McFarland & Co.

Jones, A. (1993) *Press, Politics and Society: A History of Journalism in Wales*, Cardiff: University of Wales Press.

Kaplan, E. A. (ed.) (1980) *Women in Film Noir*, London: BFI.

—— (1983) *Women and Film: Both Sides of the Camera*, London: Routledge.

—— (2000) *Feminism & Film*, Oxford: Oxford University Press.

Karpf, A. (1988) *Doctoring the Media: The Reporting of Health and Medicine*, London: Routledge.

Katz, E. (2001) 'Media Effects', in Smelser, N. J. and Baltes, P. B. (eds), *International Encyclopedia of the Social and Behavioral Sciences*, pp. 9472–79, Oxford: Elsevier Science.

—— (2004) 'Lazarsfeld's Map of Media Effects', *International Journal of Public Opinion Research*, 13: 270–79.

—— and Gurevitch, M. (1976) *The Secularization of Leisure: Culture and Communication in Israel*, Cambridge, MA: Harvard University Press.

——, Haas, H. and Gurevitch, M. (1997) '20 Years of Television in Israel: Are there Long-run Effects on Values, Social Connectedness and Cultural Practices?', *Journal of Communication*, 47(2): 3–20.

——, Docter, S., Gusek, J., Metzger, M., O'Connell, J. and Stokes, J. (1998) 'Press – conversation – opinion – action: Gabriel Tarde's public sphere', in Lautman, J. and Lécuyer, B.-P. (eds), *Paul Lazarsfeld (1901–1976): La Sociologie de Vienne à New York*, pp. 433–53, Paris: L'Harmattan.

——, Peters, J. D., Liebes, T. and Orloff, A. (eds) (2003) *Canonic Texts in Media Research. Are there any? Should there be? How about these?* Cambridge: Polity.

Kaul, C. (2003) *Reporting the Raj: The British Press and India, c. 1880–1922*, Manchester: Manchester University Press.

Keane, J. (1991) *The Media and Democracy*, Cambridge: Polity Press.

Kearney, H. (1989) *The British Isles: A History of Four Nations*, Cambridge: Cambridge University Press.

Kershaw, A. (2002) *Blood and Champagne: The Life and Times of Robert Capa*, Basingstoke: Macmillan.

Kittler, F. (1999) *Gramophone, Film, Typewriter*, Stanford, CA: Stanford University Press.

Kloppenberg, J. T. (1998) *The Virtues of Liberalism*, Oxford: Oxford University Press.

Knickerbocker, H. (1936) *The Siege of Alcazar: A Warlog of the Spanish Revolution*, Philadelphia, PA: David McKay Co.

Knightley, P. (1975) *The First Casualty*, London: Andre Deutsch.

Koestler, A. (1938) *Spanish Testament*, London: Gollancz.

Koss, S. (1981/1984) *The Rise and Fall of the Political Press in Britain*, Vols 1 and 2, London: Hamish Hamilton.

Kroker, A. (1984) *Technology and the Canadian Mind*, New York: St. Martin's Press.

Kuhn, A. (1988) *Cinema, Censorship and Sexuality, 1909–1925*, London: Routledge.

Kumar, K. (2003) *The Making of English National Identity*, Cambridge: Cambridge University Press.

Lacey, K. (1994) 'From Plauderei to Propaganda: On Women's Radio in Germany, 1924–35', *Media, Culture & Society*, 16: 589–607.

Lancaster, W. (1995) *The Department Store*, Leicester: Leicester University Press.

Landy, M. (1991) *British Genres: Cinema and Society, 1930–1960*, Princeton, NJ: Princeton University Press.

Law, G. (2001) 'New Woman Novels in Newspapers', *Media History*, 7(1): 17–32.

Lazarsfeld, P. F., Berelson, B. and Gaudet, H. (1944) *The People's Choice*, New York: Duell, Sloan and Pearce.

Leavis, F. R. (1979 [1930]) *Mass Civilisation and Minority Culture*, in Leavis, F. R. (ed.), *Education and the University*, Cambridge: Cambridge University Press.

—— and Thompson, D. (1932) *Culture and Environment*, London: Chatto and Windus.

Lee, A. J. (1974) 'The Radical Press', in Morris, A. (ed.), *Edwardian Radicalism, 1900–1914*, London: Routledge.

—— (1976) *The Origins of the Popular Press 1855–1914*, London: Croom Helm.

Legg, M. L. (1999) *Newspapers and Nationalism: the Irish Provisional Press 1850–1892*, Dublin: Four Courts Press.

LeMahieu D. (1988) *A Culture for Democracy: Mass Communication and the Cultivated Mind in Britain between the Wars*, Oxford: Clarendon Press.

Leman, J. (1980) '"The Advice of A Real Friend". Codes of Intimacy and Oppression in Women's Magazines 1937–55', in Baehr, H. (ed.), *Women and Media*, pp. 63–78, Oxford: Pergamon Press.

—— (1987) 'Programmes for Women in 1950s British Television', in Dyer, G. and Baehr, H. (eds), *Boxed In: Women and Television*, pp. 73–88, London: Pandora Press.

—— (1996) '"Pulling our Weight in the Call-Up of Women": Class and Gender in British Radio in the Second World War', in Gledhill, C. and Swanson, G. (eds), *Nationalising Femininity: Culture, Sexuality and British Cinema in the Second World War*, pp. 109–18, Manchester: Manchester University Press.

Lemish, D. (2005) 'The Media Gendering of Conflict', *Feminist Media Studies*, 5(3): 275–78.

Lepenies, W. (1992) *Between Literature and Science: the Rise of Sociology*, Cambridge: Cambridge University Press.

Leuchtenberg, W. A. (1958). *The Perils of Prosperity, 1914–1932*, Chicago, IL: University of Chicago Press.

Levinson, P. (2001) *McLuhan: A Guide to the Information Millennium*, New York: Routledge.

Lewis, J. (1984) *Women in England, 1870–1950: Sexual Divisions and Social Change*, Brighton: Wheatsheaf.

—— (ed.) (1986) *Labour and Love: Women's Experience of Home and Family, 1850–1940*, Oxford: Blackwell.

Lievrouw, L. and Livingstone, S. (2002) 'The Social Shaping and Consequences of ICTs', in Lievrouw, L. and Livingstone, S. (eds), *Handbook of New Media*, New York: Sage Publications.

Lister, R. (2003) *Citizenship: Feminist Perspectives*, Basingstoke: Palgrave Macmillan.

Livingstone, S. (1998) 'Mediated Childhoods: A Comparative Approach to Young People's Changing Media Environment in Europe', *European Journal of Communication*, 13(4): 435–56.

Llewellyn-Smith, C. (2001) *Poplife: A Journey by Sofa*, London: Sceptre.

Lloyd, J. and Johnson, L. (2003) 'The Three Faces of Eve: The Post-War Housewife, Melodrama, and Home', *Feminist Media Studies*, 3(1): 7–25.

Lotz, A.(2006) *Redesigning Women*, Urbana and Chicago, IL: University of Illinois Press.

Louw, E. (2005) *The Media and Political Process*, London: Sage.

Lury, C. (1996) *Consumer Culture*, Cambridge: Polity Press.

Lyon, D. (2003) 'Introduction' in Lyon, D. (ed.), *Surveillance as Social Sorting: Privacy, Risk and Digital Discrimination*, pp. 1–9, London: Routledge.

McChesney, R. (1999) *Rich Media, Poor Democracy: Communication Politics in Dubious Times*, Urbana, IL: University of Illinois Press.

McClintock, A. (1995) *Imperial Lather: Race, Gender and Sexuality in the Colonial Contest*, New York: Routledge.

McCombs, M. E. and Shaw, D. L. (1972) 'The Agenda-setting Function of Mass Media', *Public Opinion Quarterly*, 36: 176–87.

McDermid, J. (2000) 'Women and Education', in Purvis, J. (ed.), *Women's History: Britain, 1850–1945*, pp. 107–30, London: Routledge.

Macdonald, M. (1995) *Representing Women*, London: Arnold.

McDowell, W. H. (1992) *The History of BBC Broadcasting in Scotland 1923–1982*, Edinburgh: Edinburgh University Press.

McGillivray, D. (1992) *Doing Ride Things: The History of the British Sex Film, 1957–1981*, London: Sun Tavern Fields.

McGuigan, J. (1992) *Cultural Populism*, London: Routledge.

McKendrick, N., Brewer, J. and Plumb, J. H. (1983) *The Birth of a Consumer Society*, London: Hutchinson.

Mackenzie, J. (1984) *Propaganda and Empire: The Manipulation of British Public Opinion, 1880–1960*, Manchester: Manchester University Press.

McKibbin, R. (1998) *Classes and Cultures*, Oxford: Oxford University Press.

McLaughlin, G. (2002) *The War Correspondent*, London: Pluto.

McLuhan, M. (1962) *The Gutenberg Galaxy*, Toronto: Toronto University Press.

—— (1964) *Understanding Media: The Extensions of Man*, New York: New American Library.

McNair, B. (1996) *Mediated Sex: Pornography and Postmodern Culture*, London: Arnold.

—— (2000) *Journalism and Democracy: An Evaluation of the Political Public Sphere*, London: Routledge.

—— (2002) *Striptease Culture: Sex, Media and Democratisation of Desire*, London: Routledge.

McNicholas, A. (2003) 'Media History: Problems, Uses and Justifications', *Media Education Journal*, 34: 14–15.

McRobbie, A. (1996) 'More! New Sexualities in Girls' and Women's Magazines', in Curran, J., Morley D. and Walkerdine, V. (eds) *Cultural Studies and Communications*, London: Arnold.

—— (2005) *The Uses of Cultural Studies*, London: Sage.

—— (2006) 'Post-feminism and Popular Culture: Bridget Jones and the New Gender Regime', in Curran, J. and Morley, D. (eds), *Media and Cultural Theory*, pp. 59–70, London: Routledge.

Marchand, P. (1998) *Marshall McLuhan: The Medium and the Messenger*, Cambridge, MA: MIT Press.

Marcuse, H. (1964) *One-Dimensional Man*, Boston, MA: Beacon Press.

—— (1968 [1937]) 'The Affirmative Character of Culture', in Marcuse, H. (ed.), *Negations*, pp. 88–133, London: Allen Lane, Penguin Press.

Marshall, T. (1950) *Citizenship and Social Class and other Essays*, Cambridge: Cambridge University Press.

Martin, K. (1947) *The Press the Public Wants*, London: The Hogarth Press.

Marvin, C. (1990) *When Old Technologies Were New*, New York: Oxford University Press.

Marwick, A. (1998) *The Sixties*, Oxford: Clarendon Press.

Matheson, H. (1933) *Broadcasting*, London: Thornton Butterworth.

Mathews, T. D. (1994) *Censored*, London: Chatto & Windus.

Mattelart, A. (1996) *The Invention of Communication*, Minneapolis, MN and London: University of Minnesota Press.

—— (2000) *Networking the World: 1794–2000*, Minneapolis, MN and London: University of Minnesota Press.

—— (2003) *The Information Society*, London: Sage.

Matthews, H. (1938) *Two Wars and More to Come*, New York: Carrick and Evans.

—— (1972) *A World in Revolution*, New York: Charles Scribner.

May, C. (2002) *The Information Society*, Cambridge: Polity.

Mayhew, C. (1959) *Commercial Television – What is to be Done?* London: The Fabian Society.

Medhurst, A. (1996) 'Victim: Text as Context', in Higson, A. (ed.), *Dissolving Views*, pp. 117–32, London: Cassell.

—— (2007) *National Joke: Popular Comedy and English Cultural Identity*, London: Routledge.

Medhurst, J. (2002) 'Servant of Two Tongues: the Demise of TWW', *Llafur: Journal of Welsh Labour History*, 8(3): 79–87.

—— (2003) 'Teledu Cymru: menter gyffrous neu freuddwyd ffol?' in Jenkins, G. H. (ed.), *Cof Cenedl XVII*, Llandysul: Gomer.

—— (2004) '"You say a Minority, Sir; we say a Nation": The Pilkington Committee on Broadcasting (1960–62) and Wales', *Welsh History Review*, 22(2): 109–36.

—— (2005) 'Mammon's Television? ITV in Wales, 1959–63', in Johnson, C. and Turnock, R. (eds), *ITV Cultures: Independent Television over Fifty Years*, Maidenhead: Open University Press.

—— (2007) 'Piecing Together Mammon's Television: a Case Study in Historical Television Research', in Wheatley, H. (ed.) *Re-Viewing Television History: Critical Issues in Television Historiography*, London: I. B. Tauris.

Mercer, J. (2004) 'Making the News: Votes for Women and the Mainstream Press', *Media History*, 10(3): 187–99.

Merrin, W. (2002) 'Implosion, Simulation and the Pseudo-Event: a Critique of McLuhan', *Economy and Society*, 31(3): 369–90.

—— (2005) *Baudrillard and the Media*, Cambridge: Polity.

Meyrowitz, J. (1985) *No Sense of Place*, New York: Oxford University Press.

—— (1994) 'Medium Theory', in Crowley, D. and Mitchell, D. (eds), *Communication Theory Today*, pp. 50–77, Cambridge: Polity Press.

Miller, D. (2001) *Consumption: Critical Concepts in the Social Sciences*, London: Routledge.

Miller, M. B. (1981) *The Bon Marché: Bourgeois Culture and the Department Store 1869–1920*, Princeton, NJ: Princeton University Press.

Minihan, J. (1977) *The Nationalisation of Culture. The Development of State Subsidies to the Arts in Great Britain*, London: Hamish Hamilton.

Mitchell, C. (ed.) (2000) *Women & Radio: Airing Differences*, London: Routledge.

Modood, T. (2005) *Multiculturalism Politics: Racism, Ethnicity and Muslims in Britain*, Edinburgh: Edinburgh University Press.

—— (2007) *Multiculturalism (Themes for the 21st Century)*, Cambridge: Polity Press.

Monks, N. (1955) *Eye Witness*, London: Frederick Muller.

Moore, M. (2006) *The Origins of Modern Spin: Democratic Government and the Media in Britain, 1945–51*, Basingstoke: Palgrave.

Moorehead, C. (2003) *Martha Gellhorn: A Life*, London: Vintage.

Moores, S. (1988) 'The Box in the Dresser: Memories of Early Radio', *Media, Culture & Society*, 10(1): 23–40.

Morgan, D. H. J. (1975) *Social Theory and the Family*, London: Routledge & Kegan Paul.

Morgan, K. O. (1981) *Rebirth of a Nation: Wales 1880–1980*, Oxford: Oxford University Press.

Morley, D. (2007) *Media, Modernity and Technology*, London: Routledge.

Morris, B. (1991) *The Roots of Appeasement: The British Weekly Press and Nazi Germany during the 1930s*, London: Frank Cass.

Morrison, J. and Watkins, S. (2006) *Scandalous Fictions*, Basingstoke: Palgrave Macmillan.

Mosco, V. (1996) *The Political Economy of Communication*, London: Sage.

Murdock, G. (1988) 'Large Corporations and the Control of the Communications Industries', in Gurevitch, M., Bennett, T., Curran, J. and Woollacott, J. (eds), *Culture, Society and the Media*, pp. 118–50, London: Routledge.

—— (1990) 'Redrawing the Map of the Communications Industries: Concentration and Ownership in the Era of Privatisation', in Ferguson, M. (ed.), *Public Communication: The New Imperatives*, pp. 1–15, London: Sage.

—— (1992) 'Citizens, Consumers and Public Culture', in Skovmand, M. and Schroder, K. (eds), *Media Cultures*, London: Routledge.

—— (1999) 'Rights and Representations: Public Discourse and Cultural Citizenship', in Gripsrud, J. (ed.), *Television and Common Knowledge*, London: Routledge.

—— (2005) 'Public Broadcasting and Democratic Culture: Consumers, Citizens and Communards', in Wasko, J. (ed.), *A Companion to Television*, pp. 174–98, Oxford: Blackwell.

—— and Golding, P. (1977) 'Capitalism, Communication and Class Relations', in Curran, J., Gurevitch, M. and Woollacott, J. (eds), *Mass Communication and Society*, pp. 12–43, London: Edward Arnold in association with The Open University Press.

Murray, G. (1972) *The Press and the Public: The Story of the British Press Council*, Carbondale, IL: Southern University Press.

Murray, J. (ed.) (1996) *The Woman's Hour: 50 Years of Women in Britain*, London: John Murray.

Nairn, T. (2003 [1977]) *Break up of Britain: Crisis and Neo-Nationalism*, Melbourne: Common Ground Publishing.

Nash, M. (1995) *Defying Male Civilization: Women in the Spanish Civil War*, Denver, CO: Arden Press.

Nava, M., Barker, A., Macrury, I. and Richards, B. (1997) *Buy This Book: Studies in Advertising and Consumption*, London: Routledge.

Negrine, R. (1994) *Politics and the Mass Media in Britain*, 2nd edn, London: Routledge.

Negroponte, N. (1996) *Being Digital*, London: Hodder & Stoughton.

Nerone, J. (2006) 'The Future of Communication History', *Critical Studies in Mass Communication*, 28(3): 254–62.

Nevett, T. (1992) 'Differences between American and British Television Advertising: Explanations and Implications', *Journal of Advertising*, 21: 61–71.

Newburn, T. (1992) *Permission and Regulation: Law and Morals in Post-War Britain*, London: Routledge.

Newman, G. (1939) *The Building of a Nation's Heath*, London: Macmillan.

Nicholas, S. (1996) *The Echo of War: Home Front Propaganda and the Wartime BBC, 1939–1945*, Manchester: Manchester University Press.

North, J. (1958) *No Men are Strangers*, New York: International Publishers.

Nott, J. (2002) *Music for the People*, Oxford: Oxford University Press.

O'Malley, T. (1994) *Closedown?* London: Pluto.

—— (1997) 'Labour and the 1947–49 Royal Commission on the Press', in Bromley, M. and O'Malley, T. (eds), *A Journalism Reader*, London and New York: Routledge.

—— (1998) 'Demanding Accountability: the Press, the Royal Commissions and the Pressure for Reform, 1945–77', in Stephenson, H. and Bromley, M. (eds), *Sex, Lies and Democracy: the Press and the Public*, London: Longman.

—— (2002) 'Media History and Media Studies: Aspects of the Development of the Study of Media History in the UK, 1945–2000', *Media History*, 8(2): 155–73.

—— and Soley, C. (2000) *Regulating the Press*, London: Pluto.

Oakley, A. (1998) 'Gender, Methodology and People's Ways of Knowing: Some Problems with Feminism and the Paradigm Debate in Social Science', *Sociology*, 32: 707–31.

Offer, A. (2006) *The Challenge of Affluence: Self-control and Well-being in the United States and Britain since 1950*, Oxford: Oxford University Press.

Ong, W. (1982) *Orality and Literacy*, London: Methuen.

Oram, A. (2001) 'Feminism, Androgyny and Love between Women in Urania, 1916–40', *Media History*, 7(1): 57–70.

Orwell, G. (1965 [1937]) *The Road to Wigan Pier*, Harmondsworth: Pelican Books.

—— (1984 [1944]) 'As I Please', in Orwell. G.', *The Collected Essays, Journalism and Letters*, Vol. 3, *1943–1945*, pp. 173–76, Harmondsworth: Penguin.

Osgerby, B. (2004) *Youth Media*, London: Routledge.

Packard, V. (1977) *The Hidden Persuaders*, Harmondsworth: Penguin.

Page, B. (2003) *The Murdoch Archipelago*, London: Simon and Schuster.

Parekh, B. C. (2000) *Report of the Commission on the Future of Multi-Ethnic Britain*, London: The Runnymede Trust/Profile Books.

Park, D. and Pooley, J. D. (eds) (2007) *Ferment in the Field's History: Critical Perspectives on the History of Mass Communication Research*, New York: Peter Lang.

Park, D. W. and Pooley, J. (eds) (2008) *The History of Media and Communication Research: Contested Memories*, New York: Peter Lang Publishing.

Paulu, B. (1956) *British Broadcasting: Radio and Television in the United Kingdom*, Minneapolis, MN: University of Minnesota Press.

Peacock Report (1986) *Report of the Committee on Financing the BBC*, Cmnd. 9824, London: HMSO.

Pearson, G. (1983) *Hooligan: A History of Respectable Fears*, London: Macmillan.

Pearson, J. and Turner, G. (1965) *The Persuasion Industry*, London: Eyre & Spottiswoode.

Pegg, M. (1983) *Broadcasting and Society, 1918–1939*, London: Croom Helm.

Perkin, H. (1969) *The Origins of Modern English Society, 1780–1880*, London: Routledge and Kegan Paul.

Peters, J. D. (2000) *Speaking into the Air: A History of the Idea of Communication*, Chicago, IL: University of Chicago Press.

—— (2006) 'Technology and Ideology: The Case of the Telegraph Revisited', in Packer, J. and Robertson, C. (eds), *Thinking with James Carey*, pp. 137–55, Oxford: Peter Lang.

Pettitt, L. (2008) *Irish Media and Popular Culture*, London: Routledge.

Philips, D. (2006) *Women's Fiction 1945–2005*, London: Continuum.

—— and Haywood, I. (1998) *Brave New Causes*, London and Washington: Leicester University Press.

Philips, M. and Philips, T. (1998) *Windrush: the Irresistible Rise of Multi-Racial Britain*, London: Harper Collins.

Pilkington (1962) (a) *Report of the Committee on Broadcasting*, Cmnd. 1753; (b) *Memoranda submitted to the Committee*, Cmnd. 1819, London: HMSO.

Pimlott, B. (1998) 'Monarchy and the Message', in Seaton, J. (ed.), *Politics and the Media*, Oxford: Blackwell.

Pinchevski, A. (2005) 'By Way of Interruption: Levinas and the Ethics of Communication', Pittsburgh: Duquesne University Press.

Pittock, M. (1999) *Celtic Identity in the British Image*, Manchester: Manchester University Press

Plunkett, J. (2003) *Queen Victoria: First Media Monarch*, Oxford: Oxford University Press.

Political and Economic Planning (1938) *Report on the British Press: A Survey of its Current Operations and Problems with Special Reference to National Newspapers and their Part in Public Affairs*, London: Political and Economic Planning.

Poole, E. (2002) *Reporting Islam: Media Representations of British Muslims*, London: I. B. Tauris.

Poster, M. (1995) *The Second Media Age*, Cambridge: Polity.

Postma, J. and van der Helm, A. (2000) 'La Riegle de Libro: Bookkeeping Instructions from the Mid-fifteenth Century', Paper for the 8th World Congress of Accounting Historians, Madrid, Spain, 19–21 July, available at http://home.hetnet.nl/~annejvanderhelm/paper.html (accessed 29 March 2007).

Potter, J. (1990) *Independent Television in Britain*, Vol. 4, *1968–1980*, London: Macmillan.

Potter, S. J. (2003) *News and the British World: The Emergence of an Imperial Press System*, Oxford: Clarendon Press.

—— (ed.) (2004) *Newspapers and Empire in Ireland and Britain: Reporting the British Empire, c.1857–1921*, Dublin: Four Courts Press.

Press Council (1954) *Press and the People: First Annual Report*, London: Press Council.

Price, R. (1995) *British Society, 1680–1880*, Cambridge: Cambridge University Press.

Pronay, N. (1981) 'The First Reality: Film Censorship in Liberal England', in Short, K. (ed.), *Feature Film as History*, London: Croom Helm.

—— (1982) 'The Political Censorship of Films between the Wars', in Pronay, N. and Spring, D. (eds), *Propaganda, Politics and Film 1918–45*, London: Macmillan.

—— and Croft, J. (1983) 'British Film Censorship and Propaganda Policy During the Second World War', in Curran, J. and Porter, V. (eds) *British Cinema History*, pp. 144–63, London: Weidenfeld & Nicolson.

Purcell, H. (2004) *The Last English Revolutionary: Tom Wintringham 1898–1949*, Stroud: Sutton Publishing.

Purvis, J. (1991) *A History of Women's Education in England*, Milton Keynes: Open University Press.

—— (ed.) (2000) *Women's History: Britain, 1850–1945*, London: Routledge.

Radway, J. (1987) *Reading the Romance*, London: Verso.

Ramsden, J. (1995) *The Age of Churchill and Eden*, London: Longman.

Read, D. (1961) *Press and People, 1790–1850*, London: Edward Arnold.

Readman, M. (2005) *Teaching Film Censorship and Controversy*, London: BFI.

Reid G. F. (1971) *The British Press and Germany 1936–1939*, Oxford: Clarendon Press.

Report of the Broadcasting Committee (1949) *Appendix H. Memoranda submitted to the Committee*, Cmd. 8117 (1951), London: HMSO.

Report of the Committee on Broadcasting (1960) *Volume II. Appendix E. Memoranda submitted to the Committee (Papers 103–275)*. Cmnd. 1819–1 (1962), London: HMSO.

Rheingold, H. (2000) *The Virtual Community*, rev. edn, Cambridge, MA: MIT Press.

—— (2002) *Smart Mobs*, Cambridge, MA: MIT Press.

Richards, H. (1997) *The Bloody Circus: The* Daily Herald *and the Left*, London: Pluto Press.

Richards, J. (1981) 'The British Board of Film Censors and Content Control in the 1930s: Image of Britain', *Historical Journal of Film, Radio and Television*, 1(2): 95–116.

—— (1983) 'Patriotism with Profit: British Imperial Cinema in the 1930s', in Curran, J. and Porter, V. (eds) *British Cinema History*, pp. 245–56, London: Weidenfeld & Nicolson.

—— (1984) *The Age of the Dream Palace: Cinema and Society in Britain, 1930–39*, London: Routledge & Kegan Paul.

—— (1997a) *Films and British National Identity: from Dickens to Dad's Army*, Manchester: Manchester University Press.

—— (1997b) 'British Film Censorship', in Murphy, R. (ed.), *The British Cinema Book*, pp. 167–77, London: BFI.

Richards, T. (1990) *The Commodity Culture of Victorian England: Advertising and Spectacle, 1851–1914*, Stanford: Stanford University Press.

Richardson, J. E. (2004) *(Mis)Representing Islam: The Racism and Rhetoric of British Broadsheet Newspapers*, Amsterdam: John Benjamins Publishing.

Riesman, D. (1950/1976) *The Lonely Crowd*, New Haven, CT: Yale University Press.

Robbins, K. (1997) *Great Britain: Identities, Institutions and the Idea of Britishness*, Harlow: Longman.

Rogers, E. M (2006) *Diffusion of Innovations*, New York: Free Press.

Rolph, C. H. (1969) *Books in the Dock*, London: Andre Deutsch.

Rose, J. (2001) *The Intellectual Life of the British Working Classes*, New Haven, CT: Yale University Press.

Rose, N. (1985) *The Psychological Complex: Psychology, Politics and Society in England, 1869–1939*, London: Routledge & Kegan Paul.

Rowbotham, S. (1973) *Hidden from History*, London: Pluto Press.

Royal Commission on the Press (1948) *'Day 22' in Minutes of Evidence*, Cmd. 7398, London: HMSO.

—— (1949) *Report*, Cmd. 7700, London: HMSO.

—— (1977) *Final Report*, London: HMSO.

Ryan, M. (1986) 'Blocking the Channels: TV and Film in Wales', in Curtis, T. (ed.), *Wales: the Imagined Nation. Essays in Cultural and National Identity*, Bridgend: Poetry Wales Press.

Sampson, A. (1962) *The Anatomy of Britain*, London: Hodder and Stoughton.

Samuel, L. R. (2001) *Brought to You By: Postwar Television Advertising and the American Dream*, Austin, TX: University of Texas Press.

Samuel, R. (ed.) (1989) *Patriotism. The Making and Unmaking of British National Identity*, London: Routledge.

—— (1998) *Theatres of Memory*. Vol. II, *Island Stories: Unravelling Britain*, London: Verso.

Sandbrook, D. (2005) *Never Had It So Good*, London, Little Brown.

Sarikaskis, K. and Thussu, D. K. (eds) (2006) *Ideologies of the Internet*, Cresskill, NJ: Hampton Press.

Savage, G. (1998) 'Erotic Stories and Public Decency: Newspaper Reporting of Divorce Proceedings in England', *The Historical Journal*, 41: 511–28.

Sawers, D. (1962) 'The Sky's the Limit', in Altman W. (ed.), *Television – From Monopoly to Competition and Back?* London: Institute of Economic Affairs.

Scannell, P. (1990) 'Public Service Broadcasting: the History of a Concept', in Goodwin, A. and Whannel, G. (eds), *Understanding Television*, pp. 11–29, London: Routledge.

—— (1992) 'Public Service Broadcasting and Public Life' in Scannell, P., Schlesinger, P. and Sparks, C. (eds), *Culture and Power*, London: Sage.

—— (1993) 'The Origins of BBC Regional Policy' in Harvey, S. and Robins K. (eds), *The Regions, the Nations and the BBC*, pp. 27–38, London: BFI.

—— (2001) 'For-Anyone-as-Someone Structures', *Media, Culture & Society*, 22(1): 5–24.

—— (2007) *Media and Communication*, London: Sage.

—— and Cardiff, D. (1987) 'The BBC and National Unity', in Curran, J., Smith, A. and Wingate, P. (eds), *Impacts and Influences*, pp. 157–73, London: Methuen.

—— (1991) *A Social History of British Broadcasting: Serving the Nation, 1923–1939*, Oxford: Blackwell.

Schama, S. (2002) *A History of Britain*, Vol. 3, *The Fate of Empire 1776–2000*, London: BBC Worldwide.

Scharff, R. and V. Dusek (2003) *Philosophy of Technology*, Oxford: Blackwell.

Schot, J. and Rip, A (1997) 'The Past and Future of Constructive Technology Assessment', *Technological Forecasting and Social Change*, 54: 251–68.

Schröter, H. (2005) *Americanization of the European Economy: a Compact Survey of American Economic Influence in Europe since the 1880s*, Dordrecht: Springer.

Schumacher, D. (1973) 'Technology Assessment – the State of the Art', in Stober, G. J. and Schumacher, D. (eds), *Technology Assessment and Quality of Life*, pp. 71–88, New York: Elsevier.

Schwarzkopf, S. (2005) 'They do it with Mirrors: Advertising and British Cold War Consumer Politics', *Contemporary British History*, 19: 133–50.

Schweizer, K. (2006) 'Newspapers, Politics and Public Opinion in the Late Hanoverian Period', in Schweizer, K. (ed.), *Parliament and the Press 1689–c.1939*, Edinburgh: Edinburgh University Press.

Sconce, J. (2000) *Haunted Media: Electronic Presence from Telegraphy to Television*, Durham, NJ: Duke University Press.

Seaton, J. (2007) 'Being Objective: Changing the World', in Sambrook, R. (ed.), *Global Voice: Britain's Future in International Broadcasting*, pp. 41–55, London: Premium.

Sebba, A. (1994) *Battling for News: the Rise of the Woman Reporter*, London: Hodder & Stoughton.

Segel, H. (1997) *Egon Erwin Kisch: The Raging Reporter*, West Lafayette, IN: Purdue University Press.

Sekula, A. (1984) *Photography Against the Grain*, Halifax, NS: Press of the Nova Scotia College of Art and Design.

—— (1989) 'The Body and the Archive', in Bolton, R. (ed.) *The Contest of Meaning: Critical Histories of Photography*, Cambridge, MA: The MIT Press.

Sendall, B. (1982) *Independent Television in Britain*, Vol. 1, London: Macmillan.

—— (1983) *Independent Television in Britain*, Vol. 2, *Expansion and Change, 1958–68*, London: Macmillan.

Seymour-Ure, C. (1977) 'National Daily Papers and the Party System', in *Studies on the Press*, Royal Commission on the Press Working Paper No. 3, London: HMSO.

—— (1996) *The British Press and Broadcasting Since 1945*, 2nd edn, Oxford: Blackwell.

Shapley, O. (1996) *Broadcasting a Life*, London: Scarlett Press.

Sharr, A. (2006) *Heidegger's Hut*, Cambridge, MA: MIT Press.

Shattock, J. and Wolff, M. (1982) *The Victorian Periodical Press: Samplings and Soundings*, Leicester: Leicester University Press.

Shattuc, J. (1997) *The Talking Cure: TV Talk Shows and Women*, New York: Routledge.

Shaw, C. (1999) *Deciding What We Watch: Taste, Decency and Media Ethics in the UK and USA*, Oxford: Clarendon Press.

Shaw, T. (1998) 'The British Popular Press and the Early Cold War', *History*, 83(269): 66–85.

Shellard, D., Nicholson, S. and Handley, M. (2004) *The Lord Chamberlain Regrets: British Stage Censorship and Readers' Reports from 1824 to 1968*, London: British Library Publishing Division.

Shepard, L. (1973) *The History of Street Literature*, Newton Abbot: David & Charles.

Short, C. (1991) *Dear Clare*, letters edited and selected by K. Tunks and D. Hutchinson, London: Radius.

Siebert, F., Peterson, T. and Schramm, W. (1963) *Four Theories of the Press: The Authoritarian, Libertarian, Social Responsibility and Soviet Communist Concepts of what the Press Should Be and Do*, Urbana, IL: University of Illinois Press.

Silverman, R. (1952) *Advertising Expenditure in 1948*, London: Advertising Association.

Singer, D. G. and Singer, J. L. (eds) (2001) *Handbook of Children and Media*, Thousand Oaks, CA: Sage.

Slater, D. (1997) *Consumer Culture & Modernity*, Cambridge: Polity Press.

Slide, A. (1998) *'Banned in the USA'. British Films in the United States and their Censorship, 1933–1960*, London: I. B. Tauris.

Smith, A. (1978) 'The Long Road to Objectivity and Back Again', in Boyce, G., Curran, J. and Wingate, P. (eds), *Newspaper History: From the 17th Century to the Present Day*, London: Constable.

—— (1979) *The Newspaper: An International History*, London: Thames and Hudson.

Smith, A. D. (1983) *Theories of Nationalism*, London: Duckworth.

Smith, D. (1999) *Wales: A Question for History*, Bridgend: Seren.

Smith, M. R. and Marx, L. (eds) (1994) *Does Technology Drive History? The Dilemma of Technological Determinism*, Cambridge, MA: MIT Press.

Snoddy, R. (1992) *The Good, The Bad, and The Unacceptable: The Hard News about the British Press*, London: Faber & Faber.

Soja, E. W. (1989) *Postmodern Geographies: The Reassertion of Space in Critical Social Theory*, London: Verso.

Somerville, C. J. (1996) *The News Revolution in England*, New York: Oxford University Press.

Sontag, S. (2003) *Regarding the Pain of Others*, New York: Farrar, Straus and Giroux.

Sorel, N. (1999) *The Women Who Wrote the War*, Philadelphia, PA: Arcade Publishing.

Spar, D. L (2003) *Ruling the Waves: From the Compass to the Internet, a History of Business and Politics along the Technological Frontier*, New York: Harvest Books.

Sparks, C. (1988) 'The Popular Press and Political Democracy', *Media, Culture & Society*, 10: 209–23.

—— (1991) 'Goodbye, Hildy Johnson: the Vanishing "Serious Press"', in Dahlgren, P. and Sparks, C. (eds), *Communication and Citizenship*, London: Routledge.

Spigel, L. (1992a) *Make Room for TV: Television and the Family Ideal in Postwar America*, Chicago: University of Chicago Press.

—— (1992b) 'Installing the Television Set: Popular Discourses on Television and Domestic Space, 1948–55', in Spigel, L. and Mann, D. (eds), *Private Screenings: Television and the Female Consumer*, pp. 3–41, Minneapolis, MN: University of Minnesota Press.

Standage, T. (1998) *The Victorian Internet: The Remarkable Story of the Telegraph and the Nineteenth Century Online Pioneers*, London: Weidenfeld and Nicholson.

Starr, P. (2004) *The Creation of the Media: Political Origins of Modern Communications*, New York: Basic Books.

Startt, J. (1991) *Journalists for Empire: The Imperial Debate in the Edwardian Stately Press, 1903–1913*, Westport, CT: Greenwood.

Statistical Review of Independent Television Advertising 1 (April 1956).

Statistical Review of Independent Television Advertising 5 (February 1960).

Steer, G. (1938) *The Tree of Gernika*, London: Hodder and Stoughton.

Stratton, J. (1997) 'Cyberspace and the globalisation of culture', in Porter, D. (ed.), *Internet Culture*, New York: Routledge.

Street, S. (1997) *British National Cinema*, London: Routledge.

—— (2002) *A Concise History of British Radio, 1922–2002*, Tiverton: Kelly Publications.

—— (2006) *Crossing the Ether: British Public Service Radio and Commercial Competition 1922–1945*, Eastleigh: John Libbey Publishing.

Sutherland, J. (1982) *Offensive Literature*, London: Junction Books.

Swan, P. (1987) *The Hollywood Feature Film in Post-War Britain*, London: Croom Helm.

Tagg, J. (1988) *The Burden of Representation: Essays on Photographies and Histories*, Basingstoke: Macmillan Education.

Taplin, W. (1961) *The Origin of Television Advertising in the United Kingdom*, London: Pitman.

Tarde, G. (1898) *L'opinion et la foule*, Paris: Presses Universitaires de France.

The People & the Media (1974) London: The Labour Party.

Thomas, D., Carlton, D. and Etieene, A. (2007) *Theatre Censorship*, Oxford: Oxford University Press.

Thomas, J. (2005) *Popular Newspapers, the Labour Party and British Politics*, London: Routledge.

Thomas, N. (1970) 'The Future of Broadcasting', *Planet*, 2: 3–15.

—— (1995) 'Linguistic Minorities and the Media' in Lee, P. (ed.), *The Democratization of Communication*, Cardiff: University of Wales Press.

Thompson, E. P. (1967) 'Time, Work-Discipline, and Industrial Capitalism', *Past and Present*, 38: 56–97.

—— (1991 [1968]) *The Making of the English Working-Class*, Harmondsworth: Penguin Books.

Thompson, J. B. (1990) *Ideology and Modern Culture: Critical Social Theory in the Era of Mass Communication*, Cambridge: Polity Press.

—— (1995) *The Media and Modernity: A Social Theory of the Media*, Cambridge: Polity Press.

Thompson, K. (1998) *Moral Panics*, London: Routledge.

Thornham, S. (2000) *Feminist Theory and Cultural Studies*, London: Arnold.

Thumim, J. (1992) *Celluloid Sisters*, New York: St. Martin's Press.

—— (1998) '"Mrs Knight Must Be Balanced": Methodical Problems in Researching Early British Television', in Carter, C., Branston, G. and Allan, S. (eds), *News, Gender and Power*, pp. 91–104, London: Routledge.

—— (ed.) (2001) *Small Screens, Big Ideas: Television in the 1950s*, London: I. B. Tauris.

—— (2004) *Inventing Television Culture: Men, Women and the 'Box'*, Oxford: Oxford University Press.

Tichenor, P. J., Donohue, G. A. and Olien, C. N. (1970) 'Mass Media Flow and Differential Growth in Knowledge', *Public Opinion Quarterly*, 34: 159–70.

Tinkler, P. (1995) *Constructing Girlhood: Popular Magazines for Girls Growing Up in England, 1920–1950*, London: Taylor and Francis.

Tosh, J. (1999) *A Man's Place*, New Haven, CT: Yale University Press.

Tracey, M. (1983) *In the Culture of the Eye*, London: Hutchison.

—— (1998) *The Decline and Fall of Public Service Broadcasting*, Oxford: Oxford University Press.

—— (2003) *An Essay on Television: Part Two*, Britannia, Boulder, CO: University of Colorado.

Travis, A. (2000) *Bound and Gagged*, London: Profile Books.

Treasure, J. (1967) *As Others See Us: A Study of Attitudes to Advertising and to Television Advertisements* (IPA Occasional Paper No. 17), London: IPA.

Trend, D. (ed.) (2001) *Reading Digital Culture*, Oxford: Blackwell.

—— (2007) *The Myth of Media Violence*, Oxford: Blackwell.

Trevelyan, J. (1973) *What the Censor Saw*, London: Michael Joseph.

Tsagarousianou, R., Tambini, D. and Bryan, C. (eds) (1998) *Cyberdemocracy*, London: Routledge.

Tulloch, J. (1990) 'Television and Black Britons', in Goodwin, A. and Whannel, G. (eds), *Understanding Television*, pp. 141–52, London: Routledge.

Tunney, S. (2007) *Labour and the Press: From New Left to New Labour*, Brighton: Sussex Academic Press.

Tunstall, J. (1964) *The Advertising Man in London Advertising Agencies*, London: Chapman & Hall.

—— (1994) *The Media are American: Anglo-American Media in the World*, London: Constable.

—— (1996) *Newspaper Power: The New National Press in Britain*, Oxford: Clarendon Press.

Turkle, S. (1997) *Life on the Screen*, New York: Simon and Schuster.

Turner, F. (2006) *From Counterculture to Cyberculture*, Chicago, IL: Chicago University Press.

Turner, G. (1999) 'Tabloidization, Journalism and the Possibility of Critique', *International Journal of Cultural Studies*, 2(1): 59–76.

Turnock, R. (2005) *Did ITV Revolutionise British Television. Report for the AHRB*, available from http://www.rhul.ac.uk/media-arts/staff/AHRB%20Report.doc.

—— (2007) *Television and Consumer Culture: Britain and the Transformation of Modernity*, London: I. B. Tauris.

Tusan, M. (2005) *Women Making News: Gender and Journalism in Modern Britain*, Urbana and Chicago, IL: University of Illinois Press.

Tylor, E. B. (1913 [1881]) *Anthropology: An Introduction to the Study of Man and Civilisation*, London: Watts.

Van den Bulte, C. (2000) 'New Product Diffusion Acceleration: Measurement and Analysis', *Marketing Science*, 19(4): 366–80.

Van Zoonen, L. (2004) 'Desire and Resistance: Big Brother in the Dutch Public Sphere', in Mathijs, E. and Jones, J. (eds), *Big Brother International: Formats, Critics and Publics*, pp. 16–24, London: Wallflower.

Vincent, D. (1993) *Literacy and Popular Culture, England 1750–1914*, Cambridge: Cambridge University Press.

Vinicus, M. (1974) *The Industrial Muse. A Study of Nineteenth Century British Working-Class Literature*, London: Croom Helm.

Virilio, P. (2000) *Information Bomb*, London: Verso.

Visram, R. (2002) *Asians in Britain: 400 Years of History*, London: Pluto Press.

Waltz, M. (2005) *Alternative and Activist Media*, Edinburgh: Edinburgh University Press.

Ward. P. (2004) *Britishness since 1870,* London: Routledge.

Wasko, J. (2001) *Understanding Disney: The Manufacture of Fantasy*, Cambridge: Polity.

Watney, S. (1987) *Policing Desire: Pornography, Aids and the Media*, Minneapolis, MN: University of Minnesota Press.

Watson, R. and Blondheim, M. (eds) (2007) *The Toronto School of Communication Theory: Interpretations, Extensions, Applications*, Toronto: University of Toronto Press.

Wayne, M. (2003) *Marxism and Media Studies: Key Concepts and Contemporary Trends*, London: Pluto Press.

Webb, R. K. (1955) *The British Working-Class Reader 1790–1848*, London: Allen & Unwin.

Webster, F. (2001) *Culture and Politics in the Information Age: A New Politics*, London: Routledge.

Weeks, J. (1989) *Sex, Politics and Society: The Regulation of Sexuality since 1800*, Harlow: Longman.

—— (2003) *Sexuality*, London: Routledge.

Weight, R. (2003) *Patriots: National Identity in Britain 1945–2000*, London: Macmillan.

West, N. (1986) *GCHQ: The Secret Wireless War*, London: Weidenfeld and Nicholson.

Wheatley, H. (2005) 'Rooms within Rooms: Upstairs Downstairs and the Studio Costume Drama of the 1970s', in Johnson, C. and Turnock, R. (eds), *ITV Cultures: Independent Television Over Fifty Years*, pp. 143–58, Maidenhead: Open University Press.

White, C. (1970) *Women's Magazines, 1693–1968*, London: Michael Joseph.

White, L. T. (1962) *Medieval Technology and Social Change*, Oxford: Clarendon Press.

Whitehouse, M. (1967) *Cleaning up TV*, Poole: Blandford.

Wiener, J. (1969) *The War of the Unstamped*, Ithaca, NY: Cornell University Press.

—— (1996) 'The Americanisation of the British Press, 1830–1914', in Harris, M. and O'Malley, T. (eds), *Studies in Newspapers and Periodical History: 1994 Annual*, Westport, CT: Greenswood.

Wilkinson, G. R. (2003) *Depictions and Images of War in Edwardian Newspapers, 1899–1914*, Basingstoke: Palgrave Macmillan.

Williams, F. (1962) *The American Invasion*, London: Anthony Blond.

Williams, J. (2004) *Entertaining the Nation*, Stroud: Sutton.

Williams, K. (1996) *British Writers and the Media 1930–45*, Basingstoke: Macmillan.

—— (1998) *Get Me A Murder A Day! A History of Mass Communication in Britain*, London: Arnold.

—— (2003) *Understanding Media Theory*, London: Arnold.

Williams, L. (1999) *Hard Core: Power, Pleasure, and the 'Frenzy of the Visible'*, Berkeley, CA: University of California Press.

Williams, R. (1961) *The Long Revolution*, London: Chatto & Windus.

—— (1962 [1958b]) *Culture and Society*, Harmondsworth: Pelican Books.

—— (1966) *Communications*, London: Chatto & Windus.

—— (1970) 'Radical and/or Respectable', in Boston, R. (ed.), *The Press We Deserve*, London: Routledge & Kegan Paul.

—— (1974) *Television: Technology and Cultural Form*, London: Fontana.

—— (1976) *Keywords*, London: Fontana.

—— (1989 [1958a]) 'Culture is Ordinary', in Williams, R. (ed.), *Resources of Hope*, London: Verso.

—— (1990) *What I Came To Say*, London: Hutchinson Radius.

Williams, R. H. (1982) *Dream Worlds: Mass Consumption in Late-Nineteenth Century France*, Berkeley, CA: University of California Press.

Willis, P. (1990) *Common Culture*, Milton Keynes: Open University Press.

Wilson, E. (1977) *Women and the Welfare State*, London: Tavistock Publications.

Wilson, H. H. (1961) *Pressure Group: the Campaign for Commercial Television*, London: Secker & Warburg.

Wilson, S. (2005) 'Real People with Real Problems? Public Service Broadcasting, Commercialism and Trisha', in Johnson, C. and Turnock, R. (eds), *ITV Cultures*, Maidenhead: Open University Press.

Winship, J. (1987) *Inside Women's Magazines*, London: Pandora Press.

Winston, B. (1986) *Misunderstanding Media*, Cambridge: Harvard University Press.

—— (1998) *Media Technology and Society*, London: Routledge.

—— (1999) 'How Media are Born', in Marris P. and Thornham, S. (eds), *Media Studies: A Reader*, pp. 786–815, Edinburgh: Edinburgh University Press.

—— (2005) *Messages: Free Expression, Media and the West from Gutenberg to Google*, London: Routledge.

Wintour, C. (1972) *Pressures on the Press*, London: Andre Deutsch.

Wirth, L. (1948) 'Consensus and mass communication', *American Sociological Review*, 13: 1–15.

Wyatt, W. (1999) *The Journals of Woodrow Wyatt*, Vol. 1, S. Curtis (ed.), London: Pan Books.

Wyndham Goldie, G. (1977) *Facing the Nation*, London: Bodley Head.

Young, B. (1983) *The Paternal Tradition in British Broadcasting*, Edinburgh: Heriot-Watt University.

Index